BEHAVIORAL CASE FORMULATION
AND INTERVENTION

Wiley Series in

CLINICAL PSYCHOLOGY

Adrian Wells   *School of Psychological Sciences, University*
(Series Advisor)   *of Manchester, UK*

For other titles in this series please visit www.wiley.com/go/cs

BEHAVIORAL CASE FORMULATION AND INTERVENTION

A Functional Analytic Approach

Peter Sturmey

Queens College and The Graduate Center
City University of New York

WILEY-BLACKWELL

A John Wiley & Sons, Ltd., Publication

Other Wiley Editorial Offices

John Wiley & Sons Inc., 111 River Street, Hoboken, NJ 07030, USA

Jossey-Bass, 989 Market Street, San Francisco, CA 94103-1741, USA

Wiley-VCH Verlag GmbH, Boschstr. 12, D-69469 Weinheim, Germany

John Wiley & Sons Australia Ltd, 42 McDougall Street, Milton, Queensland 4064, Australia

John Wiley & Sons (Asia) Pte Ltd, 2 Clementi Loop #02-01, Jin Xing Distripark, Singapore
129809

John Wiley & Sons Canada Ltd, 6045 Freemont Blvd, Mississauga, ONT, L5R 4J3, Canada

Wiley also publishes its books in a variety of electronic formats. Some content that
appears in print may not be available in electronic books.

Anniversary Logo Design: Richard J. Pacifico

Library of Congress Cataloging-in-Publication Data

Sturmey, Peter.
    Behavioral case formulation and intervention : A functional analytic approach / Peter
Sturmey.
        p. ; cm. – (Wiley series in clinical psychology)
    Includes bibliographical references and index.
    ISBN 978-0-470-01889-7 (hbk : alk. paper) – ISBN 978-0-470-01890-3
(pbk. : alk. paper)
    1. Clinical psychology–Methodology.   2. Functionalism (Psychology)
I. Title.   II. Series.
    [DNLM: 1. Psychology, Clinical–methods.   2. Mental Disorders–
diagnosis.   3. Mental Disorders–therapy. WM 105 S935b 2007]
    RC467.S846 2007
    616.89–dc22   2007025162

British Library Cataloguing in Publication Data

A catalogue record for this book is available from the British Library

ISBN 978-0-470-01889-7 (hbk) 978-0-470-01890-3 (pbk)

Typeset in 10/12pt Palatino by Thomson Digital, India
Printed and bound in Great Britain by TJ international, Padstow, Cornwall

The wise see knowledge and action as one; they see truly.

Bhagava Gita

We must go work in the garden

Voltaire

CONTENTS

About the Author ix

Preface xi

Acknowledgements xvii

PART I   BEHAVIORISM AND BASIC
            LEARNING CONCEPTS 1

Chapter 1   Structural and Functional Approaches
            to Case Formulation 3

Chapter 2   Radical Behaviorism 21

Chapter 3   Respondent Behavior 37

Chapter 4   Operant Behavior I: Characteristics,
            Acquisition and Stimulus Control 53

Chapter 5   Operant Behavior II: Satiation and
            Deprivation, Extinction, Shaping,
            Variability and Punishment 79

Chapter 6   Complex Behavior I: Modeling,
            Chaining and Self-Regulation 99

Chapter 7   Complex Behavior II: Rule-Governed
            Behavior, Stimulus Equivalence and
            Verbal Behavior 117

PART II   CASE FORMULATION 141

Chapter 8   Nonbehavioral approaches to case
            formulation 143

Chapter 9   Wolpe's Tradition of
            Case Formulation 169

Chapter 10 Skinner and Psychotherapy 183

Chapter 11 Behavioral Case Formulation 195

Chapter 12 Behavioral Assessment 225

Chapter 13   Outstanding Issues and
             Future Directions 259

References 289

Index 321

ABOUT THE AUTHOR

Peter Sturmey is Professor of Psychology at Queens College and The Graduate Center, City University of New York where he is a member of the Doctoral faculty of the Learning Processes and Neuropsychology Doctoral Programs. He is also Senior Lecturer at University College, London.

He received a PhD from the Department of Psychology, University of Liverpool and subsequently trained as a clinical psychologist in the Department of Clinical Psychology, University of Liverpool. He taught in clinical psychology programs in Plymouth and Birmingham, United Kingdom, and was a visiting Professor in the Department of Psychology, Louisiana State University. He then spent 10 years working in developmental centers in Texas where he was a Chief Psychologist. His responsibilities included supervising Masters Psychologists, designing treatment plans for severe behavior problems and mental health disorders and staff training. He also consulted with community services for adults with intellectual disabilities in Texas at that time. He has spent the past seven years teaching courses in applied behavior analysis, psychopathology, intellectual disabilities, and autism at Queens College, New York and currently consults with autism services and periodically on restraint reduction and serve behavioral and psychiatric disorders in people with intellectual disabilities.

He has published over 100 peer-reviewed articles and six books, mostly in the area of assessment and treatment of severe behavior disorders and psychopathology in people with intellectual and related developmental disabilities. He is an Associate Editor for *Research in Developmental Disabilities* and *Research in Autism Spectrum Disorders* and is on the editorial board of several other journals. He has presented at many national and international conferences. His current research program focuses on applied behavior analysis and staff training.

His interest in case formulation began as a clinical psychology trainee at the University of Liverpool and developed when teaching clinical psychology trainees case formulation skills at Plymouth and Birmingham Universities in the United Kingdom. This resulted in the publication of *Functional Analysis in Clinical Psychology* (1996, Wiley). Subsequently, he taught Masters psychologists in Texas to conduct functional assessments of behavioral and mental health disorders in people with intellectual disabilities and consulted widely on this topic. Since 2000, he has returned to teaching, focusing on applied behavior analysis. This volume is the result of those experiences.

PREFACE

Case formulation is a key skill for clinicians from many clinical disciplines. Clinical psychologists, psychiatrists, counselors and social workers and other therapists all claim a special understanding of human behavior. To do so is a marker of professional skill and a point of professional pride that demonstrates one's competency as a professional. It adds something special to understanding and treatment that was not already known by the lay person.

Interest in case formulation is longstanding. Good, clinical case descriptions have always been fascinating. Their vivid description of psychopathology and clever treatment plans can be lost in data and graphs. They can be useful models to the student and practicing clinician as how to abstract and order the confusing mass of information that each client presents and how to use that abstraction to develop a treatment plan based on their own professional construction of that specific case. They are also useful teaching tools and models for professionals to use when formulating and developing a treatment plan. They can provide insight into the thinking of well-known clinicians that give us additional insight into how they work.

The idea of rational organization of clinical material has a long history in medicine. Early Greeks used systematic attempts to assess and diagnose (Eells, 1997) and such systematic approaches to collecting and organizing information continue to be used in psychiatry (Deb & Ayer, 2005; Sperry, Gudeman, Blackwell & Faulkner, 2004.) There is a long history of case presentation in psychoanalysis – much of Freud's best known work were descriptive case studies with formulations that organized and explained observable signs, symptoms and history from a psychodynamic perspective (Eells, 2007). Some of the earliest books on behavior therapy in the 1950s and 1960s used case studies and case formulations extensively (Eysenck, 1965; Ullman & Krasner, 1968; Wolpe 1958). Turkat's (1985a) classic *Behavioral Case Formulation* is an extension of this work. These and other publications proved to be useful models for behavioral case formulation and treatment for practitioners to use.

This interest in case formulation has continued, if not recently accelerated, perhaps reflecting a growing need for trainee and qualified clinicians to learn about differing approaches to case formulation. Recently there have been a number of case formulation books, from a cognitive behavioral perspective, including Waller's (2000) *Psychological Case Formulation in*

Clinical Practice; Nezu et al.'s (2004), *Cognitive-Behavioral Case Formulation and Treatment Design: A Problem-Solving Approach;* Persons's (1997) *Cognitive Therapy in Practice: A Case Formulation Approach;* Bruch and Bond's (2001) *Beyond Diagnosis: Case Formulation Approach in CBT;* and Tarrier et al.'s (1998) *Treating Complex Cases: The Cognitive Behavioral Therapy Approach.* Other case formulation volumes have been published from other theoretical perspectives including volumes on *Multiperspective Case Formulation* (Weerasekera, 1996), psychotherapeutic case formulation (McWilliams, 1999) and *Psychiatric Case Formulation* (Sperry et al., 2004.) Eells (1997, 2007) *Handbook of Psychotherapy Case Formulation* is a useful compendium of different approaches to case formulation. In short, there is now a minor genre of case formulation books.

In 1996, I wrote *Functional Analysis in Clinical Psychology.* It was an introductory graduate book to describe the basic concepts and methods that go into behavioral approaches to case formulation and behavioral intervention. This book grew out of teaching graduate courses in case formulation in Britain. However, other than Turkat (1985a) and Sturmey (1996), there have not been any volumes that have taken an explicitly behavioral approach to case formulation. Most publications have been in the area of cognitive approaches to case formulation. Explicit use of behavioral approaches is out of fashion.

This volume has grown out of a motivation to revisit the topic of behavioral approaches to case formulation. There are several reasons. First, much behavior analysis is poorly taught. It is often reduced to a rag bag of techniques. It is often taught incorrectly. It is often disparaged by those who teach it, even though they seem unfamiliar with Skinner's work. Its scientific basis is often omitted. Therefore, one of the aims of this volume was to place behavioral approaches to case formulation firmly within the context of behaviorism and learning concepts. A second area of concern has been the lack of emphasis on verbal behavior. Many behavioral texts present behaviorism with minimal reference to verbal behavior and private events. In so doing they omit an important aspect of behavior. This detracts from the credibility of a behavioral approach. Verbal behavior, including private verbal behavior, is an important aspect of human behavior. Skinner (1953, 1957) himself offered an extensive account of thinking and feeling which secondary texts and current professional training often omit. To do so is to make an incomplete presentation of behaviorism. Public and private language can be a key aspect of psychopathology and an integral part of case formulation and treatment for some behaviorists. Hence, any book on case formulation should address it. Third, there have been a number of new developments in behavior analysis since the early 1990s. Some of these have been incorporated into clinical work and some have yet to be incorporated. These new developments represent another motivation for this volume. These developments include clarification of the role of deprivation and satiation in operant behavior, new work on stimulus equivalence and transfer of function. A fourth trend has been the expansion of the range of problems addressed by applied behavior analysis. Turkat's work in the mid-1980s extended Wolpe's earlier work from neuroses to other kinds of adult psychopathology, such as personality disorders, substance-related disorders and work with seniors. More recently, there has been extensive work on Attention Deficit Hyperactivity Disorders (ADHD) and school refusal and revival of interest in areas addressed by behaviorism in the past, such as psychosis, depression and traumatic brain injury (Sturmey, 2007.) These developments with different populations allow us to make conceptual and technological links between the analogous treatments of different topographies based on function rather than irrelevant features, such as diagnosis, demographic variables, and so on. A fifth trend has been the expansion of behavioral technologies from one population and context to another. Often assessment methods developed with one population or for one problem form the conceptual basis for development of analogous assessments with other seemingly unrelated populations and problem. The final trend has been the development of technology to disseminate behavioral methods of assessment and treatment to a wider range of clinicians and nonclinicians.

These developments strongly suggest that behavioral approaches to case formulation have changed and that a new volume in this area is needed to keep the student, teacher and clinician abreast of new developments.

Therefore, the aims of this volume are as follows:

1. To describe the conceptual foundations of functional approaches to case formulation.
2. To review the literature on functional analysis applied to psychopathology.
3. To provide an update on developments in behavioral case formulation.
4. To describe the technology and application of behavioral assessment, case formulation and hypothesis-driven intervention.
5. To describe outstanding issues and future directions.

OVERVIEW OF THIS VOLUME

This volume is organized into two parts. Part I reviews basic concepts of behaviorism and learning and Part II reviews case formulation and behavioral approaches to case formulation.

Chapter 1 introduces these ideas by discussing the most basic distinction of structural versus behavioral approaches to case formulation. This chapter argues for the superiority of functional approaches to behavior generally as an extension of evolutionary thinking and as a useful approach to practical problems. Chapter 2 describes some of the key features of radical behaviorism, the philosophy of science that underpins both basic and applied behavior analysis, identifies and corrects common misconceptions about radical behaviorism.

One of the apparently simplest forms of behavior is respondent behavior. Respondent conditioning accounts for the acquisition of some phobic, stress and other disorders, as well as generalization of some common pathological behavior. Chapter 3 describes how these problems can be construed within the framework of respondent conditioning and describes interventions based on the respondent conditioning model including changes in stimulus control and most importantly respondent extinction. Respondent extinction has been implicated as a common mechanism for symptom relief in a variety of forms of psychopathology.

Operant behavior is one of the most common and important types of human behavior. Operant behavior is controlled by its consequences, the immediate antecedents correlated with the consequences and the more distant antecedents such as deprivation and satiation of the reinforcer maintaining the behavior of interest. Much psychopathology is, by definition, unusual. It commands a reaction from others. These contingencies may be important in how some forms of psychopathology develop, how they are maintained and in determining the form of treatment.

Operant behavior can be modified in a variety of ways. Modification of consequences maintaining the behaviors of interest is the most obvious intervention, but other less obvious interventions include modification of consequences maintaining other operant behaviors, modification of the antecedents and reinforcer deprivation and satiation. Chapters 4 and 5 describe the basic concepts associated with operant behavior, such as acquisition, maintenance, stimulus control and extinction as well as a wide variety of interventions based on operant approaches.

Respondent behavior does not account for much human behavior. Operant behavior explains more and can explain some quite complex behavior. Nevertheless, there are still complex forms of behavior to be accounted for. Chapters 6 and 7 describe other learning processes that account for more complex behavior and that give rise to other interventions. These include modeling and chaining, and learning processes that may be related to language, such as self-regulation, rule governed behavior, stimulus equivalence, and verbal behavior.

The second part of this volume (Chapter 8) begins by describing common features of case formulation and some of the more common approaches to case formulation. Chapter 9 reviews Wolpe's contribution to case formulation. Wolpe developed a variety of forms of counter-conditioning for both simple and complex anxiety disorders, some forms of depression, sexual dysfunctions and other problematic behavior. Hence much of Wolpe's clinical work involved careful interviewing to identify potential conditioning experiences in the client's history and Conditioned Stimuli (CS) in the current environment. Wolpe's influence in case formulation was important because it required clinicians to interview their client very carefully using hypothesis-driven interviewing, rather than technique-oriented standard interviewing. This hypothesis-driven form of interview lead to a formulation that directed the nature of classical extinction, which was achieved through various procedures referred to as reciprocal inhibition. Students of Wolpe, notably Turkat, expanded this approach to address a wider range of other disorders, such as substance abuse and personality disorders. This broader use of behavioral case formulation is alive in Bruch's University College London model. Less well known at the present time is Skinner's contribution to psychotherapy and case formulation. Chapter 10 described his views on psychotherapy and their implication for case formulation. This sets the scene for subsequent developments in behavioral case formulation described in Chapter 11. This chapter describes a rich variety of approaches to behavioral case formulation, a range of developing technology to make and use behavioral case formulations, as well as applications to a wide range of problems.

Behavioral case formulation is based on an individual behavioral assessment. Chapter 12 described the assumptions behind behavioral assessment and some of the commonly used methods. This chapter also discusses some of the issues related to combining and using information gathered during behavioral assessment. The final chapter discusses conceptual issues and directions for future research. It covers the reliability and validity of behavioral formulations, the efficacy of this approach and the implications for professional training.

ACKNOWLEDGEMENTS

I would like to thank my students and colleagues at the Learning Processes and Behavior Analysis Doctoral Program at Queens College for all their help over the last eight years. I have learned much from them.

Part I

BEHAVIORISM AND BASIC LEARNING CONCEPTS

Part I of this volume outlines what radical behaviorism is. Subsequent chapters describe respondent and operant behavior and their controlling variables. The later chapters outline more complex forms of behavior, such as verbal behavior. Throughout these chapters there are illustrations of the clinical applications of these concepts and their related interventions.

Chapter 1

STRUCTURAL AND FUNCTIONAL APPROACHES TO CASE FORMULATION

MIKE GALLAGER

Mr Mike Gallager says he is depressed because of his unhappy divorce two years ago. He admits repeatedly cheating on his former wife, but still believes that she should have been more understanding. He believes that she too was also unfaithful, but he just cannot pin her down yet. He claims that he also squandered money, which led to many family problems. He regrets the restrictions placed on the access to his two children, but also often feels too depressed to spend his assigned day with them. This causes further friction between his ex-wife and himself. He also bitterly resents that, as part of the divorce settlement, she has the family house, half of his pension, and that he has to pay her what he views as substantial sums of money each week.

He lost his job six months ago. His boss said his work had deteriorated. Mike denied it, saying his boss was determined to get rid of older workers and had a grudge against him. He had poor relationships with colleagues and refused to take direction from his supervisor. He was also found drunk at work. This incident finally led to his dismissal.

Over the past three years he has progressively become moody. He has experienced periods of depression when he cannot get out of bed. He is also often angry with his wife and many other people. Many minor disagreements are taken as major personal slights. He dislikes his flat which he had to take after the divorce. He has been taking anti-depressant for over two years, but with only some relief. He views his psychiatrist as incompetent and disinterested in him.

He lives mostly on take-out food and does not exercise. He has put on 50 pounds since being fired. He has periods when he is short of breath and believes he may have heart problems. Yet, he refuses to go to the doctor about it. He also has knee problems due to his weight, which sometimes limits his mobility.

Mr Gallager was the middle of three children. He has one brother and one sister. His father was an engineer working for the local railway company. His mother stayed at home. He reports that his early family life was good. He got on well with his siblings and parents. He was average at school and mostly enjoyed it. When he left school at 16, he trained to be a mechanic. He has had a string of jobs as a mechanic since then. His parents divorced when he was 20 after several years of a deteriorating relationship. This was apparent to the children when their parents argued loudly at home over money and other matters. He recalls things being better after his father left and got remarried. Mike had several girlfriends prior to his own marriage at 23 years of age. He says none of the girlfriends was very serious. He recalls being in love with his former wife during their engagement and when they were first married. He described that the relationship deteriorated after the birth of the second child. Sometimes he says it was because his wife had postnatal depression. Other times says it was because of the increasing financial burden. He reported that his infidelity began at about that time. None of these relationships was serious or romantic.

When asked why he has come for therapy he states that it is because he is depressed and because his antidepressants do not work. When asked what his goals are for therapy he says that he just wants these bad feelings to go away.

HOW SHOULD WE PROCEED?

How should we proceed with Mr Gallager? We could screen him with psychometric tests and standardized interviews to see if he meets diagnostic criteria for major depressive disorder, dysthymia or bipolar disorder. We might speculate that, since he had a response to an antidepressant, he may have an underlying biochemical vulnerability to depression. Perhaps an interview will reveal a family history of mood disorders in a relative, if we search hard enough and use a broad enough criterion we will probably find one or two. We might note the lifelong pattern of disrupted relationships. We might explore his developmental history, especially his relationships with his mother, sister and his girlfriends prior to his marriage. Noting the predominance of anger and possible abuse of alcohol, perhaps he is fixated at the oral stage. Perhaps a psychodynamic assessment and some projective tests might be able to clarify this. Alternatively, we might note that some people adapt poorly after divorce and others felt better after the release from an apparently miserable marriage. Why did this man react in this particular way? Perhaps an assessment of his cognitive structures will reveal biases in perception and attribution. Anger suggests that personal rules have been violated. We might assess what his own rules are as to how others should treat him. Objectively there are some good things in his life, yet he perceived the world as bad. Perhaps correction of the cognitive schemata following the divorce has caused his depression.

All of these approaches to formulating this case have something in common. They locate the cause of the problem inside the person – his neurochemicals, developmental history, personality or cognitive processes.

These are all hypothetical variables. Clinicians cannot observe any of them. They can only infer from Mr Gallager's behavior. Absent from these formulations is any analysis of the relationship between the environment and Mr Gallager's behavior. They are all structural, rather than functional approaches to formulation. So, what are structuralism and functional approaches to case formulation?

STRUCTURALISM

Structuralism has a long and broad intellectual history. Varieties of structuralism are present in linguistics, anthropology, literary criticism, and sociology, as well as psychology. Different varieties of structuralism have a common theme. Namely, that observed behavior or surface is only significant as an index of some more important unobserved, underlying and occult entity. This hidden structure is the real subject matter. The job of structuralists is to take the surface material to interpret it in order to reveal these hidden elements. This hidden reality is the true subject matter and that which is observed is unimportant other than as a token of the hidden structure. The job of the researcher or clinician is to select and interpret the relevant surface structure and to uncover the hidden structure (Cone, 1997; Nelson, 1977; Nelson-Gray, 2003.)

In linguistics, structuralist approaches can be seen in the work of Saussure (1916/1977), who distinguished between *parole* and *langue*. *Parole* –words – was roughly the surface structure of language. *Langue*, the specific "word acts" that linguists observed. Saussure distinguished between the surface signifier and the underlying signified or the meaning. Saussure emphasized the formal relationships between observed words. This analysis echoes the debate between Chomsky and Skinner on the nature of human language. For Skinner (1957), verbal behavior was behavior that we can study and analyze like any other behavior. It was not necessary to reify it. It was not a special class of behavior. Chomsky's (1959) structural approach was that individual specimens of verbal behavior were mere tokens of underlying grammatical structures.

There are also structural schools of anthropology. The structuralist approach to anthropology suggests that thought processes are uniform in all cultures. These underlying thought processes can be discovered by observation of kinship, myth, and language. Cultural acts are used to divine these underlying meanings and uniform thought processes. We can understand individual cultural acts within the context of the greater cultural gestalt. Levi-Strauss believed that specific cultural practices were an expression of a "deep grammar of society." He borrowed Saussure's idea of langue and parole in that specific cultural acts were seen as expression of underlying structures. The deep grammar was hidden, unconscious and represented fundamental mental structures caused such cultural practices.

A final example of structuralism comes from literature. Here, structuralism refers to the idea that specific narratives reflect underlying narrative structures. Many different narratives contain these fewer structures. The linguist analyzes the surface structure of the narrative to reveal its hidden, universal structure that is also in other narratives that have completely different surface structures. Sometimes the linguist uses notation similar to Chomsky's phrase structure grammar.

Structuralism and Psychology

Structuralism appears in psychology in a number of guises. In which ever form it appears, it emphasizes the discovery of hidden cognitive structures, such as the work of Piaget or cognitive therapists, personality structures, developmental stages or personality types that cause human behavior. Biological psychologists posit occult biological defects, such as biochemical disturbances or brain damage – observable or non-observable as causes of human behavior. Researchers sometimes observe these variables, but clinicians are hardly ever able to do so. The observable behavior results – a test score of performance on a specially selected experimental task, spoken words or motor behavior, including pathological behavior and psychiatric symptoms – are said to be signs of these unobservable constructs.

Early in the history of modern psychology Wundt proposed that the aim of psychology was to discover the "anatomy of the mind"; that is, the cognitive structures underlying human behavior. Trained observers introspected their own experience. They then verbally reported their introspections. In one of Wundt's typical experiments trained observers responded "yes" or "no", or pressed a telegraph key to indicate the presence or absence of a stimulus or some quality of a stimulus. Wundt used trained observers' reports of introspection to reveal the hidden cognitive structures of the mind. Specifically, he hoped to be able to analyze mental life into the elements of thought. Individual sensations were analyzed into their constituent parts of modality, intensity, and quality. Wundt analyzed his introspections of his own feelings that accompanied sensations analyzed into the component pleasantness–unpleasantness, excitement–calm and strain–relaxation.

Structuralism is also used in a more narrow sense to refer to one school of psychology – Tichner's structuralism. Tichner believed that the individual elements of mental life could be detected through introspection. Using the metaphor of atomic theory and the periodic table, Tichner hoped to discover the elements of mental life, to order them and to explain their combinations to describe individual conscious experiences. Mental elements were the elements of perception, ideas and emotions. These elements were thought to combine into complex mental experiences through their history of association with other mental elements (Hergenhahn, 2001.)

Structuralism and Contemporary Psychology

Much contemporary psychology implicitly embraces structuralism. Personality theorists attempt to uncover the structure of personality that causes us to behave in our own characteristic ways. Developmental psychologists attempt to discover children's mental structures or stages that cause them to behave the way they do. Biological psychologists attempt to uncover the neuroanatomical or neurochemical causes of behavior. They build circuit diagrams of the brain or mind to explain behavior. Cognitive psychologists attempt to detect the pathogenic schemata, memory or attentional processes that cause observable behavior. They build models with multiple modules representing hypothetical processes and structures that they infer. They have yet to observe them. They use the computer as metaphor for the brain. So, structuralism is alive and well in many branches of psychology!

Like academic psychology, clinical psychology, too, embraces structuralism. Neuropsychologists diagnose the brain damage that causes attention-deficit hyperactivity disorder (ADHD) in a child who does not do well in school or a learning disability in a child with reading problems. Cognitive clinical psychologists attempt to diagnose the damaged cognitive apparatus or processes in their clients. Psychoanalysts attempt to uncover the true causes of distress buried in their clients' histories. They seek the real causes of their clients' problems, or even their clients' real problems located under their clients' skins.

Critiques of Structuralism

Critiques of Early Structuralism in Psychology

Tichner's structuralism died out because it relied on introspection as its window into the mind. Introspection used highly trained observers who reported on their own experiences, such as sensations. The method failed. Despite their training, different observers reported different results when introspecting the same stimuli. Thus, the data were unreliable and depended on which person introspected and what they were looking for inside themselves. Critics of introspection noted that it depended on the observer's memory of a sensory event, even if it was a recent memory. It was also criticized because the process of observing a private sensation might change the observed stimulus. Hence, Tichner's introspection failed because it used an unreliable method of data collection, which is an absolute requirement of science (Hergenhahn, 2001.)

What is called introspection is not truly introspection. One cannot simultaneously report a private event as it occurs. Hergenhahn (2001) suggested that it might better be termed *retrospection.* This might not seem too serious a problem if one is retrospecting something that happened a few seconds ago. However, when one's clients are recalling cognitions from events a few days or weeks ago, or when they are allegedly recalling events months and years ago, the accuracy of these retrospections must be called into question. Prospective studies have shown that memory of events become inaccurate and stereotypical. Nineteenth-century introspection was also criticized because the process of introspection might change what was reported. Again there is good evidence that the process of asking people about their history changes, and actively creates, new memories, which may not be factually based. Studies of memory of alleged traumatic events may be influenced by popular literature, other mass media and therapists' suggestions, which sometimes result in people reporting memories that can not be true (Loftus, 1993, 1994.) Thus, the process of retrospecting for hidden trauma may change the original memories by inadvertently planting new memories during therapy (Loftus, 1993, 1994.)

Other criticisms of early structuralism included its turning away from applied aspects of psychology. Indeed, like much of experimental psychology, structuralism is concerned with a very narrow sample of behavior of a narrow sample of people in a peculiar setting. It ostentatiously turns its back on naturally occurring behavior in the real world. Nineteenth-century commentators noted this lack of interest in applied questions. Introspections were disinterested in higher mental processes, individual differences, education, abnormal human behavior, animal behavior, and child development. Perhaps this was because of the lack of a method that could be used with many populations and in a real-world setting. Perhaps it was also because introspectionism viewed the discovery of mental anatomy and cognitive elements, rather than everyday behavior, as the real topic of psychology.

More recently, post-modernists have criticized structuralist approaches to linguistics: anthropology and literature have been criticized for positing absolute truths and structures, and for failing to recognize the relativistic notions of knowledge; they were criticized for embracing the idea that there were absolute truths to be discovered. Structuralism has also been criticized for implicitly embracing determinism and for failing to acknowledge individual freedoms and autonomy, which were said to be outlawed if structures caused behavior (Hergenhahn, 2001.)

Critiques of Structuralism and Implications for Case Formulation

Structural approaches to psychology and clinical psychology have a number of significant weaknesses. The criticisms laid at the feet of the nineteenth-century structural psychologists, such as Wundt and Tichner, can also equally be laid at the feet of their contemporary intellectual offspring.

Introspection Again! The first weakness is that structural approaches to case formulation depend on introspection. Cognitive psychologists for example, train their clients in the new methods of introspection. Instead of training their clients to introspect their sensations, they train them to introspect their thoughts and feelings. Based on these new introspections, cognitive psychologists infer the presence of a damaged mental apparatus. It is these damaged mental structures – schemata, or mental processes, memory and attribution – that cognitive psychologists infer from these introspections. However, the cognitive psychologist cannot observe the presence of these damaged structures. They can only infer them from the client's unreliable retrospections.

Introspection has returned to psychology. We, generally, no longer ask trained subjects to introspect their sensations in experiments. However, cognitive psychologists ask their clients to introspect their minds and report on their cognitions and attributions. Psychoanalysts ask their clients to introspect their memories to keep looking for the hidden events that caused their current problems. Counselors ask their clients to introspect their feelings. Wundt introspected sensations. Cognitive clinical psychologists teach their clients to allegedly introspect their feelings. What is allegedly introspected has changed. Nevertheless, introspection is alive and well in clinical psychology.

Unfortunately, the current popularity of introspection has not resolved the method's limitations which were identified in the nineteenth century. These critiques of retrospection can all be made of contemporary use of introspection. Only one person can introspect their cognitions. Reliable data are not possible since no second person can simultaneously observe the cognition. Reliable measurement is a requirement for science. Therefore – using syllogistic reasoning – methods using introspection are not scientific.

Circularity A second weakness is that structural approaches to explain psychopathology and treatment are necessarily circular. Cognitive psychologists use behavior to infer the presence of the unobservable structures. Cognitive psychologists then use the unobservable structures to explain the observable behavior. We observe a client say "I only passed the test because I have a good memory, I am not really smart." From that we infer a defect in the client's attributions. The cognitive psychologist then explains the client's depressed behavior as being caused by the defective attribution that was inferred from the client's behavior in the first place (Skinner, 1950, 1990.) Worse yet, psychotherapists using cognitive approaches sometimes used independent variables and dependent variables that are unobservable. For example, when a therapist allegedly changes a client's schema and measures its effect on self-reports of mood. Yet, neither independent nor dependent variables can be reliably measured.

Applicability   Structural models of psychopathology are ultimately pessimistic concerning treatment. If a psychoanalyst could truly demonstrate
that some past event caused the client's presenting problem, what can
be done? The client and therapist cannot change the past. They can only
manipulate variables in the current environment. More insidiously, structural approaches to psychopathology and treatment often have an implicit
medical model in which the therapist diagnoses the client's structural
defect. The therapist then has two practical and logical problems. First,
they must remedy the alleged structural defect. Second, they must know if
they have remedied the structural defect that caused the client's presenting
problems. How can a cognitive therapist know if they changed the cognitive structures that caused their client's depression? Are the structures
still there and dormant after successful treatment waiting to be turned
back on again in the future? How could a cognitive therapist distinguish
between a cognitive structure that is dormant and one that is not there in
the first place? They only have their clients' unreliable retrospections on
which to base their inferences.

Structural approaches to psychopathology are stuck in a traditional
causal model of behavior. The structuralist assumes that the brain damage that resulted from the stroke caused the client to become disinhib-
ited and to yell a lot. While there may apparently be a tight correlation
between the stroke and the subsequent yelling, assuming that the brain
damage caused the yelling is not justified. The damage brain part, if it
can be isolated, is part of a large system. That system includes other parts
of the brain, other parts of physical organism, the client's behavior, and
the environment. Other variables may also have changed that may have
caused the yelling. If the brain damage is for ever present, how then could
that account for the increases and decreases in the rate of yelling? Must
we infer that the brain damage is waxing and waning with the behavior?
Or, shall we infer that the brain damage is always there, but the client's
unobservable self-control or inhibition waxes and wanes instead? When
the structuralist is asked to explain the behavior of a child with ADHD
they might note the possible changes in serotonin levels sometimes found
between children with ADHD and other children. But, what about *this*
specific child? The structuralist did not observe this child's serotonin
level. They only observed their behavior. Again, what of the variations in
the child's presenting problems? Must we infer that the child's serotonin
levels are changing along with the child's behavior? How can we do so
independently of the child's behavior?

Contrasting structural and functional approaches to two problems
– language acquisition and rehabilitation and theory of mind – illustrate
the limitations of structural approaches to applied questions.

Chomsky's (1959; Virues-Ortega, 2006) critique of Skinner's *Verbal
Behavior* received much attention. Some interpreted it as a damning critique of behavioral conceptualizations of verbal behavior. Unfortunately,

subsequent behavioral comments have generally not been acknowledged (MacCorqoudale, 1970; Palmer, 2006.) Yet, other than waiting for the Language Acquisition Device to mature, Chomsky had no intervention to offer people with language problems, such as people with psychotic disorders, developmental disabilities or dementias. Neither did he have anything to offer on how to promote language development in typical children. There has been no line of research producing effective language interventions based on Chomsky's views of language. In contrast, applied behavior analysis (ABA), with its functionalist approach to behavior change, is optimistic about change. Consequently, behavior analysis has contributed extensively to the area of language teaching and reha- bilitation. Examples include teaching language to children (Mann & Baer, 1970), teaching children with intellectual disabilities to read (Conners, 1992), remediation of language problems in children with autism (Lee & Sturmey, 2006), adults with schizophrenia (Wilder & Wong, 2007) or acquired brain damage (Dixon & Bihler, 2007), and Alzheimer's disease (Bourgeois, 1990.) Structuralists are notable absentees from language training and rehabilitation.

The second example of a structuralist theory is Baron-Cohen's (1997) "Theory of Mind." It posits that autistic behavior, including language, is caused by the lack of a theory of mind. The absence of a theory of mind is inferred through observable behavior, such as a child not describing other people's perspectives and beliefs that are different from their own. For example, in the Sally-Ann task the experimenter presents the child with two dolls. Sally has a basket and Ann has a box. Sally puts a marble in her basket. Ann then leaves. While Ann is away, Sally places the marble in Ann's box. The experimenter then asks the child observing this where Ann will look for her marble. If the child understands that, since Ann's belief is different from everyone's belief she will look in the basket. However, if the child does not understand that people have differing perspectives and beliefs from one another, then the child will say that Ann will look in her box for the marble.

Theory of mind is said to explain a wide range of behavior (Baron-Cohen, 2007) and is the basis for intervention to remedy children with autism's inherent "mind blindness" (Hadwin, Baron-Cohen, Howlin & Hill, 1997). Theory of mind researchers have attempted to teach theory of mind concepts to children with autism. Yet, even their own research has produced only modest evidence of efficacy. They have shown some evidence of acquisition of theory of mind skills in teaching situations in some, but not all studies (Hadwin et al., 1997.) When one looks at the intervention methods used to teach theory of mind skills they seem weakly designed and incompletely described. They use reinforcement, but prevaricate on its use and do not describe their interventions operationally (Hadwin et al., 1997.) Hence, researchers and parents cannot replicate these studies and researchers cannot measure if the treatment took place. It gives the impression that advocates of the theory of mind do not try very hard to teach theory of mind skills. Theory of mind researchers are too willing to accept the null hypothesis that theory of mind deficits can not be taught.

In contrast, behavior analysts have embraced the challenge that theory of mind skills can be operationalized, analyzed, and taught (LeBlanc, Coates, Daneshvar, Charlop-Christy, Morris & Lancaster, 2003.) Instead of seeing this as an impossible task, behavior analysis sees it as a new and interesting set of social behaviors to be taught. They may – or may not – be a little more difficult to teach than other behaviors, but they are not fundamentally different in nature.

Individual Differences   Finally, structural approaches under-emphasize individual differences. Medical models that emphasize diagnosis, or psychological models of specific disorders, all implicitly state that all members of the class of individuals are the same in some important way. The notion that there is an effective treatment for depression assumes that all people with depression have something important in common that determines treatment outcome. How then can this approach account for the large individual differences between clients with the same diagnosis receiving the same treatment? One could plausibly appeal to differences in treatment integrity to explain these differential outcomes. But what if treatment integrity was demonstrated and individual differences still remained? How would a structuralist account for such individual differences? From a functional perspective individual differences are the key to determining treatment design, even when all clients have the same diagnosis or presenting topography. Mismatching the treatment to the client's individual problems may result in ineffective treatment (Nelson-Gray et al., 1989.) or worse still, harm to the client (Iwata, Cowdery & Miltenberger, 1994.)

Structuralists in the Office

Structural approaches to human behavior deemphasize the environment. It assumes that the therapist treats an omnipresent person. The interaction between the person and the environment is deemphasized or ignored. Thus, if one is studying cognitive structures or repressed memories, one can study them anywhere. Why not study these structures in the office?

There is good reason. Human behavior is greatly influenced by the environment. However, many therapists are office-bound. They see only a small sample of their client's behavior in one setting. They either have to assume the client behavior that is seen in the office is representative of client behavior elsewhere and/or have to rely on client reports of their behavior elsewhere. These client reports may be incomplete and inaccurate.

Summary

Current structural approaches continue to suffer from the same limitations as they did in the nineteenth century. They are more likely to focus on private events revealed through self-report, to be more pessimistic about changing some structural feature of the person, such as their brain, to focus on the damaged person rather than the pathogenic environment, and to be office based, rather than interested in the rest of the world.

FUNCTIONALISM

Like structuralism, functionalism is present in many branches of science and thought. Although the applications of functionalist thinking are very varied, they share a number of features. Keller (1973, cited in Hergenhahn, 2001) noted eight features that distinguished functionalist from structuralist psychology:

1. Functionalists rejected the mentalistic approaches of structuralists searching for the elements of mental life as sterile.
2. Functionalists viewed mental life as an adaptive process that led to organisms functioning more effectively. They were interested in the purpose of mind, not its structure.
3. Functionalists embraced the idea of psychology as an applied science.
4. Functionalists broadened the applicability of psychology. They addressed novel populations, such as clinical populations, children and animals. They also used novel methods, such as puzzle boxes and mental tests.
5. Functionalists were interested in motivation. The organism behaved differently in the same environment on different occasions. Hence, even though it presumably had largely the same mental apparatus it had previously, something else had to be invoked to account for these different performances.
6. Functionalists were interested in both mental life and observable behavior. Introspection was only one of many methods of psychology.
7. Functionalists emphasized individual differences, not commonalities amongst people.
8. Darwin's evolutionary thinking strongly influenced functionalism.

Functional psychologists, such as William James, reacted against introspectionism. He emphasized empiricism and the pragmatic value of psychological ideas. So, he opened up psychology to many methods of study beyond introspection and placed great value on the usefulness of these ideas. Influenced by Darwin, he also noted that mind had an adaptive value and helped the organism adapt to its environment. He was also interested in human learning and its application to assist people to lead better lives. Many of his observations prefigure operant and respondent learning and their application to every day living. James also gave practical advice to develop better ways of living through learning and environmental design. His maxim to "[p]lace yourself in circumstances that encourage good habits and discourage bad ones" prefigured interventions based on stimulus control. Another of his maxims stated that you should "Force yourself to act in ways that are beneficial to you even if doing so at first is distasteful and requires considerable effort." This advice prefigures contemporary behavioral treatments of depression (Lejuez, Hopko & Hopko, 2007) amongst others clinical problems.

Keller's (1973) eight features of functionalism all suggest parallels with behaviorism:

1. Behaviorism, like functionalism generally, eschews searching for the elements of consciousness (Hergenhahn, 2001, p. 297.) It emphasizes the analysis of observable behavior.
2. Functionalists search for the adaptive function of the mind. Behaviorists similarly search for the adaptive function of both public and private behavior, including thinking and other private behavior. An organism's current behavior is seen as the result of selection of the most adapted forms of behavior by the environment during the lifespan of the organism. Even psychopathological behavior, that harms the organism, is painful and distressing, is seen as kinds of adaptation.
3. Behavior analysis does distinguish two branches of the science of behavior. The experimental analysis of behavior (EAB) studies basic learning processes that are of theoretical rather than applied significance. Applied behavior analysis (ABA) uses these basic principles to change behaviors of social significance. ABA also contributes to the basic science by describing new phenomena not observable in basic preparations and by extending the basic principles to applied settings. When Baer, Wolf and Risley (1968) first described the seven features of ABA, they emphasized that ABA must produce large changes in socially important behavior that are meaningful, that people recognize as being important using methods that are acceptable and valued, and that are based on the basic principles of the science of behavior, rather than on a technology of behavior change.
4. ABA has studied a very wide range of human populations, including children, people with various severe disabilities and non-human animals. It uses methods other than introspection, primarily direct observation of behavior in the natural environment.
5. Whereas early functionalists used the term "motivation" to account for the "why" of mental life, behavior analysis has used the terms such as reinforcement, reinforcer deprivation and reinforcer satiation as a central concepts accounting for the "why" of behavior.

6. Functionalists studied both mental life and behavior. Behaviorism has a range of positions on the status of mental life and how and why it may be studied. (See Friman, Wilson & Hayes 1998a, 1998b; Lamal, 1998; Taylor & O'Reilly, 1997 for a spectrum of views within behavior analysis on this issue.) In any case, behavior analysis surely studies public behavior.

7. Individual differences, coming from both genetic sources and differences in the organism's learning history, are central to behaviorism. However, ABA emphasizes those individual differences related to learning, since they can be manipulated during the analysis and treatment of behavior. The purpose of behavioral approaches to case formulation and behavioral treatment is to detect those individual differences that affect treatment. Commonalities, such as a diagnosis or demographic variables are seen as variables that do not contribute greatly to treatment design. Individual differences that cannot guide treatment design are ignored.

8. As noted previously, James's emphasis on pragmatism and applications of psychology directly parallel subsequent behavioral work. Behaviorism took the ideas of variation and selection from evolution and applied them directly to such topics as the evolution of the operant within the organism's lifespan and to cultural evolution (Skinner, 1953.)

Functionalism, Evolution and Psychology

One of the most important examples of functional approaches to explaining behavior that influenced behaviorism greatly is biological evolution. Evolution noted that the reproductive capacity of organisms vastly exceeded that which the environment can support. It also noted that there were considerable variations amongst members of a species. Some of this variation was due to genes that were passed on from generation to generation. An organism may have had adaptive features, such as physical features, physiology, reproductive strategies, and behavior, which may have contributed toward the survival of its genes in the next generation. If these adaptive features had a genetic component, then they will be more likely than other features to appear in the next generation. An organism was said to be "fit" if it could survive to reproductive age and pass on its genes to the next generation. Contemporary version of evolution, such as sociobiology and evolutionary psychology, emphasize the gene as the unit of selection. The organism is merely the hapless vehicle, a mere wrapping around genes to transport them from one generation to another. Genes can be transported into the next generation both directly through offspring and through investment in related organisms, such as siblings and cousins, since they share some genes with the organism doing the investment.

Hence, there may be selection for genes that promote behaviors, such as investment in kin (Hergenhahn, 2001; Wilson, 1975.)

Early evolutionary scientists were concerned with behavior and other issues that behavior analysis addressed in a number of ways. Behavior contributed to survival of genes into the next generation and some behaviors were heritable to varying degrees. Darwin published on the possible genetic basis of human emotional behavior and its relationship to emotional behavior in non-human animals. Darwin's description of his son's development was one of the first accounts of modern child development based on observation of behavior in the natural environment.

Darwin's contemporary and codiscoverer of evolution, Spencer, wrote about both learning and cultural evolution. Spencer assumed that the complex human nervous system contributed to human fitness by permitting better, faster learning and thus contributing to individual and cultural survival. Spencer also suggested that contiguity of stimuli and the consequences of behavior, such as "success", pleasant feelings, and painful feelings influenced learning that contributed to the organism's survival. Thus, Spencer's work prefigured Thorndike's and Skinner's work on operant behavior. Spencer was also interested in cultural evolution. He suggested that evolution meant progress toward perfection of individuals and societies. Spencer therefore advocated *laissez faire* capitalism and criticized social programs for the poor. Thus, early on, evolution was interested in its implications for design of society. Although they reached very different conclusions about what kinds of society to promote and how to design cultures, Spencer and Darwin's discussion of selection of societies prefigured Skinner and other behavior analysts' work on cultural evolution and design (Skinner, 1948, 1971.)

Summary

Functionalism is found in many branches of science and thought, including literature, sociology, linguistics, and anthropology. Evolution is one of the best examples of functionalism as it emphasizes the fit of the organism to its environment. Behavior analysis is an extension of evolutionary thinking in that it applied the notions of variations and selection to the behavior of individual organisms and cultures.

MR GALLAGER REVISITED

So what do structuralism and functionalism have to do with Mike Gallager? Structural approaches would attempt to detect the hidden structure of Mr Gallager's allegedly real problem – his hidden problem. One way or another, Mr Gallager's complaints would be used to make inferences about entities that his therapist cannot directly observe. These hidden entities might be psychiatric illnesses, disturbances in his brain or synapses, or cognitive processes or personality. Diagnosticians might debate which of many diagnoses might be most appropriate – major depression, dysthymic disorder, general anxiety disorder, adjustment disorder, a personality disorder perhaps. Psychotherapists might debate the relationship between his presenting symptoms and his distant history. Clinicians might suggest mapping of potential treatments from diagnoses or presenting problems. If he is depressed, perhaps cognitive-behavior therapy might be appropriate. This is not a bad choice. There is good evidence of the effectiveness of cognitive-behavior therapy for depression (Roth & Fonagy, 2004.) But he also experiences anger and anxiety – should his therapist put him in an anger management group or an anxiety management group. Perhaps he should be in three groups – one for mood, one for anger and one for anxiety. Is he one of the people who did not respond in the randomized controlled trials (RCTs) that evaluated these treatments? If he is, what is his therapist to do? His relationships have been disrupted for many years. His present problems are part of a larger pattern of disruptive and unsatisfactory relations. Should he not receive psychotherapy to understand this pattern better and gain insight into his real problem? There are too many solutions that might map onto all these possible diagnoses and problems. How should his therapist decide what treatment to implement?

These problematic approaches are structuralist. So what would function-alist do? A functionalist would begin by seeing the presenting problems as in some sense an adaptation by Mr Gallager to his environment. The presenting symptoms are useful. The environment has selected these forms of behavior over time, even though they are painful and limiting to him. So the first step is to discover the relationship between current environmental events and his problematic and non-problematic behavior. His assessment should identify current, modifiable environmental variables that influence his behavior. The therapist might work with Mr Gallager to agree which form of his behavior is problematic, which is not and what he would like to do if he was problem-free. His presenting problems, which are many, might be simplified into a smaller number of areas, such as relationships with others, mood, and health. Below is a preliminary list:

1. Get better relationships with other people
   - Former wife (handling disagreements)
   - Children (lack of visits, lack of satisfactory visits)
   - Former boss (taking direction)
   - Coworkers
   - Physician
   - Establish stable relationship with girlfriend
2. Improve mood management

- What to do when feeling depressed
- Not to drink when depressed
3. Better health
- Attend appointments for physical health
- Work with current psychiatrist or get a more acceptable psychiatrist
- Get antidepressants reviewed
- Eat more healthily
- Exercise more
- Drink less
4. Obtain better living situation
- Find a better flat
- Find a job or equivalent structured daily pattern of life

Given the large number of problems, it might be useful to identify which ones are priorities for Mr Gallager. When he stated the reason for referral, the prime reason he gave was to remove negative feelings. A constructionist approach might seize on this and begin to identify situations associated with positive mood (Lejuez et al., 2002.) Even the brief description at the beginning of this chapter identifies a number of aspects of his behavior that suggests he has effective ways of behaving in his behavioral repertoire or at least has had effective ways of behaving in the past. An important part of the pretreatment assessment would be to identify all of his strengths in these areas.

Since behavioral approaches emphasize not merely behavior, but its relationship to the environment, an important part of the pretreatment assessment would be to work with Mr Gallager to help him discover these relationships (Skinner, 1953.) Interviewing might help him to begin to describe some of them. For example, if poor relationships with other people was key area for him, his therapist might ask if there are relationships with some people or aspects of relationships that are successful. His therapist might also ask if there social skills he has or activities he carries out with other people that are meaningful and rewarding to him. As well as interviews, his therapist might also use self-recording and observation of his behavior to discover which interactions are meaningful and satisfactory and which are not. Perhaps there are visits with his children that go well and those that do not. His therapist might ask what the differences between these visits are. By doing this his therapist may discover relationships between environmental variables and Mr Gallager's behavior. More importantly, Mr Gallager might also do the same. The information given at the beginning of the chapter is incomplete. Yet, one might begin to frame assessment questions that reflect a functionalist perspective on these problems. For example, if appropriate interaction with others has decreased what might account for that? Has he become more punitive to others? Has interaction with others become less reinforcing for him? Has he learned patterns of interaction that are inappropriate or has he lost social skills he used to have? Perhaps the other people have changed in some way. Has he moved from one setting to another where previously effective behavior is no longer effective? Each of these possibilities suggests alternate approaches to the problem. If he has become more punitive to others and they avoid him, what can be done to make him more reinforcing to others? Can he learn social skills to make himself more interesting and reinforcing to others? Can he be taught to engage in activities with others that are more interesting to them? Are there things he is doing that are irritating to others that he should stop? What new behavior would be effective for a new setting?

Mr Gallager identified removal of bad feelings as the main reason for seeking therapy. Part of the pretreatment assessment might be again to discover the relationships between activities and his mood. Again retrospective information during an interview might give some broad information. A week or two of self-recording mood and activities might give some more useful and interesting information about activities associated with depressed and happy mood. By beginning to instruct Mr Gallager to self-record and to describe the relationship between the environment and his mood, his therapist has already begun to accomplish two important tasks. First, his therapist has begun to teach him to discriminate his own behavior and its relationship to the environment more carefully and effectively than he had previously done. In so doing, the implications and uses of the observed functional relationships between his environment and behavior might become apparent to Mr Gallager himself. Second, we have also begun to change the way Mr Gallager speaks and writes about his own behavior. Thus, pretreatment assessment has already induced significant behavior change that may make intervention more likely and more effective. Later, this might be the basis of a more overt treatment plan (Skinner, 1953.)

His behavioral repertoire and the range of environments might be quite restricted compared to his past. There may be important functional relationships that we cannot now observe. It might also be useful for his therapist to enquire as to the things he used to do that he used to enjoy, but no longer does. Additionally, it might be useful to begin mini experiments to try out activities in which he currently no longer engages that might both suggest further functional relationships and have implications for treatment. For example, if he used to take a drive when bored he might try that again to observe its effects on his mood. If that does not work, perhaps there are other strategies he could begin to try.

This assessment information might suggest lawful relationships between his activities and mood. This information can be used to help Mr Gallagher arrange the environment to increase the situations associated with positive mood and to remove or modify those situations that are associated with negative mood. If there are certain activities that he enjoys more than others perhaps he can begin to schedule these activities more frequently over a number of weeks. If there are certain ways to make visits with his children more rewarding, then perhaps he can learn to schedule more of these activities to make the visits more rewarding for both parties. If he can discriminate the onset of periods of negative mood early, he can take action early to avert his negative mood becoming more severe. Perhaps he can learn to avoid some activities that are associated with negative mood or modify them in some ways to make them less difficult for him. For example, he might be able to learn to interact with his former wife in a more effective manner or to terminate the interactions prior to them becoming aversive.

We now have the beginning of an incomplete, but partially useful, functionalist case formulation. Much information is missing. Yet, his therapist is now in a position to help Mr Gallagher.

Chapter 2

RADICAL BEHAVIORISM

Behaviorism is often the whipping boy of undergraduate textbooks. Many nonbehavioral authors attempt to strengthen their own position by presenting arguments that begin by repudiating, whilst simultaneously misrepresenting, behaviorism (e.g. Novacco, 1997; Stenfert Kroese et al., 1997; Taylor, 2005) or simply omit its contribution from reviews (e.g. Taylor & Lindsay, 2007). These criticisms are often inaccurate and unfounded. Many critics and teachers misrepresent radical behaviorism and criticize it for things that it is not (Chiesa, 1994; MacCorquodale, 1970; Palmer, 2006). Behaviorism's death has been periodically announced for over 50 years. Yet, it is still a strong, vital, and distinct discipline that continues to make contributions to our understanding of behavior and in changing behavior in important ways in a wide range of applied settings.

Let us begin by examining some terms and making some important distinctions relevant to this line of thinking. *Radical behaviorism* is a philosophy of science. It presents a coherent, unified world view that values observation as its basic datum. It deemphasizes theory (Skinner, 1950). It underlies the two related practices of the experimental analysis of behavior, or basic behavioral research, and ABA, the application of behaviorism to socially significant problems (Baer et al., 1969). Chiesa (1994) presented one of the best expositions, defenses, and corrections concerning these misrepresentations of radical behaviorism. We will use her account to begin this chapter.

AN ACCOUNT AND DEFENSE OF RADICAL BEHAVIORISM

Chiesa noted that psychology is a fragmented discipline with many different fields. We distinguish developmental and biological psychology almost as different disciplines or at least different fields of psychology. Each field has different world views. Each field identifies different kinds of questions as important and frames these questions differently. Chiesa suggested that this is not a trivial phenomenon. Rather, it reflects a more fundamental disunity about the nature of psychology. Psychology is unified perhaps only by a general, but not universal, commitment to empiricism as a method to answer questions about behavior but little else.

Radical behaviorism on the other hand is distinguished by two features. First, there is a unified world view. It is coherent. It uses similar kinds of explanations of behavior and similar methods of data collection, analysis and conceptual framework for all problems that is absent from mainstream psychology. Second, it is a kind of science that is distinct from mainstream psychology. Radical behaviorism embraces description of the phenomenon that is very close to the actual data. It uses observation, and then induces general principles from multiple observations. It places most emphasis on observation and induction of general laws, rather than theory (Skinner, 1950). In contrast, mainstream psychology, is theory-driven, often uses data collection methods other than observation of behavior, tests hypotheses with inferential statistics and ignores or deemphasizes data on individual people in preference for data on nonexistent, average subjects (Sidman, 1960.) Chiesa noted that radical behaviorism in general and Skinner's work in particular is a lightning rod for controversy in many different areas.

A SCIENCE OF BEHAVIOR

When Skinner (1953) described behaviorism, he began by defining it as a science of behavior and therefore looked at the terms 'science' and 'behavior.' He noted that science is a set of attitudes in which authority is rejected and facts are accepted as they are, even if they are inconvenient facts. Science is also characterized by honesty. Because science is public, any dishonesty in presentation of facts is likely to be detected quickly by others. Science is also tolerant of ignorance. If an answer is not known, the question is left as unanswered until the data come in.

Science also characterized by a search for order and simplicity of explanation. Individual observations are replicated, uniformities are detected, and if the observation has greater generality, a scientific law might be proposed. Scientific laws may have begun as artisan's rules of thumb. Later science systematized, formalized, and refined these practices. A good knowledge of such laws permits science to predict and control the phenomenon it studies. For example, the periodic table enabled scientists to predict the properties of hitherto undiscovered elements, and Newtonian physics can predict the behavior of objects that have not yet moved.

Skinner argued that, when it comes to the science of behavior, we are at a disadvantage. People are blinkered by their own beliefs and experiences, by their language and culture. Explanations of behavior are not wanting: anyone can offer many explanations of behavior. Indeed, people are already partially able to predict and control their own and other people's behavior quite effectively. We already have a folk-science of behavior. Biography, descriptions of personality and social customs all speak of the regularity and prediction of behavior.

People often object to a science of behavior. Naturally, many people cling to a prescientific approach to behavior, which is familiar, sometimes quite useful, and nonthreatening. For example, people sometimes object to a science of behavior because human behavior is complex. However, science has a good history of taking complex phenomenon and being able to explain them using a few principals after sufficient time. Sometimes people object to a science of behavior because studying people may change their behavior. However, the problem of the scientific method changing the thing it studies is a problem common to all sciences, which all sciences strive to overcome. Another relevant critique of the applied science of behavior is that laboratory studies of human behavior oversimplify. Hence, results found in the laboratory may be reliable, but may have no generalization to real world settings. Forty years of applied studies in the *Journal of Applied Behavior Analysis* shows that this problem can be overcome.

THE CAUSES OF BEHAVIOR

Skinner noted that the terms "cause" and "effect" are not always used in science. Rather, the term "functional relationship" is used to refer to a reliable relationship between the change in the independent variable and the associated change in the dependent variable. Unfortunately, everyday language and culture is full of explanations of behavior. Astrology, somatotypes, and numerous inner causes, such as neural, intrapsychic, and cognitive causes are just some commonly offered explanations of behavior.

Behavior analysis understands human behavior by conducting a functional analysis of behavior. That is, it examines the reliable relationships between external variables that can be manipulated systematically and produce a reliable change in human behavior – the dependent variable. Skinner (1953) wrote "The external variables of which behavior is a function provide for what may be called a causal or functional analysis" (p. 35). In a similar vein Baer et al. (1968) famously wrote that "the analysis of a behavior ... requires a believable demonstration of the events that can be responsible for the occurrence or non-occurrence of a behavior ... an ability of an experimenter to turn the behavior on and off ..." (pp. 93–94.) Haynes and O'Brien (1990) defined a functional analysis as "the identification of important controllable, causal and non-causal functional relationships applicable to a specified behavior for an individual."

Haynes and O'Brien (1990) discussed this definition in the context of clinical case formulation. They noted that this definition emphasizes causal relationships over noncausal relationships. Thus, it may be possible to turn a behavior on and off using noncausal independent variables that also produce changes in unknown causal variables. For example, Malatesta (1990) could turn a boy's tics on and off by presenting different people. Tics were very frequent in the presence of his father, were lower in the presence of his father and mother together, and were lower still in the presence of the therapist and custodian. His tics occurred least frequently when he worked alone. Thus, Malatesta observed a very reliable relationship between tic frequency and the presence of certain people. However, a causal relationship was not demonstrated as he did not identify what accounted for the differences in rate of tics in the presence of other people. In contrast, a series of studies by Woods, Miltenberger and others systematically identified specific, causal independent variables with functional relationships with tics. For example, Woods, Twohig, Flessner and Roloff (2003) and Woods, Miltenberger and Lumley (1996) evaluated a behavioral package known as habit reversal for the treatment of tics and Tourette Disorder. Habit reversal has four components. Awareness training involves teaching the client to accurately report each instant of the target behavior. In self-monitoring the client write down or otherwise records each instance of the target behavior. Habit reversal also involves social support from friends and family who are informed of the treatment and its goals, and who support treatment implementation and positive behavior change. Finally, the client is taught a competing response to use prior to or immediately after the onset of the target behavior. For example, to reduce a neck twitch to the right a competing response might be to have the client move their neck briefly and very slightly to the left 10 times. This could be used both immediately the tic and before, when the client feels a slight tension that often precedes the tic itself. Woods et al. (2001) showed that talking about tics reliably increased the frequency of tics. Woods et al. (1996) showed that the specific components of habit reversal – awareness training, self-monitoring, social support and a competing response – all influenced tic frequency reliably, in idiosyncratic combinations in four children with tic disorder. Finally, Woods and Himle (2004) demonstrated that verbal instructions not to engage in tics had no effect or increased tics. They also showed that reinforcing the absence of the tic also had large and robust effects on reducing tics. Thus, in contrast to Maltesta's study, which reported a reliable functional analysis but did not identify the controlling variables, Woods, Miltenberger and colleagues' series of studies identified the specific causal variables responsible to tic reduction. Haynes and O'Brien (2000) also noted that their definition of functional analysis emphasized independent variables that were important, that is, produced large effects on the behavior of interest. Finally, they emphasized that independent variables must be controllable to be useful in therapy. Thus, height, weight, gender and genetic syndromes might be important in controlling aggressive behavior. However, since none of them are variables that can be manipulated they cannot enter into a functional analysis. They cannot be of interest to a therapist for the purposes of treatment design, since no one can manipulate these independent variables.

SKINNER'S THREE SOURCES OF BEHAVIOR

Skinner identified three sources of behavior: biological evolution, cultural evolution, and evolution of the behavior during the organism's lifespan (Skinner, 1953; 1984, 1990). He described them as the provinces of biology, anthropology, and psychology. Each discipline described forms of evolution of behavior which occurred over different time spans. Biological evolution operated over of millions of years. Cultural evolution occurred over thousands of years. Psychology described the selection of behavior over the course of the organism's lifespan. All three sources of behavior have several features in common. Variations – whether genetic, cultural or variations in operant behavior – exist. For all three sources of behavior the environment selects the most effective, adapted or functional aspect of the organism. In all three examples potentially measurable aspects of the environment – some physical characteristic, some contingency that a society applies to all or many of its members, or some contingency operating on an organism's behavior are discernable. The conceptual borrowing from one form of selection as an explanation for behavior to another is apparent in terms such as extinction whether it refers to the extinction of a gene, a society or behavior. Let us examine all three in turn and see these parallels.

Biological Evolution and Behavior

As we noted in the previous chapter, behaviorism is an example of functionalism and shares with other forms of functionalism, especially evolutionary biology, common features. Evolutionary biology noted that organisms vary from one another in their form, physiology, and behavior. To the extent that these features have some genetic basis that contributes to the survival of the genes carried inside the organism, these behaviors will then be selected by the environment. As the selecting environment changes, the variations in inherited behavior-selected change over time will also change.

Behaviorism acknowledges the important role of natural selection in causing behavior. For example, many books on behaviorism note the role that biological limitations, such as sensory organs, place on learning (Leslie & O'Reilly, 1999). However, since biological evolution does not inform the selection of independent variables, it is not discussed extensively in many texts on behavior analysis.

Skinner and Cultural Evolution

Much of human behavior is culture-specific. Whether we stop working on Friday, Saturday or Sunday is a cultural-specific practice. We learn these behaviors from the other members of our culture through verbal behavior.

Skinner also wrote extensively on cultural evolution and design. In *Walden Two* (1948), he wrote a behavioral utopia, which became the model for several intentional communities, such as Los Horcones in the North Sonoran Dessert (1971). Cultural evolution and design were addressed in *Science and Human Behavior* (1953) and extensively in *Beyond Freedom and Dignity* (1971). Skinner's analysis of cultural practices usually begins with noting that a culture is a social environment that shapes the behavior of its members. When cultural practices emerge that induce its members to engage in behaviors that result in the survival of the culture, then that culture is more likely to survive. This is true, whether or not such behaviors result in personal harm or good to the individual members. For example, many cultures induce their members to engage in some personally lethal behaviors, such as fighting to the death, but if such self-sacrifice will contribute to the survival of that culture then the contingencies that are present in the culture to induce such self-harming behavior will survive. Novel cultural practices that contribute to cultural survival may be accidental or planned. Often cultures do engage in explicit cultural design that has the purpose of enhancing the probability of survival of that culture, such as attempts to control population growth, pollution and increase productivity.

Diamond's (1999, 2004) recent work on cultural evolution and extinction also used functional explanations of cultural evolution. Hence, it is conceptually parallel to behavioral approaches to cultural evolution. Diamond noted that the physical properties of environments, such as the physical geography, climate, growing season, number of plants and animals that can be cultivated and domesticated varies dramatically from location to location. Cultural evolution began and accelerated early in Eurasia. Although other parts of the world had broadly similar climates, they had surprisingly poor resources and hence cultural evolution began late and proceeded slowly. Eurasia's east-west is both relatively barrier-free and has a similar climate. Hence, a novel and useful plant, or technology could quickly travel from China to Portugal. In contrast, cultural evolution in the Americas, faced physical and climatic barriers and poorer resources, was slow. Once cultures begin to evolve then there are spiraling pressures, driven by competition for physical resources and increasing population density, leading to increasingly efficient food production and enabling specialization of labor. Denser populations are also susceptible to endemics of diseases, many of which derive from close contact with domesticated animals. These endemics result in significant mortality in those genetically vulnerable to the disease, but leave behind a genetically robust population that is resistant to such infections.

Diamond (2004) described cultural extinction. He described how cultural practices, such as overgrazing, and retention of cultural practices that were appropriate to former settings, but are harmful in a new setting lead to environmental destruction and cultural extinction. For example, Greenland's Norse culture faced significant resource problems and retained practices from Scandanavia, such as consumption of expensive church bells in a place when iron was not available. There may also have been a prohibition on eating fish. Instead they raised expensive cattle. Highly effective technologies were visible to the Greenlanders from their Inuit neighbors who still survive. The inflexible Norse adopted none of them. Hence, Greenland's Norse culture extinguished while Inuit culture, carefully adapted to the harsh conditions of Greenland, thrived in plain sight.

Skinner's and Diamond's analyses of cultural evolution are conceptually parallel. They both take a functional view. As an anthropologist, Diamond emphasized the physical and geographical resources of a particular location. As a behaviorist, Skinner emphasized the social contingencies in selecting cultural practices. Other behaviorists, such as Biglan (1995), Lamal (1997) and Glenn (1988) have extended Skinner's work on cultural evolution to address the understanding of a variety of societal problems, such as smoking, violence and education.

Cultures evolve because of fortuitous changes in cultural practices and intentional efforts by members. Cultures induce their members to work harder through wages and to control unwanted behavior usually by aversive contingencies, such as house arrest for culturally unacceptable forms of theft and aggression. Skinner (1971) argued that cultures involve contingencies that can be designed to promote desired behavior. The design of both utopian and dystopian communities has been the subject of literature. Yet, often these descriptions are not technological and clear, and are often necessarily simplistic. Explicit design of societies is often opposed because it is said it will not work, denies people their freedom, will produce disasters, or people will not like it. (Witness the public reaction to the charge zone in London to reduce excessive overcrowding on the roads prior to the actual introduction. Ironically, the program was so successful and acceptable that many other cities are adopting such a cultural practice.)

The controllers of contingencies are not immune from influence of the behavior of other members whose behavior is being controlled. The science of behavior should examine the contingencies that control their benevolent and malevolent behaviors. Members of society frequently enact counter-controlling contingencies. For example, in the poll tax strike during the Thatcher regime in the UK, many people refused to pay a legal, but unjust tax. Subsequently, the tax was rescinded. Other forms of societal design, such as voluntary self-taxation through lottery tickets, evoke little counter-control. Rather, because of the inclusion of intermittent schedules of reinforcement for self-taxation, many citizens enthusiastically endorse this method of taxation.

Skinner (1971) noted that the behavioral technology of cultural design is ethically neutral. It can be used by a tyrant or benefactor. There have been several real world attempts to implement behaviorally-inspired utopias. Los Horcones, Mexico, is an intentional community whose values will surprise many readers. This small experimental community uses behavior analysis to design a society that has shared goals, shared property, and shared responsibility in which members do not delegate responsibilities to others. This society is designed to enhance coopera-tion, rather than competition between members. Cultural practices in-clude shared responsibility for child rearing and a behavioral form of feminism. Los Horcones (2006) has applied behavioral principles to the assignment of work tasks. The objective of work organization is to get the required work done and to maximize people's enjoyment. The work that needs to be done has been task analyzed. The work is divided into fixed work that must be done, such as child care, and occasional work, such as fixing a broken fence. Work coordinators calculate the number of hours of work and allocate it to community members. Community members have choice over some tasks and members may do tasks for each other. If no one wishes to do an essential task it is placed on a schedule and everyone shares in the responsibility of its undertaking. Los Horcones has procedures to teach people how to enjoy tasks they currently do not like and procedures to ensure work is more reinforcing, for example, by increasing choice over work tasks and allowing community members to complete tasks for others who do not like a particular task. Members are not paid for work and any money made goes into an account for the entire community. Chapter 10 describes how Skinner linked societies' use of punitive behavior control to anxiety and anxiety disorders in individual members of those societies.

Selection of Behavior During the Lifespan

Behavior also varies and the environment selects some forms of behavior during the organism's lifespan. As the infant turns its head or moves its body consequences are delivered by the physical and social environment that progressively select and refine some forms of behavior and punish or extinguish others. Young infants emit a wide range of sounds, but by the time they begin talking their repertoire of sounds is greatly di-minished as their caregivers selectively ignore or punish some sounds and reinforce culture specific appropriate sounds (Goldstein, King & West, 2003.) Selection of variations of behavior during the lifespan is an important refinement in the adaptation of the organism. Natural selection can only prepare an organism's behavioral repertoire for the commonalities between the past and the present. However, it cannot predict exact changes in the physical and cultural environment that may occur in the future. The current environment selects adaptive forms of behavior through learning within the organism's lifespan.

FUNCTIONAL ANALYSIS AND MATHEMATICS

If you use Google or *Amazon.com* to search for the term "functional analysis" you do not find information on behavior analysis at first. Rather, you find journals and books related to mathematics. Functional analysis is a branch of mathematics that describes the shapes of functions. This connotation of functional analysis overlaps with behavior analysis and its approach to causation. Chiesa (1994) noted that Skinner (1953, 1971) sidestepped the traditional notion of causality (see Skinner, 1971), replacing it with somewhat neutral descriptions of the reliable relationship between independent and dependent variables. Thus, some forms of behavioral functional assessment and analysis merely describe the relationship between one variable and the target behavior of interest. For example, one might note that a child is more active in the morning and less active as the day proceeds. If the data are reliable then we can speak of a functional between time of day and the target behavior. It is not a complete functional analysis as it has not described which variables, correlated with time of day, are related to the child's behavior. We might refine our analysis further. We might observe that when the child is given small easy tasks the child is inactive and when the child is given no tasks or large, difficult tasks the child is much more active. Now we have a more satisfactory functional analysis, since we have now identified independent variables that we can manipulate. We might conduct still further analyses. We could manipulate number of items of work (1, 10, and 100) and task difficulty (tasks associated with 1%, 50% and 100% correct answers). We might now observe lawful relationships between both independent variables and some reliable measure of active behavior. Now we have begun a very precise and reliable functional assessment that could be used as the basis of an intervention to modify child activity. Mathematical approaches to functional analysis have some significant advantages. Such functional relationships are often simple to describe. They also have some implications for treatment. Further, they obviate the need to state what caused behavior to change. The mere observation of a lawful relationship between an independent and dependent variable is sufficient.

In discussing the mathematical connotation of functional analysis, Owens and Ashcroft (1982) and Haynes and O'Brien (1990) noted that the form of functions may vary. Functions might be linear, positively or negatively accelerating or irregular. For example, the relationship between impulsively picking an immediate small reinforcer may increase either linearly or exponentially with magnitude or the immediate reinforcer or might increase. There may be limits on the range of values to which a function applies. For example, deprivation from a break may have no effect on behavior for values of 0.1s, 1s, 10 s and 100s of deprivation. However, breaks after deprivation of 1000s and above may have large effects on behavior. This latter point is important. A true relationship may not be observed in the natural environment if the independent variable is not manipulated through a sufficiently large range of values. For example, quantity of food eaten might be an important variable controlling binge eating in someone diagnosed with bulimia. However, if one only observes behavior after eating, 50, 100 and 200 g of food no relationship may be observable. However, if one then observed the effects of eating, 1, 100 and 1 000 g of food, such a relationship might be apparent.

It is useful to contrast the first descriptive analysis of child activity with the latter analysis of vomiting in bulimia. In the first example, the independent variable selected – time – did not describe the relevant independent variable. There are multiple potential confounds of relevant independent variables with time. Thus, it is not clear which of these behavioral variables control the target behavior. Consequently, the clinician will be at sea as how to intervene. The treatment plan selects from potentially relevant independent variables. However, because the analysis is low grade, the treatment plan may hit or miss. In the second example, the independent variable can be construed as reinforcer deprivation. The degree of deprivation and satiation of food may be manipulated. If a functional relationship exists between quantity of food eaten and probability of vomiting then the implications for treatment are conceptually coherent. Specifically, the quantity of food eaten appears to be a generalization gradient. Practitioners can now use procedures to change behavior based on that generalization gradient. Such an analysis may be incomplete. For example, other variables, such as time since last food, type of food, and emotional behaviors ("low mood") may also be relevant (Lee & Miltenberger, 1997). Nevertheless, such an analysis may give rise to a reliable, if incomplete, basis for treatment.

The relationship between independent and dependent variables may not be unidirectional (Hayes & O'Brien, 1990). This may be especially true of socially mediated behavior. For example, problem behavior in children is usually construed as behavior that is maintained by reinforcement from another person such as an adult (Iwata et al., 1994). However, the child maladaptive behavior is also an aversive stimulus for the adult. It is likely that the child's aversive behavior may also have effects on the behavior of adults. This is illustrated by Carr, Taylor and Robinson's (1991) study, which evaluated the so-called "child effect" on adult behavior in children with problem behavior. They observed 12 adults teaching four pairs of children. Each pair of children included on child with problem behavior and one child without problem behavior. They compared the behavior of the adults teaching children with and without problem behavior. When the adult taught a child with no problem behavior teaching occurred at high rates and a full range of tasks were taught. When the same adult taught a child with problem behavior the adult taught less and taught a restricted range of tasks. Specifically, they were more likely to teach those tasks associated with less or no problem behavior and avoid teaching those tasks associated with problem behavior. Carr et al. concluded that this study showed the reciprocal relationship between child problem behavior and adult teaching behavior.

Behaviorism's Scientific Method

Radical behaviorism has adopted a scientific method that is at odds with mainstream psychology. Undergraduates are all taught that science is hypothetico-deductive science. It uses hypothesis testing, group designs and statistical inference to falsify the null hypothesis. Yet, this is not the only scientific method. Inductive science is a second type of science. It keeps very close to observation of the natural phenomena and the data. It tends to ask "what would happen if ...", rather than test hypotheses concerning constructs. Generality of observations are collated to permit induction of general laws of science. The preference for hypothetico-deductive over inductive science has waxed and waned and varies from one field of science to another. The kind of science associated with radical behaviorism is at odds with mainstream psychology. This results in misunderstanding concerning radical behaviorism, for example, when small experimental studies are incorrectly described as "case studies."

In hypothetico-deductive psychology variation in data is seen as a problem referred to as 'error variance', which should be controlled or eliminated. Group experiments attempt to eliminate individual differences by using large groups of subjects and focusing on group means and statistical significance. However, such an approach contains several fundamental weaknesses. First, it depends on the arbitrary 0.05 significance level for inferring causality. Yet, there is no justification for the conventional adoption of this level of significance. Second, it is open to the problem of type I errors. Journals rarely publish nonsignificant results. Hence, we cannot judge how often type I errors have occured. This method was developed in agriculture. In agriculture, the average potato or corn cob is important if one wishes to increase crop yield. People are not like potatoes and corn cobs. The average person's behavior is of little interest if you are not that average person. Of course no one is.

In contrast radical behaviorism is explicitly interested in the variability in data. Instead of seeing data variability as a problem, radical behaviorism sees it as the thing to study. When radical behaviorists see variability, they seek out variables that influence that variability within individual organisms. Hence, they take repeated observations of individual organisms, strive to identify the variables that influence that variability and to observe reliable relationships between the environment and behavior (Sidman, 1960).

In everyday language and much of science, causation is presented as a chain of events in which some agent operates a force that causes some outcome. Mainstream psychology has adopted this model when it assumes some inner self is the cause of observed behavior. Radical behaviorism adopts a different model in which causation is replaced with observation of a functional relationship between independent and dependent variables. The causes of behavior can be adequately shown by functional relationships without reference to the missing link in the chain – the inner person – causing the observed behavior.

APPLIED BEHAVIOR ANALYSIS

The experimental analysis of behavior began in the 1930s. In the 1950s ABA grew out of the experimental analysis of behavior. Many early ABA studies, such as those of patients with severe psychiatric disorders (Ayllon & Michael, 1959) and children with intellectual disabilities (Orlando & Bijou, 1960) were published in the *Journal of the Experimental Analysis of Behavior*, because there were few alternative outlets. The increasing number of publications in ABA resulted in the publication of the *Journal of Applied Behavior Analysis* in 1968.

In their seminal article, *Some current dimensions of applied behavior analysis*, Baer et al. (1968) outlines the key features of ABA, which still hold true today. Baer et al.'s six dimensions of ABA include that ABA should be applied. That is, ABA research addresses behavior that society, rather than the researcher, identifies as important. Hence, the experimental analysis of behavior can readily study bar pressing because it is uninterested in the behavior itself. However, ABA must study behavior that society deems to be of significance. Second, ABA must be behavioral. It must be pragmatic. It must measure behavior directly using reliable, quantifiable observation. Self-report data alone are unacceptable. This is because when the self-report data change it is not clear whose behavior has changed: the behavior that was reported or the verbal behavior of reporting. For example, reporting that one no longer feels anxious, not longer beats one's partner or is no longer sexually attracted to children is not the same as being relaxed, being affectionate to one's partner or not approaching children. ABA must be analytical. It must demonstrate a believable relationship between the independent and dependent variable. This is usually done using small experimental designs, such as reversal and multiple baseline designs. Next, ABA must be technological. It must operationalize its treatments as well as its dependent variables so that others can replicate the intervention. For example, saying that the client attended a relaxation training group tells us nothing about the relevant client behavior. However, observing that the client adopted and maintained a relaxed posture, including shoulders down, legs uncrossed and hands on lap for 10 minutes on three consecutive treatment sessions is operationalized and replicable. Next, ABA must be conceptually systematic. Its operationally defined treatments must be related to behavioral concepts, such as reinforcement, stimulus control, and so on. Finally, ABA interventions must be effective. That is they must produce such large changes that society and the client deem them to be highly valued and important.

In addition to these key features, ABA interventions must also address two further questions. They cannot assume that generalization of behavior change will occur without planning. Rather, ABA interventions must the plan and analyze the hoped for generalization behavior change at the beginning of intervention (Stokes & Baer, 1977). Finally, the society must deem that the goals, procedures and behavior change that ABA produces are important and valued (Wolf, 1978).

MISREPRESENTATIONS OF BEHAVIORISM

Radical behaviorism is often reviled on the basis of misrepresentation of radical behaviorism. Chiesa noted at least three common kinds of such errors. First, radical behaviorism is only one of several kinds of behaviorism. It is quite distinct from these other kinds of behaviorism. Methodological behaviorists, such as Watson, believed that private events, such as thinking and feeling were problematic for science. His solution was to exclude them from the science of behavior. Chiesa noted that Skinner agreed with Watson that private events were problematic for science. However, his solution was different from Watson. Namely, Skinner, made no dichotomy between public and private behavior. Skinner in fact stated that it would be foolish to ignore private behavior, since it is clearly an important part of the human experience. His solution was to give private behavior the same status as overt behavior. Namely, it was the thing for science to explain, but not the explanation of behavior (Skinner, 1990.) Skinner himself criticized Watson's methodological behaviorism on these exact grounds. Hence, to criticize radical behaviorism for ignoring private behavior or for equating it as treating the person as a black box (e.g. Stenfert Kroese, 1997) is to criticize radical behaviorism for something that it explicitly avows. The term "Neo-behaviorists" is used loosely to refer to such diverse psychologists as Tolman and Hull. Thus, Tolman's work prefigured cognitive psychology by explaining the behavior of rats learning mazes by reference to the rats' "cognitive maps" of the maze. Hull's work is sometimes described as S-O-R psychology in which intra-organismic variables mediate the relationship between the stimulus and response. These intra-organismic variables were not Tolman's cognitive maps, but were neurological constructs. Radical behaviorists are of course critical of neobehaviorists accounts because they include nonobservable constructs in science and raise private, nonobservable cognitive or neurological constructs to the status of the causes of behavior. Thus, both methodological behaviorism and neobehaviorism are distinct and different kinds of sciences from radical behaviorism. To confuse radical behaviorism with either is false.

Yet, critiques of radical behaviorism often misrepresent radical behaviorism as synonymous with these other positions, level criticisms of these other positions and erroneously conclude that they are valid criticisms of radical behaviorism. (See Sturmey, 2004, 2005, 2006a, 2006b, 2006c, 2006d for discussion of continuations of this problem.) For example, Stenfert Kroese (1997) wrote that "the pure Skinnerian 'black box' approach to cognitive processes has been rejected by most" (p. 5). This misrepresents Skinner's and other radical behaviorists' position on private events in that Skinner devoted extensive analysis of private behavior inside the box, such as thinking and feeling (Skinner, 1953.) Another common error is to reduce radical behaviorism to contingency management. For example, Novacco (1997) wrote that noncognitive treatments of people with intellectual disabilities involved "[r]eliance on externally controlled contingency management procedures has also proceeded with the belief that people with learning disabilities lack the capacity to self-regulate. Such an assumptive framework has been less than wise" (p. xi). Likewise, Tarrier and Calem (2002) wrote "behavioral analysis has examined behavior outside its social context except for viewing it as a reinforcement or punishment delivery system... " (p. 320). Curiously, Tarrier and Calem cite no source for this characterization of behavior analysis. These two quotations oversimplify ABA to contingency management. This is incorrect. They ignore many aspects of behavior analysis, such as antecedent control of behavior, establishing operations, respondent behavior, and self-regulation (Skinner, 1953; Taylor & O'Reilly, 1997). See Chapter 6 for further examples of radical behavioral approaches to self-regulation.

Critics have leveled the criticism against radical behaviorism that it adopts a mechanistic view of human behavior similar to Newtonian billiard ball physics. In so doing, they again misunderstand radical behaviorism's view on causality. Their conclusions that the limits of mechanistic views of behavior are criticisms of radical behaviorism are incorrect. A third and similar error has been to accuse radical behaviorism of Cartesian dualism and criticizing Cartesian dualism and attributing these criticisms as limits to radical behaviorism.

Chiesa (1994) also summarized evidence that our language comes loaded with assumptions and models of behavior and its causes. Thus, the explanations for behavior offered by radical behaviorists run counter to cultural and linguistic norms of English language. The English language requires permanent active nouns to be agents causing temporary changes. We even say "It is raining" when we cannot describe who did the raining. Who is the "it" that rained – the water, the sky or something else? Maybe we should just say that "raining happened." A similar problem is how we ascribe agency to action. We can observe our own behavior and our own environment easily. So when describing our own action we often explain it in environmental terms. We can readily say "She insulted me, so I told her to shut up." For other people's behavior we are less able to observe the person's private behavior and their environment, so we ascribe agency to the person. We say "She was so angry that she told him to shut up", implying that her anger caused her to behave. Thus, everyday English and other Indo-European languages come with hidden assumptions concerning agency, including the causes of behavior.

SUMMARY

Behaviorism is the philosophy of science that underlies basic and applied behavior analysis. Radical behaviorism should be distinguished from methodological behaviorism and neobehaviorism. These forms of behaviorism are distinct from and inimical to radical behaviorism. Radical behaviorism is characterized by remaining close to its data and by observing functional relationships between independent and dependent variables. It acknowledges the existence of private behavior, but gives it the status of behavior, not the cause of public behavior. Radical behaviorism is often taught badly and misrepresented. Chiesa (1994) and others have provided adequate rebuttals and corrections to these misrepresentations.

Chapter 3

RESPONDENT BEHAVIOR

Respondent behavior is learned from innate reflexes that are elaborated during the lifespan. Many of these reflexes have apparent survival or other biological value, as in coughing, eye blinking, salivating at the sight of food, conditioned taste aversions and lactating to the sound of a baby crying. Natural selection selects inherited unconditioned responses (URs) that adapt to relatively unchanging features of the world that will never or rarely change, such as gravity, heat loss or gain, or the effects of injury. However, natural selection cannot predict other aspects of the environment, such as illness after eating a sea urchin, chemotherapy or fear following cardiac surgery. Hence, the capacity for respondent conditioning to novel conditioned stimuli (CS) that evolution cannot predict is a useful adaptation (Skinner, 1990).

This chapter describes the basic features of respondent behavior, its acquisition, stimulus control and maintenance, and extinction in non-human and human animals and its potential relevance to psychopathology. Clinical applications of the acquisition of respondent behavior are limited, although there are one or two studies of modifying its stimulus control. More important are the myriad forms of respondent extinction that have been used to modify a wide variety of disturbing forms of behaviors, such as phobias, obsessive compulsive disorders, trauma related disorders, drug addiction, sexual dysfunction and a number of other odd reflex-based problems. The final section contrasts behavior analytic approaches to fear with behavior modification approaches and outlines the implications for case formulation.

BASIC FEATURES OF RESPONDENT BEHAVIOR

Acquisition

In a typical experiment, Pavlov or his students first habituated a healthy dog to a sound-proofed experimental cage. Once habituated, a small fistula was made in the dog's cheek. They then cemented a canula in place so that they could collect and measure saliva. The dependent variables were typically number of drops of saliva and the latency (time to the first drop after a stimulus was presented). Anrep (1920, cited in Leslie & O'Reilly,

1999) conducted a prototypical experiment. Anrep sounded a tone for 5 seconds and 2–3 seconds later delivered food. In order to measure the acquisition of respondent behavior, Anrep presented the tone alone periodically. Over 16 days Anrep presented the tone and food together 50 times and the tone alone was presented six times. Over time, the latency to respond decreased and the quantity of saliva increased in response to the tone alone. Anrep showed a functional relationship between the number of food-tone parings and the acquisition of a conditioned response.

Respondent conditioning has been demonstrated in a very wide range of nonhuman animals and humans. Some examples of human conditioned responses include the infant sucking unconditioned response (UR) following an object touching the infant's lips unconditioned stimulus (US), withdrawal of a body part and autonomic arousal (UR) following noxious stimulation (US), and erection or vaginal lubrication (UR) following sexual stimulation (US). Notable is the possibility that an organism can acquire a conditioned response (CR) by few or even one pairing under certain circumstances. This may occur if the unconditioned stimulus is very intense, such as a very hot surface.

Conditioning can also take place to a range of public and interoceptive stimuli. For example, classical conditioning can take place to carbon dioxide and associated interoceptive blood pH. This may be relevant for classical conditioning of fearful behavior, as these physiological stimuli may be CS. Classical conditioning may also take place in response to verbal stimuli. For example, even brief pairings of neutral words with positive or negative meanings, of which subjects are unaware, result in affective responses to formerly neutral words (De Houwer, Baeyens & Eelen, 1994).

Stimulus Control

Discrimination   Pavlov extended acquisition studies, such as that described above, by presenting two stimuli. Pavlov paired one stimulus with the US but did not pair the second stimulus with the US. Only the stimulus paired with the US came to elicit the CR. The second stimulus did not. Since the organism emitted the CR in response to one stimulus, but not another, discrimination had occurred.

Generalization   Respondent conditioning takes place to a limited range of stimuli. However, the organism may emit a CR in response to stimuli that the experimenter did not directly condition. For example, a cardiac phobic might acquire a fear during a medical procedure that involves stopping their heart while conscious, eliciting an extreme fear response. However, a CR of fearful behavior might subsequently occur whilst running for a bus or walking up a hill when the person's heart accelerates.

Blocking   Not all stimuli that the experimenter consistently paired with a CS come to elicit a CR. Suppose a US has already been repeatedly paired with a UC before conditioning and now functions as a CS. Suppose that these conditioning trials continue, but now a second stimulus is presented simultaneously with the original CS. Although this new stimulus is repeatedly paired with the US, it does not some to elicit the CR when presented alone. This is known as "blocking."

Overshadowing When the experimenter presents two stimuli simultaneously from the beginning of conditioning trials and one of the stimuli is more intense than the second, then only the first stimulus may function as a CS. Some studies have presented two stimuli in different modalities, such as a sound and an odor. Which of these two stimuli comes to function as CS depends on the UR. For example, some studies have observed that noise but not taste come to function as CS for pain. Other studies have shown that tastes, but not sounds, function as CS for upset stomach.

In the natural environment when respondent conditioning take place there are many stimuli present simultaneously. For example, during radiotherapy for cancer odors, visual stimuli and noises characteristic of the treatment setting are all present. Yet, patients typically report conditioned nausea to smells or the people administering treatment, rather than lights or hospital signs.

Extinction and Spontaneous Remission

Once a CR is acquired it may be extinguished if the CS-US pairing is broken. For example, if the CS is repeatedly presented without the US the CR gradually reduced in frequency and intensity. However, after the CR disappears it may spontaneously reappear. This phenomenon is called spontaneous remission. This has practical importance. If a clinical problem is treated using classical extinction (see below) the CR may reoccur. Clinicians should be alert to this phenomenon. If it occurs in the context of treatment, additional respondent extinction treatment sessions may be required (Hermans et al., 2005).

ACQUISTION OF PSYCHOPATHOLOGY

Respondent conditioning has been implicated in the acquisition of a wide range of forms of psychopathology (Bouton, 2002). These include phobias, obsessive-compulsive disorders, post traumatic stress disorders, adjustment disorders, psychological problems following sexual abuse, traumatic nightmares, morbid grieving, and psychophysiological disorders, such as asthma, problematic sexual behavior, as well as a variety of odd reflex-related problems. Failure to acquire certain conditioned reflexes is also problematic, as in failure to acquire bladder and bowel control. Hence, interventions to teach continence are based on acquisition of respondent behavior. Respondent conditioning is also important in changing stimulus functions, for example as in the acquisition of secondary reinforcers and secondary punishers. People for whom conventional secondary reinforcers and punishers are ineffective are considerably disabled. For example, they do not learn from consequences such as human interaction, money, or other conventional consequences. Hence, they cannot learn in typical environments. Here, respondent conditioning may also be important in establishing conventional secondary reinforcers and punishers so that people can learn quickly, participate in society more readily and ensure that public programs are effective and efficient.

Conditioning of Respiratory Behavior

Van den Buergh and colleagues (1999) demonstrated that various respiratory behaviors, such as rapid breathing, can be acquired through respondent conditioning. Carbon dioxide-enriched air elicits rapid breathing and increases the quantity of air breathed. Subjects described it as increasing arousal and a variety of physiological sensations, such as warmth and tingling. Thus, since carbon dioxide is odorless, the interoceptive stimuli it produces can be the basis of respondent conditioning.

Carbon dioxide-enriched air can act a US that can be classically conditioned to a variety of odors, such that these odors alone subsequently elicit conditioned response. This model of respondent conditioning of respiratory behavior may be a useful model of panic disorder, asthma and multiple chemical sensitivities (De Peuter et al., 2005, Devriese et al., 2000; Van Den Bergh et al., 1995, 1999). This suggests that these at least some of symptoms are CRs acquired by classical conditioning. This notion is consonant with a number of observations that environmental cues can elicit panic attacks, asthma attacks and respiratory symptoms of multiple chemical sensitivities.

APPLICATIONS

Interventions based on respondent behavior have focused on conditioned responses that are problematic. Hence, there are few applied studies on the acquisition of respondent behavior. Although a few intervention studies have been based on modifying or eliminating the problematic CS, almost all applications based on respondent behavior have involved respondent extinction. Many treatment packages and behavior therapy technologies that are not explicitly based on ABA, such as flooding, sensate focus, and so on, incorporate respondent extinction as an important, and perhaps the effective component of their intervention. This section briefly reviews nonclinical applications of respondent behavior. It then describes procedures based on acquisition of respondent behavior. Finally, there is a review of a wide range of interventions procedures, all of which may be forms of respondent extinction.

Nonclinical Applications

Words, images, and music can all be CS for a wide range of responses, including positive and negative emotional responses (De Houwer et al., 1994). Words like "true love" and "terminal cancer" can elicit strong emotional responses in a way parallel to CS and CR. Before the formal science of ABA evolved, novelists, poets, advertisers and film directors carefully placed conditioned stimuli to elicit laughter, fears and tears; a good movie or book can indeed bring us to tears. After Watson left academia he worked for New York advertising agencies and developed the Marlborough Man as a CS originally to sell cigarettes to women.

Another form of folk technology based on CS is the way we manage a variety of aversive CS. We cover corpses and graves with flowers and pictures of the living person in idealized youthful form. We surround out toilet with pictures of the sea and seahorses. We mask the CS with a toilet lid, remove even higher order conditioned stimuli by covering toilet paper with something else and add odors that elicit images of beautiful flowers rather than the alternative. We cover our trash cans with lids to eliminate or minimize exposure to the CS or purchase scented bin liners to elicit alternative CRs. Taking Mary Poppin's advice, we sugarcoat pills to eliminate CS that would make us retch. When we wish to increase the likelihood of avoidance or escape we present loud aversive US, such as fire alarms that elicit URs, such as heart racing, as well as operant avoidance. We also present CS, such as the color red (depending on your culture) and words such as "danger!", "stop!" Although this folk technology is only indirectly related to clinical applications, it is suggestive of the potential efficacy of a technology of behavior changes based on respondent conditioning.

Acquisition of Respondent Behavior

There are relatively few applied studies of the acquisition of respondent behavior. One comes from Whitehead, Lurie and Blackwell (1976) who classically conditioned the carotid sinus reflex. In the carotid sinus reflex, the US is a 15 degree head-down tilt and the UR is a modest drop in blood pressure. In this study, the CS was a quiet noise, ding of a timer and the noise of the tilt table. Modeled on Pavlov's procedures described earlier, experimental subjects experienced conditioning trials that consisted of paring 30 s of the CS following by the US and UR. There were 30 trials over 90 minutes. The first 20 trials consisted of 15 conditioning CS + US trials and five CS-only trials. These first 20 trials were then followed by 10 extinction trials of CS only. Three groups of subjects participated: There were six nonhypertensive subjects, four patients with essential hypertension and four control nonhypertensive subjects. The control group received US-only and CS-only trials, but no pairing of the US and CS. In both experimental groups, presentation of the CS resulted in little change in blood pressure. After 20 trials the CS alone elicited as large a drop in blood pressure as the US. The results were the same for both nonhypertensive and hypertensive subjects. No changes were observed in the control group. This study suggests that respondent conditioning could be used to reduce blood pressure. See also the discussion of Paunovic (1999) below for an example of the use of acquisition of a CR in treatment of a complex trauma-related disorder.

Removing Conditioned Stimuli

One approach to modifying respondent behavior based on its stimulus control is simply to remove the conditioned stimulus that controls the respondent behavior. Greene and Seime (1987) reported an ingenious application of this approach to treat anticipatory nausea in a 61-year-old woman undergoing chemotherapy for breast cancer. After several months of chemotherapy she began to complain of an unpleasant taste associated with injection of her drugs used for chemotherapy. Subsequently she reported nausea and would gag and retch cough and spit. These latter behaviors were the study's target behaviors. Antinausea medications were ineffective and she sometimes refused chemotherapy because of these problems. Based on the formulation that the unpleasant taste was a CS that elicited the CR of nausea, Greens and Seime used lemon squirted into the client's mouth to block the unpleasant taste, thereby removing the putative CS. This treatment eliminated three of the five problematic target behaviors.

Respondent Extinction

Respondent conditioning occurs when a CS is repeatedly presented without the US until the CS no longer elicits the CR. This learning process may underlie a wide range of clinical treatments that involve presentation of CS until they no longer elicit problematic emotional responding. This learning process may involve a variety of different procedures depending on the context.

Flooding for Phobias

Flooding consists of several sessions of in vivo exposure to the maximally fearful stimuli for prolonged periods of time (90–180 minutes) until the stimuli no longer evoke anxiety. Flooding requires accurate identification of maximally traumatic stimuli and prevention of avoidance, including reduction of the experience of anxiety through relaxation, medication, alcohol, cognitive rituals, etc. It also requires the full cooperation of the client and a therapist who can work with clients suffering extreme anxiety. Flooding has been used for simple phobias, complex phobias, obsessive compulsive disorders (OCD) post traumatic stress disorders (PTSD) and recurrent nightmares.

Simple Phobias   Houlihan, Schwartz, Miltenberger and Heuton (1993) reported treatment of an unusual simple phobia – fear of the noise of balloons popping. The participant was a 21-year-old student, Bill, who was referred by his girlfriend because his nearly lifelong fear of balloons interfered with their social life. Although Bill has several other fears, his fear of balloons was problematic because of avoidance of social occasions, such as family occasions and parties when balloons were likely to be present.

Treatment consisted of three sessions, held one day after another, each of which lasted up to three hours. Two therapists were necessary, one to support Bill and one to guide exposure. In these sessions Bill was exposed to rooms filled with approximately 100 balloons. During the sessions the experimenter, and eventually Bill, popped the balloons with a pin or by stepping on them. The experimenter used client reports of subjective units of discomfort (SUDs) rating of anxiety to judge the effectiveness of exposure during and between sessions and to identify the most fearful stimuli.

In the first session, Bill huddled near the door, shook, cried, and turned pale. He avoided looking at the balloons by looking away and shielding his eyes. Stepping on the balloons evoked greater fear than popping them with a pin. During the sessions the therapist eventually instructed and shaped Bill's behavior to look at the balloons, pop them with a pin and step on them himself. Both SUDs rating during sessions and behavior approach test measures showed large improvements during the three treatment sessions and at one-year follow-up. Additionally, Bill was now confident, was able to attend a wide variety of social situations that he formerly avoided, and reported a reduction in anxiety in many aspects of his life.

Obsessive Compulsive Disorder   Foa et al. (2006) reported a multi-site randomized controlled trial (RCT) of exposure and ritual prevention and clomipramine for treatment of OCD. They randomly assigned 122 adult outpatients with OCD to one of three conditions: exposure plus ritual prevention alone; exposure plus ritual prevention plus clomipramine; and exposure plus ritual prevention plus placebo. The study was conducted blind as to whether participants were given drug or placebo. Exposure plus response prevention consisted of 15, two-hour sessions scheduled over three weeks and daily exposure and prevention homework for up to two hours per day. The authors used both imaginal and in vivo exposure, beginning with less threatening objects and situations. They moved to the most fearful situation by the sixth session. Therapists also discussed the disconfirming nature of anxiety reduction during treatment sessions. Homework included further exposure and response prevention and self-recording at home using the objects and situations from that day's treatment session. There were also two home visits, which lasted a total of four hours in which the therapist conducted exposure in the home. There was then eight weeks of maintenance, which consisted of 45-minute exposure sessions. Participants in the clomipramine group received up to 250 mg of clomipramine per day and were encouraged to expose themselves and refrain from rituals. The main dependent variable was the Yale-Brown Obsessive Compulsive Scale. Of 149 participants who entered the trial, 27 dropped out before treatment began. At week 12, all treatment groups were doing better than the placebo only group. The exposure and ritual prevention groups both did better than the group that only received clomipramine. The group that received exposure and ritual prevention only was equivalent to the exposure and ritual prevention plus clomipramine group. Foa et al. classified participants as "responders" and "excellent responders." There were more responders and excellent responders in the treatment groups and significantly more excellent responders in the exposure plus ritual prevention group than the exposure plus ritual prevention plus clomipramine group. Seventy-eight per cent of participants who received clomipramine reported a moderate or severe side effect as did 46% of the placebo group. Twenty-nine per cent of participants dropped out during treatment mostly because they disliked the medication side effects or because they wished to terminate the exposure treatment. Patients who dropped out did not differ from those who remained in the study on a number of measures. The authors concluded that exposure and response prevention was superior to the clomipramine alone. They were cautious about the lack of difference between the two exposure and response prevention groups, as the study may have been insensitive to any true difference between the two treatments.

Post Traumatic Stress Disorder

Paunovic (1999) reported successful treatment of a 34-year-old man with PTSD. Prior to the current problem he had experienced multiple traumatic events, including his fiancé having life-threatening burns after which he wrecked his car and broke his arm, combat trauma following killing two people at close range, walking over their bodies and recognizing one of them as someone he knew. The current precipitating event was a severe assault in which he was kicked, resulting in broken ribs and concussion. These traumas left him depressed, guilt-ridden, unemployed, and they interfered with current relationships.

Treatment consisted of multiple components based on both respondent extinction and counter-conditioning using positive conditioned emotional responses (CERs). First, he practised imagining neutral visual images to enhance his visual images. Second, Paunovnic identified images that elicited positive conditioned emotional reactions and the client practised imagining these images, such as great moments with his friends and son. These positive CERs were conditioned to a neutral stimulus – pressing the client's fingernail moderately hard. In this way, positive CERs could be readily elicited later in therapy for counter-conditioning. Third, Panovnic used prolonged imaginal exposure to trauma-related cues. Fourth, Paunovnic used counter-conditioning by having the client imagine the trauma-related cues and then eliciting the positive CERs using the fingernail pressing as the CS. Treatment took place over 17 sessions. Following treatment and at six-month follow-up the client reported large reductions in symptoms of PTSD, anxiety, depression and anger.

Traumatic Nightmares

Traumatic nightmares consist of highly fear-provoking nightmares that may relate to actual trauma or imagined scary imagery. They are often accompanied by anxiety and depression and anticipatory anxiety may occur prior to sleep. Traumatic nightmares may occur at varying frequencies and may persist for many years or may re-emerge or increase in frequency during periods of stress or repeated trauma. Exposure therapy for nightmares consists of identifying the images that evoke fear and exposing the person to them in imagination, verbally, or using drawing until they no longer evoke a negative CER.

Schindler (1980) reported a case of a 29-year-old Vietnam veteran who had a recurrent traumatic nightmare. The nightmare consisted of an actual event in which he witnessed a fellow soldier physically disintegrate as he stepped on a mine. This occurred nine years prior to treatment. The nightmare occurred at least monthly and more frequently prior to military service. He experienced sleep-related anxiety every night. Treatment consisted of counter-conditioning using positive emotional imagery to elicit relaxation and graded exposure to seven progressively more anxiety provoking elements in the dream, including both visual and olfactory imagined cues. He practised exposure both in the office and at home. There was also a two-week booster session. The dream no longer occurred after therapy, nor did it occur at three- and seven-month follow-ups. There have been several randomized controlled trials of exposure therapy for traumatic nightmares indicating the efficacy of this approach. For example, Grandi, Fabbri, Panattoni, Gonnella and Marks (2006) demonstrated that exposure therapy for nightmares was superior to a waiting list control. Treatment effects were maintained at four-year follow-up.

Morbid Grieving

A small proportion of people react to the death of a loved one in a way that is unusually distressing, judged excessive and is culturally inappropriate. This is often associated with depression and anxiety. It often involves avoidance of stimuli associated with the dead person, either by physical avoidance of the cues, such as not visiting the person's room or grave, by anxiety-reducing strategies, such as alcohol or psychotropic medications, or by avoiding grieving over the person and thinking about them and the events surrounding their death. It is possible to construe the avoided stimuli, both public and private, as CS that were paired with the US associated with the loss of the loved person and the various forms of avoidance.

Various forms of guided mourning have been based on a respondent extinction model of treatment. Vogel and Peterson (1991) presented three cases of a form of guided grieving, two of which were highly successful and one of which failed. The first participant was 30-year-old man who was depressed following the break up of his engagement when his fiancé left him for another man. He cried to exhaustion when something reminded him of his fiancé and had stopped dating. His work suffered and he experienced depression. For one year he had undergone psychodynamic psychotherapy without symptom relief. Guided mourning consisted of requiring the person to spend 30 minutes per day to isolate himself in a closed room and to focus on his loss, pain, and unhappiness, and to mourn his loss. He was to continue this without interruption for the entire 30-minute period. He had weekly appointments, mainly to review progress. One month after treatment began, he no longer could cry when thinking about his fiance and she no longer intruded in her thoughts.

Vogel and Peterson's failed case is instructive. A 34-year-old widow lost her husband. He died because of an undetected congenital coronary defect. He died suddenly following a 10-year happy marriage. One year later she was still mourning, was isolated, frequently talked to her husband, and became withdrawn. Help from her clergyman, who specialized in treatment of grief, did not produce any change. After 30 days of following the Vogel and Peterson's exposure treatment no change occurred and the treatment was stopped. The authors noted that in her case the treatment sessions ended with her being comforted by the memory of her husband and she never actually grieved over his loss. Thus, it appeared that exposure to the relevant conditioned stimuli and respondent extinction never occurred for this client. Two randomized control trials of treatment of exposure for morbid grieving have found it to be effective (Mawson, Marks, Ramm & Stern, 1981; Sireling, Cohen & Marks, 1988).

Some Forms of "Anger"

"Anger" is an imprecise term that refers to behaviors with many different functions. Some forms of angry behaviors may be CRs. One of the earliest examples of respondent aggression came from animal studies which showed that when an animal received an electric shock it will aggress to another nearby conspecific (Ulrich & Azrin, 1962). Thus, the electric shock appears to act as an US for the UR of aggressive behavior. Thus, parings of electric shock or other painful stimuli with other CS, such as certain people, their actions or certain words, might result in the acquisition of respondent forms of "anger."

Some clinical observations are consonant with the notion that anger is sometimes elicited automatically as a CR in humans. For example, some people with extreme anger specific stimuli seem to evoke extreme feelings of anger and angry behavior. For example, other people staring at the client, criticism from specific people or certain forms of critical comments might trigger angry behavior. Further, arguing and blaming others may be forms of avoidance behavior that are negatively reinforced by the termination of criticism (Grodnitzky & Tafrate, 2000). Therefore, exposure to these CS as a form of respondent extinction might be one form of therapy for anger.

Grodnitzky and Tafrate (2000) developed a group format of exposure therapy for anger in a group of clinic-referred clients, including clients referred by the courts for anger problems related to domestic violence. Six clients participated in treatment. They assigned three to a waiting list control procedure. Clients identified anger-producing scenes, wrote them down and read them aloud to the group whilst group members practised visualizing the scenes. Group members then rewrote the scenes, based on group feedback. Participants then recorded their scenes on audiotapes and listened to the tapes for at least 30 minutes per day, every day, and recorded their responses to the scenes. As sessions progressed, they revisited the scenes to include more detail or make them more anger-provoking. Each participant exposed themselves to two anger-provoking scenes during the 10-session group. Untreated participants made no or minimal progress on measures of anger and mood. Participants who had self-exposed made progress on these measures. This was judged to be clinically significant for 5 of 6 group members. At 15-month follow-up, three group members could be contacted and all reported maintaining treatment gains.

Cue-Dependent Extinction

Addictive drugs often elicit responses suggesting that, in part, they function as US. Over time, US associated with ingestion of addictive drugs also come to elicit related conditioned responses. People with alcohol problems may begin to crave alcohol at certain times of the day or at the sight of drinking-related cues. Cocaine addicts may remain clean for extensive periods of time when they avoid the people and places associated with use, but may relapse when they return to places where they formerly used. If cues associated with drug use are CS then respondent extinction might be a promising treatment or component of a treatment package for substance related disorders.

Drummond and Glautier (1994) conducted an experimental evaluation of cue exposure for 35 detoxified men with severe alcohol dependence. They randomly assigned participants to either cue exposure or relaxation training. In the cue exposure treatment, subjects identified a preferred alcoholic drink, a less preferred alcoholic drink and a soft drink. Subjects exposed themselves to alcohol-related cues for 40 minutes and the neutral stimuli for 10 minutes for 10 consecutive days. The experimenters presented low salience cues in the first five days and high salience cues for the last five days. They presented stimuli in the manner that the subjects preferred. The relaxation treatment group received a standardized progressive relaxation training procedure. Outcome measures included self-reports of drinking behavior and latency collected directly from the client and interviews with family members and health professionals where appropriate. They followed up the participants at one, three, and six months.

When compared with participants in the relaxation group, participants who received cue-exposure did better after treatment. At six-month follow-up they had longer latencies to drink, lower self-reports of drinking and lower scores on the *Alcohol Problem Questionnaire*, a measure of the impact of alcohol use on people's lives. Notably physiological responsivity to the presence of alcohol also significantly predicted alcohol reduction. This observation is consonant with the notion that the extent to which respondent extinction took place predicted alcohol reduction. The authors concluded that cue-exposure was more effective than relaxation.

Cue exposure has been used for a wide variety of substance-related problems. For example, Loeber, Croissant, Heinz, Mann, and Flor (2006) demonstrated that cue exposure was superior to standard cognitive behavior therapy during detoxification of inpatients with alcohol abuse problems. Substance-related disorders are complex and have a wide variety of effects on people's behavior that may require other treatment components to address treatment adherence, vocational and social functioning (Higgins, Heil & Sigmon, 2007). However, cue exposure seems to be one component of an effective approach to treatment of substance related disorders.

Exposure Therapy For Delusions

Delusional beliefs and other psychotic phenomena often elicit extreme fear in people with psychotic disorders. Consequently, some people with such fear-evoking beliefs engage in extensive avoidance behavior. For example, (Morrison, 1998) described how a man with persecutory male voices that threatened him with violence elicited extreme fear and panic attacks. He engaged in a variety of avoidant behaviors, such as leaving the house when drinking, crouching down to hide from possible aggressors and drinking to reduce anxiety.

Townend (2002) extended this idea and earlier work on exposure therapy for delusions by treating a 71 year-old man's delusions with exposure therapy. The man had believed that electromagnetic rays from household equipment would cause him cancer. To prevent this be avoided using equipment, wore a magnet around his neck and "earthed" him self at night by chaining himself to a radiator pipe. Intervention consisted of weekly 30 to 60 minute exposure sessions in which he gradually increased his use of household electrical equipment and refrained from engaging in safety behaviors, such as wearing the magnet. (The treatment also included self-monitoring and cognitive therapy.) Within 6 sessions ratings of discomfort and belief reduced significantly and were maintained at 3 month follow-up.

Unusual Reflex-based Disorders   A wide range of reflexes can become exaggerated, be conditioned to inappropriate stimuli and be stigmatizing or interfere with daily functioning in a number of ways. For example, Fulcher and Celluci (1997) reported case formulation and treatment of a chronic cough in a 13-year-old boy who had coughed apparently on every single breath for two months. The cough began following 'flu but had persisted. Physicians could not identify and current medical etiology. Fulcher and Celluci hypothesized that, during the 'flu episode, coughing was an unconditioned response to the unconditioned stimulus of mucus in his throat, and subsequently the cough had become classically conditioned to airflow. They observed that he had some control over the cough if he breathed through pursed lips. Hence, when they asked him to breathe through several straws, he could take several breaths without coughing. This suggested that the rate of airflow was the relevant generalization gradient. Based on this hypothesis, treatment in the first sessions consisted of breathing through four coffee straws and increasing the number of breaths without a cough from two to 14 breaths. Over six treatment sessions, the number of breathes taken without coughing, breathing through more narrow tubes and breathing without coughing without straws gradually increased. They also gave him daily homework assignments. In this way, the authors hypothesized that desensitization to progressively faster air flows took place. After the first treatment sessions the boy reported less intense coughing in several public places. By the end of the treatment sessions, he was able to breath without coughing for up to an hour at a time. At eight- and 24-month follow-up, the cough had disappeared. This paper shows a nice combination of careful case formulation and idiographic treatment development based on learning principles. Foster, Owens, and Newton (1985) presented a similar analysis and treatment of a problematic gag reflex.

BEHAVIOR ANALYTIC APPROACHES TO FEAR

The literature reviewed in the preceding sections is primarily behavior modification, not behavior analysis. Almost all the studies described here do not include pre-intervention observational analysis of the presenting problems, identification of some socially significant problem in the real world, observational data, inter-observer agreement, single-subject experimental design, and generalization data, etc. This literature has focused on behavior during extinction sessions in clinical rather than everyday settings. When it has done so, it has accepted client reports of behavior change, rather than observation of behavior. Consequently, this literature has not identified which replacement behaviors should be exhibited in the presence of the (former) CS. Presumably in many cases clients should be brave, assertive, and confident in the presence of these formerly fear-provoking conditioned stimuli. Some of this research has anecdotally described what appears to be important broad changes in the client's lives, but has not observed these appropriate forms of behavior in the natural environment.

Behavior Analytic Approaches to Phobias

Jones and Friman (1999) began addressing these problems in a preliminary study when they presented a functional analysis and treatment of
an insect phobia in a 14-year-old school boy. Mike's head teacher referred
him because his intense fear of insects disrupted his academic performance and resulted in teasing by his peers. Mike himself complained that
he had difficulties working and concentrating when he thought insects
might be near by. The main reason the phobia was problematic was poor
academic performance. Hence, the dependent variable was the number of
math problems completed in the presence of insects. The pre-intervention
assessment consisted of comparing the number of math problems completed in three conditions. The three conditions were *Bugs, Say Bugs, and
No Bugs*. Figure 3.1 contains the data for this study. In the *Bugs* condition
the experimenters released three live crickets into the centre of the room.
During the *Say Bugs* condition, the experimenter told Mike "There are
bugs somewhere in this room." During the *No Bugs* the experimenter said
"There are no bugs anywhere in the room." Jones and Friman compared
Mike's rate of completing math problems during these three conditions
using a multi-element design. Mike's rate of academic work was highest in
the *No Bugs* condition and approximately 50% lower in the *Bugs* condition.
Thus, the pre-assessment functional analysis identified some variables
that controlled Mike's academic performance. Intervention compared two
conditions. Graduated *in vivo* exposure involved Mike spending 15–20
minutes exposing himself at his own pace to a variety of stimuli arranged

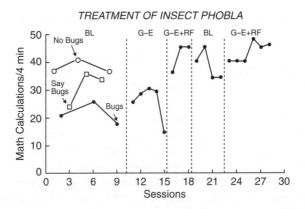

Figure 3.1. Mean number of correct problems per 4-min probe across assessment (BL), graduated exposure (G-E), and exposure plus reinforcement (G-E+RF)
conditions. Reproduced from K. M. Jones & P. C. Friman (1999). A case study of
behavioral assessment and treatment of insect phobia. *Journal of Applied Behavior
Analysis,* **32,** 95–98.

in a nine-step hierarchy. The least fear-provoking stimulus was from holding a jar of crickets. The most fear provoking stimulus was holding a cricket in his hand for an extended period of time. Graded exposure plus reinforcement was the same as graded exposure, but included points for completion of each problem exchanged for back up reinforcers. In the graded exposure condition, Mike completed a similar number of math problems as in the *Bugs* assessment condition. However, in the graded exposure plus reinforcement condition he completed twice as many math problems. Recall that these data were taken in the presence of crickets. Jones and Friman concluded that pre-intervention functional analysis was important since it contradicted the information from the functional assessment. Specifically, although teachers identified taunts from peers as the primary antecedent that interfered with academic performance, the functional analysis identified the presence of insects as the antecedent. Second, Jones and Friman noted that this study focused on the deficits in adaptive behavior rather than self-report of fears, such as Wolpe's SUDs ratings. Third, they noted that exposure alone was insufficient for remedying the deficits in adaptive behavior. Rather, they had to add contingencies in order to increase academic performance. They also reported anecdotal evidence that after treatment his peers teased much less and that he did not respond when peers taunted him. There was some possible stimulus generalization in that Mike was observed to crush a spider, although treatment did not include spiders.

In some ways, Jones and Friman's study is unremarkable: They treated a simple phobia with exposure and when this was ineffective they added reinforcement of another behavior. On the other hand, some of its features do distinguish it from a classic behavior therapy approach to a phobia. First, the authors focused on the socially valid problem – disruption in academic performance – rather than subjective ratings of fear. For this reason, and in order to measure behavior reliably, they measured the product of academic behavior rather that subjective ratings of fear. Second, they conducted a pre-intervention functional analysis. Although interviews were used to identify the relevant stimuli, they did not stop there. Indeed, their functional analysis produced reliable data that contradicted the impressions of the teachers. Finally, no reference was made to the problem history. They did not report how the phobia developed. Hence, current stimuli rather than client history, influenced treatment design.

Future studies could build on this study in a number of ways. For example, most clinicians would be more impressed if they had also shown that some observable fearful behavior co-varied with academic behavior, thereby validating the case formulation. Their case description did describe behaviors such as "ignoring his work, pulling the hood of his jacket over his head, or yelling" (p. 96). These appear to be valid fearful behaviors that the experimenters could also have observed. As the authors themselves noted, they could have observed generalization across untreated insects that he also feared. They could also have probed for generalization across academic tasks as well as observe his behavior in response to peer taunts in the classroom setting. Finally, the authors did not report social validation data. Specifically, the study would be even more convincing if the head teacher, other teachers, peers and Mike himself had reported that this was a successful acceptable intervention. It would also have been nice to see that Mike's rate of academic behavior was similar to his peers and that the change in rates of academic behavior resulted in some meaningful improvement in grades. Future research should address these issues.

IMPLICATIONS FOR PRACTITIONERS

Respondent extinction is applicable to a very diverse range of clinical problems It varies tremendously in form, depending upon the natures of the CS, the manner in which extended contact with the CS occurs, and the kinds of participants and contexts. This suggests the general applicability of this approach.

Whatever the form of respondent extinction, practitioners must do three things. First, the practitioner must accurately and comprehensively identify the relevant CS. Wolpe's case studies testify to the problems and subtleties in doing this. Case formulation must identify interoceptive stimuli, such as sensations of dizziness, lightheadedness, tension, gastro-intestinal mobility, etc., that may be CS. The case formulation must also identify private stimuli, such as words, visual imagery, as well as imagined smells, if necessary. The case formulation must also identify the public social and physical CS. Thus, it is not enough to say that someone fears shopping alone in a crowded grocery store. The functional assessment must identify all the relevant CS, such as feeling faint and wobbliness in the knees, worrying that people are going to see that the client is tense and sweating, and strangers looking at the client. Second, the clinician must develop some method of bringing the person in prolonged contact with CS, so that respondent extinction can occur. This can be done through relaxation, in vivo exposure, modeling, humor, tickling, play, writing, drawing, reading descriptions of the CS aloud, or shaping approach behavior. Third, the clinician must have a sufficiently good relationship with the client and the clinical skills to ensure that exposure to all relevant CS occurs. These skills include the ability to observe the client's closely during treatment sessions, and accurately and rapidly identify the exact nature of the stimuli avoided and novel forms of avoidance behavior that the client may not have described. Houlihan et al.'s (1993) description of the treatment of the balloon phobia nicely demonstrates a number of these clinical skills.

Chapter 4

OPERANT BEHAVIOR I: CHARACTERISTICS, ACQUISITION AND STIMULUS CONTROL

CHARACTERISTICS OF OPERANT BEHAVIOR

The idea that behavior is governed by its consequences was recognized in the nineteenth century by early evolutionary scientists. In the nineteenth and early twentieth century much progress was made on understanding respondent behavior through the work of Pavlov and his contemporaries. Yet, this work failed to account for much behavior that was apparently voluntary, rather than reflex-based. Thorndike's work on cats escaping from puzzle boxes and Skinner's work on operant conditioning expanded this understanding of behavior to account for a much broader swath of behavior.

Acquisition of Operant Behavior

Leslie and O'Reilly's (1999) account of operant behavior will suffice to illustrate the nature of operant behavior. In everyday language we describe operant behavior by reference to the organism's "intent." For example, they use the example of an ordinary language account of operant behavior using the example of Russian dogs in World War II who blew up tanks. Russian soldiers trained the dogs, which carried magnetic mines, to hide and run next to the tanks, resulting in the tanks being destroyed. What did the dogs have in mind when they did this? Did their loyalty to Mother Russia or their plan to kill the invaders cause them to blow themselves up? This is both unlikely and illogical. Rather, than explain the dogs' purposive behavior with reference to its inferred intentions or events in the future, one can better explain it by reference to their past learning history. Why did the dogs run toward the tanks? The dogs ran toward the tanks because previously the soldiers reinforced the dogs' behavior of running toward the tanks.

What happens during the acquisition of operant behavior? Consider a typical Skinner box operant experiment. A rat that is food deprived and that has been habituated to the chamber moves around the chamber. It sniffs grooms, walks, and rears. The experimenter cannot identify stimuli that elicit these behaviors, so we say that the animal emits these behaviors. Periodically, the rat depresses a lever and a food pellet is delivered. The rat's behavior changes. It consumes the food and temporarily stops emitting many other behaviors, such as those that are incompatible with eating. More subtly at first, other changes also occur. The rat tends to stay nearer the lever and moves away less. These behaviors that occurred prior to the introduction of a programmatic contingency are temporarily strengthened. Over a variable period of time four effects of this contingency on operant behavior occur. First, after a period of time the rate of lever pressing increases dramatically from a very low rate to a new higher and stable rate. There are individual differences between organisms before this occurs and there is an initial period of varied rates of responding that may be lower than the final operant rate. After a while a steady rate of responding emerges. Second, the rate of other responses that were not reinforced change. The rat wanders around and grooms much less frequently. Other behavior, such as orienting to the bar and moving back and forth between the bar and food dispenser increase in frequency greatly. Third, the sequencing of the rat's behavior becomes stereotypical and invariant. The rat cycles through an orderly sequence of behaviors of repeatedly pressing the lever, approaching the tray, entering the tray and consuming the food in a highly predictable manner. Finally, the response emitted by the rat is highly stereotypical in topography. The rat could press the lever in many different places, with many forces and many different body parts. Yet, it only presses the bar in a very narrow range of locations with one body part. Over time the force reduces to approximate to the minimum force necessary to operate the lever. Thus, the outcomes of operant conditioning include increasing the rate of the operant response relative to baseline and relative to other response and increasing stereotypy of sequencing and topography of behavior. The properties of operant behavior, the outcomes of operant conditioning and the mechanisms necessary to produce operant conditioning are all highly suggestive of implications for case formulation and very useful methods of intervention.

Maintenance of Operant Behavior

Once operant behavior is acquired, its rate is affected by many variables. These include the schedule of reinforcement, response effort, reinforcer magnitude, reinforcer quality, and reinforcer deprivation. This section will briefly describe some of these variables.

A schedule of reinforcement described the relationship between the reinforcer and behavior. Schedules may be either simple or compound. In a simple schedule the schedule can be described in a single rule, for example "the first response after 120s will be reinforced." A compound schedule combines two or more simple schedules, for example "When the red light is illuminated an Fixed Ratio-10 operates, when the green light is illuminated an Fixed Interval-30 seconds operates."

Simple Schedules

In ratio schedules the *n*th response is reinforced. In interval schedules the first response after a specified period of time is reinforced. During fixed schedules the response is always reinforced after a criterion is met. During varied schedules the response is reinforced after various values of the criterion that meet an average. Thus, there are four kinds of simple schedules: fixed ratio (FR), variable ratio (VR), fixed interval (FI) and variable interval (VI).

Each of the schedules is associated with a characteristic pattern of behavior (see Figure 4.1). VR schedules are associated with consistent high rates of responding. FR schedules are also associated with very high rates of responding, but involve a post-reinforcement pause in which the organism temporarily does not respond. In FI schedules the organism shows a characteristic scallop pattern of responding, in which the rate of responding is modest after reinforcement and gradually accelerates until reinforcement occurs. VI schedules are associated with steady, slow rates of

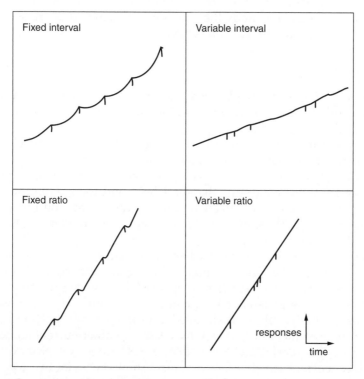

Figure 4.1. Typical cumulative records of performances maintained by four schedules of intermittent reinforcement. J. C. Leslie & M. F. O'Reilly (1999). *Behavior analysis: Foundations and applications to psychology.* Amsterdam, Netherlands: Harwood. p. 65.

responding. When a new schedule is introduced it is often done gradually. For example, when transitioning from an FR-1 to an FR-100 schedule the value of the schedule is gradually changed in small increments, contingent on the organism maintaining high rates of responding.

There are other simple schedules that are clinically important. In a differential reinforcement of other (DRO) schedule the organism's behavior is reinforced for a specified period of time with no responding. For example, a reinforcer may be delivered after 30 s of not pressing a lever. This schedule results in reduction in one response and increases in unspecified other behaviors. In a differential reinforcement of lower rates of responding (DRL) only low rates of responding result in reinforcement. For example, in DRL-30s schedule only the first response after 30 s is reinforced. By contrast, in a differential reinforcement of higher rates of responding (DRH) a response is reinforced before a maximum interval. For example, in a DRH-10s the first response within 10 s is reinforced. DRH schedules are associated with high rates of responding. In time-based schedules reinforcement is delivered independent of the organism's behavior. For example, on a Fixed Time 60-s schedule reinforcement is delivered every 60 s independent of the organism's behavior. Such schedules are sometimes used to study the effects of satiation and deprivation and "environmental enrichment" on behavior.

Compound Schedules

There are many compound schedules. This section will only describe concurrent schedules, as research has investigated these most extensively in applied human studies.

The experimenter designs a clear and explicit schedule of reinforcement for the rat pressing a level in the Skinner box, but that is not the only schedule that is present. Occasionally the rat sniffs, rears up, scratches, and looks around, suggesting that these behaviors too are reinforced, albeit only weakly compared to the powerful, experimenter-designed operant environment. Thus, even in the Skinner box there is more than one schedule of reinforcement.

A concurrent schedule exists when more than one schedule operates simultaneously. The phenomenon of multiple concurrently available schedules of reinforcement has been formalized in Herrnstein's (1961) equation and the generalized matching law (Baum, 1974). Herrnstein's equation states that "the time allocated to an activity is proportional to the rate of reinforcement of that activity relative to other current sources of reinforcement" (Leslie & O'Reilly, 1999, p. 318.) After extensive exposure to two concurrent schedules, an organism shows behavior in a way typical of each schedule. It distributes its responses in a lawful way between the two schedules as it appears to chose between the two concurrently available schedules.

HUMAN OPERANT BEHAVIOR

There are many basic and applied examples of operant human behavior. These include operant conditioning of verbal behavior in students (Greenspoon, 1955) and the development of culture-specific vocal behavior in infants (Halle, De Boynson-Bardies, & Vihman, 1991). Additionally, operant mechanisms have been implicated in the acquisition of a wide range of forms of psychopathology (Sturmey, 2007) including depression (Hopko, Lejuez, LePage, Hopko & McNeil, 2003; Lam, Marra & Salzinger, 2005), psychotic behavior (Ayllon & Haughton, 1964; Ayllon, Haughton & Hughes, 1965; Patterson & Teigen, 1973), school refusal (Kearney & Silverman, 1990; Kearney & Albano, 2004), anxiety (Jones & Friman, 1999; Friman, 2007), self-injury (Oliver, Hall & Murphy, 2005; Richman & Lindauer, 2005; Schaeffer, 1970) and stereotypical behavior (Kennedy, 2007). Research has demonstrated operant processes maintaining factors in problem behaviors in a wide range of populations including adults with traumatic brain injury (Dixon & Bihler, 2007), chronic pain (Flor, Knost & Birbaumer, 2002; Joliffe & Nicholas, 2004), people with intellectual disabilities (Didden, 2007), autism spectrum disorders (Sturmey & Fitzer, 2007), people with eating disorders (Farmer & Latner, 2007; Redin, Miltenberger, Crosby, Wolff, & Stickney, 2002), and older adults (Fisher, Drossel, Yury & Cherup, 2007.)

Lam et al. (2005) provide an example of how symptomatic behavior could be shaped through social contingencies. They noted that different cultures tend to favor either somatic or psychological presentation of depression. This suggested that different contingencies embedded in different cultures may shape different reporting of psychopathology (see Skinner, 1953, 1971). Thirty-six, nondepressed American undergraduates participated in an analog study in which they had to read a sentence on a computer screen and endorse either a psychological, somatic or neutral word. After a baseline condition the experimenter made comments such as "most people would experience _____", or "Mm-hum." After, conditioning extinction took place. Lam et al. observed that all three classes of words could be conditioned and extinguished, although they also observed large individual differences between subjects. This study suggests that social contingencies can shape culture-specific behavior similar to depressive symptoms.

Operant phenomena in psychopathology are robust, widespread and well established. Unfortunately, generally clinicians cannot observe client's learning histories. The clinician may see current behavior, or hear reports of recent behavior in the clinic from the client or from third parties. The behavior observed or reported may be strange and apparently self-defeating and thus it may seem unlikely that such behavior could be learned. It is import to note that professional staff who are unaware of the true origin of operant behavior attribute it to a variety of underlying psychiatric and psychodynamic processes (Ayllon & Haughton, 1964; Ayllon et al., 1965.)

Implications for Case Formulation and Intervention

The operant nature of some behavior, including psychiatric symptoms, in people with psychiatric and behavioral disorders has a number of important implications for case formulation and intervention. First, operant mechanisms are important in both acquisition and maintenance of a wide variety of forms of psychopathology. This is hardly surprising. Much psychopathology is likely to affect that of other people in a variety of ways. Others may avoid a client's unusual behavior or offer assistance. Thus, unusual behavior is likely to have social consequences, some of which may be important in operant mechanisms maintaining that unusual behavior. This suggests that case formulation should assess this possibility and identify the possible contingencies maintaining problematic behavior. Second, since operant behavior is a function of schedules of reinforcement for other adaptive behavior, the clinician should also ask themselves why current contingencies do not support adaptive behavior to compete with the presenting problem. For example, when working with a housebound person with agoraphobia, one might readily observe the obvious contingencies maintaining staying at home, such as avoidance of anxiety, work and responsible adult role behavior. One might also observe any secondary gains in the forms of assistance from family members and friends. The clinician should enquire as to what has happened to the contingencies that used to support independence. Perhaps they are no longer present or perhaps there are stronger contingencies maintaining problematic behavior. Third, these observations suggest that interventions based on operant mechanisms identified in the case formulation may be indicated. Fourth, since the acquisition of operant behavior can reduce other behaviors, this may be a viable mechanism to simultaneously increase some appropriate behavior, while simultaneously reducing ineffective behaviors. Fifth, in situations where the person's behavior is disorganized, random or chaotic, operant conditioning can organize the client's behavioral repertoire in ways that may be desirable. Sixth, in situations where response stereotypy, such as consistent performance of behavior within certain limits is important, operant conditioning might be a mechanism to achieve this outcome. Finally, where behavior is inappropriately invariant, then operant mechanisms might be applicable to induce behavioral variability.

An additional set of implications of operant conditioning comes from identifying variables that must be manipulated in order to implement operant conditioning. First, assessment must focus on careful analysis of behavior and its consequences. The office-bound clinician is at a distinct disadvantage here, as they have to reply on client reports and recollections and observations of behavior in the office, which may be a very limited sample of behavior. Second, some appropriate operant behavior probably exists in the client's behavioral repertoire. If it is absent, or so very low in frequency that it cannot come in contact with the contingencies, then operant conditioning is difficult or cannot occur. The clinician must identify all these appropriate forms of operant behavior. Third, an effective reinforcer must be both available and must be readily manipulated. For basic behavioral researchers this is not an issue. They can deprive their subjects of food and water and impose a contingency through the physical mechanisms in a Skinner box. For practitioners none of these assumptions can be made. Indeed, identifying and manipulating reinforcers appropriately can be highly problematic in clinical settings. Finally, operant behavior is a function of reinforcer deprivation and satiation. Again, although basic researchers can readily manipulate these variables, practitioners may require an extensive technology, as well as good luck, to do so.

Application: Preference and Reinforcer Assessment

Clinicians have a great challenge in identifying and manipulating stimuli that function as reinforcers. In order to address the first question, researchers have developed a range of reinforcer questionnaires. Because of their limitations, researchers have gone on to develop stimulus preference assessment methods.

Reinforcer Surveys

A wide range of psychometric instruments have been developed to assess potential reinforcers. For example, Cautela and Kastenbaum (1967) developed the *Reinforcer Survey Schedule* for use in adult mental health settings. This was the model for many variants of this scale designed to be used with children, adolescents, seniors, psychiatric patients, children with autism, intellectual disabilities, people with visual impairments and for use in contexts such as marriage, social behavior, sexual dysfunction, work, and school (Cautela and Lynch, 1983). Copies of these schedules are available in Cautela (1990) and Cautela, Cautela and Esonis (1981). Discussion of these scales in detail is beyond the scope this chapter (see Cautela, 1972, 1977, 1981; Cautela & Brion-Meisels, 1979; Cautela & Lynch, 1983, Galeazzi, Franceschina, Cautela, Holmes & Sakano, 1998; Holmes, Heckel, Chestnut, Harris & Cautela, 1987; Jacobs, Daly, King & Cheramie, 1984; Keehn, Bloomfield and Hug, 1969; Kleinknecht, McCormick & Thorndike, 1973; Matson, Bielecki, Mayville, Smalls, Bamberg & Baglio, 1999; Phillips, Fischer & Singh, 1977; Thorndike & Kleinknecht, 1974; Dewhurst & Cautela, 1980). This line of research has been a model for the subsequent development and elaboration of a wide range of similar measures. There are reinforcer surveys for people with intellectual disabilities (Bihm, Poindexter, Kienlen and Smith, 1992; Fisher, Piazza, Bowman & Amari, 1996; Fox & DeShaw, 1993; Northup, 2000; Sturmey, Matson & Lott, 2003), autism (Atkinson et al., 1984), inpatient children (Jones, Mandler-Provin, Latkowski & McMahon, 1988) and children with attention-deficit hyperactivity disorder (ADHD: Northup, 2000; Northup, George, Jones, Broussard & Vollmer, 1996.)

These schedules are quick and easy to administer to most populations and can readily be incorporated into clinical interviews. In general terms these schedules often, but not always, proved to have adequate inter-rater and test–retest reliability, although the internal consistency of the scales was often variable. Factor analytic studies have not always replicated the proposed scale structure (Baron, Dewaard & Galizio, 1981; Holmes et al., 1987; Sturmey et al., 2003; Thorndike & Kleinknecht, 1974). These surveys are limited in that both third-party reports, such as from family members and staff, and even self-reports may not accurately identify functional reinforcers. Sometimes, they may identify stimuli that are only moderately powerful as reinforcers and hence may not be sufficiently powerful to change behaviors of concern.

This literature had generated a number of outstanding issues that continue to be addressed. First, the content and format of the scales should be carefully considered. Although items may sometimes be generated by researchers, parents and staff, others have used large scale sampling of items nominated by clients (Houlihan et al., 1991; Jones et al., 1987). Fisher et al. (1997) compared stimuli generated from a standard list with stimuli generated from a structured interview with caregivers. Caregiver generated stimuli were modestly more effective than those identified from a standard list. Some scales have excluded items because of ethical or practical concerns over the use of particular items (Houlihan et al., 1991). Over time the availability, cost and appropriateness of items changes. Thus, some of the surveys developed in the 1960s are outdated as they omit important potential reinforcers. A related issue is that almost all of these scales have implicitly sampled only positive reinforcers. Few scales assessed potential negative reinforcers, such as being left alone or avoiding chores. Clinicians should also consider what stimuli clients avoid and consider how this may be incorporated into intervention. Future research should address this important gap. Finally, these scales vary considerable in length, administration time and ease of administration. For some purposes, relatively brief, standardized reinforcer assessments that include the most commonly identified stimuli and adequately samples a variety of stimulus domains may be sufficient. This may especially be so if they are supplemented with an open-ended question to name any other stimuli that are not on the list (Fisher et al., 1997.) For other purposes longer, more time-consuming schedules may not be worthwhile.

A second issue is the organization of items into scales. Almost all instruments assemble their items intuitively into scales. This may have distinct advantages in terms of face validity and acceptability, but may beg important questions as to the nature of reinforcers. This is reflected in the variable and sometimes low internal consistency of intuitively developed scales. Currently there are relatively few factor analytic studies available to guide empirical development of scales (Baron et al., 1981; Holmes et al., 1987; Sturmey et al., 2003; Thorndike & Kleinknecht, 1974)

A final and important issue is that of validity. Some early studies observed poor, and sometimes no, agreement between child- and teacher-nominated reinforcers (Jacob et al., 1984.) Several studies have reported similar problems with a variety of populations. (Fisher et al., 1997; Green et al., 1988, 1991; Northup, 2000; Northup et al., 1996; Reid, Everson, & Green, 1999). For example, Northup (2000) found that a reinforcer schedule correctly identified stimuli that subsequently functioned as reinforcers in only 57% of assessments with children with ADHD. They found both false negatives and false positives. It is also well know that self-reports of behavior and reinforcers may be very inaccurate (Bernstein & Michael, 1990; Risley & Hart, 1968). Thus, even self-nominated reinforcers may be inaccurate, if naming these stimuli as reinforcers has a history of punishment. For example, in staff motivation programs, staff may be reluctant to name time off from work as a reinforcer. There are also a variety of potential reinforcers, such as violence, inappropriate sexual behavior, and so on, that people are unlikely to report accurately for the same reason.

There is now a substantial body of empirical studies that have consistently shown stimuli names as reinforcers by third parties as reinforcers for clients may or may not function as reinforcers. The inaccuracy of psychometric checklists creates a potential problem for practitioners that research has yet failed to address. Psychometric instruments are quick and easy to administer, because many people have the skills to use them. In contrast, using other more accurate methods, such as stimulus preference assessments (SPAs) requires specific skills that staff may not possess unless they receive specific training (Lavie & Sturmey, 2002; Roscoe, Fisher, Glover & Volkert, 2006). If the cost of inaccurately identifying a stimulus as a reinforcer is not great, then a simple remedy would be to select another high ranked item from the checklist and continue with the procedure until an effective reinforcer was found. Alternately, stimuli identified from checklists could be efficiently and rapidly evaluated to investigate if they function as reinforcers (DeLeon et al., 2001; De Leon, Iwata, Goh & Wordell, 1997; Fisher et al., 1996.) However, in order to do this, staff would have to be trained to conduct these procedures and the additional costs for staff training and time to conduct the procedures would have to be worthwhile compared to alternate procedures. However, in some situations, incorrectly identifying stimuli as reinforcers may have substantial personal costs, for example in the case of reducing a life-threatening or dangerous maladaptive behavior. In such situations, SPA methods are to be preferred because of their greater accuracy and the higher costs of errors.

Stimulus Preference Assessments

Researchers developed SPAs to identify reinforcers for people with severe disabilities. They did this, in part because of the limitations of surveys noted above and in part because of the need to identify very powerful reinforcers to compete with the reinforcers maintaining severe behavior problems. SPAs typically involve presenting various potential reinforcers and observing the frequency of the number of approaches to each stimulus. The stimuli may be presented individually or in groups. Research has also extended SPA methods to include simply presenting multiple stimuli and recording the length of time that the person interacts with each item. SPAs have been extended for use with children with ADHD, and adults with dementia and psychosis. A study by Northup, George, Jones, Broussard & Vollmer (1996) illustrates this. He compared three methods of reinforcer assessment in children with ADHD. A reinforcer survey was verbally administered to each child. In the verbal choice method the child was given a verbal choice between two alternative stimuli. For example, the experimenter asked "Would you rather get things to eat ... or ... go to the library?" (p. 204). In the pictorial presentation method the child selected one token from a pair of tokens, each representing one of the two items. Northup then assessed the validity of these methods by measuring the number of coding tasks the child would complete for each identified item. The survey method only identified reinforcers on 55% of occasions. In contrast, the verbal and picture choice methods did so on 70% and 80% of occasions respectively. This, and other research with various populations, suggests that surveys are often less accurate than direct stimulus preference assessments in identifying reinforcers.

Manipulating Potential Reinforcers

Clinicians must also manipulate reinforcers. Reinforcers can be manipulated directly by the therapist. This can be done during therapy. The therapist can also manipulate reinforcers indirectly through the behaviors of other people, such as family members, peers and staff. The client may manipulate their own reinforcers if the client has good self-regulation skills and can accurately reinforce their own behavior.

Summary

Reinforcer surveys are available for many populations and contexts and can readily be incorporated into clinical interviews. They may be effective in identifying reinforcers for some clients, but not others. SPAs are more accurate than surveys in identifying reinforcers. Therapists must also manipulate reinforcers accurately contingent on client behavior. This requires accurate client reports of their own behavior or effective training of others to do so.

Increasing Desirable Behavior With Reinforcement

In most applied studies the intervention naturally consists of many components. Reinforcement is often combined with instructions, modeling and other procedures. For example, Hollandsworth, Glazeski and Dressel (1978) treated poor interview skills in a 30-year-old college student with a history of a severe and disabling anxiety disorder, which had resulted in hospitalization and as needed stelazine. The client had participated in over 60 job interviews during the past five months and had received no job offers. Instead, he worked as a sales clerk. Baseline observations in role plays of interviews revealed that his answers were rambling. He stared blankly. He had emotionless expressions and speech dysfluencies. In order to improve his social skills, the client was taught to give focused, unambiguous and concise answers to questions, to use coping statements, such as "let me start again" and to generate his own questions of the interviewer. The intervention used behavioral skills training, which consisted of instructions, modeling, rehearsal and social reinforcement in the form of verbal feedback. Additionally, his therapist taught him that when the interviewer asked a question he should pause, briefly look away, look back in a few seconds and begin a focused response. Observational data showed that he learned these social skills rapidly. Observers rated him as more focused. He was also physiologically less responsive, as measured with galvanic skin response. Unobtrusive ratings of other social skills, such as eye contact and personal appearance also improved. Following intervention, he participated in three job interviews. Each interview resulted in a job offer. The job he took resulted in a 2353% increase in salary. Follow-up phone contacts at two-monthly intervals for eight months indicated that he maintained his job, began reading in church before his congregation and participated in public organizations in a way he had previously never been able to.

Decreasing Undesirable Behavior With Reinforcement

As mentioned earlier simple reinforcement schedules may be used to decrease undesirable behavior, by reinforcing the absence of the target behavior, or specific alternate or incompatible behaviors. For example, Heard and Watson (1999) used a DRO procedure to reduce wandering in four seniors with dementia aged 79–83 years. Wandering was defined as "aimless, disoriented, continuous ambulation that occurred when the individual moved from their immediate, specifically assigned area to another area within the facility's physical structure" (p. 381). Inter-observer agreement was over 90% for all observations. Prior to intervention, they kept six sessions of ABC logs. They used these to identify the possible consequence of maintaining wandering. For example, wandering appeared to be maintained by access to sweet food for one person. For a second person, access to sensory stimulation, such as touching items to face, appeared to the reinforcer maintaining wandering. DRO consisted of restricting access to the consequence hypothesized to maintain wandering and presenting this consequence contingent upon 14–30 s intervals when no wandering occurred. For all four participants DRO resulted in 65–75% reduction in wandering. Two features of this study are noteworthy. First, the authors empirically identified reinforcers using direct observation before intervention. They did not use staff reports. Presumably it was not possible to use self-reports. Second, the therapist manipulated the consequences that appeared to maintain the problem behavior. Third, behavior that is usually attributed to some unknown and unspecified biological mechanism was very responsive to contingency management.

Schedules of Reinforcement

Applications

Relatively few studies have compared schedules in clinical settings. However, Van Houten and Nau (1980) compared the effects of FR and VR schedules of the same value (i.e. FR-8 versus VR-8 and FR-12 versus VR-12) on attentive and disruptive classroom behavior. Five children with hearing impairments, behavior problems and language delays participated. They made reinforcement contingent on attending without disruptive behavior. VR schedules consistently resulted in higher rates of attending and less disruptive behavior than FR schedules. These results mirror basic research with nonhuman animals that have shown that VR schedules are associated with higher rates of responding and fewer breaks in performance than FR schedules, which are characterized by post-reinforcement pauses. This study, in conjunction with basic research on FR and VR schedules, suggest that therapist should chose VR over FR schedules because VR schedules produce more consistent and higher rates of responding.

Concurrent Schedules of Reinforcement

Pierce and Epling (1995) noted that the generalized matching law has important implications for applied work, including behavioral case

Table 4.1. Implications of generalized matching law for behavioral intervention

Parameter	Unhealthy behavior	Healthy behavior
Immediacy	Reduce	Increase
Rate	Reduce/eliminate	Increase
Quality	Use low quality	Use high quality
	Eliminate high quality	Eliminate low quality
Effort	Increase effort	Reduce effort

formulation and intervention. When we observe high rates of unusual behavior there are strong contingencies maintaining it. A clinician's job is to identify those contingencies and incorporate them into the case formulation. Low rates of appropriate behavior suggests that the reinforcement schedules for appropriate behaviors are weak, or perhaps appropriate behavior is even punished. Again, the clinician's job is to identify these contingencies and incorporate them into the case formulation. Once the formulation has identified both sets of contingencies, then interventions can be designed based on manipulating one or more sets of contingencies. For example, it may be possible to increase desirable behavior indirectly and without intervention, by weakening the contingencies for inappropriate behavior. Table 4.1 summarizes the implications of the generalized matching law for intervention in clinical situations.

Of course in the real world, clinicians can only rarely exert such strong control over their client's behavior. Much of the business of behavioral approaches to intervention reflects the problems of multiple completing schedules – some strong schedules of reinforcement maintaining the undesirable behaviors and some weak schedules maintaining desirable behavior. Part of the job of the therapist is to reverse these schedules so there is greater reinforcement for appropriate behavior and less or no reinforcement for undesirable behavior.

Clinicians have incorporated concurrent schedules of reinforcement into interventions in many clinical situations. The following sections illustrate with reference to drug abuse, depression, ADHD and autism.

Application: Drug Abuse

Many drugs provide powerful positive and negative reinforcing effects for their use by providing pleasant or euphoric consequences and terminating or attenuating aversive consequences, such as pain or anxiety. Comer,

Collins and Fishman (1997) illustrate the reinforcing effects of drugs and the interaction between concurrent schedules of reinforcement. They recruited five morphine-maintained adults to a study that compared the effects of the availability of various amounts of money on the reinforcing value of differing doses of morphine, placebo, and money. They evaluated the reinforcing value of the stimuli using progressive ratio (PR) schedules. In PR schedules the subject emits progressively more and more responses to access the reinforcer. Eventually the subject no longer responds. The "break point" is the value of the last PR schedule that the subject completes. Stimuli that are weak reinforcers have low break points and powerful reinforcer have high break points.

As might be expected, larger doses of morphine and larger quantities of money had higher break points. More interestingly, Comer et al. also found that as larger quantities of money were available the break point for the same dose of morphine fell. Likewise, as the dose of morphine increased the breakpoint of the same quantity of money fell. This study replicated many other studies showing that many addictive drugs are positive reinforcers. Further, increasing the availability of other reinforcers, in this case money, decreased the reinforcing value of drugs (Carroll et al., 1996; Higgins, Heil & Sigmon, 2007.)

These observations are the basis of behavioral approaches to treatment of drug addiction that incorporate reinforcement of healthy behavior to compete with drug use. For example, Higgins et al. (2007) developed a community reinforcement approach plus voucher program for cocaine addiction. This program included urinalysis to measure cocaine use accurately and the use of vouchers to access nondrug reinforcers. Additionally, the program included numerous skills training programs, such as job finding, relationship counseling, increasing recreational skills, increasing a social network of nondrug using people, mood management skills and sleep hygiene procedures, teaching functional assessment to clients to understand the variables controlling their cocaine use, and teaching functional healthy alternatives to drug use. Program staff gave clients vouchers for clean urine specimens. They also used progressive fines for each day of positive toxicology screens. Clients did not receive cash; instead staff members bought requested items in the community for the clients with vouchers.

A series of RCTs has shown that this program is superior to traditional drug counseling using a disease model resulting in higher abstinence rates and lower drop out, including at 6- and 12-month follow-up (Higgins et al., 1991, 1993, 2000). Further, a component analysis, which compared the program with and without the voucher component, found that vouchers were associated with higher abstinence rates and lower drop out at the end of treatment and at six-month follow-up (Higgins, Budney, Bickel & Badger, 1994). In another component analysis Carroll et al. (1998) showed that the community reinforcement approach component was also effective in promoting positive outcomes that were maintained at one-year follow-up. Studies of other reinforcement-based approaches to drug addiction have also found that adding motivational components to existing rehabilitation programs result in more job seeking-related behaviors, better abstinence, greater chances of employment and higher incomes in veterans with mental health and substance abuse problems (Drebing et al., 2005.)

Application: Depression

Contemporary behavioral approaches to depression also reference the general matching law as a model for understanding and treating depression (Hopko, Hopko & LeJuez, 2007.) Here again the relative balance of reinforcement for depressed and nondepressed behavior is the focus of attention. Behavioral approaches note that many of the stressful life events involve loss of reinforcement and increased punishment for adaptive behavior, such as painful medical conditions. People with depressed mood also report fewer enjoyable activities (Hopko et al., 2003), have low rates of adaptive, healthy behavior, little persistence and high rates of complaining and symptom-related talk.

Based on these observations, Lejuez, Hopko and Hopko (2001, 2002) developed *Brief Behavioral Activation Treatment for Depression* (BATD). BATD is a manualized treatment approach to depression. The aim of behavioral activation is to set small specific goals that bring the client in contact with the available reinforcement for healthy, nondepressed behavior. The potential reinforcing activities and long-term personal goals are individually assessed. Further, the treatment of individual cases is based on individual formulation based on individual functional assessments. See Hopko et al. (2003) for an example. Several RCTs have demonstrated the efficacy of BATD with depressed cancer patients (Hopko, Bell, Armento, Hunt & Lejuez, 2005) and psychiatric inpatients (Hopko et al., 2003.)

Application: ADHD

Behavioral approaches to ADHD have formulated ADHD in terms of concurrent schedules. In particular, impulsivity has been analyzed as a concurrent choice between a smaller, sooner reinforcer (SSR) or a larger later reinforcer (LLR.) For example, if a child with ADHD has two concurrent schedules available: emitting an inattentive behavior resulting in immediate removal of a work task (the SSR) or working on a sheet of academic tasks (the LLR.)

Neef et al. (2005) manipulated several aspects of available reinforcers for completing academic tasks in 58 children with and without ADHD. For example, children chose between an immediate low quality reinforcer and a high quality reinforcer that was delivered the next day. Children with ADHD were more likely than children without ADHD to choose

SSRs than LLRs. Therefore, behavioral interventions for impulsivity often involve substituting immediate for delayed reinforcers, graduated introduction of difficult tasks, and teaching progressively tolerating delays in reinforcement (Neef & Northup, 2007). For example, initially, the therapist may reinforce appropriate, nonimpulsive responding with a larger, high quality reinforcer. Once, responding to that choice occurs consistently, a small time delay is introduced. Once responding maintains with a modest time delay, the delay is progressively increased over time until the child responds nonimpulsively and waits for a longer later reinforcer. See Neef and Northup (2007) for an illustrative case study.

Application: Teaching New Behavior to Children with Autism

Teaching new skills to children with autism often takes place in the context of existing skills that have recently been taught and which may be maintained on rich schedules of reinforcement. For example, a child may be taught a conventional form of communication, such saying "Coke," when the child already has other means of requesting the item, such as pointing or tantrums. In this example, novel effortful responses with low certainty or reinforcement compete with existing, easy responses that have a strong history of reinforcement. Thus, the purpose of language interventions may sometimes be to reduce and eventually eliminate current communicative behaviors and replace them with other more advanced conventional forms of communication (Sigafoos, O'Reilly, Schlosser & Lancioni, 2007)

Bernstein, Brown and Sturmey (2007) conducted a study that addressed a somewhat different version of this issue – how to teach play when children had learned and frequently uses requests (mands). The practical problem was how to teach play responses without eliminating the mands, which therapists had laboriously taught and were effective forms of communication. They investigated the effects of the schedules of reinforcement for mands on the frequency of play responses in tree children with autism. In one condition, both responses were on an FR-1 schedule. In another condition, the mands were on an FR-10 and the play was on an FR-1 schedule; that is, only every 10th mand was reinforced. Thus, play responses were always on an FR-1 schedule. When the schedule for mands was thinned to an FR-10, the frequency of play responses systematically increased, even though play was always on an FR-1 schedule. Thus, changing the schedule value for the mands resulted in changes in the frequency of play responses. This study demonstrates that increases in one adaptive behavior can result from thinning the schedule for some other dominant response class.

Summary

Concurrent schedules are the rule, not the exception, in the real world. The generalized matching law can be used to model interventions based on the notion that there are at least two schedules of interest operating at any time – one for healthy, desirable behaviors and one for unhealthy, undesirable behaviors. This model seems useful for a wide range of problems including drug use and depression, amongst others. Although schedule value is one important parameter in concurrent operants it is not the only one. Neef et al.'s work identified reinforcer immediacy (immediate versus delayed), rate of reinforcement, reinforcer quality (high versus low preferred stimuli), and responses effort (easy versus effortful responses.) These ideas may be useful in behavioral case formulation and intervention. For example, when formulating a case, one should look at immediacy, rate, quality and effort involved in both unhealthy and healthy behavior. If may be that manipulation of some of these parameters may not be possible, but manipulation of others may be sufficient to produce the desired behavioral change.

STIMULUS CONTROL OF OPERANT BEHAVIOR

So far we have only discussed two aspects of operant behavior – the response and its consequence. However, antecedent stimuli that are correlated with the presence or absence of a contingency are also important. Suppose that in a Skinner box a green light is illuminated when reinforcement is available and a red light is given when reinforcement is not available. After a period of time the presence of these antecedent stimuli greatly affect behavior. When the green light illuminates the animal immediately emits high rates of operant behavior and when the red light illuminates the animal quickly stops responding. When this occurs the lights are said to be discriminative stimuli that exert stimulus control of operant behavior. Note that when the experimenter presents or withdraws discriminative stimuli, the rate of behavior changes abruptly and there is no acquisition curve or extinction. Such rapid behavior change is very desirable in many applied situations.

Stimulus generalization occurs when the effects of reinforcement in the presence of one stimulus spreads to other similar stimuli. For example, red lights that differ in color, brightness and saturation from the training stimulus might also affect operant behavior. This is true, even though no training has occurred with these stimuli. Stimuli that are most physically similar to the training stimulus usually result in most rates of responding that are most similar to the training stimulus. Stimuli that are physically very different from the training stimulus usually result in rates of responding that are most different from the training stimulus.

Discrimination training is used to establish stimulus control. In discrimination training reinforcement is made available for some stimuli and is not available for other stimuli. For example, to bring a pigeon's behavior under stimulus control in the above example, we might only make reinforcement available during the green light and ensure that no reinforcement occurred during the red light.

Stimulus control of behavior is gradually modified by procedures that involve transfer of stimulus control. In typical procedures that involve transfer of stimulus control discriminative stimuli that currently control behavior are gradually modified. For example, the color, saturation, shape or duration of a conditioned stimulus might be progressively and slowly modified until new stimuli that are different from the original stimuli now exert stimulus control over behavior. For example, a large, bright red illuminated circle might be gradually transformed in size, brightness, color and shape over many trials to become a small, light, yellow triangle. If this new stimulus now exerts stimulus control over the operant behavior, then transfer of stimulus control has occurred.

Human Operant Behavior

Operant behavior in verbal humans sometimes differs from operant behavior of nonhumans. For example, schedule performance in human infants resembles that of nonhuman animals (Bentall, Lowe & Beasty, 1985). As children get older and acquire language their performance on operant schedules may differ from that of nonhumans and nonverbal infants. Linguistically competent humans may form verbal rules. These rules can be acquired from instructions from other people. Verbally competent people can also form rules that describe contingencies. For example, during a FI 20 schedule a person might form the rule "count to 18, then press the button" (Leslie & O'Reilly, 1999.) Such private verbal behavior is difficult to study. It might appear that stating such as rule may be a discriminative stimulus that controls subsequent operant performance, although such behavior may also serve other functions. Chapter 7 deals with verbal behavior and how behavioral therapies account for and use verbal behavior during therapy.

Clinical Implications

Examples of stimulus control of human behavior are very common. The boss walks in, everyone stops talking and looks busy. The boss leaves, everyone relaxes and goes back to chatting and surfing the web. This suggests that the presence of the boss has history of punishment for goofing off and reinforcement for work-related activities. The absence of the boss has a history of reinforcement for goofing off and punishment for working too hard in front of coworkers. There are many clinical examples like this. Stimulus hierarchies for systematic desensitization describe the relationship between stimuli and the likelihood of a wide range of clinically relevant behaviors, such as relaxing and avoidance. Generalization problems, such as a client who can relax in the office, but not when traveling on a bus, again suggest stimulus control of clinically relevant behaviors. Behaving aggressively and angrily when people look at you, instead of when you are in imminent danger, can be construed as another example of inappropriate stimulus control. A client who can never relax is an example of lack of stimulus control of relaxation.

Stimulus control of operant behavior has some important implications for intervention. Interventions based on stimulus control have a distinct advantage over contingency-based methods because they can change behavior much more rapidly than contingency-based interventions. For example, if a client behavior can be brought under control of written instructions, audio prompts or other antecedents, then behavior change can occur very rapidly. Similarly, if clinically relevant behaviors are under inappropriate stimulus control, then transfer of stimulus procedures may be effective in helping the client change their behavior.

Lack of stimulus control and inappropriate stimulus control suggest two kinds of remedies. If the behavior of interest is not under any stimulus control the intervention must consist of establishing stimulus control. If the problem is inappropriate stimulus control then the remedy is to bring the behavior of interest under appropriate stimulus control.

Application: Establishing Stimulus Control

Establishing stimulus control of behavior may be an essential component of many interventions. For example, Functional communication training (FCT) is an intervention strategy to reduce challenging behaviors in people with ID and other populations. In FCT, the function of the challenging behavior is identified. Functions might include positive reinforcement by access to attention, food, drinks or tangible items, or escape from aversive stimuli, such as teaching or work tasks or environments that are too noisy or crowded, etc. FCT consists of teaching a conventional communication response that serves the same purpose as the challenging behavior to compete with the challenging behavior.

Fisher, Kuhn and Thompson (1998) taught FCT to two participants, Amy, a 13-year-old girl with mild ID and Ned, a 9-year-old boy with autism, moderate ID and ADHD. Initially, each child learned to request either attention or a toy using either words or gestures. Discrimination training consisted of teaching the children to only request those consequences in the presence of a discriminative stimulus indicating the availability of that consequence. For example, the therapist used pictures of Amy's preferred toys and Amy interacting with a therapist as discriminative stimuli. Amy learned to ask "I want my toys, please" and "Excuse me, please." During a 10-minute session the therapist hung the pictures on the wall where they were clearly visible. The therapist only reinforced requests that corresponded to the discriminative stimulus on the wall. During baseline both children emitted high rates of destructive behaviors, such as scratching, pinching and kicking objects. Following discrimination training the children emitted high rates of communication responses almost exclusively only in the presence of the relevant discriminative stimulus. Additionally, destructive behavior reduced to zero or near-zero levels. This study showed that discrimination training was effective in establishing stimulus control of requesting. This was of great practical value, since it is not always possible to ensure that all consequences are available at all times. Thus, if a classmate is using the child's preferred toys, the discriminative stimulus for the availability of attention could be used to reduce destructive behavior.

Application: Modifying Stimulus Control of Operant Behavior

An example of changing stimulus control comes from Allen and Evans (2001). Hypoglycemia is an aversive experience in which a person with diabetes experiences headaches and other unpleasant physical symptoms, as well as potential embarrassment. Thus, avoidance of hypoglycemia is negatively reinforced by avoidance or removal of aversive consequences. Likewise, in children with diabetes, their parents are also actively involved in the management of these symptoms and their behavior may also be negatively reinforced by avoiding or removing their child's medical discomfort. However, the various strategies used, such as repeated checking of blood sugar and consuming sugar, can result in dangerously high levels of blood sugar with attendant risks of medical problems, such as blindness and renal failure.

Amy was a 15-year-old girl who had poorly controlled diabetes. Her parents were very concerned about the negative effects of hypoglycemia. Her blood sugar was poorly controlled. Amy checked her blood sugar approximately 80–90 times a day. This cost $600 per week in reagents. Hence, an inappropriate generalization gradient existed whereby the probability that Amy would retest herself increased after too short an interval of time since the last check. Allen and Evans developed an intervention so that Amy and her parents could progressively tolerate longer periods of time without testing and without hyperglycemic episodes. The intervention consisted of setting targets for the number of tests Amy would conduct each day. They progressively lowered the goals from 60 to 12 tests per day in seven steps. Since testing was obviously a powerful reinforcer, Amy could earn a small number of additional test strips for completing household chores for 30 minutes. The intervention was successful in reducing the number of blood checks from 80–95 per day in baseline to less than 12 per day. The behavior change of Amy and her parents was maintained at 3-month follow-up. Amy's blood sugar levels improved to safe levels.

Hence, the contingencies of reinforcement changed the stimulus control of checking blood levels to progressively longer interval since the last check.

Generalization: A Stimulus Control Problem

A criticism often charged against behavior analysis is that "behavioral interventions do not generalize" (Chiesa, 1994). Such a generalization is unfounded and unwarranted. It also misses an important point: nonbehavioral interventions often do not assess generalization. However, since nonbehavioral interventions often do not assess generalization, we do not know if generalization occurred or not. There are many examples of generalization problems in many therapies. When a physician changes the doses of a child's Ritalin and the child's academic performance deteriorates, this is failure to generalize across drug doses: an inappropriately narrow range of drug doses control appropriate behavior. When a client recites a correct cognitive strategy in an anger management group and walks out of the therapist's office and assumes he is being slighted by the secretary who keeps them waiting to schedule their next appointment, there has been a failure to generalize. Generalization across settings, people and responses of anger management has not occurred. In both of these examples the client has the appropriate behavior in their behavioral repertoire, but they failed to show appropriate behavior in the appropriate circumstance. It is ironic, then, that ABA – the one approach that measures, analyzes and has a conceptual system to understand the issue of generalization more than any other approach – should receive this false accusation.

Generalization is a naturally occurring behavioral phenomenon that behavior analysts have studied extensively. Generalization is also an important aspect of intervention. Prior to intervention, therapists should analyze generalization, plan and measure it. There are two forms of generalization: stimulus and response generalization. Stimulus generalization refers to producing the same response in novel, untrained stimulus conditions. For example, a person may learn to emit an assertive response, such as disagreeing with their psychologist in role play on what to eat at night. An example of stimulus generalization would be emitting the *same* response, but in novel stimulus conditions, such as in response to a son's request to cook a favorite food when some other meal is already available. Response generalization refers to producing novel, untrained responses. For example, suppose a therapist taught a client with social skills deficits to say "no thanks." If the client later said "let me think about that" in a similar situation, even though the therapist had not taught them to say that, then that would be an example of response generalization.

ABA has explicitly conceptualized, developed and evaluated a technology of generalization (Stokes & Baer, 1977) As noted above, a failure to generalize is conceptualized as a problem of stimulus control in which too narrow a range of discriminative stimuli control behavior. Remediating problems of generalization therefore consists of procedures to transfer stimulus control from an inappropriate, narrow range of controlling antecedent stimuli to a broader, appropriate range of stimuli. Generalization of behavior change could be promoted by simple strategies, such as reinforcing instances of generalization when they occur, widening the range of appropriate stimuli included in training, and instructing the client to generalize the skills from one environment to another, or reinforcing examples of generalization. A more sophisticated strategy might include general case training in which sufficient exemplars are taught that sample all the relevant stimuli that control behavior and all the responses that the person might make. Table 4.2 summarizes and gives examples of Stokes and Baer's nine strategies to promote generalization of behavior change.

Application

Interventions often depend on the performance of third parties, such as family members and staff. We may train staff in one situation, such as in a workshop using role play. However, we also expect their behavior to change elsewhere, for example when working with clients with problems a little different from the ones taught in the workshop in a regular work setting. We may change one aspect of staff behavior, such as describing treatment principles in a class. However, we expect generalization to occur to novel, untrained behaviors, such as implementing a treatment plan in a day treatment setting. Hence, we often hope for extensive generalization of staff behavior in clinical work.

In order to illustrate this let us consider Feldman and Ducharme's study of generalization of staff performance. Ducharme and Feldman (1992) investigated the problem of generalization of teaching skills in staff who worked with adults with intellectual disabilities. The staff target behavior was an observational measure of staff teaching skill. This measure included 10 staff behaviors, such as using least intrusive prompts and correct data recording. In order to assess generalization of staff skill, Ducharme and Feldman observed staff performance with clients and programs that they had not taught to staff. The experiment compared staff teaching skills in five conditions. In baseline they told staff to teach the clients as they typically would. In the written instructions condition staff members read written descriptions of correct teaching and asked questions of the experimenter. In the single case training procedure Ducharme and Feldman taught staff one specific teaching program for one specific client using role play. In the common stimuli condition one actual client participated in staff training. In the general case training condition Ducharme and Feldman used role

Table 4.2. Stokes and Baer's (1977) nine strategies for promoting generalization

Strategy	Description	Example
1. Train and hope	No specific strategy is used	A client is taught relaxation training in the office and uses it subsequently on the bus without any further intervention
2. Sequential modification	This is an empirically driven strategy whereby the therapist systematically observes for generalization to occur; when it does not, some additional intervention is made where generalization failed to occur	The therapist notices that the client does not use relaxation training in the car; they go and practise it in a parked car and generalization occurs when the client drives a car
3. Introduce natural contingencies of reinforcement	Teaching skills that are maintained by the therapists' contingencies early on are readily transferred to the control of naturally occurring contingencies, such as those from family members and staff	A child who is taught to smile in a social skills group smiles with her peers who are now more friendly to her after she smiles
4. Train sufficient exemplars	Teach multiple examples, until sufficient generalization to nontrained examples occurs	Teach enough examples of different kinds of greeting responses to enough different social partners until the person interacts appropriately with all novel people desired
5. Train loosely	Train loosely refers to varying all the irrelevant stimuli, such as the trainers, materials, and settings as much as possible.	Teach several variants of social greetings with adults and children in several different settings and with several different trainers.

(*continued*)

Table 4.2. (*Continued*)

Strategy	Description	Example
6. Use of indiscriminative contingencies	Shift from continuous to intermittent schedules of reinforcement that increase resistance to extinction	Fade schedules of reinforcement very gradually rather than abruptly. For example, initially comment on each client's goals achieved several times during an appointment. Over time gradually only comment on some
7. Program common stimuli	Specifically insert a common stimulus into the initial training that will be present in the generalization setting	Include a classroom peer in the training of social smiling when that peer will be present in the generalization setting
8. Mediate generalization	Program a response in training that will be present in the generalization setting, such as a self-instruction	Teach clients to accurately describe and reinforce their behavior in the teaching environment and in the generalization environment
9. Train to generalize	Consider generalization as a behavior that can be taught	Instruct and reinforce examples of generalization

play to teach staff to correctly implement 12 programs. They selected the 12 programs from 40 potential teaching programs. The programs that they selected sampled all the possible variations in skills taught and all the different staff skills, such as different levels of prompting.

In the baseline, written instruction, single case training and common stimuli conditions, staff never performed teaching novel clients and programs to criterion. Ducharme and Feldman did observe modest improvement in staff performance in the single case and common stimuli conditions. Nevertheless, staff never taught proficiently and often had some problems teaching novel clients or programs. Only after general case training did staff consistently and correctly teach novel programs and novel clients.

This study showed the need to conceptualize generalization of behavior change early during a behavioral intervention and to assess generalization as treatment progresses. For example, teaching a client to use relaxation exercises in the psychologist's office and at home does not sample the relevant universe of discriminative stimuli for the use of relaxation. At the beginning of treatment planning the treatment plan should identify all the relevant stimuli and their dimensions. This might include use of relaxation in various degrees of crowded settings and with nonthreatening and threatening other people. Generalization of client use of relaxation is most likely if the treatment plan *begins* by identifying the relevant dimensions of generalization and includes intervention that samples all the relevant situations.

A second example that addresses analyzing and promoting generalization comes from Kale, Kaye, Whelan, and Hopkins (1968.) They investigated transfer of stimulus control and generalization of greeting behavior in three people with chronic schizophrenia. Initially, the participants did not greet people. During the initial reinforcement and prompting condition, the experimenter approached the participant with a pack of cigarettes. If the participant greeted them, they offered them a cigarette and interacted with them briefly. If the participant did not great the experimenter within 10 s, then the experimenter prompted them to greet them and reinforced the greeting in the same way. In the reinforcement and fade prompt condition, the experimenter asked the client to greet them next time he approached them. Fading consisted of gradually increasing the time between the initial instruction and the experimenter's second approach. Kale et al. progressively increased the gap between instruction and the next approach to 10 minutes. In the reinforcement condition, Kale et al. used reinforcement alone without prompts.

During baseline, none of the participants greeted the experimenter. However, with the introduction of prompts and reinforcement, greetings increased in frequency. Few were spontaneous. When Kale et al. introduced prompt fading, spontaneous greetings increased. However, when they conducted generalization probes with a second experimenter, they observed little generalization. Therefore, they used additional generalization training in which five new experimenters conducted training sessions. This procedure is an example of multiple exemplar training (Stokes & Baer, 1977; see Table 4.2). Only when training occurred with multiple other people did the participants show generalized greeting to the second experimenter. This study shows the importance of assessing and programming for generalization of any behavior change (Stokes & Baer, 1977).

SUMMARY

Operant behavior is a fundamental consideration in case formulation. Much behavior that is distressing to clients and much appropriate behavior that we wish to strengthen is operant behavior. Operant behavior is controlled by its consequences, discriminative stimuli and reinforcer deprivation and satiation. Schedules of reinforcement do not operate independently. Rather, many schedules operate simultaneously and may affect behavior or other schedules of interest. Interventions using discriminative stimuli and modification of stimulus control are important aspects of intervention. The next chapter goes on to explore other aspects of operant behavior including satiation and deprivation, extinction, shaping, variability and punishment.

Chapter 5

OPERANT BEHAVIOR II: SATIATION AND DEPRIVATION, EXTINCTION, SHAPING, VARIABILITY AND PUNISHMENT

SATIATION AND DEPRIVATION

Operant behavior is affected by the degree of recent deprivation or satiation of the reinforcer maintaining the operant behavior in question. Satiation refers to the recent delivery of large quantities of the reinforcer and deprivation refers to the recent withholding of that reinforcer. Deprivation and satiation can occur in a number of ways. First, the change agent can deliver large quantities of the reinforcer independent of the person's behavior. This is a simple schedule of reinforcement. It is known as a time based schedule, since the delivery of the reinforcer is only dependent on time, not the organism's behavior. It is also sometimes also referred to as noncontingent reinforcement (NCR) in the applied literature. Reinforcer deprivation can occur when access to the reinforcer is restricted. Note also that each time an operant is reinforced a certain amount of satiation has also occurred. Likewise, if an operant has not been reinforced, then a degree of reinforcer deprivation has occurred. Thus, we may expand the three-term contingency to the four terms contingency. Figure 5.1 illustrates this.

The applied literature sometime refers to deprivation/satiation and other events that occur more distantly in time prior to the operant behavior as establishing operations (EO). EOs may have at least two distinct effects on behavior. The most obvious one is that an EO temporarily changes the value of a stimulus as a reinforcer. However, an EO may also *evoke* changes in behavior. For example, deprivation temporarily increases the power of a stimulus as a reinforcer. However, behavior that has a history of reinforcement with that stimulus may also increase in frequency. For example, if someone is deprived of water, not only will they work harder for access to water, but they will begin to look for water, approach areas where water was previously delivered and talk a lot about water. By contrast, if someone has recently drunk a great deal of water, the water may

Establishing Operation → Discriminative Stimulus → Response → Consequence

(Deprivation/satiation, etc.)

Figure 5.1. The four term contingency

only be a weak reinforcer, a neutral stimulus, or even a punishing stimulus. Thus, they may avoid water and not talk about it. Walters and Ray (1960) and Walters, Marshall and Shooter (1960) demonstrated that deprivation and satiation of social interaction increased or decreased the efficacy of social interaction in typical children.

Implications for Practice

It is not unusual to observe that in applied settings a stimulus that recently functioned as a reinforcer now no longer functions as a reinforcer. This may be especially true for primary reinforcers, such as food and drink. It may also be true for other consequences, such as attention. The varying value of stimuli as reinforcers may in part reflect recent deprivation or satiation. A clinical formulation should examine information relating to possible satiation or deprivation. For example, in eating disorders, binging may lawfully occur after long periods of not eating. One might construe this long period of not eating as an example of reinforcer deprivation. This EO may result in evocative effects on behavior. For example, the client may spend more time thinking about and looking for food. It may also results in a temporary increase in the value of food as a reinforcer. Hence, food can now effectively reinforce costly or unpleasant behavior, such as binge eating (Farmer & Latner, 2007).

Satiation and deprivation also have implications for intervention. For example, satiation could be used to reduce the reinforcing value of the target behavior's consequence. Similarly, deprivation could be used to increase the reinforcing value of the consequence maintaining an alternate desirable behavior. In the previous example, the regular scheduling of small snacks throughout the day may reduce the value of food as a reinforcer. This may result in a reduced frequency of binge eating. Likewise, reserving the use of the most powerful reinforcers for engaging in some desirable behavior, such as relaxing gardening to compete with increased anxiety prior to binge eating, might be a good example of using reinforcer deprivation to promote some alternate desirable behavior.

Deprivation and satiation have a second set of implications for practice. Primary reinforcers, and especially excessive use of a single primary reinforcer, are associated with satiation. Hence, programmatic interventions that depend on primary reinforcers may be weak. Interventions should use secondary reinforcers, vary primary reinforcers, and reserve the most powerful primary reinforcers for high levels of appropriate behavior.

Application: Reinforcer Satiation

Ayllon (1963) conducted a classic study of satiation as a treatment for hoarding towels in a psychiatric patient. The patient hoarded towels in her room. Thus, hoarding appeared to be reinforced by access to towels. Ayllon delivered extra towels everyday. Over time the patient stopped hoarding towels. Indeed, she began to remove towels from her room. It seems that noncontingent delivery of the reinforcer maintaining hoarding resulted in a reduction in hoarding.

A more common approach to reinforcer satiation is to identify the reinforcer maintaining the behavior of interest and then deliver that same reinforcer independent of behavior in a NCR schedule. Thus, noncontingent attention, tangibles, escape, and so on, have been used as treatments for a variety of behavior problems (McGill, 1999.) O'Callaghan, Allen, Powell and Slama (2006) reported an interesting variation of this procedure. Five children, aged 4–7 years, who had been referred to a pediatric dental clinic because of behavioral issues participated. Two children were so disruptive that they were restrained up to eight times per visit. In baseline, treatment proceeded as usual. This included topical and local anesthetic and a prize at the end of each session regardless of the child's behavior. During NCR, a pager was used to prompt the dentist to give the child a short break from treatment. The child was told that when the pager buzzed there would be a break. Initially, breaks were frequent. The dentist gave breaks on a Fixed Time 15 seconds (FT-15 s) schedule; that is, the child had a break every 15 seconds. The dentist then gradually thinned the schedule to a FT-60 s schedule. During breaks the dentist removed all dental equipment and the child was free to move around.

During baseline, the children emitted disruptive behavior more frequently as the visit progressed. The children also emitted more disruptive behavior when the dentist implemented more invasive treatments. During the FT schedule, disruptive behavior markedly reduced as the visit progressed. The amount of disruptive behavior was lower than during baseline. Reduction in physically disruptive behavior was especially marked. The FT schedule resulted in almost complete elimination of restraint. Thus, escape satiation using a FT schedule resulted in effective reduction of disruptive behavior and in near elimination of restraint.

Another example comes from Buchanan and Fisher (2002), who conducted functional analyses and other procedures to identify the reinforcers maintaining disruptive vocalization in two people with dementia. The pre-assessment functional assessment and analysis of the first participant's behavior suggested that attention and music may have reinforced her disruptive vocalizations. Therefore, initially, intervention included providing both attention and music continuously. Later, this was faded to a FT-30 s schedule. First, Buchanan and Fisher compared continuous music with combined continuous music and continuous attention. They found that continuous music did not produce reductions in disruptive vocalization, but the combined treatment did. They then compared continuous with FT-30 s schedules of noncontingent reinforcement. They found that only the continuous schedule of reinforcement reduced disruptive vocalization. Buchanan and Fisher conducted functional assessments and analyses of the second participant's disruptive vocalization. They found that this person's disruptive vocalization was more frequent when staff made comments contingent on disruptive vocalization. Therefore, intervention consisted of noncontingent attention. They found that an FT-40 s initially produced reductions in disruptive vocalizations. They then successfully faded this schedule progressively to an FT-160 s schedule. They noted that this approach was promising, but further work was needed to develop a more practical method of intervention and to establish social validity.

Application: The Token Economy

The token economy is one of the most widely adopted procedures designed to address the problem of reinforcer satiation. In a token economy, arbitrary stimuli, such as points, poker chips or marks on a piece of paper, are paired with primary reinforcers. Tokens are then delivered contingent on predetermined behavior. Some token economies also include punishment procedures, such as token fines for undesirable behavior. Clients exchange tokens for primary or other secondary at a later time. Over time the therapist fades these very structured procedures. For example, the therapist may introduce progressively greater delays between behavior and tokens or may teach self-monitoring, so that tokens are no longer needed.

Ayllon and Azrin (1965) showed that a token economy was highly effective to increase attendance in rehabilitation activities in 44 psychiatric inpatients. They compared contingent with noncontingent tokens. Only during the contingent token condition did patients attend rehabilitation activities. Thus, the token alone could not account for the change in behavior. Only when there was a contingency between the tokens and the patients' behavior did the patients' behavior change.

Token economies, especially group token economies, require extensive staff monitoring of token use and extensive staff training to ensure accurate implementation. The token economy is an incredibly robust procedure. It has been implemented on an individual and group basis, been incorporated into self-management and implemented in a wide variety of settings, such as classrooms to address disruption and mines to address worker safety (Kazdin, 1982). Thus, it is one of the most robustly effective behavioral interventions.

OPERANT EXTINCTION

Operant extinction is the learning process whereby the contingency between an operant behavior and its maintaining consequence is disrupted, resulting in the reduction of the future probability of the behavior. Thus, extinction requires that therapist has identified the consequences of maintaining the behavior. The therapist must also be able to manipulate that consequence. The therapist can disrupt the contingency between the behavior and its maintaining consequences in two ways. First, the therapist can remove the consequence contingent on the behavior completely. Second, the therapist can program the consequence to be noncontingent. There are many everyday examples of extinction. Machines that usually work then suddenly no longer work and disruptions in formerly reliable social contingencies are two common examples.

Operant extinction has a number of effects on behavior. The most obvious one is the reduction in the frequency of operant. There are others. Operant extinction is often accompanied by an increase in novel behavior. It is also accompanied by increased variability in the topography and sequencing of behavior. Operant extinction is sometimes accompanied by a temporary increase in the target behavior, as well as increases in emotional and aggressive behavior. After extinction has occurred, the response may increase in frequency without any planned intervention. This is known as spontaneous remission. Once extinction has occurred the behavior may subsequently be reconditioned if the contingencies are reinstituted. If extinction is subsequently implemented extinction may take place more rapidly than on the first occasion. If a behavior is reinforced and extinguished many times, then extinction takes place very rapidly. This may sometimes result in "one trial extinction." It seems that after repeated exposure to extinction, the introduction of the extinction schedule exerts stimulus control of behavior. Extinction also occurs more rapidly for effortful responses than for low effort responses (Leslie & O'Reilly, 1999.)

Extinction is both a naturally occurring process and, if the environment is deliberately manipulated, it is also an intervention method.

Thus, extinction has relevance to at least three aspects of case formulation. First, the client's history should be examined for reductions in behavior that may appear to be extinction. This may be shown by reductions in behavior that may have formerly been reinforced. Many of the life events related to depression appear like this. Bereavement, disruptions in relationships, such as divorce, children moving from home, unemployment, retirement, moving house, changing job, leaving school, or even promotion may all involve changes in environmental contingencies. Sometimes, behavior that was previously effective and reinforced is no longer effective. If new, effective, alternate behavior is not learned then previously effective behavior may be extinguished. This may present as depression, lack of goals or indifference (Skinner, 1971.) Alternatively, as previously effective behavior extinguishes, novel potentially problematic behavior might arise. Examples might include drug use, complaining, hyperchondriasis or agitation. If these new behaviors come into contact with contingencies than reinforce these problematic behavior, then these new, problematic behaviors may increase. Thus, behavioral excesses may also occur following extinction of adaptive behavior. A second implication for case formulation is that the therapist should carefully examine the client's current environment to see if current contingencies support adaptive behavior. For example, an "unmotivated" student who continues to receive passing grades and financial support from their family may fail to work because of the absence of contingencies. A final implication for case formulation relates to the effects of repeated exposure to extinction. "Resistance to extinction" refers to the degree of persistence in responding after a contingency no longer operates. Resistance to extinction is greatest when (1) the behavior has been reinforced many times in the past; (2) when the pre-extinction schedule was an intermittent, rather than continuous; (3) when the response is easy; and (4) when the organism has not been exposed to repeated periods of extinction in the past. Resistance to extinction and the variables that control it sound like variables related to resilience. Being able to continue to respond in the absence of immediate reinforcement may be quite adaptive. In contrast, being highly sensitive to brief disruptions in schedules of reinforcement may leave the person vulnerable to extinction and its negative side effects.

The form of an extinction procedure depends crucially on the function of the behavior. A common error is to equate extinction with specific procedures. For example, planned ignoring is a procedure in which other people do not interact with a client contingent upon a target behavior. This procedure is often erroneously equated with extinction. This procedure is only extinction when it disrupts the contingency between the target behavior and its maintaining consequence. Iwata, Pace, Chowdry and Miltenberger (1994) conducted the classic study demonstrating the importance of matching the form of extinction to the function of the target behavior. They evaluated the efficacy of three putative extinction procedures and their relationship to the function of the behavior. Four children with intellectual disabilities and self-injurious behavior (SIB) participated. During attention extinction, the experimenter discontinued attention contingent on SIB and delivered attention on a Differential Reinforcement of Other Behavior 30 seconds (DRO-30 s) schedule for the absence of SIB. Escape extinction took place during a teaching task. It consisted of preventing escape from the task by gently guiding the participant to complete the task. During sensory extinction, the experimenter attenuated the sensory consequence maintaining the SIB. For example, the experimenter placed a heavily padded helmet on the child's head to reduce the stimulation that might result from SIB. For all four children, when the form of extinction matched the consequence maintaining the child's SIB, SIB reduced from 99.5% to 85.5% of the baseline. When the form of extinction did not match the function of the behavior, SIB *increased* by 26% for one child and reduced by only 24–29% of baseline for the remaining three children. Hence, only when the form of extinction matched the function of the child's SIB did SIB reduce. Further, when treatment procedures did not match the function of the child's SIB, the treatment was not merely ineffective; in some cases, treatment was harmful. In a subsequent study, Iwata al. (1982/1994) analyzed data from a 152 children and adults with intellectual disabilities and SIB. This analysis of data from a large cohort confirmed the paramount importance of matching treatment procedure to function.

Researchers and practitioners have used extinction procedures for a very wide range of problems. Extinction has been used to treat school refusal, food refusal, sleep disorders, a wide rage of behavioral problems in many populations, depression, psychosis, etc. It has also been used in almost every conceivable population, including typical and a wide range of atypical children, adolescents, people with acute and chronic psychiatric disorders, acquired brain damage and dementias. These observations confirm the robustness of procedures incorporating extinction into treatment of problematic operant behavior.

There are a variety of practical considerations in the use of extinction. First, there are many alternatives to extinction which practitioners should consider that may be more convenient, safer or result in quicker behavior change. These include differential reinforcement, NCR and antecedent interventions, such as instruction and various forms of prompting. Under certain circumstances these may be better treatment options. Second, extinction can be difficult to implement accurately. For example, if intermediaries are not well trained it may not be possible to implement extinction. Again, if the therapist is not able to train intermediaries effectively, they may do more harm than good. For example, if intermediaries inadvertently reinforce the target behavior on an intermittent schedule instead of extinction, they may inadvertently strengthen the target behavior. Third, if extinction is accompanied by reinforcement of alternate or other behavior, the target behavior decreases more rapidly than with the use of extinction alone. Additionally, combining extinction with differential reinforcement may permit teaching an alternate, functional behavior. This may reduce the likelihood of accompanying emotional problems and extinction bursts. Hence, extinction alone is generally not a desirable intervention. However, it may be one element in a treatment package. Finally, once extinction has been implemented the therapist should monitor the client's behavior for relapses perhaps due to spontaneous remission or problems with treatment implementation.

Application: Extinction

Piazza, Patel, Gulotta, Sevin and Layer (2003) compared the effects of differential reinforcement of alternate behavior (DRA) alone, escape extinction alone and combined DRA and escape extinction. Four children, aged 2–4 years, who were diagnosed with pediatric feeding disorder participated. Their problem behaviors included food and fluid refusal. All children had associated medical problems. They were still bottle fed or were tube fed. During the DRA condition a therapist presented a preferred toy or other item which had been identified using an SPA for 15 s contingent on eating a bite of food. During escape extinction, the therapist never removed the spoon from in front of the child until the child swallowed a bite of food. In the DRA and extinction procedure the therapist implemented both procedures simultaneously. Piazza et al. found that DRA alone was ineffective. Only when they used escape extinction did the children learn to eat.

Application: Extinction Plus Differential Reinforcement

Liberman, Teigen, Patterson, and Baker (1973) promoted appropriate and contextual speech and reduced delusional speech in four patients with schizophrenia. These patients had been hospitalized for 17 years. Liberman et al. evaluated the effects of two combined schedules during four, daily 10-minute interviews. First, the interview was stopped if the patient emitted delusional speech. Second, they made the number of minutes of snacks and evening conversation directly proportional to the number of minutes of rational speech during the daytime interviews. Thus, if we assume that attention maintained delusional speech these two contingencies represent attention extinction and differential reinforcement of rational speech respectively. On introduction of these two contingencies rational speech increased between 200–600% for each participant. Thus, combining extinction and differential reinforcement of appropriate speech was an effective treatment to reduce delusional speech and to promote appropriate speech.

Application: Infant Cholic

It is often tempting to assume that certain problems are necessarily biomedical and are resistant to behavioral interventions, but this may not always be the case if such assumptions are not tested. Larson and Ayllon (1990) used simple extinction and DRO procedure to reduce behavior associated with colic in eight infants. They used direct observation to measure infant crying, which was their dependent variable. Intervention consisted of reinforcing behavior that was incompatible with crying, such as quiet alertness with contingent music and parental attention. Crying was followed by a brief time out from reinforcement. Intervention resulted in reduction in crying in all eight infants by approximately 75%.

SHAPING

One may sometimes observe complex behavior which is unlikely to result only from reinforcement of the target behavior. This may be because the complex behavior presumably occurred at such low frequency or was rarely never emitted. Thus, the complex behavior could not come in contact with contingencies of reinforcement. Sometimes the behavior of interest may be the first and only time that such particular responses have been emitted. For example, a psychopath might commit an elaborate murder of several people (Gresswell & Hollins, 1992), or a person might kill themself.

One process by which people learn complex behavior is shaping. Shaping involves two processes: extinction and differential reinforcement. During shaping, some current behavior which had previously been reinforced is extinguished. Simultaneously, some responses that more closely approximate to the final responses are differentially reinforced. Extinction induces response variability. The therapist can then differentially reinforce some of these novel responses which more closely approximate to the final target behavior. Shaping can be applied to many parameters of a response. For example, one could shape the frequency, latency, intensity, force, or topography of a response.

Research has implicated shaping in the development of a number of forms of psychopathology. For example, Schaeffer (1970) shaped up self-injury resulting in lacerations in rhesus monkeys. Inadvertent shaping has been implicated in the development of such diverse problems as infant sleep problems (Blampied & France, 1993), bizarre behavior in people with schizophrenia (Ayllon et al., 1965) and attempted murder (Gresswell & Hollin, 1992).

Research has shown shaping to be effective in treating a wide range of problems. Examples include treatment compliance (Hagopian, Farrel & Amari, 1996; Hagopian & Thompson, 1999), wearing contact lenses in young children who have had their lenses surgically removed (Mathews, Hodson, Crist & LaRoche, 1992), self-initiating toileting in young infants (Smeets, Lancioni, Ball, & Oliva, 1985), developing more elaborate language in a variety of typical and atypical children (McGee, Krantz, Mason, & McClannahan, 1983) and reinstating speech (Sherman, 1965) and work (Mitchell, & Stoffelmayr, 1973) in people with psychoses, increasing voice volume (Fleece, Gross, O'Brien, Kistner, Rothblum, & Drabman, 1981), reinstating fluent speech in people who stutter (Ingham, & Andrews, 1973), shaping deep relaxation responses (Budzynski, & Stoyva, 1969), increasing activity levels in people with depression (Hopko et al., 2003), and so on. Thus, shaping is an intervention method that can be applied to remediate a wide range of problems in many populations.

Clinical Implications

Shaping has several implications for case formulation and treatment. First, if a client presents with unusual behavior that seems baffling, one should consider the possibility that such as behavior is the product of shaping. For example, Gresswell and Hollin (1992) describe a detailed history of a forensic client who attempted to kill two people and had developed a plan to kill 20 people. At first the client appeared to have attempted murder out of the blue. They reported an analysis of the client's history as a series of ABC analyses, which is suggestive of shaping. The progression from one step to another involved modest changes in behavior. For example, in response to criticism at work he began to take a knife to work. Next he began to eat lunch alone in the car at work. He then began to take a club to work. All of these forms of behavior involved avoidance of people at work or criticism. Later, he began to prowl the streets for unidentified victims. He then began to identify and later search for specific victims. He found this to be exciting. Thus, behavior that began modestly enough as avoiding colleagues at work, was eventually shaped into stalking specific victims. Early on the reinforcer maintaining the problem behavior may have been avoidance of other people evaluating him negatively. Later, the reinforcer appeared to be the excitement involved in stalking other people. Thus, different environments may have shaped different topographies and frequencies of disturbing behavior over time.

An important implication of shaping is that the clinicians should review the client's background for a history of shaping problematic behavior. This might identify potential reinforcers and earlier, less problematic forms of behavior. This information might be useful in developing a treatment plan. As with other reinforcement-based paths to problematic behavior, one should also ask why other competing adaptive behaviors were not supported during the client's history. For example, Gresswell and Hollin's (1992) case study described how the client failed to learn appropriate social behavior and warm relationships early in life. Subsequently, he learned to lie to present himself as normal as a typical adult, but did not learn more typical adult relationships with people at work.

A second implication of shaping for case formulation is that one should examine the client's current behavioral repertoire and environment and detect any adaptive behavior that the client has that may be shaped into useful behavior. This strategy might eventually result in a larger repertoire of adaptive behavior. Another implication is that the clinician should also observe the client's environment in order to detect the contingencies that inadvertently shaped problematic behavior. For example, if other people to not reinforce appropriate behavior early on, then they may differentially reinforce other, more intense, forms of problematic behavior. If the clinician does observe such contingencies, then it may be possible to train others to respond more appropriately early on in order to avoid shaping maladaptive behavior.

Strengths and Limitations of Shaping

Shaping can be used to establish many new repertoires of behavior in many populations and contexts. However, shaping has significant limitations. First, use of shaping alone typically produces slow behavior change. If behavior change can be achieved by other methods that are more rapid and simple, such as instruction or modeling, the therapist should not use shaping. Second, shaping may require relatively precise discrimination of client behavior on the part of the therapist. The therapist must also effectively use differential reinforcement, extinction and judicious assessment, and use of reinforcers to avoid reinforcer satiation. Poor skill in these areas will results in suboptimal behavioral change. Third, shaping necessarily involves extinction, including extinction of recently reinforced responses and thus may involve some of the undesirable features of extinction. Hence, the application of shaping should be limited to those occasions when other approaches are unlikely to be effective, when variations in the behavior can be accurately measured, and when there are competent therapists who can accurately implement shaping.

Application: Treatment Compliance

Fitterling, Martin, Gramling, Cole and Milan (1988) treated vascular headaches by shaping compliance with exercise regimes. They measured exercise behavior using "Cooper points," a standard measure of aerobic exercise. They measured headaches with a self-report Likert scale. They first took baseline data in order to establish pre-intervention level of exercise. Shaping involved a cash deposit. They refunded portions of the deposit contingent on completion of the prescribed number of exercise points. Once a given target number of Cooper points had been achieved, the target was progressively increased in small increments. Subsequently, self-reported headache intensity decreased. The number of headache-free days also increased as shaping of exercising progressed. These changes were not due to changes in medication for headaches. At six-month follow-up, three of six participants maintained this level of exercise. Relapse in compliance resulted in return to baseline levels of headache intensity and frequency.

Application: Smoking

Smoking is a behavior that is difficult to observe. People are highly motivated to lie or otherwise report smoking inaccurately. Yet, shaping requires careful measurement of behavior in order to detect variations in behavior to differentially reinforce and extinguish accurately. Hence, applying shaping to smoking behavior is particularly challenging.

Dallery and Glenn (2005) obviated this problem by using on-line technology to measure smoking. They measured smoking behavior indirectly by measuring its product – carbon monoxide in the clients' breath. The participants were heavy smokers. They had to videotape themselves on line whilst providing breath samples of carbon monoxide twice a day. Once Dallery and Glenn observed stable baseline concentrations of carbon monoxide, they differentially reinforce lower levels of carbon monoxide. Eventually, they could reinforce not smoking. Participants could exchange vouchers on line for merchandise that the participants chose for themselves from a variety of web sites. All four participants greatly reduced smoking. Three stopped smoking in a four-week period. This study suggests that shaping might be a useful component to achieve initial reductions in smoking, although it did not address the issue of maintenance.

RESPONSE VARIABILITY

Most contemporary accounts of behavior emphasize its topography, frequency, rate, duration, and permanent products. However, behavior has another important property: variability. Early accounts of behaviorism devoted considerable space to response variability (Keller & Schoenfeld, 1950, Chapter 6). However, subsequent research has deemphasized this essential aspect of behavior. More recently, both theoreticians and practitioners have rediscovered variability as an important and clinically significant aspect of behavior (Lee, Sturmey & Fields, 2007; Neuringer, 2002, 2004.) For example, Hopkins and Neuringer (2003) showed that depressed undergraduates emitted more invariant responding on an operant task. This study suggested that invariability may be related to psychopathology.

No organism ever emits a response in precisely the same manner on every occasion. However, the variability in responses itself varies from highly stereotyped behavior to behavior that is highly varied. Highly stereotypical behavior includes precise, accurate and reliable performance. Accurate proof reading and quality control performance are all examples of valued invariant behavior. Highly variable behavior includes brainstorming, in which a person generates many novel solutions to a problem, and creativity, in which a person emits novel and valued responses, such as art, literature or music. Thus, sometimes highly variable behavior is appropriate. Response variability may apply to different parameters of behavior. For example, the form of the behavior may be stereotypical – the person emits the response in the same way constantly – or variable – the person never emits the response in the same way. Alternatively, the sequencing of behavior may be stereotypical – the person emits a sequence of responses in an invariant sequence – or variable – the person switches from one behavior to another in different orders every time.

During the acquisition of operant behavior that behavior becomes highly stereotyped. Only a few of the possible response topographies, forces and locations that could result in reinforcement are ever emitted. Over time and during reconditioning, behavior tends to become more, rather than less stereotyped. For example, the Law of Least Effort describes that, over time, an organism emits less and less forceful behaviors during operant conditioning. These observations suggest that response variability is influenced by environmental events. Neuringer (2002, 2004) showed that variability itself is subject to operant conditioning. For example, operant behavior can become more stereotypical if we reinforce only similar responses. Likewise, if we extinguish similar responses and reinforce varied responses, then behavior can become more variable. Thus, we can conclude that response variability is an operant.

What has all this to do with case formulation? We have already noted that certain clients' behavior may be chaotic and disorganized. If they fail to focus on any one thing: their behavior is too variable. Aspects of response variability are characteristic of certain forms of psychopathology, such as depression and autism. For example, a person with depression who ruminates on one topic, an obsessive compulsive patient who repeatedly checks, the person with autism who constantly emits the same invariant response "peanut butter and jello", and the person with intellectual disability who body rocks in the same manner for years, all emit behavior that is unusual in part because it is invariant. Thus, interventions should address response variability.

There are a wide range of variables that can be manipulated to influence variability (Lee, et al., 2007.) Intervention can address variability directly by reinforcing variability, novel, or low frequency responses. Some studies have used lag schedules in which a response is only reinforced if it differs from the last *n* responses (see below). Procedures such as extinction can be used to induce response variability and operant conditioning can be used to induce response stereotypy.

Lag Schedules and Autism

A series of studies from Lee and colleagues have evaluated the efficacy of lag schedules to increase response variability in the language of children with autism. Autism is characterized by invariant behavior in a number of domains, including motor stereotypy, such as hand flapping and body rocking, unusual fixed interests and resistance to changes in routines. One facet of this is relatively invariant verbal behavior. For example, a child with autism may perseverate on the same topic or always give the same answer to a question much more often than a typical child. Such invariant verbal behavior can be stigmatizing and may inhibit progress on learning new language.

McComas, Lee and Jawor (2002) compared the effects DRA with a combined DRA/lag-1 schedule in two children and one adults with autism. The target behavior was appropriate, varied verbal responding to the question "What do you like to do?" During DRA, they reinforced correct responses. Following incorrect responses, the therapist said "no" and turned away. During the DRA/lag-1 they used the same contingency, except a correct response also had to be different from the previous response. DRA alone was ineffective at increasing variability. Indeed, during DRA alone the participants emitted the same one or two responses. Thus, DRA induced response invariance. During DRA/lag-1 two of the three participants made many novel, appropriate responses. One participant continued to emit many new responses throughout the DRA/lag-1 schedule. Additionally, during generalization probes in novel settings and novel trainers, these two participants also emitted varied appropriate responding. The third participant did not emit novel responses during the DRA/lag-1 schedule. The experimenters then provided him additional training to ensure that he had other responses in his repertoire. However, this was also ineffective. Lee and Sturmey (2006) replicated this study. They showed that lag-1 schedules were effective at increasing variability in responding to a question in two of three teenagers with autism.

Lee and Sturmey (in preparation) extended this line of research again by evaluating the effects of script fading and lag-1 schedules on appropriate verbal behavior in three children with autism. Script fading is a procedure used to transfer stimulus control from imitating a recording of a conversation to just the presence of another person. Initially a complete statement is played. This prompt is then faded by progressively shortening how much of the statement is recorded, although the child must still make the complete correct answer. This procedure has been shown to be highly effective in teaching children with autism to initiate conversation without prompts from adults. It also results in children making novel, untrained statements (McClannahan & Krantz, 2006). Lee and Sturmey extended earlier studies by including a more complex three-question conversation, rather than a single question. During scripting and script fading, not only did the three children make more correct responses, but responses were more variable than baseline. They added a lag-0 schedule; that is, the experimenter reinforced responses that were the same as previous responses. This resulted in decreased variability in all three children. When they added a lag-1 schedule, all three children's response variability increased. Independent observers rated transcripts of the conversations of the children's conversations during the lag-0 and lag-1 conditions. They rated the conversations during the lag-1 conditions as more competent, linguistically and socially skilled than the conversations during the lag-0 condition.

Taken together, these three studies show that lag schedules can be implemented in applied settings. These studies also show that lag schedules may be effective in increasing variability in a clinically important behavior – language and conversation skills in children and adults with autism. Further, other people recognize these changes in variability as socially valid.

Other applications include the use of lag schedules to induce variability in the performance of martial arts students (Harding, Wacker, Berg, Rick, & Lee, 2004) and selecting variable activities in typically developing children (Cammilleri & Hanley, 2005). So far, no studies have applied lag schedules to clinical problems other than autism. Thus, future research should explore the effectiveness of lag schedules in other areas of clinical application. These could include both increasing variability in behavior in other populations and behavior, such as depression and OCD. These future studies could also decrease variability in behavior, for example, in people with chaotic or unfocused behavior, for example in children and adults with ADHD.

PUNISHMENT

Punishment is a controversial issue. The use of the term "punisher" is unfortunate. ABA would have been better off if a better term had been used. ABA is committed not only to changing behavior, but to doing so through means that are also socially valued (Wolf, 1978).

Despite this commitment, punishment procedures have been used inappropriately. For example, punishment has been used in the absence of alternate procedures, without adequate training and supervision, and for target behaviors that are too mild to warrant the use of punishment. There are examples of the unethical use of punishment that are illegal and involve depriving clients of their basic rights. However, ABA is committed to increasing the behavioral repertoire and skills, rather than only reducing problematic behavior (Goldiamond, 1974; Skinner, 1953.) Hence, ABA generally opposes the use of punishment procedures, especially when there are alternative effective procedures that are available. Indeed, research on functional analysis may have contributed to the reduction in the use of punishment procedures in research (Pelios, Morren, Tesch, & Axelrod, 1999) Additionally, ABA-based procedures may eliminate punishment procedures through staff and parent training and implementing effective procedures using reinforcement and positive procedures (O'Callahan et al., 2006; Sturmey & McGlynn, 2003).

Despite all this protestation concerning punishment, it would be both incomplete and dishonest not to address the issue directly. Punishment is a naturally occurring phenomenon. As Vollmer (2002) put it "Punishment happens. To ignore a natural phenomenon and its implications for a technology of behavior is akin to ignoring the physical nature of the universe. A science and a technology of behavior are incomplete without research on punishment" (p. 469). Punishment is an inherent property of the natural environment. When the ground is icy and we walk carelessly, slip and hurt ourselves, we are less likely to walk carelessly in the future. Much behavior that is punished contributes to our survival by ensuring our health and safety. It is adaptive that we learn to avoid such dangerous situations through punishment. When people are insensitive to consequences that typically function as punishers they suffer injury and significant medical risks. For example, people with leprosy or other medical conditions involving loss of pain sensation injure themselves unwittingly and expose themselves to infections and life-threatening situations because of their insensitivity to stimuli that typically function as punishers. Punishment is also a commonly occurring social phenomenon. It may be related to the development and maintenance of psychopathology. Often therapists are called into situations where punishment is a naturally occurring phenomenon. Examples here include child abuse, violence in relationships and excessive use of restrictive management practices in treatment settings. If we wish to eliminate punishment and replace it with more acceptable and effective interventions, we should begin by striving to understand it.

Punishment occurs when as aversive stimulus is made contingent on a response and results in a reduction in the frequency of the response. Two forms of punishment are commonly distinguished. Positive punishment involves the presentation of a stimulus and negative punishment involves the removal of a stimulus. A primary punisher is a consequence that acts as a punisher without any learning. Examples include painful stimuli and naturally occurring aversive consequence of behavior, such as nausea and vomiting after eating rotten food. A secondary punisher is acquired through pairing a primary punisher with an arbitrary stimulus. For example, a parent may pair a word such as "stop" with primary punishers such as painfully grabbing their child by the arm.

Behavioral treatments are explicit about their use of punishment. This is a necessary corollary of being both technological in describing exactly what we do. It is also necessary if we are to be conceptually consistent about our treatments and describe them with reference to the learning that underlies them (Baer et al., 1968). Other treatments generally refrain from acknowledging punishment procedures, even deny their use. However, punishment probably occurs in all therapies and all environments. When the cognitive therapist uses cognitive restructuring they ask the client for the strength of their maladaptive cognition. If the client reports that they still hold that belief strongly, then the therapist requires them to engage in an effortful task, such as coming up with more evidence for and against the belief. If the client reports progress by stating that they now hold the belief less strongly, then the therapist uses both negative reinforcement, by removing or reducing the magnitude of the effort, and positive reinforcement by praising the client's progress. The apparently nondirective counselor, who briefly pauses, furrows their brow and asks "Is that appropriate?", may also present secondary punishers contingent on client report of inappropriate behavior or noncompliance with treatment. Some teachers, parents and other family members frequently use reprimands, suspensions, expulsions, threats and humiliation in the classroom and in the home. All of these may be examples of punishment. So, punishment may be a widespread, naturally occurring phenomenon that we should seek to understand.

Punishment may be a significant component of a case formulation and may have important implications for treatment. For example, decreases in adaptive behavior may be related to punishment in the natural environment. The significant other who ridicules and sneers at each of their partner's initiation or independent action and the teacher who only controls a student's behavior through sarcasm and public humiliation may be important parts of some case formulations. In both examples, the client's adaptive behavior is punished by another person's aversive behavior applied contingent on the client's independent behavior. If these observations are accurate, then it may be possible to teach the punishing other to reinforce and not punish. If this is not possible, it may be necessary to remove the punisher or the client from that setting.

Malatesta (1990) presented an interesting case formulation and functional analysis example of such a problem. Mark, a nine-year-old boy had multiple problems, including tics. During assessment, Malatesta noted that Mark appeared hypervigilant to criticism by others, especially his father. His father was severely critical of his son and his apparent lack of achievement. Observation of Mark's tics with different people and when he was alone showed that his father specifically, was associated with high rates of tics. Malatesta summarized his formulation as follows:

> All seven problems were formulated as manifestations of a hypersensitivity to criticism ... related to the boy's relationship with an insecure, demanding and critical father ... hypersensitivity to his father's criticism ... then generalized to other evaluative situations ... (pp. 224–225)

Thus, the aim of intervention was to change the value of the father from an aversive stimulus associated with punishment to an appetitive stimulus associated with reinforcement. Therefore, Malatesta instructed the father to engage in nonevaluative tasks with his son. Malatesta also instructed the boy's father to make errors during these tasks, such as knocking over a can of paint. He further instructed his father to engage in pleasurable, nonevaluative activities with his son, such as going to a baseball game. This procedure resulted in elimination of Mark's tics. This was maintained at 18-month follow-up. Malatesta's case report illustrated how a history of punishment can be incorporated into a behavioral case formulation and be used to direct treatment.

Application: Positive Punishment

Lang and Melmed (1969) reported treatment of life-threatening rumination in a nine-month-old infant. He had regurgitated his food for four months and weighed only 12 pounds. He was starving and in danger of dying. Anti-emetic drugs, physical restraints, psychotherapy for the mother had all failed. He also had undergone exploratory surgery. That surgery was a potentially life-threatening procedure in such a medically fragile infant. Lang and Melmed carefully identified appropriate and inappropriate behavior. Appropriate behavior included chewing. Inappropriate behavior included the beginnings of reverse peristalsis as well as actual rumination. During treatment, they delivered brief painful shocks to the infant's leg contingent on the first sign of regurgitation. They conducted five treatment sessions. At two-weeks follow-up the infant had gained over 20% body weight. At 6-month, 1- and 2-year follow-up, the infant was physically and psychologically sound.

Application: Negative Punishment

Response cost, such as loss of points, is a commonly used negative punishment procedure. An example comes from Siegel, Lenske and Broen (1969),
who modified the speech dysfluencies of five college students. They conducted a series of 10–17 intervention sessions. They defined a dysfluency as
a repetition or interjection of a sound, syllable or word, etc. During the point-
loss condition, each dysfluency resulted in the loss of a penny. A screen in
front of the subject indicated this. Response cost resulted in reduction of
dysfluencies which remained at very low levels for four of the subjects. The
experimenters subtracted points only during speech sessions. However,
there was also a trend for dysfluencies to decrease during reading probes.

Application: Combining Punishment with Reinforcement

Punishment procedures are often combined with reinforcement procedures. The combination of procedures may make intervention more effective and more acceptable. For example, Reisinger (1972) combined token
reinforcement and response cost (loss of tokens) to treat behaviors associated with depression and anxiety. The client was a 20-year-old inpatient
in a psychiatric facility. The client was depressed and anxious. She spent
much of the day crying and withdrawn from others. She had been hospitalized for six years. None of her previous treatments has been effective.
She was admitted to a behavior modification unit that used a group token
economy. The target behaviors were crying and smiling. During baseline, observers recorded the number of episodes of crying and smiling
in 10-minute sessions. Treatment consisted of positive reinforcement and
response cost. During token reinforcement, tokens were delivered contingent on smiling, and crying resulted in the loss of one token.

   In baseline, she did not smile. Crying occurred 28 and 30 times per
week. Intervention resulted in a rapid increase in smiling and near elimination of crying. In the final phase, Reisinger faded the tokens. Reisinger
then used praise and then faded the response cost procedure. This procedure also resulted in near elimination of crying and high rates of smiling.
The client was discharged to the community. There she functioned independently for at least 14 months without readmission.

SUMMARY AND IMPLICATIONS FOR PRACTIONERS

This chapter shows that operant behavior can be used to model many
aspects of psychopathology. Case formulation can incorporate ideas based
on operant behavior and can use this information to design interventions

based on that formulation. Case formulations can incorporate processes such as reinforcer satiation and deprivation, extinction, shaping, response variability and punishment into understanding how the presenting problem may have developed and how the current environment may maintain the problem. These concepts can also be used to identify which variables in the current environment may influence the presenting problem. The case formulation can then be used to identify which variables can be manipulated to bring about desirable change in client behavior through a treatment plan that incorporates these concepts.

Chapter 6

COMPLEX BEHAVIOR I: MODELING, CHAINING AND SELF-REGULATION

The earlier chapters have focused on behavioral approaches to deal with relatively modest behavioral changes, such as the modification of a single operant or respondent behavior. Now, these apparently simple learning processes may result in change in more than one response or sometimes even large behavioral change. For example, the acquisition and extinction of operant behavior results in many changes in the organism's behavior. Nevertheless, much human learning involves the rapid acquisition of behavior that is more complex that has been discussed so far. Much applied work requires large changes in the client's behavioral repertoire, rather than changing a single response.

This chapter will discuss three processes that account for some of this more complex behavior. The next chapter will deal with another set of learning processes and interventions that result in complex behavior change – verbal behavior.

In modeling, the learner's behavior comes under the stimulus control of the model. In this way, the learner may rapidly acquire many new responses that may be complex in topography or sequencing, and that have previously never been learned or even observed. In chaining, many different topographies of behavior are learned in a certain sequence. These sequences may be quite short or very extensive over time. They may involve either few or many different responses. Chaining is important in teaching sequences of new skills to people who have few chains of complex behavior in their repertoire. Thus, chaining may be very helpful when working with people with severe psychiatric disorders, intellectual disabilities and young children. Chaining may also be useful when teaching some complex novel chain of responses to a client, for example, in habilitation of adult mental health disorders, where the therapist and client must identify sequences of adaptive behavior, such as going to work, engaging in leisure activities and other chains of appropriate behavior, such as social behavior, to replace the existing undesirable behaviors. Finally, in self-control procedures, a controlling response, such as writing a reminder or a private self-instruction, comes to control some subsequent controlled response, such as completing a task on a list. Skinner (1953) placed greatest emphasis on self-control procedures in treatment of mental health and behavioral issues. This was because self-control procedures bring the client's desirable behavior under the stimulus control of either portable discriminative stimuli, such as reminder lists or diaries, or portable private verbal stimuli, that can be carried outside the therapists office and control behavior in the natural environment. Behavioral approaches to self-control focus on independent variables that control the controlling response. If a client can learn generalized self-management strategies, then the client may benefit from a generalized set of self-management skills that can be applied to future problems that cannot be identified in current therapy.

MODELING

Modeling is learning process that can be used to establish complex behavior. In modeling the behavior of the model becomes the antecedent stimulus that controls the client's behavior. Simple modeling required that the client imitates specific taught behaviors of the model. Generalized imitation refers to the skill of imitating novel models that have not been previously observed and are not currently reinforced (Young, Krantz, McClannahan & Poulson, 1994). During intervention, modeling is almost always combined with some form of reinforcement in order to maintain the model as an effective antecedent for client behavior. Modeling has been implicated in the development of a wide range of psychopathology. For example, rate of alcohol consumption may be controlled by the rate of a confederate's alcohol consumption (Caudill & Lipscomb, 1980; DeRicco, & Niemann, 1980.)

Modeling combined with reinforcement obviously has considerable clinical application. A client who discriminates and models accurately may learn a wide range of appropriate behaviors from their peers in the natural environment. Models can be presented through therapists, peers, fellow clients, and videotaped models. Modeling is a common component of many behavioral skills training interventions. Behavioral skills training combines modeling with instructions, rehearsal, and feedback. Behavioral skills training has been used widely to teach social skills, and to teach staff, parents and therapists a wide range of skills.

Application: Enhancing Independence of Children with Physical Disabilities

Dowrick and Dove (1980) increased the independent functioning of three children with spina bifida. They used video self-modeling to teach the children to swim independently. The authors videotaped the children swimming. They then edited the videotape so that only correct swimming responses were shown. Using videotapes of the child themselves maximized similarity between the child and the model. During the baseline, the children watched another videotape prior to swimming. During intervention the children watched the edited videotape. The dependent variable was the number of steps of correct swimming taken from a task analysis of swimming.

During intervention, the number of correct steps that the children showed systematically increased. However, the number of independent steps completed increased to only to a moderate degree. This suggested that modeling alone may be one complement of a multi-component package to increase independence.

Application: Reducing Aggressive Behavior

Frederiksen, Jenkins, Foy and Eisler (1976) reduced abusive verbal outbursts in two psychiatric inpatients using modeling, instructions and feedback. Pre-intervention functional assessment indicated that the first participants often became abusive when other people did not comply with his requests for help and when other people asked him to do something, such as stop smoking. The second participant had lost six jobs in the eight months prior to intervention. After a supervisor criticized his work he would comply with their instruction, but then become verbally abusive. Frederiksen et al. assessed the participants' social skills in role play situations that reconstructed previous challenging interpersonal interactions and on the ward. They identified specific target behaviors, such as looking at the other person and making irrelevant or hostile comments and making inappropriate and appropriate requests. Intervention consisted of instructions, modeling, rehearsal, and feedback. Instructions were brief, positive statements that described what to do and why. For example, "look directly at the person when you talk to him ... It makes you look more confident" (p. 120). Modeling was done using videotapes, with the experimenter modeling the skill. In rehearsal the participant practised in role play. Feedback consisted of immediate performance feedback that both emphasized the positive aspects of the performance and described the deficiencies.

Intervention resulted in consistent improvement in all target behaviors during role play. Generalization of behavior also occurred to the ward and to novel people who did not participate in training. After training, professional and other ward staff rated the participants as more socially skilled.

CHAINING

Definition and Teaching Response Chains

A response chain is a sequence of responses in which each response functions as the discriminative stimulus for the next step in the response chain and as a conditioned reinforcer for the previous response. A reinforcer is delivered at the end of the response chain. Figure 6.1 shows an example of a response chain analyzed in these terms. In order to identify a response chain, a therapist must conduct a task analysis. This task analysis specifies each of the behaviors, their discriminative stimuli and sequence. This is usually done by directly observing competent or expert performance of the task concerned. In clinical work with verbal clients, a chain of appropriate responses might be identified during an interview. Steps in response chains are sometimes classified as essential and non-essential. For example, Haring and Kennedy (1988) conducted a task analysis of a leisure activity of looking at a magazine and listening to a radio. Steps such as "gets radio and magazine" were classified as essential. Steps such as "puts headphone on appropriately (i.e. forward rather than backward)" were considered non-essential. Hence, one could perform the leisure task competently as long as one completed all the essential steps.

Teaching a new response chain also includes discrimination training so that each response can be brought under the stimulus control of the previous response. That is, the client must learn which response to emit after which discriminative stimulus (i.e. the previous response). Teaching new response chains can be done by forward, backward and whole task teaching methods. In forward chaining, teaching begins at the beginning of the response chain. When the client reaches criterion mastery, teaching

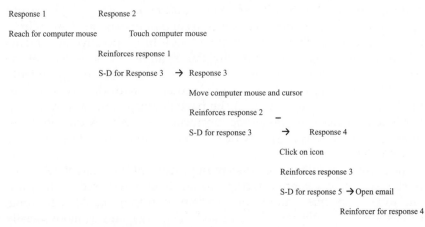

Figure 6.1. An example of a task analysis describing both the responses and discriminative stimuli. Reproduced from Miltenberger (2003).

proceeds to steps one and two. In backward chaining, the last step closest to the reinforcer is taught. Once the client reaches criterion mastery teaching proceeds to the last two steps. In the whole task method, the entire chain is taught simultaneously often using errorless learning methods by beginning with hand-over-hand prompting and fading out these prompts up the arm to the shoulder and then fading out the presence of the trained. In verbal clients it may be sufficient to instruct each step in the chain and then fade out the verbal instructions once each step is mastered. Backward chaining and whole task methods are preferred. This is because in forward chaining, once the first step is mastered, correct responding is placed on extinction as the reinforcer is withheld for correct performance of the step and is only delivered for correct performance of steps one and two. Hence, forward chaining may introduce error, and the undesirable side effects of extinction, such as response variability and the emotional side effects of extinction within a response chain.

The Unit of Analysis in Task Analysis

Progress in acquisition of a response chain is almost always represented as the percentage of steps performed correctly. However, Haring and Kennedy (1988) pointed out that, although the percentage of steps performed correctly indicates day-to-day variation in performance, this metric has several significant disadvantages. For example, it does not indicate whether or not the entire task was performed competently. It also does not indicate which steps were performed correctly and which incorrectly. Finally, it converts an ordinal scale into a ratio scale, when it cannot be assumed that all steps of the task analysis are of equal difficulty.

Haring and Kennedy proposed an elegant solution. Figure 6.2 illustrates this. This approach nicely illustrates daily variation in performance, whether or not the task has been performed independently each day, as well as the performance of each step. Such an approach is potentially quite useful in teaching response chains. However, for long tasks analyses it might be impractical unless multiple steps are combined into single steps.

Applications

Response Acquisitions

An essential component of behavioral approaches to case formulation and intervention is to enhance client's behavioral repertoire. Chaining is one approach to do this. Researchers have used chaining to teach a wide range of clinically relevant skills such as self-help skills including food

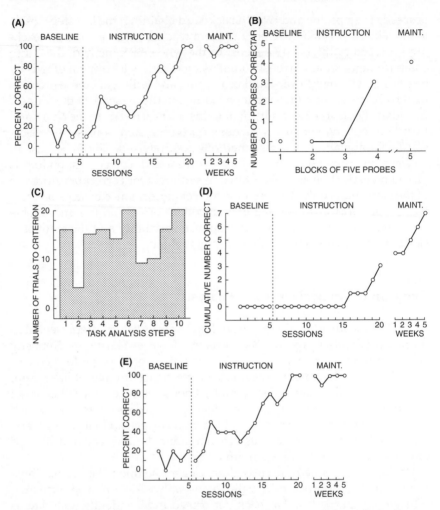

Figure 6.2. Different methods of scoring behavior using task analysis. Reproduced from Haring and Kennedy (1988).

preparation (Griffen, Wolery & Schuster, 1992), laundry skills (Thompson, Braam & Fuqua, 1982), social skills (Wong & Woolsey, 1989), and self-help skills in people with psychiatric disorders (Ayllon & Haughton, 1962). These procedures have been used most commonly with young children, people with severe psychiatric impairment and people with intellectual disabilities. Chaining has also been used to teach independent engagement for extended periods of time using activity schedules. Chaining can be an important approach to establishing appropriate behavior in a wide variety of rehabilitation settings. It might be a useful model to consider when supporting appropriate behavior in a range of clients. For example, one could easily imagine chaining pleasurable activities in a client with depression.

Self-catheterization Skills

Children with disabilities often have chronic medical problems that require the performance of treatment regimens varying in complexity from taking medicine to drinking enough water to more complex skills. Neef, Parrish, Hannigan, Page and Iwata. (1989) developed an interesting procedure to teach self-catheterization to two girls with spina bifida. The girls were aged four and eight years. First, Neef et al. task analyzed self-catheterization into four components: preparation, mirror placement and adjustment, catheter insertion, and removal and clean up. Each component consisted of six to nine steps. The experimenter then modeled the procedure with a doll whilst describing the steps. The girls then completed the task with the doll whilst also describing the step she was doing. The experimenter praised correct completion of each step. Once the girls mastered one of the four components the experimenters held a review session. During the review session the girls performed all the previously mastered steps, beginning at the first step of the task analysis of the entire chain. The experiments also used additional in vivo training with one girl using verbal and physical prompts and praise for completion of certain steps that were difficult without further practice in vivo.

The experimenters took data on both simulated sessions with the doll and in vivo sessions in which the girls self-catheterized. During baseline the girls showed very few correct, independent steps with either the doll or themselves. After training one girl was completely independent. The second girl needed help with one step of the procedure. At three-month follow-up both girls were independent in self-catheterization. This study is notable because it taught a highly complex response chain to young children using combinations of task analysis, modeling, instruction, and self-instruction, as well as in vivo training for steps that were not learned during simulated training.

Complex Response Chains in Children with Autism

Chaining has also been used to teach extended complex chains of ongoing unprompted activity to children with autism. This intervention generally does not teach skills that the children do not already have in their behavioral repertoire. Rather, the intervention brings existing skills under more appropriate stimulus control and organizes them into long chains of adaptive behavior.

McClannahan and Krantz (1993) noted that children with autism rarely displayed the skills they processed except when other people instruct or otherwise prompt them to do so. This might be perhaps because the children's learning history had inadvertently taught them to wait for extended periods of time, or even indefinitely, for instructions or other prompts from other people. Hence, lack of skill is not the only problem that these children may have. In addition, their behavior may be under inappropriate stimulus control. Therefore, they designed an intervention known as *activity schedules*. One of the purposes of this approach was to bring the children's behavior under appropriate stimulus control.

McDuff, McClannhan and Krantz (1993) taught four children participants with autism aged 9–14 years to follow a photographic activity schedule. The photographic activity schedule is a series of photographs displayed in a three-ring binder. Each activity schedule typically contains approximately six photographs depicting a leisure or homework activity. They taught activity schedules using graduated guidance delivered from behind the child. That is, if the child did not perform a step within 10 s, the experimenters used hand-over-hand guidance without verbal instruction to prompt the step. They used graduated guidance from behind the child in order to minimize social antecedents. This approach also increased the likelihood that the child's behavior will come under the stimulus control of the picture it enhances. The task analysis of using an activity schedule included (1) going to pick up the activity schedule; (2) placing it on the table; (3) opening the book; (4) pointing to the picture; (5) obtaining the materials depicted in the picture; (6) completing the activity depicted in the picture; and (7) turning the page to the next activity, and so on until all the activities were completed. The only social interactions were an initial instruction to "find something to do" and social reinforcement when the activity schedule was completed. If programmatic reinforcement was necessary during teaching, they delivered a candy silently from behind the child. Once the child no longer needed graduated guidance the experimenters used spatial fading and they gradually increased the distance between the teacher and child.

MacDuff et al. found that during baseline the children exhibited variable, low or no independent engagement. The children also did not engage in the tasks on their activity schedule. Following teaching, all four children remained on task for nearly 100% of the time. They also engaged in the activities specified in the schedule nearly 100% of the time. When the experimenters reordered the picture sequence, the children followed the activities in the new order in the activity schedule. This indicated that the pictures exerted stimulus control of the child's behavior. Further, when the experimenters introduced new photographs of similar, but novel activities, the children engaged in these novel activities, even though they had received no training to do so. This indicated generalization of schedule following skills.

Activity schedules result in children with autism engaging in varied activities for extended periods of time without prompting from other people. Parents have learned to use activity schedules at home with their children (Krantz, MacDuff & McClannahan, 1993). Once acquired, activity schedules can be elaborated in a number of ways. For example, therapists can embed choice-making, individual teaching sessions and social activities within the activity schedule. The photographs can be gradually faded to other stimuli, such as words. Eventually some children with autism can independently select their daily activity schedule from a menu and write their own activity schedule. This is much like many of the ways in which typical people organize their own behavior with to-do lists and calendars.

Behavior Reduction Procedures and Chaining

Some forms of psychopathology can be construed as response chains. Accurate identification of the various responses in the chain can be used to identify early points of intervention. If intervention occurs early in a response chain the probability of the terminal problematic behavior may be reduced. For example, it is maybe a lot easier to reduce the probability of drinking by not going to a bar, rather than teaching a self-management strategy to drink non-alcoholic drinks in a bar.

Seizure disorders. It is easy to mistakenly construe seizure disorders as inherently biological phenomena caused by the dysfunctioning brain. But, to paraphrase Skinner (1990), what the brain does is the behavior to be explained, not the explanation itself! Behavioral treatment of seizure disorders exemplifies that approach by modifying the behavior of the brain as well as motor behavior. In behavioral assessment and treatment of seizures the motor behavior during a seizure and the correlated activity of the brain are construed as the terminal behavior in a response chain. People with seizures often report pre-seizure behavioral and sensory phenomena. Some people with seizure disorders report being able to control their seizures in various ways before their seizures occur. This suggests that it may be possible to design interventions to modify seizure behavior based on a response chain model.

Zlutnick, Mayville and Moffat (1975) reported an analysis of seizure behavior as a response chain and behavioral treatment based on interruption of the responses early in the chain. There were six participants. The first subject was a seven-year-old boy with a five year history of seizures. His naturally occurring response chain included: (1) a fixed state at a table or wall; (2) his body became rigid; (3) violent shaking; and (4) falling to the floor. Based on this response chain analysis, they targeted the earliest response in the chain – staring. Contingent on each stare, the experimenters taught the staff to shout "no" loudly, grasp and shake the child vigorously. In baseline, seizures occurred approximately 12 times per day. Following intervention, the frequency of seizures fell to 1–2 per day. By the seventh week they had eliminated seizures completely. Seizures only occurred when staff could not implement the procedure within 10–15 seconds of the child staring. At 38 weeks his seizures had stopped. His physician had eliminated his seizure medication.

Zlutnick et al. (1975) also reported similar, but less dramatic results, using the similar procedures with three other participants. These interventions variously targeting individually identified responses early in the response chain, such as minor motor seizures and lowered activity. In a fifth subject, a response interruption and differential reinforcement procedure was used to decrease arm raising. This resulted in near elimination of seizures at nine-month follow-up.

Severe Maladaptive Behaviors.   Many studies have noted that some severe maladaptive behaviors, such as aggression and self-injury, may be the terminal responses in response chains. Several studies have identified these response chains and developed interventions based on these analyses. For example, Lalli, Casey and Kates (1995) conducted functional analyses of SIB in two adolescents and aggressive behavior in a third. All three participants were adolescents with moderate intellectual disabilities, who were referred to a special behavioral inpatient unit. Functional analyses (Iwata, Dorsey, Slifer, Bauman & Richman, 1994) showed that escape from task demands was the reinforcer maintaining self-injurious behavior (SIB) and aggression for all three participants. The authors used functional communication training (FCT) extinction and response chaining to reduce the maladaptive behaviors and to teach alternate functionally equivalent adaptive behaviors. FCT consisted of prompting an appropriate way to escape demands, such as shaking the head for "no." The experimenters removed the demand contingent on appropriate escape behavior. Extinction consisted of not permitting escape from the task contingent on the target behavior. The treatment innovation consisted of including response chaining using escape as the reinforcer to teach progressively larger number of work responses. For example, initially the experimenters required the participant to emit one task response and an appropriate escape response for escape from the task. Later they systematically increased the number of task responses required to two, four, eight, and 16 task responses. Hence, they taught a chain of 16 task responses and a request to escape using escape from the task as a negative reinforcer.

All participants showed high rates of target behaviors in the baseline. After treatment they all showed substantially lower rates of maladaptive behavior. Additionally, the rates of the communication response systematically increased during the treatment sessions. In the final treatment sessions, communication responses had replaced maladaptive responses. By the end of the treatment sessions, all three participants showed near-zero levels of the target behavior and emitted the 17-step response chain consistently. This study is notable not only because of its successful treatment if severe maladaptive behaviors, but also because it taught an extensive chain of appropriate behavior using the reinforcer that maintained the maladaptive behavior.

Analyses of response chains of maladaptive behaviors have important treatment implications. Figure 6.3 illustrates some examples. First, it is probably more effective to intervene early in the response chain. This

Functions	Example(s)
A chain of client maladaptive behaviors are all part of the same response class, and are all maintained by the same reinforcer (e.g. Lalli et al., 1995)	A1 → B1 → C1 Request / Scream / No presented / / escape C1' Escape A2→ B2 → C2 No / Aggression / Escape escape C2' Escape A3 → B3 → C3 No / Self- / Escape escape injury
A chain of staff behaviours maintained by termination of client mand and resumption of ongoing staff activity (Bowman et al., 1997)	A1 → B1 → C1 Client / Staff / Termination of aversive mand mand / reinforces / Staff resumes previous activity / manding A1 → B1 → C1 Client / Staff / Client mand / ignores / aggression A2 → B2 → C2 Client / Staff / Aggression aggression / reinforces / terminated / aggression
Access to a second behavior reinforces first behavior (Fisher et al., 1996; Silverman et al., 1984; Smith et al., 1992)	A1 → B1 → C1/B2 Removal / Aggression / Self-restraint of restraint A2 → B2 → C2/B2 Block / Aggression / Self- Self-restraint / / restraint
Access to second high probability behavior that is automatically negatively reinforced (Fisher et al., 1998; Sugai & White, 1986)	A1 → B1 → C1/B2 Unbroken / Break / Taps material / object / broken materials A1 → B1 → C1/B2 Request / Comply / Access to / / stereotypy

Figure 6.3. Examples of response chains in a variety of clinical contexts.

could be done by reinforcing earlier innocuous rather than later distressing members of the response chain. Second, some other, perhaps functionally equivalent adaptive behavior could be taught early in the response chain. In this way the therapist can teach an adaptive response to compete with the terminal response. Third, since the analysis identifies the reinforcer maintaining the response chain, the therapist could also use a number of consequence-based interventions. These could include teaching a functionally equivalent request, non-contingent reinforcement, or differential reinforcement using the consequence maintaining the target behavior.

A second form of response chains related to challenging behavior concerns chains of staff behavior that are negatively reinforced by termination of aversive client behavior. Bowman et al. (1997) demonstrated that when a staff member failed to reinforce a client request, then a client maladaptive behavior occurred. The client maladaptive behavior was subsequently consequated with the same reinforcer maintaining both the request and maladaptive behaviors.

A third mechanism maintaining response chains is that access to a second behavior negatively reinforces a first behavior. For example, following removal of restraint, a client may self-injure and access the second response of self-restraint. This second response may negatively reinforce self-injury by termination of the aversive, painful self-injury.

A final mechanism that may maintain response chains is that a behavior early in the response chain may be positively reinforced by access to some high probability automatically reinforced behavior, such as stereotypy. For example, Fisher et al. (1998) demonstrated that property destruction was maintained by access to a subsequent behavior, engaging in stereotypy with the broken materials, such as tapping them to produce noise.

Case Formulation and Response Chains

It may be tempting to assume that therapists can only apply response chain analysis and interventions to people with more severe disabilities because most research has been done in this population. This would be a mistake. For example, Koerner and Linehan (1997) used response chains in case formulation and intervention with people with borderline personality disorder and suicidal behavior. Further, Farmer and Latner (2007) used this model to formulate a case of bulimia. Consider, for example, a client with bulimia who first withdraws socially, drinks, feels depressed, then cuts herself and feels somewhat less depressed. This sequence of behaviors may also be a response chain. It too can be analyzed and be used as the basis for intervention in a way analogous to those described in Figure 6.3. An intervention might start before or immediately when social withdrawal occurs. If the reinforcer maintaining the response chain is removal of negative mood, then the intervention would be to teach skills to identify these situations early on and to engage in some alternate pleasurable activity in order to improve mood (Hopko et al., 2003). Several non-behavioral and behavioral case formulations implicitly or explicitly identify response chains and interventions based on them.

SELF-CONTROL

Self-control at first blush seems to be a special problem for behaviorism. If behaviorism recognizes no autonomous self that initiates and causes behavior, how does behaviorism account for self-control? Skinner (1953, 1971) noted that people often modify each other's behavior. Skinner construed self-control as simply an special case of modifying another person's behavior. However, in self-control the person doing the modifying and being modified are the same. A person can modify their own behavior in at least two ways. First, they can avoid aversive stimulation and the behaviors associated with aversive stimulation, by arranging their environment to make doing something else more probable. Thus, doing something else is likely to be behavior that is reinforced. Since this is behavior that avoids aversive consequences, the conditioned pre-aversive stimulus and their unpleasant consequences will also be avoided. Much clinical work uses this principle in a number of ways. We exhort our client's to "try another way." In problem solving, we ask our clients to generate many alternative solutions to a problem. We tell them initially not to be concerned about the quality of their possible solutions. Later we ask them to evaluate the solutions, then engage in the selected solution and evaluate the results. Such a strategy facilitates doing something other than the problematic behavior.

Skinner (1953) defined a second form of self-regulation that is more significant, as follows:

> The organism may make the punished response less probable by altering the variables of which it is a function. Any behavior which succeeds in doing this will automatically be reinforced. We call such behavior self-control ... one response, the controlling response, affects variables in such a way as to change the probability of the other, the controlled response. (p. 230)

Skinner then went on to describe a variety of strategies that we learn to avoid aversive stimuli and their negative affects. These are summarized with examples in Table 6.1. Let us consider a few examples. We learn to avoid punishment from others for fidgeting in public by self-restraining. Other people teach us to sit on our hands, put them in our pockets or fold then. The controlling response – self-restraint – is negatively reinforced by avoidance of verbal punishment from others. Interestingly, Skinner cites suicide as an example of self-control. By killing oneself, a person does indeed change the future probability of behavior and avoids future aversive stimuli. This example is interesting on a couple of counts. First, it is suggestive that some forms of psychopathology, such as depression and other forms of psychopathology associated with risk of suicide, involve deficient self-regulation. This implies that teaching self-regulation skills might be an appropriate form of intervention for suicidal behavior. In this way, Skinner (1953) anticipated several later forms of effective intervention for suicidal behavior. These include dialectical behavior therapy, where clients with Borderline Personality Disorder learn other ways of dealing with provocative situations and emotional pain (Linehan, 1993) and cognitive behavior therapy, which teaches "coping skills" that can

Table 6.1. Some of Skinner's (1953) types and examples of self-control strategies

Type	Example
Physical restraint	Put hand over mouth to stop coughing Put hands in pocket to reduce fidgeting Present self at institution to reduce symptoms Walk away from trouble to reduce anger
Supply physical aid	Have devices nearby to facilitate behavior Have pen and paper handy to increase likelihood of writing
Change the stimulus	Sugar coat a pill Remove a discriminate stimulus e.g. remove food to reduce likelihood of eating
Deprivation	Skip lunch to eat more at a party where there is free food
Satiation	Drink water before a party to decrease drinking alcohol
Manipulate	Count to 10 to reduce likelihood of angry behavior emotional conditions
Drugs	Take a pain killer to facilitate working Drink alcohol to "feel less guilty"
Operant	Associate with friends who only reinforce appropriate behavior conditioning
Self Punishment	Tighten belt to reduce eating
Do something else	Talk about an acceptable topic in order to avoid talking about something difficult or embarrassing

readily be construed as the controlling responses that make suicidal behavior less probable and other forms of behavior more likely (see Skinner, 1953, pp. 223 and 232). Second, it is suggestive of naturally occurring learning processes that may contribute to the development of psychopathology, such as the failure to acquire effective controlling responses. Third, it links directly to Skinner's recommendations for treatment of clinical problems. Namely, therapists should teach their clients to discriminate and describe their own functional assessment and to learn self-control to arrange their environment, so that the problem behavior is less likely to occur.

Other examples of self-control that Skinner outlines seem paradoxical and odd. Examples such as extinction and punishment of one's own behavior seem strange at first glance. Yet, we do seem to practice extinction of our own behavior when we deliberately arrange for our own behavior that was previously reinforced to no longer be reinforced. We cancel our credit card inadequate internet provider and do not buy a new TV when the old one breaks. In this first example, perhaps we avoid the aversive stimulus of getting further in debt. When we change out internet provider perhaps we avoid the slow service and get access to a faster cheaper service. When we do not buy a new TV, perhaps we avoid arguments over breakfast TV and discover the joys of radio and conversation with other people.

Self-punishment might seem strangest of all. Do people arrange the environment to punish their own behavior? Under certain circumstances it seems that this is indeed the case. To terminate even more aversive guilt over sin or immoral behavior, a person may engage in various forms of self-punishment, such as flagellation. A person with depression might cut themselves to avoid even greater pain or to reduce their current aversive mood state.

This analysis of self-control has much to offer people to modify their own behavior. In the end the self-regulation is behavior that should be explained like any other behavior and in the same terms as other behavior. Thus, the independent variables that control and modify self-controlling responses are in the end a function of environmental variables like any other behavior. But therein lies the good news. We can analyze and modify self-control like any other behavior. This can be a highly effective tool to help clients modify their own behavior without reliance on therapist prompting and reinforcing their each and every move.

Self-regulation skills have been used to treat many problems. Neef and Northup (2007) used self-regulation to treat impulsivity in children with ADHD as did Binder, Dixon and Ghezzi (2000). Other applications include reduction of smoking (Newman & Bloom, 1971), trichotillomania (Keijsers et al., 2005), living better in old age (Skinner & Vaughn 1983), severe behavior problems in people with intellectual disabilities (Dixon, Hayes, Binder, Manthey, Sigman, & Zdanowski, 1998; Dixon & Holcoumb, 2000; Vollmer, Borrero, Lalli & Daniels, 1999) and in people with brain damage

(Dixon, Horner & Guercio, 2003). It has also been used in the treatment of such diverse varied problems as obesity (Loro, Fisher, & Levenkron, 1979) and teach skills such as regulation of shopping in adults with intellectual disabilities (Taylor & O'Reilly, 1997).

Applications

Skinner Self-Manages

Skinner's applied this model of self-regulation to control his own behavior (Epstein, 1997). He arranged his desk to increase the likelihood of working. He made working easier by having frequently needed items to hand. He used magnifying glasses and lights to overcome poor eyesight resulting from glaucoma. He posted reminders to take medicine. He removed distractions to make writing more likely, for example covering up the clock when he wrote. Further, he only did serious writing at this desk. He also scheduled fun activities at other times and places.

One of Skinner's only publications in the *Journal of Applied Behavior Analysis* was on self-control. Ironically, he entitled the article "A thinking aid." In this article, Skinner described his own self-management strategies to make writing more likely to occur. This included a clipboard with cards attached. Each card corresponded to a section of a writing project. As soon as ideas occurred to him, he wrote them in the appropriate section. Later, when he wrote part of a project, he selected a section that interested him at that time. The card that corresponded to that section acted as a discriminative stimulus to make writing those things that were important more likely. Thus, making the clipboard, placing it close to hand, writing down ideas and selecting sections that were currently likely to be reinforcing were controlling responses. These behaviors all resulted in a greater probability of writing and completing the project, but presumably also greatly influenced his thinking behavior.

Promoting Rehabilitation Activities

Let us consider an example of applying this model to engaging in rehabilitation activities. Many people, after injury or surgery, refuse to engage in rehabilitation activities. Their low effort avoidance behavior is immediately negatively reinforced by avoidance of effort and pain. The delayed but larger reinforcer of recovery in the future is not chosen. Dixon and Falcomata (2004) taught self-control skills to a 31-year-old man with acquired brain injury who refused to participate in physical therapy. An initial assessment indicated that when given a choice between an immediate 10 s access to a videotape versus a delayed 30 s access to a DVD he always selected the immediate, smaller reinforcer. Self-control training consisted of offering a choice between the previous two options and a new option involving progressively delayed 30 s reinforcer. Initially, the large reinforcer was available after no delay. A progressive delay procedure increased the delay in access to the large reinforcer by 10 s contingent on three selections of the current delay value. Teaching progressive tolerance for delay resulted in vastly improved better engagement in physical therapy.

Treatment of ADHD

Neef and Northup (2007) described an application of self-control to ADHD. The participant was Chang, a 10-year-old boy with ADHD, referred because of disruptive behavior and academic failure. Analysis of his behavior consisted of giving him choices between different math problems that resulted in immediate or delayed reinforcement. This pre-intervention assessment showed that Chang always chose immediate over delayed reinforcement, even when the delayed reinforcer was of higher quality or larger. Thus, Chang showed impulsive behavior. Therefore, intervention involved teaching Chang to tolerate delays of reinforcement.

During baseline Chang was off task most of the time, and when he attempted math problems the answers were mostly incorrect. The first intervention was a modified worksheet. The questions were on one side. On back were the answers, and Chang could reveal the answers after completing the question on the front by coloring in the space, thus providing some immediate reinforcement for correct responses and on task behavior. This intervention alone resulted in improvement in both on-task behavior and number of correct responses. Neef and Northup then added further self-control strategies. First, one in four math problems was associated with earning a point. If he earned four points he could earn a back-up reinforcer. The experimenters told Chang that if he revealed the answer before making his own answer he would lose a point. They never observed him doing so. Further, before beginning each lesson, Chang chose between an immediate low-ranked reinforcer or a delayed, high-ranked reinforcer. This intervention resulted in very high rates of on-task behavior and nearly all questions were answered correctly. Thus, teaching Chang controlling responses of selecting a delayed, highly preferred reinforcer resulted in improvement in impulsive behavior. Additionally, he also learned to tolerate delayed reinforcement.

Treatment of Compulsive Gambling

Dixon and Johnson (2007) described treatment of compulsive gambling in Pat, a man with a 20-year history of gambling. This case study includes elements of Skinner's (1953) advice that the therapist should assist the client in discovering his own functional assessment and using that as the basis of intervention using self-management. Assessment included clinical interviews, ABC charts and a brief questionnaire to describe the function of gambling. After this initial assessment, Pat was able to describe that gambling occurred after stressful days of work and after arguments with his wife. He could also describe that gambling resulted in relaxation. Review of his ABC records revealed that after one occasion after arguing with his wife he did not gamble. Instead, he went to the barn, worked on some woodwork projects and felt relaxed. Therefore, the self-management strategy consisted of Pat writing a note to himself and looking at it on Tuesdays and Thursdays, when he often experienced stress at work. After he used this strategy, Pat reported that he almost completely stopped gambling and used working on woodwork projects as an alternate way to manage stress. Thus, teaching the client to (1) describe his own functional assessment and (2) emit a controlling response (writing and reading the reminder on stressful days) resulted in a reduction in the controlled response (gambling) and an increase in an effective way of avoiding aversive stimulation (going to the barn.)

SUMMARY

Modeling, chaining and self-control are all learning processes that relate to the development of problematic behavior. Therapists can use them to develop intervention methods based on a case formulation in a wide range of clinical situations. The next chapter goes on to consider other forms of complex behavior, namely those related to client verbal behavior.

Chapter 7

COMPLEX BEHAVIOR II: RULE-GOVERNED BEHAVIOR, STIMULUS EQUIVALENCE AND VERBAL BEHAVIOR

Behavior therapies have traditionally been associated with doing, rather than talking: This is one of its virtues. Behavior analysis treats verbal behavior, especially verbal behavior as a measure of private verbal behavior, with considerable skepticism. Social contingencies influence verbal behavior considerably (Greenspoon, 1955; Lam et al., 2005) including contingencies from therapists (Truax, 1966) and other interviewers (Antaki, Young & Finlay, 2002). Thus, verbal behavior may be a completely inaccurate measure of actual behavior. As a measure of private behavior – thinking and feeling – it becomes most suspect. Since there is only one observer, there is no way to conduct reliability observations. Thus, behavior analysis reluctantly lets in self-report of behavior as a last resort, only where other measures are not possible, such as self-reports of headaches. Such self-reports should be augmented with reliable and public measures of behavior, such as frontalis tension, brow furrowing and activity level, etc. This skepticism over the meaning of verbal behavior has lead many, including some behavior analysts, to be quite dissatisfied with clinical applications of behavior analysis. To some, it appears to miss an essential aspect of behavior in clinical work – private behavior. This chapter addresses how behavior analysis accounts for verbal behavior. In particular it discusses Skinner's (1957) *Verbal Behavior* and its implications for clinical work and contemporary theories of verbal behavior, such as relational frame theory (Hayes, Barnes-Holmes & Roche, 2001a). This chapter goes on to describe a variety of relatively new psychotherapies that behavior analysts have developed, including acceptance and commitment therapy, dialectic behavior therapy, functional analytic psychotherapy and contemporary approaches to language interventions in children with autism and other developmental disabilities. Before addressing these more complex aspects of verbal behavior we will begin by considering two other kinds of verbal behavior: self-instruction and stimulus equivalence.

RULE-GOVERNED BEHAVIOR

Earlier in Chapter 5, we noted that operant behavior is influenced by the antecedent stimuli that are associated with the contingencies that control that behavior. We also noted the inefficiency of operant learning, since behavior must come into contact with contingencies, which laboriously differentially reinforce, extinguish and shape behavior. Obviously, under some circumstances some human behavior is like that, but not all. A friend tells us the best route to drive home. We covertly instruct ourselves to take the suggested route home. Perhaps we read the instructions and try that route out. Thus, our behavior changes rapidly and in complex ways as we emit novel behavior without a history of reinforcement for this particular response. We arrive home quickly and avoid traffic jams. We tell ourselves "that's the best route home." Subsequently, we rarely drive home any other route, even when the regular route is slow and sub-optimal. How did this self-instruction come to control out behavior so effectively and efficiently?

Skinner (1969) defined a rule as a verbal discriminative stimulus. Leslie and O'Reilly (1999) defined rule governed behavior as:

> the general name for those occasions where verbal behavior, in the form of a rule, is acquired either through verbal instruction or through direct experience of some reinforcement contingencies, and then determines other behavior ... (p.147)

We may acquire rules from direct instruction, as in the example, of acquiring a rule about which way to drive home. Alternatively, we may learn to generate our own rules. For example, when through experience we learn to state a rule describing a possible contingency. Rule-governed behavior is relatively insensitive to its consequences. For example, we may never come into contact with the contingencies stated in the rule "eat foods rich in antioxidants to prevent a heart attack." We may even experience many trials of aversive consequences where driving along the freeway on the alleged best route home. Yet, we continue to follow our rules unless the price of fruit increases astronomically or we drive home with a friend more quickly via another route.

Application: Rule-Governed Versus Contingency-Controlled Behavior in ADHD

Bicard and Neef (2002) investigated the effects of rules and contingencies on the behavior of four 10-year-old boys with ADHD. They manipulated both instructions and contingencies. The boys worked on two concurrent tasks (computer math problems) which delivered independent schedules of reinforcement. In the tactical instructions condition they instructed the boys to spend more time on one schedule, rather than another. In the strategic instructions condition they instructed the boys to sample both schedules and to state their own rule. When the experimenters gave the boys tactical instructions and contingencies changed, the boys continued to respond as if the old contingencies were in place. However, when the experimenters gave the boys strategic instructions and contingencies changes, then the boys were much more likely to be sensitive to the change in contingencies. Neef and Bicard also asked the boys to describe any rules they used during the sessions. The rules the boys stated corresponded to their performance whether their performance accurately or inaccurately matched the contingencies. The authors concluded that, since the boys' behavior was insensitive to contingencies when they stated inaccurate rules and was sensitive to contingencies when they stated accurate rules, the boys did indeed show rule-governed behavior.

There are few applied studies of rule-governed behavior. If research can demonstrate such phenomena robustly, then teaching clients to engage in rule-governed behavior might be quite useful. For example, for clients who have a history of rapid extinction of behavior, inducing rule-governed behavior might make them behave more persistently in the face of extinction.

STIMULUS EQUIVALENCE

Chapter 5 described how a stimulus that is correlated with a schedule of reinforcement eventually comes to influence behavior itself – it exerts stimulus control over that behavior. Many everyday observations of stimulus control quickly show that the stimuli that exert stimulus control of our behavior are physically very different. We even often respond to novel antecedent stimuli without direct learning. Thus, a baby may respond to the visual stimuli of its caretaker, as well as to the caretaker's sounds and odors. Over time, a child may respond to photographs, line drawings and the telephone voice of its caretaker as if it were the same as the actual caretaker. Likewise, a client with a clinical anxiety disorder who responds with fearful behavior to the place where trauma took place might also respond fearfully when hearing the trauma discussed, the smells associated with trauma, and so on. In these examples, a variety of disparate stimuli are *functionally equivalent* in that they all control the same behavior. How can behavior analysis account for this?

Formation of Equivalence Classes

When experimental behavior analysts study stimulus equivalence, they use match to sample (MTS) training. MTS training often uses stimuli presented on computer screens (see Figure 7.1). In MTS training a

Figure 7.1. The relationships that emerge when a person forms a simple equivalence class. W. H. Aheam, R. MacDonald, R. B. Graff & W. B. Dube (2007). Behavior analytic teaching procedures: Basic Principle, empirically derived Practices. In P. Sturmey & A. Fitzer (Eds.) *Autism spectrum disorders. Applied behavior analysis, evidence, and practice.* Austin, TX; ProEdInc. p. 49.

comparison stimulus (A1) is presented at the top of the screen and several comparison stimuli (B1, B2 and B3) are presented below. For example, A1, A2 and A3 might be line drawings of a tree, a cat and a house and the comparison stimuli might be the words "tree", "cat" and "house." The subject hits a key to indicate which of B1, B2 or B3 is the correct answer. A correct response is followed by feedback, such as the word "correct" displayed on the screen. No such feedback is delivered for an incorrect response. Many non-human organisms can learn many surprising human-like discriminations using MTS training. For example, Watanabe, Sakamoto, and Wakita (1995) taught pigeons to discriminate between paintings by Monet and Picasso accurately. The pigeons also accurately discriminated between novel, untrained pictures by Monet and Picasso. Remarkably, they showed generalized responding from Monet to pictures by Cezanne and Renoir and from Picasso to pictures by Braque and Matisse.

Suppose now that a subject meets some predetermined criterion on the task described above, such as 90% correct responding on 10 trials for each of the three A stimuli and that further training now takes place. In this second stage, the experimenter now uses the old B stimuli as sample stimuli with a new set of comparison stimuli C1, C2 and C3, which are photographs of a tree, cat and house. Verbally competent humans who acquire this new set of discriminations also learn a large number of new sets of *emergent relationships*. Thus, although not trained, they will also learn to match the stimulus to itself (A1-A1), which is termed *identity*. When the subject matches B1-A1 and C1-B1 these relationships are termed *transitivity*. Finally, when the subject matches C1-A1, this relationship is termed *equivalence* (Sidman, 1994). In everyday language, we might say that a person who can match all combinations of line drawings, written words and photographs of trees, cats and houses understands the concepts of "tree", "cat" and "house."

Further training of this sort can lead to many new untrained emergent relationships. Suppose now we train a set of D-stimuli (spoken English words) to the C-stimuli and a set of E-stimuli (spoken French words) to D-stimuli. Now many more untrained relationships may emerge for relatively little training (Fields & Verhave, 1987). In everyday language we might say that someone who can match line drawings, written words, photographs, English and French spoken words correctly, *really* understands these concepts. If still other classes are also taught, for example, that tree and cat are both members of another equivalence class – natural things – then not only do all the members of these two equivalence classes enter into equivalence relationships with each other. They also do so with all other members of the equivalence class "natural things." Any new equivalence classes that form then enter into equivalence relationships with the class "natural things" also form equivalence relationships with our earlier classes "tree" and "cat." In this way we may come to learn that perceptually very different stimuli such as a line drawing of a squid, the written word "nematode" and the spoken word "aardvark" are all members of the equivalence class "natural things." (See Figure 7.1.)

Equivalence training is important as an explanation of generalization of behavior. Material in the last chapter addressed generalization through stimulus similarity and the effects of discrimination training modifying stimulus control. Stimulus similarity is unlikely to account for all generalization of human behavior because it is limited only to stimuli that are physically similar. Likewise discrimination training may account for some further generalization of human behavior, but it implies an enormous amount of training would be necessary to achieve it through this mechanism. Stimulus equivalence is learning process to account for massive amounts of generalization and the emergence of many new forms of behavior that may underlie language and education.

Application: Teaching Face Recognition to People with Acquired Brain Damage

Cowley, Green and Braunling-McMorrow (1992) taught three men with acquired brain injuries to name their therapists using stimulus equivalence training. At baseline the participants could match dictated to written names. However, they could not produce names to photographs, locate offices given their therapists' names or produce their therapists' names when looking at their therapist. Cowley et al. then taught the conditional discriminations between dictated names and photos (see Figure 7.2). After the men had acquired this discrimination they also acquired novel, untrained relationships. For example, they learned to match photos to names, even thought the experimenters never trained this. This study suggests that equivalence training may be useful in rehabilitation of people with brain damage.

There is extensive research on use of equivalence training to many academic and functional academic tasks, such as reading, spelling, coin recognition, and mathematics. This has been applied to typically developing children, and children and adults with intellectual disabilities (Sidman, 1994).

Transfer of Function

Equivalence classes offer another additional, potentially very powerful explanation of generalization of behavior. Stimuli may serve various functions. For example, they may be reinforcers, aversive stimuli, discriminative stimuli, etc. An interesting phenomenon is that if one member of an equivalence class acquires a function, this function may be transferred to other members of a class without direct training.

Auguston and Dougher (1997) taught eight students to form two equivalence classes using MTS training. Next they used classical conditioning in which one stimulus from the first equivalence class was paired with shock.

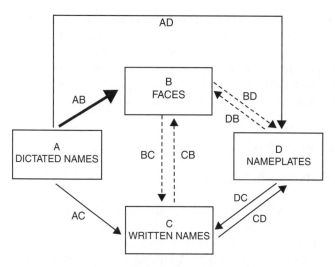

Figure 7.2. Schematic representation of conditional relations demonstrated on pretests (solid arrows), those trained (bold arrow), and those posttested (broken arrows). Arrows point from stimuli used as samples to stimuli used as comparisons in match-to-sample procedures. Reproduced from Cowley et al., 1992, Using stimulus equivalence procedures to teach name-face matching to adults with brain injuries, *Journal of Applied Behavior Analysis,* **25,** 461–475.

A stimulus from the second equivalence class was not paired with shock. In the third step, participants learned to avoid the shock to the stimulus in class one by pressing a key. In the final phase, Auguston and Dougher tested participants to see if they emitted an avoidance response to other stimuli. Indeed, the participants emitted the avoidance response to *all* the members of the first equivalence class and to *none* of the members of the second equivalence class. This demonstrated that as a member of one equivalence class acquires a function that function may transfer to other members of the same class, but not to members of different equivalence classes.

This and other studies that have demonstrated transfer of function have a number of possible clinical implications. First, transfer of function may be a powerful explanation for generalization that may occur when some clinical problems are acquired. For example, if a client learns to avoid stimuli that are members of a class "critical people" and they then learn from a colleague "Mike is very critical of others, but Jane is nice", then they may learn to avoid Mike, without direct experience of contingencies with Mike. They may also learn not to avoid Jane, again, even though they have not experienced contingencies associated with Jane. Second, transfer of function within a member of an equivalence class may also account for generalization that may occur during therapy. For example, suppose during therapy that respondent extinction occurs to certain words, such as "Mike", "Jim", etc, which are all members of an equivalence class "critical people." Then generalization may occur to other members of that class, including other people and stimuli, to which respondent extinction has not yet directly occurred. Clinical examples here might include the generalization that may occur during systematic desensitization. Here respondent extinction occurs to various words and images used during systematic desensitization. Generalization may occur to actual people or situations outside of therapy that may enter into equivalence relationships with these stimuli.

VERBAL BEHAVIOR

Skinner's *Verbal Behavior*

Skinner had been working on the applications of behavior analysis to language from as early as 1934. He took another 20 years to publish these ideas in *Verbal Behavior*. Skinner distinguishes verbal behavior from other behavior – not on the basis of its form, such as spoken or written words – but on the basis if its function. He rejected terms, such as "speech" and "language" because they are imprecise and laden with existing meaning that obstruct careful analysis. For example, "speech" suggests that all forms of spoken behavior are mediated through other people, which they are not. The term "speech" suggests that other forms of behavior, such as sign language and writing are fundamentally different, because they do not involve speech. This is also untrue. Likewise he rejected the term "language" because it seems to refer to the behavior of a community, rather than an individual. Therefore, Skinner proposed the tem "verbal behavior" because it was new, emphasizes the behavior of the speaker and implies the possibility that verbal behavior is operant behavior that was shaped by its consequences.

In defining verbal behavior Skinner distinguished between behavior that is effective by acting directly on the environment, such as picking up a glass of water, and drinking, and behavior which is mediated by other people, such as asking someone for a glass of water. Thus, Skinner (1957) defined verbal behavior as "behavior reinforced through the mediation of other persons " (p.2). Skinner proposed that the distinction between behavior that is reinforced directly and behavior that is reinforced through the mediation of other people is a fundamental one.

Skinner also introduced the notion of the speaker and the listener as part of the analysis of verbal behavior. The behavior of the speaker that is mediated by the listener is verbal behavior. The part of the listener's behavior that controls the verbal behavior of the listener permits a functional analysis of verbal behavior. The combined behavior of the speaker and listener constitutes a verbal episode. He noted that the speaker is often also a listener. What the speaker does after emitting verbal behavior may control verbal behavior. When this is all done privately we call this "thinking" in everyday language. Thus, Skinner's account of verbal behavior addressed both public verbal behavior involving two people, as well as private thinking involving one person.

Skinner also offered an analysis of conversation in which the speaker and listener are entwined in a dance of mutual stimulus control and reinforcement of verbal and non-verbal behavior. Consider the following example:

Person A: Coming through!
(The Speaker emits verbal behavior specifying an aversive consequence for Person B's failure to move. Person B functions as listener at this point.)

Person B: Sure!
(Person B as speaker reinforces Person A's verbal behavior with his verbal response and by stepping aside. Person A functions as the listener.)

Person A: Thanks!
(Person A as speaker reinforces Person B's previous verbal response and stepping aside. The "thanks" also is a discriminative stimulus that the threat of an aversive stimulus is no longer present. Person B functions as listener.)

Thus, the notions of verbal behavior were immediately extended to describe the contingencies of reinforcement and stimulus control that occur during typical verbal episodes that occur between two people.

Traditional formulations of language suggest that verbal behavior originates inside the speaker – from the speaker's goals, ideas, meaning and intensions. Skinner rejected such formulations because of their circular and untestable nature and because they are not useful to develop a science of verbal behavior. Instead, Skinner proposed that we should define the topography of verbal behavior and identify its controlling variables. That is, we should conduct a functional analysis of verbal behavior, just like any other behavior. Skinner identified four main verbal operants. These are defined by the types of contingencies that maintain them and by related reinforcer deprivation and satiation. A *mand* is a verbal operant that specifies its own reinforcer. Its controlling variables are deprivation of the reinforcer it species and aversive stimulation. In everyday language, *mands* are requests. For example, if saying "Can I have copy paper" is reinforced by access to the copy paper and influenced by deprivation of copy paper, then this is a mand. An example of a mand controlled by aversive stimulation might be "Could you turn the heating on," as it is controlled by removal of aversive cold stimulation. A *tact* is reinforced by its social consequences. For example, if speaker says "the opera was good" and the listener says "Yep, I liked it too", and the response from the speaker is the reinforcer maintaining this response, then it is a tact. An *echoic* is reinforced by the match between the utterance and the verbal behavior prior to what the speaker said. Thus, if a person said "Say thank you" and the next person said "thank you" and the match between the two utterances was the reinforcer maintaining the second person's response, then this was an echoic. Finally, *intraverbals* are responses that are under the stimulus control of the previous speaker's verbal behavior, but are not identical to it. For example, if the first person asks "What do you like to do?" and second person says "I like the opera", then the second response is an intraverbal. Note that the same topography of verbal behavior may have different functions. For example, the spoken word "apple" may be a mand or a tact. Only by analyzing the effects of reinforcers and reinforcer deprivation can we know what the function of such an utterance is.

Another functional category of verbal behavior is *autoclitics*. Autoclitics are verbal behavior which "is based upon or depends upon other verbal behavior" (Skinner, 1957 p.315). Autoclitics alter the behavior of the listener in some way. There are several kinds of autoclitics. One example is where the autoclitic indicates that kind of verbal operant that it is associated with. For example, if a speaker says "I remember ... " that autoclitic indicates that the person is tacting an object that is absent. Another class of autoclitics is that which indicate the strength of a response. For example, if a speaker says either "I am sure that John is there... ", or "Perhaps John is there", then these verbal behaviors indicate the strength of the speakers response.

Skinner also extended verbal behavior to analyze thinking and self-control of verbal behavior. Thinking is covert, private verbal behavior. Skinner speculated that private verbal behavior comes about through a history of punishment in which adults and peers progressively punish children's loud verbal behavior. He noted that when the punishing audience is absent, as in people who live alone and the nonjudgmental psychotherapist, people gradually begin to talk aloud. Likewise, when talking aloud has advantages to the person, such as self-instructing in a difficult task, people do indeed "think aloud." When it is to the advantage of the speaker to speak covertly, as in hiding secrets from others, people think rather than speak. Skinner suggested that "[t]he range of verbal behavior is roughly suggested, in descending order of energy, by shouting, loud talking, quiet talking, whispering, muttering 'under one's breath,' subaudible speech with detectable muscular action, subaudible speech of unclear dimensions, and perhaps even the 'unconscious thinking' sometimes inferred in instances of problem solving" (p. 438.) Skinner went on to suggest that private verbal behavior can be very useful. For example, we may emit private mands – one might think "Stop wasting time, get one with it! Only 30 minutes left!" – and private tacts such as "I'm getting tense now." Private verbal behavior may also be very important in self-control of behavior, including both public as well as private verbal behavior. Thus, one may learn to control one's thinking and overt verbal behavior in the same way as one controls other behavior. Thus, Skinner extended the analysis of self-control of public behavior to private verbal behavior. For example, one may reject saying things aloud, if one has said them privately. We often tell people to "stop and think before speaking." In a similar way, under certain circumstances we may learn to modify our private verbal behavior. When increasing the probably of certain kinds of thinking, one might learn to remove distracting stimuli that occasion thinking about other things, but closing the office door, putting the phone and clock in the drawer and turning off the music, and to only present the stimuli likely to occasion the desired private verbal behavior, such as a carefully highlighted article to promote thinking and writing about a certain topic. Thus, Skinner took a functional approach that emphasized the adaptive value and utility of some forms of thinking as private operant behavior.

Clinical Implications

The most important implication of Skinner's conception of verbal behavior, including private verbal behavior, is that it requires no special analysis that is different from the analysis of non-verbal behavior. Verbal behavior is subject to the same kind of conceptual analysis and functional analysis as other behavior. It is not necessary to elevate it to the status of the cause of behavior. Rather, it is behavior that can be understood in the same terms as other behavior.

Accessing private verbal behavior may be an ultimately insurmountable problem. One may believe that as a clinician one is being non-punitive and that clients are indeed speaking or writing their minds. However, it is hard to truly know this. Some behavior analysts have attempted to conduct functional analyses of private behavior (Taylor & O'Reilly, 1997) and to conduct clinical interventions by changing private verbal behavior (Wilson, Hayes, Gregg & Zettle, 2001), but others doubt it can be done (Lamal, 1998.)

Verbal Behavior: Critique and Replies

Skinner's *Verbal Behavior* is perhaps more famous for apparently being demolished by Chomsky's critique than its actual content. Few people have read Chomksy's critique. Fewer have read Skinner's rather long and tedious *Verbal Behavior*. Few outside the behavior analytic community have read MacCorquodale's (1970), Stemmer's (1990) and Palmer's (2006) replies to Chomsky. Hence, the notion that Chomsky disproved Skinner's *Verbal Behavior* has drifted from academic gossip to the myths of introductory psychology textbooks.

Chomsky's criticisms of *Verbal Behavior* include that its technical terms, such as mand, are merely everyday concepts that add nothing to our understanding. Chomsky also criticized the use of animal studies, which he viewed as being contrived. Chomsky contended that these animal studies cannot be extended to account for human behavior, including verbal behavior in general, but especially human grammar and novel forms of language.

MacCorquodale (1970) noted Chomsky's review was at least half a more general critique of behaviorism and half a critique on its application to verbal behavior. His first criticism of Chomsky's review was that it criticized Skinner for things he did not say, such as drive reduction explanations of reinforcement, which was not part of *Verbal Behavior*. Second, MacCorquodale pointed out that Skinner's book was a speculative book. At the time there was little data on application of behavioral concepts to human verbal behavior. Chomsky erroneously concluded that because the data had not yet been collected, that it could not be done. (The subsequent application of these ideas has justified Skinner's assertion that these ideas could be applied to verbal behavior.) Third, in response to Chomsky's critique that Skinner's new technical language is mere paraphrases of everyday language, MacCorquodale noted that these terms are much more precise than the everyday language and potentially amenable functional analysis in ways that the everyday terms they replace are not. Finally, in response to Chomsky's assertion that speech is too complex for functional analysis and can only be explained in terms of mediation through genetics and neurology, MacCorquodale noted that apparent complexity can emerge out of the combined effects of more than one simple process. Skinner did indeed suggest several functions of verbal behavior. However, it was the *combined* effects of these several processes, rather than any single process acting alone, that may account for complex verbal behavior, such as grammar.

Perhaps the most damning critique of Chomsky's review of *Verbal Behavior* is that in 50 years it has lead to no useful developments in therapy, rehabilitation or other forms of intervention.

The Influence of *Verbal Behavior*

Verbal Behavior caused considerable controversy when it was published. However, at first its influence was modest. There were relatively few citations and even fewer citations in empirical papers (McPherson, Bonem, Green & Osborne, 1984). There was a series of empirical studies from Baer, Bijou and other colleagues in the 1960s and 1970s demonstrating contingency effects on a wide range of language behaviors in typical children and children with developmental disabilities (Baer & Guess, 1971; Guess, Sailor, Rutherford & Baer, 1968; Mann & Baer, 1971). However, although some work was done using concepts such as mands, as in work on incidental teaching, Skinner's concepts were not used extensively until the 1990s (Dymond, O'Hora, Whelen & O'Donvan, 2006). Verbal behavior has now become a very active field of practice and research with children with autism spectrum disorders. Thus, the influence of *Verbal Behavior* has gradually increased over time, especially in the area of Relational Frame Theory (RFT) and recent language interventions for children with autism spectrum disorders.

Relational Frame Theory

Since the mid-1990s, Hayes and colleagues extended Skinner's work to psychotherapy. RFT has become an active area of research on verbal behavior, which has also resulted in new verbal psychotherapies (Hayes et al., 2001a). RFT claims to be, as Hayes et al. (2001a) subtitle their book, "a post-Skinnerian account of human language and cognition." Hayes, Blackledge and Barnes-Holmes (2001b) began by acknowledging Skinner's contribution. However, they also noted some of the limitations of Skinner's *Verbal Behavior*. These included the difficulty in converting these speculations into a research program and the excessively broad definition of verbal behavior. They also noted two historically new developments in verbal behavior research that occurred since Skinner (1957), namely rule-governed behavior and derived relational responding.

Derived relational responding deserves some amplification. As we saw in the earlier section, one such derived stimulus relationship is equivalence. We also saw that functions may transfer from one member of an equivalence class to another. Stimulus equivalence and transfer of function seem to be behavioral models of language and cognition. However, RFT expands on these ideas in a number of ways (Hayes et al., 2001b). They noted that operants are often defined topographically, such as pressing a bar, or saying "door." However, in principal, all operants are defined functionally, rather than topographically. That is an operant is defined by its relationship between its antecedent and consequence. For example, the verbal mand "door" includes any response that is occasioned by the door being closed and that is reinforced by the door opening. Thus, pointing and clicking one's fingers, might also be members of the mand "door." Hayes et al. (2001b) noted several common examples of operants that cannot be defined topographically. For example, teaching someone to produce novel responses, random numbers or imitating new models all involve operants that cannot be defined topographically, since the topography that is reinforced is different on each occasion.

Responding to the relationship between stimuli is also common. For example, when reinforced for selecting the taller of two stimuli, A, B, and C, an organism must respond "B", when presented A and B. However, the organism must respond "C", when presented A and C or B and C. Relational responding, such as discriminating brighter, higher, etc., is common. Hayes et al. pointed out that the context of the learning determines the relationship to which one responds. Thus, in one context one might respond to the relationship "taller" and in others to "brighter" for the *same* set of stimuli.

One of the main expansions that RFT proposes is that equivalence is only one specific form of derived relationship. Many other derived relationships are possible. Examples could include "older", "smarter" and "cuter", etc. Relationships between sets of stimuli often imply other relationships. Thus, saying "A > B" and "B > C" implies both "A > C" and "C < A." These relationships may not be taught directly. Rather, the subject can derive then by combining several relationships. This is called "combinatorial entailment." Thus, Hayes et al. (2001b) go on to define a relational frame as:

> A specific class of arbitrarily applicable relational responding that shows the contextually controlled qualities of mutual entailment, combinatorial mutual entailment, and transformation of stimulus functions. (p.33)

There are many ways in which stimuli could relate to each other. These include coordination, such as "A is the same as B," such as "This is a cup," "This is called a cup" and "A cup is similar to a bowl." Other relational frames include opposition (" pretty is the opposite of ugly"), distinction ("this is not warm water"), comparison ("A is twice as fast as B") and hierarchical and temporal relationships.

As a behavioral theory of language and cognition, RFT emphasizes the role and characteristics of verbal behavior (Hayes et al., 2001b). RFT attributes several properties to verbal behavior. Verbal behavior is said to be indirect because many relationships can be derived without direct contact with the events themselves. Verbal behavior is said to be arbitrary, in that the form of verbal behavior – spoken or written words, signs – have no necessary relationship to the stimuli they "refer to" or have equivalence or other relationship to other stimuli. Verbal behavior is also said to vary in specificity and is very flexible. Verbal behavior is a pervasive part of behavior, which intrudes into many non-verbal aspects of behavior. Verbal behavior expands social influence on behavior and enables us to contact the past and imagine the future. Thus, animals and non-verbal humans, such as infants, live in a world of direct contingencies. In contrast, verbally competent humans live the two worlds of direct contingencies and of verbal behavior. Hayes et al. (2001a) summarizes RFT as follows:

> Relational Frame Theory is a behavior analytic approach to human language and cognition. RFT treats relational responding as a generalized operant, and this appeals to a history of multiple-exemplar training. Specific types of relational responding, termed relational frames, are defined in terms of the three properties of mutual and combinatorial entailment and the transformation of functions. Relational frames are arbitrarily applicable, but are typically not necessarily arbitrarily applied in the natural language context. (p.141)

The interested reader is referred to an online website for interactive tutorial in RFT (Fox, 2006) as well as to Hayes et al. (2001a) for further information.

VERBAL BEHAVIOR THERAPIES

Clinical Behavior Analysis

RFT theorists have explored the possible implications of RFT for psychopathology and verbal forms of psychotherapy, such as acceptance and commitment therapy (ACT) described below. RFT implies that for verbally competent humans intervention that only emphasizes current contingencies addresses only half of human behavior. Thus, accounts of psychopathology and psychotherapy must also address the role of verbal behavior in the etiology and maintenance of psychopathology, and psychotherapy and should also address verbal behavior, including private verbal behavior, as a target behavior and vehicle to produce behavioral change.

Since the early 1990s, clinical behavior analysts have begun to address clinical areas, such as anxiety, depression, abuse and pain (Dougher, 1999). Traditional ABA has ignored or underplayed these topics. Further, these new verbal behavior therapies have often been done in the context of traditional therapeutic settings, such as a therapist and client in an outpatient setting, rather than in an institutional, educational or some other public setting where behavior can be readily observed. Dougher's (1999) volume, *Clinical Behavior Analysis* summarized these developments. Its chapters address clinical problems that are not typically seen in behavior analytic journals. Chapters included topics such as sexual abuse, depression, anxiety, marital problems and alcohol abuse. Further, this volume also covered topics such as language in therapy, problems of self, emotion, relationship and interpretation in psychotherapy.

In the introductory chapter of this volume, Dougher and Hayes (2000) distinguished two branches of behavioral approaches to clinical problems. The first was an operant, primarily American, school of behavior analysis. This school tended to deal with people with developmental disabilities and children in institutions, residential and educational settings. Interventions were often contingency-based. The second school was a British and South African school of behavior therapists who dealt with adult mental health issues in outpatients. Both approaches share certain commonalities, such as empiricism and an interest in learning. However, Dougher and Hayes believed that there were significant philosophical differences between these two approaches. Behavior analysis emphasizes context and the development of behavior within its context. Behavior therapy was not contextualist, but mechanistic. Thus, in the 1970s it incorporated the computer metaphor of human behavior and spawned cognitive-behavior therapy and cognitive therapy, in which the component parts of the human computer – its perceptions, memory, recall, and so on – are damaged. Therefore, therapy consisted of diagnosing the damaged human computer and repairing the damaged parts through changing how people think and feel.

Dougher and Hayes claimed that the new field of clinical behavior analysis is an outgrowth and expansion of behavior analysis, rather than behavior therapy. This is because it shares with behavior analysis recognition and use of reinforcement, punishment, schedule effects, and stimulus control. More importantly, it also emphasized the role of verbal behavior in human behavior generally, and its application to clinical problems in particular. They emphasized that clinical behavior analysis was not just a new set of intervention methods. More fundamentally, it involved a new focus on verbal behavior in psychotherapy. This is illustrated nicely by the following quotation:

> 'Psychotherapy' is dominantly verbal therapy and the 'mind' is a name for a collection of verbal processes. In that sense, 'psychopathology' is dominantly verbal pathology and 'mental' illness is verbal illness ... (pp. 22–23)

Clinical Application of Transfer of Function

We saw in the preceding section that when a stimulus, which is a member of an equivalence class, acquires a function, that function may transfer to other members of that stimulus class (Auguston & Dougher, 1997). Wilson and Blackledge (1999) suggested that this might have implications for psychotherapy. They proposed that words may be members of equivalence classes with traumatic events. For example, the word "rape" may enter into an equivalence relationship with the actual events to which the word refers. The word "rape" already has multiple equivalence relationships with a wide variety of other words, such as "sex," "immoral," and other stimuli, such as images and sounds. Therefore, these other equivalent stimuli may also come to elicit the same emotional behavior as the actual event. This may hold true, even though these words and images were not directly paired with the actual traumatic event itself. Hence, Wilson and Blackledge speculated that the generalization of the effects of trauma to other situations might occur through transfer of function within an equivalence class.

They went on to speculate that, since transfer of function, such respondent extinction, can occur among members of an equivalence class, then psychotherapy may work in precisely that way. Namely, by talking about the traumatic event and the related material, respondent extinction to these stimuli – trauma-related words – may occur. As these words progressively elicit less and less emotional responding, then avoidance of these stimuli should also reduce. More importantly, if respondent extinction and reduction of avoidance do indeed take place to these stimuli, then this change in function may also transfer to other members of that equivalence class. Hence, talking about aversive histories during therapy may result in improvement of functioning outside of therapy because of transfer of function within equivalence classes.

Acceptance and Commitment Therapy

ACT is a behavior analytic therapy said to be based on the RFT model of verbal behavior and the role of verbal behavior in psychopathology. ACT addresses verbal behavior including thoughts, and the labels applied to emotions, memories, bodily sensations and other private behavior. According to ACT, problem contexts are contexts in which people struggle to control their thoughts, rather than simply experience them. For example, trying to control one's impulses is the maladaptive solution to the problem of an unpleasant thought. This solution is not merely ineffective: It *causes* the problem to continue and worsen. According to ACT, psychopathology arises when people struggle to control verbal behavior by avoiding unpleasant thoughts, when people attend more to what they think than what they experience, and when people are unclear about their core values.

ACT includes two components: acceptance and commitment. Acceptance includes verbal strategies that teach clients to merely experience and accept their private behavior, rather than fight or change dysfunctional patterns of thinking. ACT therapists use metaphor to illustrate this. An example is the metaphor that private verbal behavior is like quicksand. If you fight it you go deeper into the quicksand. If you spread out and contact it, you do not sink. Another metaphor ACT therapists use is the tiger metaphor. At first you feed the small hungry tiger that might eat you. It goes away. Unfortunately, over time you end up with a large tiger that will eat you. Trying to control thoughts and impulses is said to be like feeding the tiger. The thoughts may go away for a while, but eventually, they too, like the tiger, eat you whole. ACT therapists also try to loosen stimulus control of behavior that thoughts may have in a number of ways. They use the metaphor that private events are the furniture in the house. Thoughts are not the house itself, merely the furniture within. They also use language exercises which again try to loosen the control that private events may have over behavior. For example, instead of saying "I wanted to go out with my friends, but I was too depressed", clients learn to say "I wanted to go out with my friends *and* I felt depressed." Describing one's behavior this way may negate the link that feelings cause and behavior.

Commitment is the second component of ACT. It is a fairly traditional behavioral approach. It involves identifying core values that are important to clients. Once the client and therapist identify core value, then they change client behavior to that which is consonant with these values and goals (Hayes, Masuda, Bisset Luoma and Guerrero, 2004; Wilson et al., 2001).

Evaluations of ACT

There have been a number of case studies, case series and at least eight RCTs evaluating ACT (Hayes et al., 2004.) For example, Bach and Hayes (2002) conducted a RCT for 80 inpatients with auditory hallucination or delusions that were not substance induced or related to delirium or dementia. The patients were mostly diagnosed with psychotic disorders and a few with mood disorders. They randomly assigned the participants to either treatment as usual (TAU) or ACT. TAU included active treatment and consisted of psycho-educational groups, individual psychotherapy and case management services. The ACT group received four sessions of ACT that they modified for this population. The sessions addressed: (1) the ineffectiveness of previous strategies used to avoid distress by controlling thoughts; (2) that thoughts do not have to control behavior; (3) exercises on the futility of trying to control one's thoughts, including negative ones; (4) identifying valued goals, such as living independently; (5) the strategies that can be used to obtain those goals; and (6) a final review session. The main outcome measure was the percentage of participants readmitted, following discharge over a four-month period. At four-month follow-up, 20% of ACT participants and 40% of TAU participants were readmitted. This was a statistically significant difference. The authors argued that this was also socially significant. At follow-up, ACT participants were also less likely to believe their psychotic symptoms when these symptoms were present. This suggested that the change in belief due to ACT was the mechanism of change.

Researchers have evaluated ACT for a wide range of problems. There are uncontrolled studies evaluating ACT to treat co-morbid substance abuse and post traumatic stress disorder, public speaking anxiety in college students, promotion of wellness and reduction of stress at work, depression, psychotic symptoms, enhancing athletic performance, chronic pain, smoking, eating disorders, bereavement, alcoholism, survivors of child sexual abuse, reduction of high-risk sexual behavior in adolescents, erectile dysfunction, stress in a cancer patient, exhibitionism, generalized anxiety disorder, agoraphobia, trichotillomania, and improving the effectiveness of mental health clinicians (www.contextualpsychology.org, 2006). Additionally, there are at least eight RCTs for a wide range of problems (Hayes et al., 2004), including panic-related symptoms in highly anxious undergraduate students (Eifert & Heffner, 2003), anxiety in college students (Zettle, 2003), and polysubstance abuse, stress and pain symptoms in workers with chronic disabilities. Some of these RCTs have shown ACT to be superior to other established effective treatments, such as nicotine replacement therapy for smoking and cognitive-behavior therapy for anxiety (Heimberg, Salzman, Holt & Blendel, 1993). ACT training has also been used to reduce stigmatization and burnout and increase a sense of personal accomplishment in behavioral health counselors.

Corrigan (2001) criticized ACT and other new behavior analytic therapies because they were "getting ahead of their data" (p. 192). In response, Hayes, Masuda et al. (2004) found that although there were eight RCTs for ACT, and there were at least three RCTs for DBT, other verbal behavior analytic therapies, such as functional analytic psychotherapy (FAP), had more much more limited empirical support.

Dialectic Behavior Therapy

Linehan (1993) developed dialectical behavior therapy (DBT) to treat parasuicidal behavior in people with borderline personality disorder. DBT conceptualizes change as a result of a dialectic and eventual synthesis between two contradictory, alternative positions. The most common dialect is between acceptance that one's life will continue to be painful and change that invalidates the current person as not being good enough and in need of change.

DBT is a manualized treatment that includes weekly individual therapy, group skills training and telephone contact in between meetings. DBT includes four stages. Stage 1 focuses attention on decreasing suicidal behavior, substance abuse, eating disorders and homelessness, and increasing skills, such as mindfulness and tolerating distress. Stage 2 focuses on emotional problems and uses exposure to treat trauma-related affect. Stage 3 focuses on acquisition of living skills, such as employment and education. Finally, stage 4 addresses accepting life's struggles and enhancing living skills with contentment and joy (Linehan, 1993).

DBT has been applied to a wide range of problem, such as borderline personality disorder, including with concomitant substance abuse disorders, and eating disorders. Hayes, Masuda et al.'s (2004) review identified eight RCTs which showed the efficacy of DBT. Impressively, participants in all of these RCTs were actual patients with apparently difficult clinical problems, such as outpatients with repeated suicidal attempts and veterans with borderline personality disorder, rather than distressed students. Another impressive feature of these studies is that several compared DBT to TAU or currently used treatments, such as 12-step programs.

Functional Analytic Psychotherapy

Another radical behavioral verbal psychotherapy is Kohlenberg and Tsai's (1991) functional analytic psychotherapy (FAP). FAP is intriguing because it focuses on the interactions during one-on-one psychotherapy sessions as the vehicle of behavioral change, including behavioral change outside of the therapy session. During FAP, the therapist must (1) carefully observe potentially problematic client behavior during therapy sessions; (2) identify the context in which these problematic behaviors occur; and (3) reinforce instances of improvement during the session. Thus, the FAP therapist must accurately discriminate and differentially reinforce client behavior during therapy.

FAP identifies three kinds of clinically relevant behaviors (CRB). CRB1 is the actual problematic behavior that occurs during therapy. An example might be when a client reports "feeling really bad" during the therapy session. CRB2s are improvements on CRB1s, such as being assertive with the therapist instead of angry. CRB3s consist of a client describing the functional relationship of his own CRB.

FAP involves five principles. First, the therapist must discriminate CRBs so they can be used during therapy. Second, the therapist should deliberately provoke CRB1s, so there is clinical material to work with during therapy. Third, the therapeutic relationship must be real and genuine. That is, the therapist must use naturalistic reinforcers for client progress. For example, after a client reveals personal information, rather than telling a client "good sharing," a therapist should show more attention and emotional behavior. Fourth, the therapist should observe progress in client behavior, as CRB1s are replaced with CRB2s and CRB3s. Finally, the therapist gives the client interpretations out loud by describing the observed functional relationships during therapy. Kohlenberg and Tsai (1991) described the process of FAP in detail. FAP has been incorporated into various other kinds of therapy, such as cognitive therapy and ACT (Hayes, Masudo et al., 2004.)

There has been much less outcome research on FAP than ACT: Hayes, Masudo, et al. (2004) identified *no* controlled outcome studies of FAP. A key question relating to FAP is whether the behavior changes that occur in CRBs in therapy sessions do indeed generalize to real life setting. Thus, at this time empirical support for FAP is very limited.

Radical Verbal Psychotherapies: Are They Behavior Analytic?

Hayes, Masudo et al. (2004) showed there is good evidence from RCTs that ACT is more effective than both TAU and in some cases current established effective treatments. This is positive and permits evaluation of ACT in terms that non-behaviorists find acceptable. Evidence for the effectiveness of DBT is, if anything, *more* compelling because the RCTs for DBT involve patients with severe problems. However, when one compares these outcome studies against the criteria for evaluating behavior analytic interventions (Baer et al., 1968; Wolf, 1978) these studies are wanting.

For example, group designs to evaluate treatment are very limited: they emphasize statistical significance, data from the nonexistent average subject at only one point in time and do not evaluate the effect of treatment at the level of individual subjects. Further, because these studies do not use small experimental designs and do not measure the independent variable using observational data, they do not demonstrate functional relationships between independent and dependent variables, which is the hallmark of behavior analysis (Baer et al., 1968; Skinner, 1953).

An additional problem is identifying what the effective components of the ACT and DBT packages might be. Naturally, ACT authors emphasize the use of novel acceptance-related procedures involving alleged changes in private verbal behavior. However, no studies have investigated the effects of the various components of ACT. Setting goals and receiving weekly feedback from the therapist and oneself may function as contingency management for client progress. The acceptance component of ACT includes nonspecific treatment components including talking about one's problems with a nonpunitive audience. Finally, the commitment component includes traditional behavior therapy procedures that have extensive research indicating their efficacy. The commitment component alone might explain any change that occurs during ACT. The RCTs have not shown if the change is due to specific components of ACT, behavior therapy, nonspecific components of acceptance, or the acceptance procedures themselves. Future research should conduct component analyses of the ACT package to separate out these elements and use placebo control conditions for the acceptance.

Similar comments can be made concerning DBT. DBT includes many components. Some components are traditional behavior therapy skills teaching, such as interpersonal skills teaching, exposure therapy and self-regulation. Others, such as mindfulness training, are not traditional behavior therapy methods. Thus, it is unclear which of these components are responsible for producing change. The RCTs for DBT, like other studies that use group designs, fall foul of the potential limitation of overemphasis on statistical rather than clinical significance and fail to show functional relationships between independent and dependent variables.

FAP appeals to many behavior analytic concepts. However, its empirical basis is weak. Recently, Kanter et al. (2006) reported two nonexperimental case studies evaluating the efficacy of FAP in treating two adults with depression and other disorders. In the first phase the therapist used standard Beck-like cognitive behavior therapy, but did not use FAP methods. In the second condition the therapist switched to using FAP by "blocking" or punishing CRB1 and differentially reinforcing CRB2. The participants collected data on their own behavior outside of therapy using diary cards. Examples of target behaviors included histrionic behavior, such as flirting with men, worrying about what others thought about them, and poor communication with spouse. The first participant reported that during

12 sessions of CBT, target behaviors were frequent and occurred on a daily basis. Following the introduction of FAP they were nearly eliminated during the next eight sessions. Observation of the therapist's behavior indicated that during cognitive behavior therapy the therapist emitted no FAP-related contingent responses. During the FAP condition the therapist made some FAP-related contingent responses in every session, although the frequency was variable. The second participant's data were incomplete and difficult to interpret. This study is suggestive of that FAP may be effective for some clients, but because of the incomplete data and lack of experimental control, no firm conclusion can be drawn. More evidence is needed as to the efficacy of FAP and its effects on behavior outside of therapy setting.

Verbal Behavior and Developmental Disabilities

Many early behavior analysts and behavior therapists were very interested in language interventions. However, some of these early interventions occurred without reference to the function of the words or signs that they taught, or by inadvertently mixing the functions of the words. This might account for the limited success of some early behavioral intervention programs (Sigafoos, O'Reilly, Schlosser & Lancioni, 2007). Thus, verbal behavior has recently influenced the development of language acquisition programs for children and adults with developmental disabilities, such as autism and intellectual disabilities. Some studies have begun to teach different functions of each word separately. For example, some interventions first teach the form of the word as an echoic, then teach the function of that word as a mand, and then teach the function of that spoken word as a tact (Partington & Sundberg, 1998.)

Application: Teaching Mands and Tacts

Partington, Sundberg, Newhouse and Spengler (1994) reported an experimental study in which a 6-year-old nonvocal girl with autism had acquired 30 signs as mands (requests), but could not tact (label) the objects when asked "what is this?" When asked "what is this?" she often responded with the sign for "ball" or "hat" and engaged in maladaptive behavior. Partington et al. speculated that this was an example of "stimulus overselectivity." That is, one element of a complex stimulus exerted inappropriately narrow stimulus control over responding. Thus, when presented with the compound stimulus "what is this?" and an object, the object did not exert stimulus control, so that the child responded with a tact that correctly labeled the object. To remediate this, Partington et al. initially eliminated the antecedent "what is this?" Instead they only presented child's name and pointing as the antecedent stimuli. If the child made a correct response they praised the correct response and gave the child one minute access to a preferred item. If the child made an error or no response, they then modeled the correct tact. This and other related procedures were effective in teaching the child to tact both actual items and pictures of the items, and in reducing maladaptive behavior. This study showed that merely teaching a child to produce the form of a language response (emitting the sign) was insufficient to teach functional language. Indeed, teaching mands did not help teach the child tacts for the same stimuli. Thus, the different functions of words appear to be independent of one another, and must be taught separately. Sigafoos et al. (2007) provide a good summary of the impact of functional approaches to language teaching in children with autism.

SUMMARY

Verbal behavior has become influential in both traditional adult psychotherapy and language interventions for people with developmental disabilities. In adult psychotherapy the ideas of verbal behavior have been used to develop new treatment procedures and have been combined with traditional behavior therapy and cognitive behavior therapy procedures for a very wide range of problems. For DBT and ACT there is a reasonable and growing number of RCTs that support their use. The literature on these therapies is limited because they do not use the methods of behavior analysis to demonstrate functional relationships and to evaluate the clinical significance of behavior change for individual clients. The application of verbal behavior to people with developmental disabilities has also generated new treatment procedures. However, this literature is much closer to behavior analysis conceptually and methodologically.

Part II

CASE FORMULATION

Part I of this volume laid the foundations as to what behaviorism is and described some basic learning concepts that may account for the acquisition and maintenance of psychopathology, and that can be used to intervene. Part II goes on to examine case formulation and various nonbehavioral and behavioral approaches to case formulation. The latter chapters illustrate various approaches to behavioral case formulation and describe some of the technology and conceptual issues in behavioral case formulation.

Chapter 8

NONBEHAVIORAL APPROACHES TO CASE FORMULATION

Nonbehavioral approaches to case formulation refer to a variety of quite different theoretical approaches, including psychodynamic, psychiatric, and cognitive case formulation. It is useful to contract other approaches to case formulation with behavioral approaches. Such contrasts identify the dimensions along which approaches differ and identify the relevant issues that distinguish different approaches to case formulation. This chapter will begin by reviewing the history and definitions of case formulation. Subsequent sections illustrate various nonbehavioral approaches to case formulation including psychoanalytic, psychiatric, cognitive, and eclectic approaches.

HISTORY OF CASE FORMULATION

The notion that information concerning clinical cases, or people more generally, should be organized rationally and systematically is a very old one. We often turn to technicians and professionals to give us an explanation of something we do not understand with the hope that this specialist knowledge will help us solve an important problem. Being able to make such a pronouncement is a professional skill that our guilds jealously guard on our behalf.

Eels (1997, 2007) described how both individual case studies and systematic and unsystematic collections of case presentations have had a long and important contribution to the history of medicine and psychology. Publications of series of case studies can be found throughout the course of history. Ancient Egyptian medical treatises report cases of depression and dementia. The Ancient Greeks collected information on humors by systematic examination of their patient's various excretions and symptoms. Based on their individual formulation idiographic recommendations were made to correct imbalances in humors. (They were structuralists, I suppose, since they could not observe imbalances of humors directly and so had to infer the alleged imbalances in humors through observations of behavior and their products.)

The systematic examination of individual cases has made a significant contribution to psychotherapy, neurology and behavior analysis alike. The work of such diverse authors as Freud, Watson and Reyer, Wolpe and Luria all use vivid presentation of case study material from different theoretical perspectives. These case studies often include commentary as to the thinking and analysis from these experts. Such descriptive case studies can be excellent teaching tools and useful models for practitioners to use with their own cases. They are also often useful because they may describe in detail assessment procedures, individual modifications to assessment and treatment procedures, as well as problems and problems solving that are usually absent from journal articles and group experimental designs.

Recent Developments in Case Formulation

Since the early 1960s, there has been more formalized interest in case formulation. Early behavior therapy produced numerous books of case formulations illustrating the then new and exciting methods of behavior therapy (Eysenck, 1960; Eysenck & Rachman, 1965; Marks, 1981), including such classics as Wolpe's (1958) *Psychotherapy by Reciprocal Inhibition.* Such case studies, although often data-based, generally did not use single subject experimental designs and hence did not demonstrate causality. In the late 1950s and early 1960s a number of classic articles in the application of behavior analysis to severe psychiatric disorders were published in the *Journal of the Experimental Analysis of Behavior.* These included Ayllon and Michael's (1959) classic "The psychiatric nurse as a behavioral engineer," as well as similar publication in intellectual disabilities (Ellis, Barnet & Pryor, 1960), and stuttering (Goldiamond, 1959). *The Journal of Applied Behavior Analysis* was first published in 1968. It has since become the primary repository of published single subject applied and single subject experimental research. Other notable journals such as *Journal of Behavior Therapy and Experimental Psychiatry,* and *Behavior Modification* and *Behavior Therapy* have also published single subject experimental research, including behavioral work with a wide variety of populations. Turkat (1985a) published an important volume of descriptive case studies, including formulations of anxiety disorders, alcohol abuse, various forms of personality disorders, and problems in later life. Behavioral approaches to case formulation continue to be of interest, as shown in Haynes and O'Brien's (1990) volume on behavioral assessment, Sturmey's (1996) account of some of the methods of behavioral approaches to case formulation, as well as recent work on the application of relational frame theory to a variety of clinical problems (Wilson et al., 2001), and in the recently burgeoning field of clinical behavior analysis, which has addressed behavioral approaches to sexual abuse, depression, anxiety, marital problems, alcohol, and marital conflict (Dougher, 1999.)

Alongside the tradition of behavioral approaches to case formulation has been an active line of research on cognitive-behavioral and cognitive approaches to case formulation (Bruch & Bond, 1998; Dryden, 1998; Nezu, Nezu & Lombardo, 2004; Persons, 1997; Persons & Tompkins, 2007; Tarrier, Wells & Haddock, 1998.) This approach to case formulation can be distinguished from behavioral approaches in a number of ways. Although many of these accounts include behavioral concepts and methods of intervention, their primary focus is on identifying and changing putative cognitions processes such as attributions, perception or schemata to change behavior. These approaches have been applied to a wide range of clinical problems, but most prominently in adult mental health including problems, such as depression, anxiety, psychosis, and hyperchondriasis. Alongside behavioral and cognitive approaches to case formulation other less active strands of activity are also apparent. These include integrative and eclectic approaches (Lane, 1997; Weeraskera, 1996), psychoanalytic (Henry et al., 1997; McWilliams, 1999) and psychiatric approaches (American Psychiatric Association, 1996). Eels (1997, 2007) edited volumes on case formulation from a wide range of theoretical perspectives provides an excellent survey of the differing approaches to case formulation.

DEFINITIONS OF CASE FORMULATION

Several authors have provided definitions of case formulation. Eells (1997) defined case formulation as "a hypothesis about the causes, precipitants, and maintaining influences of a person's psychological, interpersonal, and behavioral problems..." (p. 1). McWilliams (1999) defined psychoanalytic case formulation as "[a method] to suggest how a person's symptoms mental status, personality type, personal history, and current circumstances all fit together and made sense" (p. vii). Meyer and Turkat (1979), coming from a behavioral perspective, defined case formulation as "an hypothesis which (1) related all the client's complaints to one another, (2) explains why the individual developed these difficulties, and (3) provides predictions concerning the client's behavior given any stimulus conditions" (pp. 261–262.) Along the same lines, Wolpe and Turkat (1985) specified that a case formulation must include "1. all of the patient's problems, 2. the onset of each problems, 3. the development of each problem, and 4. the predisposing factors" (p. 8.) Coming from a cognitive-behavioral perspective, Persons (1997) wrote that " [t]he case formulation model conceptualizes psychological problems as occurring at two levels: the overt difficulties and the underlying psychological mechanisms. Overt difficulties are real life problems, such as depressed mood...Underlying psychological mechanisms are the psychological mechanisms...often expressed in terms of one (or a few) irrational beliefs about the self..." (p. 1). Later she wrote that "The case formulation is a hypothesis about the nature of the psychological difficulty (or difficulties) underlying the problems on the patient's problem list" (p. 37). Tarrier and Calem (2002) wrote that "Case formulation…involves the elicitation of appropriate information and the application and integration of a body of theoretical psychological knowledge to a specific clinical problem in order to understand the origins, development and maintenance of that problem. Its purpose is both to provide an accurate overview and explanation of the patients problems that is open to verification through hypothesis testing, and to arrive collaboratively with the patient at a useful understanding of their problem that is useful to them…"(pp. 311–312). This definition emphasizes the use of psychological concepts, the treatment utility and using a formulation with a client.

These definitions share a number of common elements. They all involve abstraction of information from large quantities of disorganized and specific client data. They involve some statement that condenses this information coherently. The case formulation usually attempts to link development, presenting symptoms and other currently available information together. They also imply that the formulation will guide treatment to develop an individually based treatment that will match the formulation. Eells, Kendjelic, and Lucas (1998, p. 144) suggested that the three common elements in different approaches to case formulation were:

1. They emphasize levels of inference that can be readily supported by a patient's statements in therapy.
2. The information they contain is based largely on clinical judgment rather than patient self-report.
3. The case formulation is compartmentalized into preset components that are addressed individually in the formulation process and then assembled into a comprehensive formulation.

COMMON FEATURES OF CASE FORMULATION

Definitions of case formulation differ significantly in a number of ways but share a number of common features. First, a case formulation condenses and organizes disparate information into some conceptually unified whole. Whether it is a 700 word narrative or a score on a checklist, the final formulation is much shorter than all the assessment information gathered. Second, the manner in which the assessment information is condensed is rational, rather than intuitive. There is some overarching set of psychological concepts that defines which variables may and may not enter into the formulation and their permissible relationships with each other. Third, a case formulation acts as a map to guide further assessment, if needed. More importantly yet, a case formulation should act as a guide to indicated and contra-indicated interventions. Most approaches advocate sharing the formulation with the client and perhaps actively incorporating it into treatment. All of the examples of case formulation concur that formulations are not set in stone but may be revised.

Approaches to case formulation do differ from each other significantly. The most notable area of differences related to the variables that are conceived as being legitimate ones to enter into the formulation and their status as causal or non-causal. Thus, behavioral formulations emphasize the current environment as the cause of presenting problems. Some approaches to behavioral case formulation de-emphasize history because of the impossibility of obtaining reliable data from the past. Other behavioral approaches (Salzinger, 1996) set great store on learning, such as Wolpe's searches for conditioning events. In contrast, psychoanalytic case formulations emphasize history as the cause of the presenting problems and downplay the current environment as causal. Likewise cognitive formulations emphasize underlying beliefs and cognitive structures as the cause of presenting problems. Cognitive approaches place less emphasis on social aspects of psychopathology (Tarrier & Calem, 2002). Behavioral case formulations would consider private events as behavior to be explained, but not the cause of behavior (Skinner, 1953, 1990). Different approaches to case formulation also tend to be associated with different methods of data collection. Thus, psychoanalytic formulations emphasize interview, therapist reaction to the client material and perhaps projective testing. Cognitive formulations emphasize assessment of beliefs, attributions and cognitive processes. Behavioral approaches emphasize objective data, such as observation of behavior, behavior avoidance tests and self-recording of behavior. A final difference is the emphasis placed on parsimony versus complexity in case formulation. Behavioral approaches explicitly value scientific approaches that reduce explanations to the most simple and smaller number of learning processes. Cognitive formulations value one kind of complexity: adding inferences concerning a client's underlying beliefs. Finally, some forms of psychoanalytic approaches to case formulation appeal to the greatest level of inference, minimizing or denying the possibility of objectivity and appealing explicitly to art, rather than science (McWilliams, 1999.)

Eells (1997) documented five tensions in case formulation that are reflected in these different approaches to case formulation. The first is immediacy versus comprehensiveness. Authors such as Wolpe, Turkat and Persons emphasized immediate formulation: when you receive a referral, when the client walks in the room, make a hypothesis. Some behavior analysts, noting the extensive amount of time to implement analog baselines, have developed protocols for assessing the functions of maladaptive behaviors that can be used within in single half-day appointment (Derby et al., 1994) or through telemedicine technology (Barretto, Wacker, Harding, Lee & Berg, 2006). Others, such as psychoanalytic formulations and to some extent, some forms of functional assessment (Hayes & O'Brien, 1990; O'Neill et al., 1997) emphasized the use of a comprehensive and systematic assessment protocol. To some extent, this may reflect the skill level of the clinician and the number and variety of different clinical problems that they have had to solve. Perhaps after effective training with multiple exemplars clinicians could acquire case generalized formulation skills.

Eells's second tension is complexity versus simplicity. As noted earlier, behavioral formulations seek out simplicity and abstraction, whereas other approaches embrace varying degrees of detail and complexity. Part of the tension between simplicity and complexity reflects whether or not explanations of human behavior can be reduced to a few simple and robust principles, or whether it is so complex that simplification does it an injustice. Complexity can take a number of different forms. For example, much of the case formulation literature notes that clinical cases apparently do not correspond to clinical trials. Individual clients present with multiple diagnoses, physical health, social and financial problems. Clinical trials neatly report treatment of a single diagnosis and only report measures of symptoms related to that diagnosis and perhaps some measure of global functioning. Yet, they do not report each individual's own complex set of problems, which may meet criteria for multiple or no diagnoses.

Another kind of complexity is the degree of complexity of explanation. Wolpe (1958) was happy to reduce the causes of clinical problems that often included multiple presenting problems to simple explanations, such as respondent conditioning. This approach has the virtue of simplifying the case formulation and link between formulation and treatment – identify the conditioning experiences and the reciprocal inhibition it implies will be simple to conceive. In contrast, Tarrier et al.'s (1998) *Treating Complex Cases* apparently addresses both complexity of presentation and complexity of explanation. For example, in this volume Wells (1998) presented a cognitive formulation and treatment of social anxiety. Wells evoked the complexity of identifying the social situations that provoke social anxiety (encountering a work colleague), identifying the negative automatic thoughts, such as "He'll think I am weird", processing oneself as a self-conscious person and by noting one's physical tension and flushing. This is then followed by safety behaviors, such as avoiding eye contact and somatic and cognitive symptoms, such as tachycardia. These processes are linked with each other by a variety of feedback loops.

What does all this cognitive complexity add to treatment utility? What would Wolpe say? I think Wolpe would have no problem in taking a history of social anxieties and identifying a number of conditioning events in which high levels of fear were paired with certain social situations. Subsequently, avoidance would be shaped by negative reinforcement by avoiding or removing discomfort. Treatment would be based on reciprocal inhibition using a hierarchy of progressively socially challenging situations representing a generalization gradient from least to most anxiety-provoking stimuli. Imaginal exposure using relaxation training followed by in vivo exposure using relaxation or perhaps assertiveness training as vehicles for reciprocal inhibition would then be used.

Wells's (1998) approach evoked complex cognitive explanations with multiple unobservable constructs and unobservable and undefined feedback loops. It implied complex cognitive and behavioral treatments. Wolpe's approach would evoke the simplicity of classical conditioning and negative reinforcement and a straightforward mapping of case formulation to a simple treatment. What is gained by Wells's complexity here?

Eells's third tension in case formulation is clinician bias versus objectivity. Noting the extensive research on clinician inaccuracy and judgment biases, Eells notes that such biases have long been acknowledged by a variety of clinical traditions. Here we may note that behavioral formulations are explicit in aiming toward the greatest degree of objectivity, through reliability of measurement, reliability of formulation, use of publicly available knowledge and discount clinician intuition. In contrast, some approaches to psychoanalytic case formulation are explicit in embracing of subjectivity and the art of therapy (McWilliams, 1999). Wilson (1996a, 1996b) raises another aspect of this question, by questioning whether clinicians have good enough clinical skills to accurately individualize formulations and treatment to be more effective than empirically established manualized treatments.

Eells's fourth tension overlaps with the third – observation versus inference. Again, behavioral formulations place greatest emphasis on direct observation of the client's behavior, not just in the office, but also in a variety of natural settings. As well as the client's behavior, behavioral case formulation emphasizes observation of the natural environment, both physical and social, and its relationship to the client's behavior. Inference does occur in behavioral formulations when multiple observations and other sources of data are combined into some statement about the target behavior(s) of interest, their relationship to the environment, and some abstraction as to the function of the target behavior and its implication for intervention. Nevertheless, the observer behavior is simply seen as a sample of behavior, but not as an index of anything else. In contrast psychoanalytic case formulation is highly inferential. Current behavior is only of interest because it is seen as determined by psychological history, because of its symbolic value, because its value as an example of recapitulation of previous patterns of relationships and unconscious motives that the therapist must uncover (Messer & Wolitzky, 1997).

The final tension that Eells outlines is that of individual versus general formulations. For example, behavioral formulations have been proposed of specific clinical problems, such as school refusal (Kearney & Silverman, 1990), anorexia (Slade, 1982), chronic pain (Lethem, Slade, Troup & Bentley, 1983; Slade, Troup, Lethem & Bentley, 1983), arson (Jackson, Glass & Hope, 1987) and more recently have been extended to address all the major DSM-IV diagnostic categories (Sturmey, 2007.) Yet behavioral formulations emphasize the analysis of the individual's behavior, not of a diagnostic category. General formulations of diagnostic categories may guide the clinician to seek certain information from a limited number of options. For example, school refusal might be motivated by positive reinforcement at home, avoidance of travel, social anxiety, academic demands, bullying by peers or punitive teachers (Kearney & Silverstein, 1990). Such a limited menu of options can be useful in guiding the clinician and simplifying the task of case formulation and treatment selection

PSYCHOANALYTIC CASE FORMULTAION

Perhaps the longest history of case formulation comes from psychoanalysis. Many of Freud's classic texts are elaborate formulations of individual cases. Eells's (1997, 2007) volumes on case formulation contains several examples of psychoanalytic case formulation including Luborsky's (1997) *Core Conflict Relational Theme* and Curtis and Silberschatz's (1997) *Plan Diagnosis Method*. Horowitz (1997) and McWilliams (1999) both dedicated entire volume to psychoanalytic case formulation.

Messer and Wolitzky (1997) stated that "[we] define psychoanalytic case formulation as a hierarchically organized set of clinical inferences about the nature of a patient's psychopathology, and, more generally, about his or her personality structure, dynamics and development" (p. 26). They go on to note the variety of schools of psychoanalytic psychotherapy, but stated that psychoanalytic case formulation has a number of common elements. They maintained that in a clinical formulation the clinician "creates a narrative structure...[which] is an attempt to provide a coherent, comprehensive, plausible and hopefully accurate account of the individual's personality development and current functioning that is based on the life history of a particular patient..." (pp. 32–33.) Thus, psychoanalytic case formulation emphasizes history leading to the presenting problem and personality.

Messer and Wolitzky noted that psychoanalytic case formulation does not follow a typical format. Rather, it usually presented a continuous narrative of 500–700 words based on the psychoanalytic interview. In their format, the psychoanalytic case formulation includes a summary of the structure of the person's personality, such as ego functions, defenses, the client's central conflict and its developmental antecedents, as well as the client's assets and strengths. This formulation is used to identify treatment goals, such as accepting mixed feelings. The formulation may be shared in various ways with the client in a jargon-free way.

McWilliams (1999) was more obtuse about the elements of a psychoanalytic case formulation. She noted that a formulation should include information on personality structure, stressors accounting for the client presenting at this time, unique vulnerabilities, and that it should be used to increase the likelihood that psychotherapy would be helpful. She also noted that this formulation is used to derive recommendations about how to interact with the client based on this formulation. However, in emphasizing the subjective art of psychotherapy, its complexity, and the apparent limitations of objective methods of case formulation she avoided prescription of specific elements in case formulation.

Others working in the psychoanalytic framework have been more prescriptive in the elements that go up to make a psychoanalytic case formulation and in the methods used to develop such as case formulation. For example, Luborsky (1997) developed the *Core Conflict Relationship Theme* as a method to score interviews to identify recurring themes within relationships and to identify the main conflict. Levenson and Strupp (1997) developed a series of steps that go to make a case formulation in time limited dynamic psychotherapy as well as the *Cyclical Maladaptive Pattern* to identify recurrent problems with relationships. Horowitz (1997) also provided more systematic guidelines as how to structure psychotherapeutic case formulation. These included using a grid of content area and time focus. For example, content areas included external orientations such as symptoms, recent stressful life events and internal orientation such as conflicted topics and defensive controls and identity and relationships. Time focus included four domains including the current situation, the therapy situation, past developmental and future planning issues. This four by two by three grid resulted in 24 possible cells representing issues that a formulation could address. Thus, there are both relatively unstructured and fairly structured approaches to psychoanalytic case formulation.

A Psychoanalytic Case Formulation of Obesity

McWilliams (1999), contrasting psychodynamic approaches to case for-mulation with traditional DSM-IV diagnosis, noted that psychoanalytic case formulation is based on hunches, subjectivity and the search for the meaning of behavior. She described case formulation as an art that is not formulaic. Noting the possibility of multiple causality of human behavior, she rejected parsimony as a principle for evaluating case formulations.

McWilliams presented a formulation of a woman who was obese. McWilliams noted that the client was aware that:

- she had a genetic predisposition to obesity
- her mother has been over-concerned about her eating and put her on a rigid feeding schedule, but acted hurt if she did not eat all her food
- she had a family history of using food to reduce anxiety and shame
- she identified with her obese grandmother
- she had a history of child abuse leading her to deliberately appear unattractive

- she reduced negative mood by eating alone
- her self-esteem was related to intelligence rather than appearance
- she had a concern that if she lost weight she might die like her father, who had died of cancer.

McWilliams stated that the task of psychodynamic psychotherapy is to identify the historical causation of the client's problems and to change behavior. The aims of psychoanalytic therapy was not merely to remove symptoms, but also "the development of insight, agency, identity, self-esteem, affect management, ego strength and self-cohesion, a capacity to love, work and play, and an overall sense of well-being" (p. 28). McWilliams described this as "transforming suffering into mastery" (p. 27).

According to McWilliams, her formulation of the case had the following implications for therapy:

- her client had to modify her pattern of mealtime behavior
- early in development she had learned to eat everything available immediately in case food was removed
- she also had to learn ways of managing anxiety other than through eating, for example, by taking a hot bath, etc.
- she also had to "[grieve] over the many unfortunate aspects of her life"
- the client also felt that if she remained obese she would retain her grandmother's positive qualities and that if she lost weight she would have her mother's negative qualities
- McWilliams noted that her client was in a post traumatic state in which she saw others as potential molesters
- she also noted that her client should also be able to enjoy a normal degree of vanity
- finally, she commented that her client became panicky when she lost weight and believed she might die like her father (pp. 26–27.)

Comment

McWilliams's psychoanalytic case formulation is explicitly unscientific, if not anti-scientific. It rejects rationality in favor of intuition, and rejects mechanism over mystery. McWilliams presents the method of developing a case formulation as intuition-based. Her approach relies extensively on inferring historical events that are the underlying cause of the presenting problem, begging many empirical questions. For example, if we look at the above case study it is unclear how the client and therapist discovered that her meal pattern as an infant or child truly was as described. Likewise, how they discovered the causal link between the alleged history and the presenting symptoms were established is unclear. Does it matter that a case formulation be based on true, established facts? For some, this is not an issue.

Some parts of McWilliams's formulation seem more like goals than explanations that lead to intervention. For example, it seems likely that the client knew before therapy that "she needed to replace eating with other means of handling anxiety" (p. 27). Yet, the formulation presented this as a new discovery. It did not specify how this new way to avoid anxiety is to take place and how it is related to the client's current or historical problems. The formulation also posits something referred to as a "post traumatic mental state" (p. 28). Does this refer to DSM IV's post traumatic stress disorder? Nothing about the description of the client indicates what this "post traumatic mental state" was. Its meaning is unclear. Further, such language reifies a problem, uses language that tells the client it's a very serious and horrible problem, while simultaneously neither truly describing the problem nor identifying what can be done to help the client.

Psychoanalytic case formulation is weak. The basis for the formulations is explicitly speculative, intuitive and depends on divining the distant history of events that can neither be confirmed nor linked to current problems in any satisfactory way. The availability of other more simple, economical and efficient forms of therapy with strong empirical bases documenting their effectiveness, challenge psychoanalytic case formulation to demonstrate if it has any place in current therapeutic practice.

PSYCHIATRIC CASE FORMULATION

Like other approaches to case formulation, psychiatric case formulation emphasizes the rational collection and organization of material and its use in directing treatment. The American Psychiatric Association (APA, 1996) described case formulation as

> information specific to the individual patient that goes beyond what is conveyed in the diagnosis. The scope and depth of the formulation vary with the purpose of the evaluation. Elements commonly include psychosocial and developmental factors that may have contributed to the present illness; the patient's particular strengths and weaknesses; social resources and the ability to form and maintain relationships; issues related to culture, ethnicity, gender, sexual orientation, and religious/spiritual beliefs; likely precipitating or aggravating factors of the illness; and preferences, opinions and biases of the patient relevant to the choice of a treatment ... additional elements may be based on a specific model of psychopathology and treatment, e.g., psychodynamic or behavioral. The diagnosis and case formulation together facilitate the development of a treatment plan.

Thus, this psychiatric approach to case formulation emphasizes the comprehensive listing and integration of all potentially relevant information that should guide treatment. Winters, Hanson and Stoyanova (2007) described this process in the context of child and adolescent psychiatry using a grid of biologic, psychological, social and social-environmental factors, each with predisposing, precipitating, perpetuating and protective aspects.

Perhaps the most sophisticated approach to psychiatric case formulation comes from Eells et al. (1998). They reported on the development and evaluation of a case formulation content coding method (CFCCM) to evaluate psychiatric case formulations. This method attempted to be theory neutral in that it could code formulations from a variety of theoretical perspectives. Their measures illustrate what constitutes a psychiatric case formulation. They coded four content areas of case formulations: (1) symptoms and problems; (2) precipitating stressors or events; (3) predisposing life events or stressors; and (4) a mechanism that links the preceding categories together and offers an explanation of the precipitants and maintaining influences of the individual's problems (p. 144). They coded each of the four dimensions on a three-point scale as 'absent', 'somewhat present' or 'clearly present'. The CFCCM also codes positive treatment indicators, such as personal strengths and adaptive skills, and negative treatment indicators. The CFCCM also includes three codes for quality. These include five-point rating scales for the complexity, degree of inference and precision of language used. Complex case formulations included several aspects of the person's life that were integrated into a meaningful account. Degree of inference refers to the extent to which the formulation goes beyond the immediate facts that the client provides and refers to more hypothetical and "deep structure" aspects of the case formulation. Formulations with a high degree of precision of language were those that referred to the specific individual, rather than a generic formulation.

A Psychiatric Case Formulation

Nelson and Hastie (2005) presented a psychiatric case formulation of an 11-year-old boy diagnosed with ADHD, mood disorder Not Otherwise Specified and a history of possible brain damage at birth due to oxygen insufficiency. Presenting problems include slight social delays, some academic problems, including a great deal of coaxing to complete homework assignments resulting in temper tantrums, kicking and screaming, poor hygiene skills. His mother reported attempting to use punishment methods such as loss of video games, but without success.

Using their case conceptualization grid they assessed all 10 domains. For example, they noted an IQ of 81 and possible organic basis, perhaps frontal lobe damage, to cognitive and motor delays. They noted strengths, including a loving but highly stressed mother, good health and lack of substance use. Using this case formulation they suggested the need for parenting skills, social skills training, perhaps in a group, building on strengths such as good community interface, cognitive behavioral treatment, medication for depression, and relational treatment for social and emotional delays.

Comment

These psychiatric approaches emphasize the collection of comprehensive information in many domains and the need for comprehensive and individualized treatment based on that case formulation. Psychiatric case formulations usually contrast case formulation with diagnosis, often in terms of emphasizing the individuality of each client's presentation and the limitations to psychiatric diagnosis.

Psychiatric case formulation has several important weaknesses. Although it emphasized the importance of a comprehensive assessment, it does not present a rationale for why this is important or how this influences treatment design. This approach seems to give indiscriminate and equal weight to all information without considering which information is important in determining treatment and which is not. A related problem is that although this approach requires the clinician to collect information from different domains and integrate the information, it does not define what "integration" is. Presumably listing information from all the required domains is not integration, but what the clinician must do to produce an integration of this information is unclear. For example, Eells et al. (1998) used five-point ratings of quality of case formulation which appear to be quite reliable. However, they did not operationally define "quality", rather they described it in general terms. Thus, even this reliable approach to measuring the quality of psychiatric case formulations did not define high and low quality formulation. As might be expected, the APA's guidelines on case formulation explicitly endorse a medical model by referring to the "patients", "illness" and the role of diagnosis in formulating a treatment plan. Such a position perhaps reflects the ambiguity that an essentially structuralist-medical approach has to take in simultaneously implicitly defending diagnosis as the basis for treatment and also attempting to individualize treatment through case formulation without making explicit how this should occur.

If we revisit Nelson and Hastie's case formulation these strengths and weakness become apparent. On the one hand the interventions suggested are indeed tailored to the specific problems and situations that the adolescent presents. However, what is lacking is a theoretical framework to organize the case formulation, its assessment and implications for treatment. Thus, all 10 domains are assessed and where any one of them might have an implication for treatment, that plan is added to the list of treatments. The formulation does not question whether or not the diagnoses of ADHD, depression and brain damage are valid or related to the presenting problems. For example, it is unclear how diagnoses could explain why tantrums occurred at home, but not at school. Further, because the formulation is not conceptually driven, many of the recommendations are somewhat non-specific. For example, they correctly identify that the problems that occur at home imply the possible usefulness of parent training. However, without a conceptual framework the nature of the parent training needed is unclear. Finally, because there is no overarching conceptual framework, the resulting treatment plan is a list of treatments – medication, parent training, education and social skills training – that are not conceptually linked into some coherent whole.

COGNITIVE APPROACHES TO CASE FORMULATION

Since the late 1970s cognitive and cognitive behavior therapies have been developed for a wide variety of problems and they have an extensive evidence base for many common applications (Fonagy, Target, Cottrell, Phillips & Kurtz, 2002; Roth & Fonagy, 2004). Thus, there has been considerable activity and interest in cognitive approaches to case formulation since the 1980s (Bruch & Bond, 1998; Persons, 1997; Persons & Tompkins, 2007; Tarrier et al., 1998).

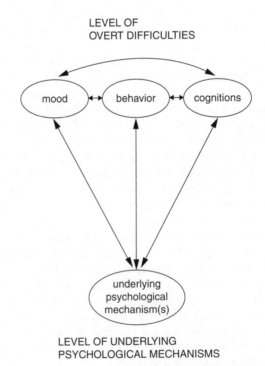

Figure 8.1. Person's two-level model of psychological problems. J. B. Persons (1989). Cognitive therapy in practice. *A case formulation approach.* New York: Norton, p. 5.

Persons (1989) gave a detailed prescriptive and very practical protocol to conduct cognitive case formulation. In her approach, the presenting problem (generalized anxiety) is reflected in cognitions ("I'm trapped"), behaviors (palpitations) and mood (anxiety). Mood, behavior and cognitions are all reflective of some underlying psychological mechanism. For example, they may reflect a dysfunctional belief, such as "unless I am perfection in everything I do, I'll fail" (p. 1). Figure 8.1 illustrates this approach. Persons's approach to cognitive case formulation has six parts. First, the therapist and client generate a problem list. Second, the therapist identifies an underlying cognitive mechanism for each individual client. Third, the therapist proposes the way in which this cognitive mechanism causes the presenting symptoms. Fourth, the therapist identifies the precipitants of the current problems. Fifth, the therapist describes the origins of these mechanisms in the client's personal history. Finally, the therapist identifies the obstacles to treatment based on this formulation (p. 48). Figure 8.2 shows how Persons used this formulation to contrast the client's old plan for life with the new treatment

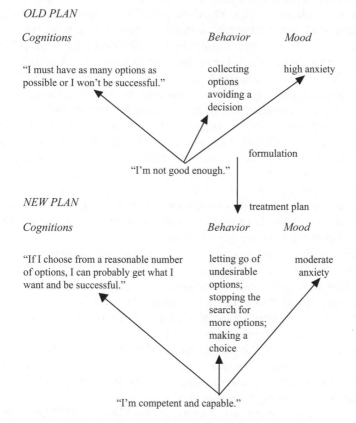

Figure 8.2. Persons's old plan/new plan intervention. J. B. Persons (1989). *Cognitive therapy in practice. A case formulation approach.* New York: Norton. p. 69.

plan based on developing a replacement core belief. Thus, in this model the formulation is not only a tool for the clinician to use to conceptualize the case. It is also an intervention method to explain the conceptualization of the presenting problems to the client and to use as a tool to guide intervention. Persons and Tompkins (1997) also provided an example of this approach to cognitive case formulation.

A Cognitive Case Formulation

Cognitive therapy has been applied to an ever-expanding set of problems. Recent randomized controlled trials of cognitive therapy for psychoses (Tarrier & Wykes, 2004) have caused considerable excitement, since they challenge traditional assumptions that psychoses are illnesses to be treated with medication. Thus, it is appropriate that we should illustrate cognitive approaches to case formulation with an example of its application to schizophrenia.

Morrison (1998) reviewed the literature on cognitive approaches to psychoses and reported a case formulation of auditory hallucinations in a man with schizophrenia. Morrison noted that cognitive approaches to case formulation are based on a good therapeutic relationship which is necessary for change and a collaborative working relationship between therapist and client, which is problem- and symptom-oriented. Cognitive approaches are also structured, time-limited and directive, since they use an educational model that involves the therapist guiding discovery by the client. For psychotic disorders, sessions may be shorter and be spaced out over longer periods of time because of the greater severity of disability of many people with psychoses compared with anxiety and mood disorders. Individual cognitive therapy sessions for psychotic disorders are structured. They include a review of previous work, elicit feedback concerning the last session in part to check for comprehension and agreeing a short, manageable agenda. The session concludes with setting homework assignments, feedback about the current session and a written summary of the session for the client to take away.

Morrison illustrated this approach by a case formulation of a man with a psychotic disorder. Mr B had been hearing two voices for the past year. The voices were persecutory and abusive to him. For example, the voices would threaten to attack him with a beer glass. Mr B believed the voices to be those of real people. He engaged in various avoidant behaviors, such as not going outside. He also engaged in a variety of so-called "safety behaviors", such as checking the attic and under the floorboards in order to find the two people. He was also very fearful, had panic attacks, was vigilant and drank to reduce anxiety. He also had another disturbing belief that he was "loosing his marbles".

The case formulation is summarized in Figure 8.3. Prior to hearing the voices, Mr B was hyper-vigilant and preoccupied with the voices.

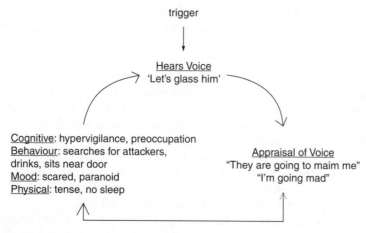

trigger

Hears Voice
'Let's glass him'

Cognitive: hypervigilance, preoccupation
Behaviour: searches for attackers,
drinks, sits near door
Mood: scared, paranoid
Physical: tense, no sleep

Appraisal of Voice
"They are going to maim me"
"I'm going mad"

Figure 8.3. Morrison's cognitive-behavioral formulation of psychosis (Tarrier et al., 1998, Figure 9.4, p. 209). A. P. Morrison (1998). Cognitive behavior therapy for psychotic symptoms in schizophrenia. In: N. Tarrier, A. Wells & G. Haddock (Eds.) *Treating complex cases*. The cognitive behavioral therapy approach (pp. 195–216). Chichester, UK: Wiley UK.

His behavior included searching for attackers and sitting near the door where he could escape. His mood was scared and paranoid. Physically he was tense and sleep deprived. The disturbing experience was hearing one of the voices saying "Let's glass him". His appraisal of the voice was that he was about to be maimed and that he was going mad.

Like other approaches to case formulation, one of its key functions is to guide the development of treatment for each individual. This cognitive case formulation does exactly that. The formulation identified two key inappropriate beliefs: (1) that there are real persecutors; and (2) that Mr B is truly going mad. Using classic methods of cognitive therapy, Morrison identified the evidence for and against each belief. For example, the evidence that the voices were real included that (1) the voices sounded real; and (2) the content indicated they were real voices. Mr B reported believing this with 90% confidence at first. The evidence against the belief included (1) observations such as his family could not hear the voices; and (2) that they had not actually harmed him in the past, etc. After reviewing this evidence, Mr B now reported believing this with only 50% confidence. The therapist and client also generated additional beliefs. For example, that the voices were due to stress, a result of a road traffic accident that he had been in or due to medication side effects. In considering the evidence in favor of medication side effects Mr B noted that (1) he had begun medications at the same time as the voices began; and (2) medication do indeed make people hallucinate. Counter-evidence included that many people who take medications do not hallucinate. Initially he reported believing this with 0% confidence and after consideration of the evidence for and against the belief he reported believing it with 10% confidence. Cognitive therapy took place during therapy sessions and included homework assignments and diaries of beliefs and behavior.

Morrison also included behavioral experiments to test the veracity of the beliefs. For example, the most distressing belief was that the voices were real people who were about to come and harm him. This belief was supported by his various checking strategies, which appeared to be effective in preventing harm occurring. Hence, Morrison developed a test of these beliefs. The test included staying at home and not engaging in any safety behaviors to test if the people would actually come and harm him. The cognitive explanation for the efficacy of such behavioral experiments is that they generate evidence that contradicts the belief.

A final component of Morrison's approach was a so-called "blueprint". The blueprint is a written summary of the formulation including the disturbing symptoms, their development and maintenance, strategies for intervention, including cognitive therapy and behavioral experiments and summaries of the evidence for and against each core belief. Morrison stated that the client themselves should be encouraged to write as much of the blueprint as possible during homework assignments.

Comment

Cognitive formulations and cognitive therapy have a number of distinct strengths. Perhaps the greatest and most obvious is the extensive evidence for the effectiveness of cognitive and cognitive behavior therapy for a wide range of disorders (Fonagy et al., 2002; Roth & Fonagy, 2004), including in this example multiple randomized controlled trials of cognitive therapy for psychosis (Tarrier & Wykes, 2004). Cognitive therapy may sometimes make inferences concerning the client's history and how the schemas that they currently possess developed. Yet, therapy is focused on the here and now, on current private verbal behavior, such as attributions and cognitive processes, and on changing current problematic symptoms and other behavior in a focused and time-limited fashion. Another important virtue of cognitive therapy is that it is structured and technological. Cognitive therapy can be readily specified, task analyzed and potentially observed. This makes it relatively easy to teach to therapists and relatively easy for therapists to self-monitor their own behavior. Similar virtues accrue to the client, especially clients such as Mr B, who's cognitive and motivation limitations might make it difficult for him to engage in therapy requiring complex verbal or social skills, such as those in psychotherapy or group therapy. The adoption of a collaborative, educational relationship requires the client to change the way they talk and the way they behave during and between therapy sessions when they begin to observe and record their own behavior and environment. This also seems to be an important practical way of beginning to address client behavior change. Such initial behavior change might be an important start to induce other more significant behavior change that might be difficult if the preliminary behavior change had not already begun in early sessions (Skinner, 1953).

Cognitive approaches are clearly concerned with behavior change. They are explicit in their concern for changing problematic behavior in the current environment as well as increasing desirable behavior. They are also concerned with the relationship between the current environment and behavior. Witness, for example, that Morrison noted the relationship between certain settings and behavior, such as the pub and experiencing auditory hallucinations, and the use of behavioral experiments to change behavior. All of these are important virtues that may well account for the positive behavior change that occurred.

Cognitive therapy's explanation for the observed client behavior change is, of course, in terms of changes in the underlying cognitive structures that are said to cause behavior. Hence, Morrison might have concluded that Mr B's behavior changed because cognitive therapy and behavioral experiments caused a change in his attributions concerning the delusional voices. The radical behaviorist would note the limitations of such explanations, such as their circularity, the unnecessary elevation of private behavior as the cause of the observed change of public behavior and their dependence on client self-report as a measure of outcome.

However, cognitive therapy often does result in behavior change. The radical behaviorist should ask what learning processes there might be that could explain Mr B's behavior change during cognitive therapy. One key feature of Mr B's treatment is the similarity of the behavioral experiment to respondent extinction. (See Chapter 4 for a more extensive discussion of respondent extinction and therapy.) The experiment required Mr B to remain in a situation that in the past had often evoked disturbing, fearful private behavior, such as thinking he was about to be harmed or go mad. The hallucinations and associated stimuli, such as remaining in the house, may be considered to be conditioned stimuli that evoke conditioned responses called fearfulness and hyper-vigilance. His safety behavior appears to be operant behavior. These safety behaviors were negatively reinforced by termination of the aversive stimuli of telling himself he is about to harmed or go mad and reduction in fear. Hence, Morrison's treatment of requiring Mr B to remain in the house without engaging in safety behavior could readily be construed as form of exposure and response prevention, similar to that used in clients with obsessive compulsive disorder.

Verbal behavior during therapy may also have resulted in symptom relief. During cognitive therapy sessions Mr B was exposed to verbal stimuli, such as his own words and the therapist's word about the fear of going mad, that evoked anxiety. Therapy sessions involved repeated exposure to these stimuli that formerly had been avoided or minimized, for example through drinking. The therapist's encouragement may also have differentially reinforced client verbal behavior. Cognitive therapy involved several techniques with potential learning processes embedded within them. For example, identifying alternate attributions for hallucinations involved prompting and shaping client non-psychotic, public and perhaps private verbal behavior. When the client reported no change in the strength of a belief, two kinds of punishment contingencies may have followed. First, it is possible that various forms of subtle therapist verbal and non-verbal disapproval may occur contingent on client verbal behavior reporting of lack of progress. Second, a response cost procedure may be inadvertently invoked when the therapist requires the client to engage in a mildly effortful, difficult task of reconsidering the evidence and generating alternate explanations for his inappropriate attributions. On the other hand, if the client emits a verbal response indicating progress, the therapist removes this mildly aversive consequence. Hence, this aspect of cognitive therapy involves shaping client non-psychotic verbal behavior which is similar to the verbal behavior prior to psychosis and to typical non-psychotic people.

INTEGRATIONIST APPROACHES TO CASE FORMULTAION

There is a long tradition of aversion to proclaiming allegiance to any particular school of psychotherapy. Adherents' critics usually note the apparent rigidity of explanations, the technical inflexibility, and the apparently reasonable benefits of taking the best from all approaches. At least two kinds of integration or eclecticism can be distinguished. A technical eclecticism uses techniques traditionally associated with different schools of therapy. For example, some therapists freely use psychodynamic, cognitive, behavioral and other interventions, depending on the perceived client needs, practical limitations, the therapist's skills and so on. Such technical eclectics may use a single theory to explain and conceptualize the case. Other eclectics attempt to integrate explanations from different schools of psychotherapy into some overarching set of concepts. For example, Prochaska and Norcross (2002) maintained that all schools of therapy include common concepts and processes, such as hope, insight and catharsis. Hence, according to this view, catharsis is the common process in therapy that accounts for recovery of traumatic material in psychoanalytic psychotherapy, implosion and flooding. Prochaska and Norcross (2002) maintained that all schools of therapy can be unified by these overarching concepts.

Recently, Ingram (2006) presented a volume designed to teach integrated case formulation. This volume presented formulation from biological, learning, cognitive, existential and spiritual, psychodynamic perspectives. Ingram used each of these perspectives to generate 28 core clinical hypotheses which are linked to possible treatment plans.

For example, if there is a biological cause then medical treatment should be sought and psychosocial help for dealing with disability and illness. Ingram also proposed 33 standards as to what constitutes an adequate case formulation. For example, case formulations should comprehensively specify problems, include quotations from the client, uses only the useful hypotheses and include a plan that is focused on client outcomes, follows logically from the assessment and is tailor-made for the specific client.

There are numerous approaches to integrating material from different schools of psychology (Horowitz, 1997). In the remainder of this section we will consider just two examples, but examples that are quite different. In Weerasekera's (1996) approach, concepts are taken from many different approaches and considered one after another in parallel. Finally, they are integrated. In Ryle's (1982) integrationist approach, concepts from psychoanalysis and cognitive psychotherapy are integrated into a new approach to psychotherapy known as cognitive analytic psychotherapy (CAT).

Weerasekera's Multi-perspective Approach

Weerasekera (1996) proposed a format for multi-perspective case formulation. Weerasekera developed this format to train psychiatric residents in Canada. This approach attempted to integrate biological, behavioral, cognitive, psychodynamic, couples, family, occupational and social formulations of a case. The therapist identifies precipitating, perpetuating and protective factors for each of these eight aspects of a case. This results in an eight-by-four grid to structure assessment and guide treatment.

Weerasekera used this grid to formulate the problems presented by an 18-year-old adolescent, Susan. Susan presented with repeated vomiting, panic disorder and agoraphobia. Figure 8.4 illustrates how Weerasekera used this grid. Weerasekera's method was in two parts. First, formulations are presented from each perspective corresponding to each column of Figure 8.4. Then, a final integrated case formulation is drawn up.

Weerasekera presents fully eight, non-integrated formulations of this case. These are followed by one final, integrated formulation. For example, from a psychodynamic perspective vomiting is a symptom of her guilt over her affair with a married man. Vomiting represents an attempt to purge herself of repressed material and disgust. The fact Susan rejects such an interpretation is evidence of repression of the guilt. Her attachment to a bad object, such as a married man, is evidence of an unresolved oedipal complex, recapitulating her childhood relationship with an unavailable father whom she longed for but could not obtain, etc. The biological formulation noted that Susan may have various genetic

	INDIVIDUAL FACTORS				SYSTEMIC FACTORS			
	BIOLOGICAL	BEHAVIORAL	COGNITIVE	PSYCHO-DYNAMIC	COUPLE	FAMILY	OCCUPATIONAL/SCHOOL	SOCIAL
PREDISPOSING	• Fam history - anxiety - agoraphobia - gastrointestinal vulnerability	• Classical conditioning married man (CS) → anxiety vomiting • poor*R history	• EMS - worthlessness - autonomy • NAT - failure	• arrest in oedipal stage • attchm't to bad objects • ↑ mirror/ideal fun'c • insecure attachment	• relationship with father • difficulties with intimacy	• dysf'nc structure • poor affective communication • triangulation • intergenerational family dysf'nc	• underachiever in school • poor occupational hx • no career aspiration • poor family modeling	• poor social hx • shyness • poor social support
PRECIPITATING		• loss of *R - rel'ship • generalization of CR to "out of house"	• affair/loss of → activate EMS → ↑ NAT	• affair/loss of → guilt/unresolved issues → anxiety/vomiting • time to individuate	• ? ↑ demands for intimacy (sexual) in current rel'ship	• impending separation from family → leaving mother alone	• need to develop career plans	• loss of rel'ship • loss of friends after "affair"
PERPETUATING		• *R of avoidance via ↑ anxiety • *R of vomiting via ↑ attention	• NAT → EMS self-perpetuating → ↓ challenging environment → ↑ NAT	• repression/suppression • poor self-objects • attachment to bad objects	• collusive projective identification interaction • ongoing ambivalence re: relationship	• chronic dysf'nc system • triangulation • parental marital discord	• *R of illness behavior at work • no work demands	• avoidance of social situations
PROTECTIVE	• good health	• work → avoidance	• perceives self as attractive	• ? current object choice (boyfriend)	• Supportive rel'ship	• good instrumental functioning	• good relationship with employer	• attractive • good verbal skills
COPING-RESPONSE STYLE	• somatizer • anti-meds	• action-oriented • "do-er"	• not reflective • not introspective	• not reflective • not introspective • no insight	• Rel'ship gives some support	• support from mother for "vomiting" → not a familial coper	• not an occupational coper	• not a social-support seeker
TREATMENT	• anti-dep • anti-anx ↓ but • anti-med	• Relaxation/systematic desensitization • exposure	?	• currently unavailable → not initial approach	• Not as initial approach → ? later	• unavailable for intervention (? Reassess)	• vocational counseling	• social skills • exposure ↑ support

* R = reinforcement; P = punishment; ↑ = increase; ↓ = decrease; tx = therapy; hx = history; NAT = negative automatic thoughts; beh = behavior; EMS = early maladaptive schemas; dysf'nc = dysfunction; rel'ship = relationship; CR = conditioned response mirror; ideal = idealizing; fun'c = functions; attachm't = attachment; CS = condition stimulus

Figure 8.4. Weerasekera's grid to organize eclectic case formulations. P. Weerasekera (1996). *Multiperspective case formulation. A step toward treatment integration.* Malabar, Florida: Krieger Publishing Company, pp. 276–277.

vulnerabilities to these disorders. For example, both her mother and herself have panic attacks. Her gastrointestinal symptoms may also be due to a genetic vulnerability to expressing emotional problems in this way. Her good physical health would be a biological protecting factor. The integrated formulation consists of taking elements from all eight formulations. For example, when presenting the integrated formulation of her history Weerasekera noted that her biological vulnerability to anxiety lead to its expression at an early age. Further, her anxious mother and distant father put her at risk for separation anxiety. She was unable to internalize a sufficiently good object leading to a negative self-view and an early negative schema that she was unworthy and unable to function independently (p. 282.)

Susan's treatment was also multi-modal. Initially, behavior therapy was used because she opposed taking medications, did not want family involvement in her therapy but wanted to take action to resolve her symptoms. She learned relaxation exercises and undertook exposure to anxiety provoking situations. She also kept a diary of her behavior, anxiety level, and thoughts and feelings. After three months her vomiting decreased from three times per day to 2–3 times per week. At this point, Weerasekera noted that Susan's vomiting was related to anxiety. This was apparently related to the ambivalence of her sexual feelings to her boyfriend. At this Weerasekera used both behavior therapy, along with psychodynamic work to explore her feelings of guilt related to attraction to men. Over a total of three years of therapy, Weerasekera dealt with a variety of other issues mostly by greater emphasis on psychodynamic therapy and with less emphasis on behavior therapy. Later in therapy, they addressed occupations and vocations as therapy was terminated and Susan began to consider leaving her family home. At the end of therapy she was virtually symptom free. Susan enjoyed a sexual relationship with her boyfriend. She also engaged in a number of mature, independent adult roles, such as going to a night course and going out with friends.

Comment

Weerasekera's approach attempted to be both conceptually and technically eclectic. It borrowed explicitly and freely from multiple theoretical perspectives. It made multiple formulations and then attempted to integrate them into one overarching, integrated case formulation. The grid was completed and was used to integrate the formulation case and guide treatment, which consisted of various treatment options derived from the grid. Hence, it was eclectic in the technical sense of using treatments from multiple approaches. Such an approach might be quite useful as a teaching tool to assist novice clinicians write multiple formulations from several perspectives of the same case.

Cognitive Analytic Case Formulations

CAT originated with Ryle's dissatisfaction with classic dynamic psychotherapy, use of Kelly's repertory grids, and patterns observed in psychotherapy referred to as "dilemmas", "traps" and "snags". Dilemmas are situations in which a client's options are narrowed down to two polarized opposites, such as either caretaking or being dependent. Traps are circular negative patterns of behavior that confirm the client's negative self-perception, such as someone worthless avoiding challenging affirming experiences and concluding that they are worthless. Snags are self-defeating actions that avoid negative evaluation from others.

Ryle observed that clients appeared to benefit from participating in the development of their case formulation. Hence, one of the key features of CAT is development of a reformulation of the clients' problem in these terms. This written case formulation is finalized by the fifth therapy session. The therapist and client then use it to understand the client's behavior and suggest ways to change their behavior, for example, by monitoring repetitive negative patterns of behavior. Diagrams summarize recurrent patterns of interaction with others. These diagrams summarize shifting between opposing states, such as polar opposite ideal and pathological states. The current patterns of interaction with others are presumed to originate in infant patterns of interaction with caregivers.

A CAT Case Formulation of Depression and Anger

Ryle and Bennett (1997) presented a CAT case formulation of a 32-year-old man with anger, depression, a history of drug overdosing and personality disorder. Using information from self-monitoring and unstructured therapy sessions, the therapist wrote a letter reformulating Nick's problems and summarizing them in a diagram summarizing repeated patterns of interaction (see Figure 8.5). The formulation identified two states, one in which Nick was in an idealized closeness state of "cloud cuckoo land" and the polar opposite state of abusive contemptuousness. One example of a recurrent a pattern of interaction began with avoiding feeling abused and angry, striving to please others, being taken advantage of by others and then returning to the state of abusive contemptuousness. Hence, one point of intervention included identifying examples of the early steps of this loop and taking other action to avoid the negative outcome involved in that loop.

Comment

CAT is indeed eclectic. It borrows ideas freely from psychoanalysis and Russian psychologists, such as Vygotsky and repertory grids. It also uses behavioral methodologies, such as self-monitoring, identifying behavioral chains, changing behavior early in response chains and so on. Ryle shares

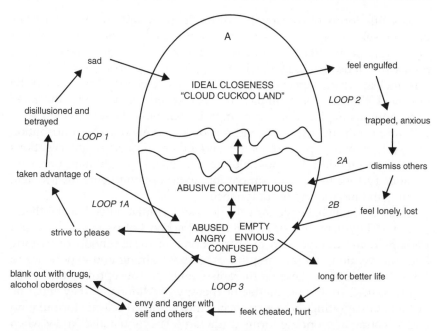

Figure 8.5. Ryle O's (1995) diagram summarizing a cognitive analytic case formulation (From A. Ryle (1995). Transference and counter transference variations in the course of the CAT of two borderline patients: Relation to the diagrammatic reformulation of self states. *British Journal of Medical Psychology*, **68**, 109–124).

with Skinner the emphasis on involving the client in developing their own formulation early on, rather than having the therapist deliver the formulation to the client.

Issues for Integrationist Approaches to Case Formulation

Eclectic case formulations have a number of appealing features. They involve looking at a client's problem from multiple perspectives and leave the door open to as many forms of intervention as therapist and client see fit. Much of this has face validity and may be appealing to some therapists. Flexibility in selection of therapy methods may also have benefits for some clients if the intervention methods associated with the therapist's theoretical orientation are ineffective for that particular client.

Despite these strengths, eclectic case formulation has many challenges. Unlike cognitive and behavioral approaches to therapy the empirical support for integrated approaches is very weak. For example, Prochaska and Norcross (2002) – advocates of eclectic approaches to psychotherapy – noted that there is little evidence that such approaches are effective beyond nonspecific forms of therapy. For example, there are no empirical trials of Weerasekera's approach yet and the evidence base for CAT consists of only a few case studies and one RCT for diabetes (Fosbury, Bosley, Ryle, Sonksen & Judd, 1997). Even when eclectic case approaches are effective it is unclear which aspect of the treatment package may have caused the observed change. For example, in Weerasekera's case study, the most parsimonious explanation for change is that bulimia was treated with relaxation training, exposure and response prevention. The contribution of psychodynamic psychotherapy and other subsequent interventions were, if any, modest. It is possible that this change might have occurred without further therapy or simple follow-up appointments for problem solving and monitoring of compliance.

An additional challenge for eclectic case formulation is that the therapist must be fluent and skilled in several schools of psychotherapy and perhaps many intervention methods. Some of these schools of therapy and intervention methods require extensive training and experience to achieve competence. Eclectic therapists must be conceptually and practically skilled in several modes of therapy. Additionally, they must be skilled at integrating these approaches into a unified eclectic formulation and selecting appropriate forms of therapy. They must also know when and how to switch from one form of therapy to another. Thus, such eclectic approaches may be difficult to teach and it may be difficult for therapists to monitor their own performance.

SUMMARY

The status of nonbehavioral approaches to case formulation is quite varied. Psychoanalytic and eclectic case formulations are complex and highly inferential. Both are complex for therapists to implement and both have weak empirical support. Psychiatric approaches lack overarching concepts to guide how the clinical material should be ordered and abstracted and how the formulation should influence treatment. Of the nonbehavioral approaches to case formulation, cognitive approaches are the most promising. They are most technological, provide explicit guidelines to the practitioner to follow. Importantly, they have the greatest evidence base to support their use. Like behavioral approaches they are symptom- and solution-focused, time limited, involve a collaborative educational relationship between the therapist and client and emphasize the current environment. Their consistent use of client data such as diaries, gives feedback to the client and therapist. This is likely to provide contingencies that may refine the current formulation and shape therapist and client behavior towards effective practices.

Chapter 9

WOLPE'S TRADITION OF CASE FORMULATION

Wolpe's Approach

One important early strand of interest in behavioral case formulation comes from a tradition deriving from Joseph Wolpe's work. It is influenced by respondent models of neuroses based on careful and skillful detective-like interviewing. In this model, the therapist is always keeping an eye out for respondent conditioning events in the client's history, or at least attempts to identify the precise focus of the client's fear that may be conditioned stimuli (CS). The aim of the clinical interview is identify stimulus-response relationships in order to develop stimulus hierarchies for reciprocal inhibition (Wolpe, 1986). This approach relies heavily on skillful clinical interviewing to derive and test clinical hypotheses. It uses both what is said during an interview and very careful observation of the client's appearance and nonverbal behavior.

Wolpe's (1958) pioneering book, *Psychotherapy by Reciprocal Inhibition*, described the treatment of a variety of clinical problems, including anxiety disorders, depression, sexual dysfunction, lack of assertiveness and so on using the general principal of reciprocal inhibition. Wolpe became interested in the treatment of neuroses when he was a physician in 1943 treating battle neuroses in North Africa. At that time, battle neuroses were treated with narcoanalysis based on a kind of psychoanalytic model. Soldiers were placed in a stuporous state using medication. The recovery of the alleged suppressed memories of the battle was supposed to lead to recovery from the battle neurosis. Noticing that such treatment was ineffective, Wolpe began reading Pavlov's work on human neuroses and related work on experimental models of neuroses in cats. He then completed a doctoral thesis on treatment of experimental neuroses in cats using feeding as a so-called counter-conditioning response. This thesis and subsequent work was the basis of his book, which was a citation classic (Wolpe, 1980a.)

One of Wolpe's commonly used methods was to identify potential conditioned stimuli through careful interviewing of his patients. He then developed a hierarchy of fear-evoking stimuli, taught the client to relax using Jacobsonian deep muscle relaxation and to use systematic desensitization in order to progressively reduce anxiety evoked by stimuli higher in the hierarchy. Unfortunately, Wolpe's work is often mischaracterized as treating phobias with relaxation training, which is a gross oversimplification. In fact *Psychotherapy by Reciprocal Inhibition* described an inventive variety of approaches to treatment. The book described many case studies – some of which today might be described as "complex cases" – reduced the complexity to a few simple learning principles. Wolpe (1986, 1989) went to great lengths to warn against technologically driven intervention. He wrote against the use of technique-oriented interventions, such as exposure therapy, relaxation training or cognitive therapy, which were not based on an understanding of each client's own individual stimulus-response relationships. This approach is illustrated in the case study below.

Identifying Stimulus-response Relationships

Wolpe published a number of annotated clinical interviews that illustrate his approach. One key element is that his approach is driven by clinical hypotheses from the beginning. For example, even a referral letter might give sufficient information on life events and symptoms to begin making some hypotheses before the client is even seen (Sturmey, 1996, p.81). In Wolpe's case study the client had just taken a seat and, Wolpe noted:

> the patient is very neatly dressed and appears stiff in walk. When seated the patient's posture is formal as well. She sits on the edge of the seat … lipstick is fresh … this information is used to begin the hypothesis testing process … Is she generally cautious … why? … [Does she] demand perfection in herself? Is she excessively concerned abut how she appears to others. Is she afraid of criticism? (Turkat & Wolpe, 1985, p.11)

After the client spelled out her name letter-by-letter and stated her age as "thirty-four and a half", Wolpe makes a tentative hypothesis:

> The clinician adopts a preliminary hypothesis, namely, that the patient is a perfectionist. Accordingly, he expects her to be fearful of making mistakes and being criticized, failing. He further expects interpersonal difficulties and perhaps depression. With this beginning hypothesis, the clinician moves on with the inquiry (Wolpe & Turkat, 1985, p.12)

The patient has only uttered three sentences. Yet, Wolpe can state a tentative formulation. From this tentative formulation one can already derive a treatment plan that might use systematic desensitization to poor appearance, criticism by others and failure. This is only a preliminary hypothesis. Later information in the interview might negate it, but the information is sufficient to guide the assessment process.

This hypothesis-driven approach to interviews requires an active interviewer who, prior to the initial interview, has a conceptual framework to guide assessment. In Wolpe's case the respondent conditioning model guided the clinicians to ask about what *precisely* is feared. Merely knowing that a person fears dogs or crowds is insufficient. Does the person fear dogs because of being bitten, being ashamed or because of harm that might occur to someone else? Without this information it is unclear what the relevant stimuli are for desensitization. Likewise, does the person with a fear of crowds, fear criticism from others, fainting, vomiting, screaming, a stroke, being trapped, talking to strangers, other people staring at them, other people thinking bad things about them, traveling, sweating, other people noticing that they are sweating, etc? Identifying some CS may be difficult. For example, identifying interoceptive stimuli may be difficult if the client is unable to report the stimuli or stimuli that are closely correlated to them. For example, Wolpe (1986) noted that panic attacks may often be due to hyperventilation and hence the interoceptive stimuli, such as the plasma carbon dioxide level, could be the relevant discriminative stimulus. Treatment that exposes the person to these relevant stimuli is essential if exposure is to take place. Such formulations indicate that interventions such as breathing concentrated carbon dioxide or graduated exposure to rapid breathing are appropriate. However, plasma carbon dioxide level is just one of many interoceptive stimuli which might be conditioned stimuli and one that is correlated with an observable response – rapid shallow breathing. The client and therapist might find it much more difficult to discriminate other interoceptive stimuli. However, until the clinician can identify these stimuli, they cannot begin an intervention based on a formulation.

Making these inferences is not always easy. For example, Levine (1987) reported an annotated assessment interview of an initial interview of an adolescent referred for an injection phobia. Adopting a Wolpe-model, Levine listened carefully for the exact nature of what was feared. What Levine immediately noticed was that the client did not describe fear. Rather the client described being *angry* over being made to have injections. As the interview unfolded more and more material related to how other people forced the client do certain things and the resentment he had relating to that came out. Nevertheless, it was the early interview material that Levine noticed – being angry rather than fearful about an injection – that was unusual. This observation that Levine made in the first few sentences of the interview guided the rest of the interview. In a similar vein, Goldiamond (1974) noted, when observing a psychotic patient engaged in strange behavior, that her symptoms related to electricity, that her admission to hospital coincided with her being concerned about house bills being paid on time. When he told her that the hospital social worker could help sort this problem out she immediately relaxed. A final example comes from Wolpe's case study, described in more detail below, in which he identifies that the stimuli which evoked anxiety in a person with social anxiety were not other people being critical of her, but rather her *imagining* other people being critical of her. Being able to discriminate such subtleties might reflect good training and good luck on the part of the clinician. A series of annotated clinical interviews provide good models for a variety of disorders such as eating disorders (Chioda, 1987), anxiety and depression (Levine, 1987; Morganstern, 1988; Wolpe, 1980b) and behavior problems (Sturmey, 1991). Turkat (1985a) reported case studies that make excellent models for case formulation. They address problems such as substance abuse, a variety of personality disorders and problems in later life.

The Role of History

In Wolpe's approach to case formulation considerable emphasis is given to client history. This is because the clinical history is a search for conditioning events that will inform treatment (Wolpe & Turkat, 1985). Finding the exact conditioning events and precisely what occurred at that time may also give clues as how to guide the rest of the interview and exactly what hierarchy of stimuli should be developed for systematic desensitization. For example, Wolpe and Turkat described a case study of a woman with a fear of passing out related to feeling dizzy. Initially, they could not identify any event to this phobia. Only with careful and probing questioning did they eventually trace the history to a childhood surgery in which she was given surgery without warning. At that point she recalled the traumatic event as a sensation that was similar to the one that was currently problematic. Likewise, in the case of Jane described below, Wolpe traced her sensitivity to criticism to an incident in which her teacher humiliated her. Thus, Wolpe gives history relative prominence in case formulation.

Note that in this approach history is only important in so far as it illuminates the learning that has lead to the current problem. Unlike some nonbehavioral approaches, there is no dark, repressed secret to be uncovered and merely uncovering the history does not change behavior. Rather, this information is used to direct the future learning that will take place in therapy.

Sharing the Formulation

Wolpe and Turkat (1985) recommended presenting the formulation "in certain cases" (p. 31). They described that the main reason for doing so was to confirm the accuracy of the formulation. In this approach, the formulation is derived primarily during the interview and, at least in Wolpe's accounts, less emphasis is given to homework assignments or in the patient discovering the formulation themselves.

A Case Formulation from Wolpe

Wolpe's analytic style of thinking and hypothesis-driven approach to case formulation is illustrated in a case report he published in 1989. Jane was a 27-year-old single woman. She complained of lack of confidence and self-esteem. She was fearful of other people looking at her critically. She dated this to an occasion when she was in the 12th grade when she was evaluated harshly by a teacher.

She had previously been treated unsuccessfully by cognitive therapy. Cognitive therapy had convinced her intellectually that she should not be fearful. However, it left her fearful of criticism. She had also been instructed to expose herself to difficult social situations. She received no benefit from this.

Wolpe interviewed Jane. His assessment indicated that she was fearful of being watched, of superiors, of criticism, of shortcomings in her appearance, and that her feelings were easily hurt. However, Wolpe's assessment interview revealed that what truly provoked anxiety was not other people being critical of her. Rather, what provoked anxiety was *thinking* about other people criticizing her. It appeared that it was her *thoughts*, not other people being critical of her, that were the CS. Hence previous therapy was ineffective because it failed to conduct respondent extinction to the relevant CS. Thus, systematic desensitization consisted of exposure to hierarchies of her own thoughts. From least to most anxiety–provoking they included: thinking about others thinking she has poor taste, thinking about others thinking she was aloof, and thinking that other people thought that she was nervous. The person that she imagined doing the thinking about her was also relevant. Hence, imagining that the doorman was thinking about her was much less anxiety-provoking than thinking about Mr Black thinking about her.

Based on this new hypothesis, treatment consisted of systematic desensitization using deep muscle relaxation to these hierarchies of stimuli. In addition, Wolpe used in vivo desensitization to treat fear of being praised and admired. Ten months later Jane as able to socialize without anxiety, was minimally anxious when imagining what others thought about her and was considering marriage.

Wolpe commented that the key to this case formulation was the care that had been taken during assessment to identify precisely what stimuli evoked anxiety. Previous therapies – all of which had a good evidence base – failed because they failed to identify these stimuli accurately.

Turkat's *Behavioral Case Formulation*

Turkat's (1985a) *Behavioral Case Formulation* is a key work in this field. Building on Wolpe's earlier work he extended the application of behavioral case formulation to numerous clinical problems. The chapters in this book address behavioral formulation of anxiety and mood disorders (Wolpe & Turkat, 1985), alcohol abuse (Maisto, 1985), chronic headache (Adams, 1985), several kinds of personality disorder (Brantley & Callon, 1985; Turkat, 1985b), as well as problems in older adults (Malatesta, 1985). Thus, quite early on behavioral case formulation had moved beyond apparently simple clinical problems, such as simple phobias, to address more complex problems.

Turkat's model of case formulation included three steps. The first step was a hypothesis that linked all the presenting problems. The second step was a hypothesis concerning the development of the problems. The third step was that the formulation should predict the client's future behavior. Turkat recommended sharing the formulation with the client and asking for confirmation and clarification of the formulation.

A Behavioral Formulation of Histrionic Personality Disorder

In Turkat's volume, Brantley and Callon (1985) presented a behavioral formulation of 32-year-old single woman diagnosed with a histrionic personality disorder. She referred herself at the suggestion of a coworker after she had become depressed following the break-up of a recent relationship. During the call to make an initial appointment she made a veiled suicide threat which she immediately denied. Her appearance was unremarkable, expect for some overuse of makeup and jewelry. She complained of depression and gastro-intestinal distress. During depression she had bad moods that involved crying, insomnia, boredom, irritability, a history of suicidal threats, but no suicide attempts, etc. Her gastro-intestinal distress included stomach pain and diarrhea, which a recent medical consultation indicated were probably stress-related. She had poor social relationships. These included arguments with her mother, poor relationships with co-workers and no sustained relationships with friends or men. Her parents divorced when she was young and she knew little about her father. Her mother gave her a great deal of attention, although she regarded her mother as interfering and opinionated. During the initial interview she explained that she was dubious about seeing a therapist, but was willing to let him prove himself. She showed inappropriate affect during the interview. For example, she constantly smiling during the beginning of the interview and was somewhat seductive at other times. She explained most her own problems away in terms of the shortcomings of other people, her own physical illnesses or simplistic explanations. She was dramatic at times and often demanded that the clinician agree with her explanations of her own problems.

Early on during the initial interview the therapist noted that she lived very close to her mother and was single, suggesting a lack of independent mature social behavior, over-involvement in her mother's life and vice versa, and a failure to establish typical adults roles. She was generally unable to identify antecedents or consequences of her bad moods. However, she agreed that she was generally better when active, worse when around her mother, and had gotten worse two months ago after breaking up with a boyfriend of six months. A problem list identified 33 problems, including 11 related to depressed mood, physiological symptoms of stress, and a large number of problems related to poor relationships with other people. There were no examples of a good relationship with anyone.

Brantley and Callon presented a developmental analysis as part of their behavioral assessment. They noted that her mother has divorced when she was aged one year. Her parents assisted her financially. She had also no good relationships with men, of whom she was very critical. She said that her mother spoiled her, planned all her activities and often left work to spend time with her. During high school she was socially active, dated, but never steadily, and had friends who were less attractive than herself. She attended university away from home but for only one year because of illnesses and gastro-intestinal distress. She had her first serious relationship at university. It began well. Then she realized that her boyfriend was getting bored with her and she responded with anger. After a while he left her for another girl. Although she denied it, she appeared to experience an episode of depression at that time. This pattern was repeated with several relationships through out her adult life.

The Formulation   Brantley and Callonn summarized their formulation in a diagram reproduced in Figure 9.1. They noted that during her early development Ms H was the center of her mother's and grandparent's attention. Through this over-rich schedule of reinforcement and modeling of inappropriate behavior by her mother she also learned similar ways of behaving. Although she acquired some socially appropriate behavior, she also learned to be extraverted and seductive. She also learned to respond to lack of attention with tantrums and eventually social withdrawal, which were maintained by intermittent schedules of reinforcement, as she would sometimes get her own way. Her mother remained her only important source of social reinforcement.

When she left home for university her primary source of social reinforcement was no longer present. She initiated intimate relationships but could not maintain them. In the past, her mother's attention sustained her through this. Hence, her depression and gastro-intestinal problems might be viewed as extinction and its side effects. This observation parallels Skinner's earlier generic formulation of psychological dysfunction, which will be discussed in Chapter 11. These symptoms brought her into contact with new schedules of reinforcement, especially from her mother. Her mother's behavior appeared to maintain her symptomatic behavior. This pattern was repeated throughout her subsequent adult life. Further examples of work on behavior analytic conceptions of personality

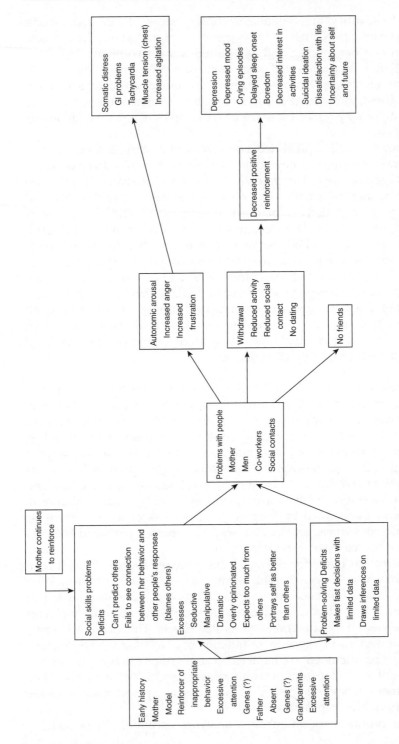

Figure 9.1. Brantley and Callon's formulation of histrionic personality disorder (from Turkat, 1985, p. 246, Figure 2) P. J. Bantley & E. B. Callon (1985). Historionic personality. In: I. D. Turkat (Ed.) *Behavioral case formulation.* New York: Plenum, p. 246.

disorders can be found in Bissett and Hayes (1999) and Nelson-Gray and Farmer (1999a, 1999b).

Implications for Treatment   In a case like this with 33 problems on the problem list, where to start would be a daunting task for anyone. Indeed, the possibility that the client's mother may gain so much out of her daughter's problems – being the heroine mother who fixes all her poor, sick, yet frequently ungrateful, daughter's problems one more time when no one else can do it – suggests another serious challenge to developing an intervention. Brantley and Callon observed that it is tempting to address some of this client's most obvious sources of distress – her somatic problems and depression. However, their analysis shown in Figure 9.1 suggested that, if one construes these problems as a response chain (see Chapter 6), to do so would be least efficient and effective. Hence, they recommended intervening early in the response chain. For example, intervention might take place by decreasing autonomic arousal, increasing activities associated with positive mood, and increasing social reinforcement from sources other than her mother. The earliest parts of the chain related to social behavior, problem solving and her mother's behavior. Thus, intervention here might lead to the greatest treatment gains. Rather than a generic skills intervention package, the skills selected must carefully match the deficits and functions identified in the formulation. For example, skills such as learning how to interact with her mother when her mother irritates her in some way other than throwing things at her, learning how to maintain relationships after the first few weeks, and learning what to do when she feels mildly depressed might all be key skills.

A Case Formulation of Alcohol Abuse

Maisto (1985) provided an interesting case formulation within the Wolpe tradition. The presenting problem was unusual. The man was initially referred for depression following separation from his wife, loss of his job and excessive drinking. During the initial interview he was overly formal and concerned with rules and unable to describe why his wife and co-workers might have problems with him. He had a very religious upbringing. Consequently, following rules and high standards of performance were important to him. Subsequently, he was also diagnosed with alcohol abuse and compulsive personality disorder.

Maisto based his formulation on interview, observation of the patient during the interview, and some diagnostic testing. His main complaints were depression, loss of employment, separation and impending divorce and excessive drinking. Maisto's formulation noted that he had learned to be indiscriminately rational, lacked experience in expressing emotions and in recognizing emotions in others. His depression resulted from losses, including loss of his job and family, both due to his insensitivity toward other people and poor social skills. These factors lead to social isolation and anger relieved by drinking excessively. Based on this formulation Maisto recommended social skills training and various alternatives to deal with drinking. See below for further details.

Commentary

This formulation is notable in a number of ways. One striking feature of the formulation is that it addresses a complex case involving multiple psychopathologies. This is indeed a complex case, not a simple phobia. Second, the formulation is rational and flows directly from the functional assessment. Finally, its treatment recommendations are also closely linked to the formulation. Hence, this approach to behavioral case formulation has many positive features. A closer analysis of this approach to formulation identifies two weaknesses. The formulation implicitly and occasionally explicitly uses behavioral concepts. However, the majority of the formulation is not explicit in its conceptual foundations (Baer et al., 1968). As a consequence of this lack of conceptual clarity, some of the treatment recommendations are not as precise as they could be and are limited to changing the client's behavior, rather than his environment, especially other people. Let us examine these two critiques further.

Maisto's formulation is easy to read and appears rational. This is partly because it uses the vernacular language of clinicians and generally avoids the technical language of behavior analysis. For example, in describing Mr S he described him as:

> ... indiscriminately rational ... rigid ... [he failed] to observe that he made other employees uncomfortable at work ... often initiated sex at inauspicious times and persisted despite his wife showing her displeasure ... often failed to perceive occasions when his wife may have desired to have sex ... was insensitive to his wife about non-sexual matters ... did not perceive how the secretary was feeling ... he would often appear to act incongruously with the emotional aspects of settings ... (1985, pp. 74–75)

The use of mentalistic language such as "observe" and "perceive" should alert us that the analysis is incomplete as it does not describe the client's behavior precisely and implicitly places the problem inside the person in terms of deficits in observation and perception, rather than observable client behavior. Further, Maisto did not frame these accurate observations in the conceptual language of behavior analysis. All the examples above can be reframed as deficits in stimulus control. He has sex with his wife, but only on a few occasions, and not on many other appropriate occasions. He sometimes interacts appropriately with his workmates, but often does not. He responds to his wife's upset sometimes, but often does not. All of these suggest that at least some of the required skills are in his repertoire, but not under appropriate stimulus control.

A similar example is that Maisto notes that "sexual encounters ... were perfunctory in manner and lacking in emotion to an unusual degree ... it would be predicted that Mr S saw marriage solely in non-emotional terms ... although the failed sexual encounter disturbed Mr S he failed to do anything about it" (pp. 74–75.) These descriptions appear to be pure skill deficits and refer to behaviors that were not present in Mr S's repertoire. Maisto also noted that "he made other employees feel uncomfortable .. it did not take long for his wife to habituate to him sexually ... Mr S would have few, if any, close friends, .. [as] others would view him as a poor candidate as a close friend ... and since he would tend to extinguish other's expression of feelings by not responding to them... " (pp. 74–75). In this example, the last part of the quote does refer to extinction of other people's social behavior because of his failure to respond in a reinforcing manner to intimacy, but the earlier parts are not so explicit. All these examples could be linked by the notion that his failure to reinforce other people's social approaches extinguished their social behavior. Indeed, that his coworkers felt uncomfortable might reflect the emotional side-effects of extinction.

As a final example, Maisto noted that "Mr S's heavy drinking is related to the occurrence of negative affect like anger and depression ..." (p. 75). Again, this described a correlation between anger and depression and drinking. Yet, it did not specify the behavioral process that may underlie it. We could rephrase it as "drinking excessively was negatively reinforced by the termination or attenuation of the aversive private behavior of anger and depression".

This technical precision is important in at least three ways. First, the use of such technical language changes the clinician's private verbal behavior and the public spoken and written behavior. The use of this technical language makes the clinician think in behavioral terms and steers them away from the imprecise vernacular language. It makes us sound like psychologists who have something to contribute beyond everyday understanding problems. Second, it may make a difference in treatment planning. Consider Maisto's treatment plan. It is not a bad plan, but perhaps it is imprecise. Maisto recommended that Mr S receive social skills training to "(a) gauge more accurately others' behaviors (and feelings), (b) permit himself to react emotionally, and (c) express these emotional reactions appropriately" (p. 80). Such a plan fails to distinguish between problems of lack of stimulus control from skills deficits. Further analysis of the stimulus dimensions that controls these behaviors is needed. What social stimuli does he respond to appropriately? What social stimuli should he respond to and how can we conceive of them along some dimension that we might call "unsubtle – subtle social cues". Without such an analysis, treatment cannot proceed adequately.

This reflects the problem that treatment has not conceptualized as a problem of stimulus control and because the teaching cannot proceed by teaching him to respond to progressively more subtle skills. Thus, this formulation fails to specify targets such as learning to respond sexually to his wife when she makes approaches that he currently does not respond to with the implication that the intervention should be discrimination training to broaden stimulus control of his behavior. Third, this formulation does not recognize the skill deficit resulting in him being more reinforcing to other people, which in turn results in isolation, depressed mood and drinking. Thus, Mr S needs social skills training to make small talk and to respond positively to emotional expression in other people.

A third element of the treatment plan is that Mr S "should learn alternate responses to drinking alcohol, such as relaxation, jogging or meditation" (p. 80). Maisto based this recommendation primarily on nomothetic behavioral research on treatment of alcohol abuse. Thus, it is consonant with Skinner's (1953) recommendation that one way to self-control a problematic behavior is to do something else (see Table 6.1). So this strategy might work as a generic DRO intervention. However, this approach is not function-based. If drinking is negatively reinforced by termination or attenuation of anger or depression then the function-based intervention would be to teach Mr S better ways to avoid or terminate his mood or anger. Better yet, if we consider the behavior chain that consists of extinction of other people's social behavior, followed by social isolation, followed by depressed mood, resulting in drinking, then perhaps the most economical intervention for problem drinking would be to intervene earlier in the chain by teaching social skills to reinforce other people's behavior and to avoid depressed or angry mood more effectively.

A final limitation of Maisto's analysis is that it emphasizes Mr S's behavior. The role of other people's behavior is underplayed. If part of his problems result from the extinction of other people's prosocial behavior, then some intervention with others to reduce this might be appropriate. For example, other people could be taught to be more patient, to reinforce any socially appropriate behavior from Mr S, and so on.

Bruch's University College of London Model

Bruch (1998) described the British tradition of case within clinical psychology as growing out of Eysenck's work in the 1950s. This work showed the ineffectiveness of psychotherapy and advocated the use of behavior therapy. Following this approach, Shapiro developed a variety of idiographic methods to measure and understand each individual client as a scientific puzzle to be solved by the systematic application of scientific methods and learning theory. For example, Shapiro used card sort tasks and other idiographic methods of case assessment. Shapiro saw each client as a novel scientific puzzle to be solved. Clinical psychologist did not adopt Shapiro's methodology, although his ideas were influential. Bruch (1998) argued that Shapiro's methods were too labor intensive and beyond the skills of most clinicians. Thus, they never caught on in practice. In contrast, Meyer shifted away from Shapiro's systematic empiricism to emphasize – like Wolpe – clinical interviewing, general guidance from the principles of learning, and integration of this information into a formulation that is shared with the patient.

Bruch (1998) presented one current version of this methodology. He described this as the University College of London five-step model of case formulation, which is the continued elaboration of this approach. The five steps are (1) definition of problems, (2) exploration, (3) formulation, (4) intervention, and (5) evaluation. Thus, Bruch's model extends Turkat's model to include intervention and evaluation as part of the ongoing formulation. In phase 1, *descriptive analysis*, the purpose is to understand the client's problems and goals and to specify problems. In phase 2, *exploration*, the aim is to identify causes and maintenance mechanisms, to conduct a cognitive behavioral assessment and to collect data to test hypotheses. This assessment included the tri-partite model of assessing verbal-cognitive, automatic-somatic and behavioral-motor aspects of the problem. Additionally, the therapist also assessed organismic variables, which were said to mediate the stimulus and response, including biological variables. These three systems may be synchronous or desynchronous (Lang, 1979). Phase 2 also included a developmental analysis of the problem, much like Wolpe's work. Additionally, Phase 2 included an analysis of schema, including unconscious schema, which may be responsible for the maintenance of the problem. Finally, phase 2 included an analysis of the client's personal assets. In phase 3, *problem formulation*, the therapist integrated data into a coherent case formulation that accounts for the development and maintenance of the problem. This problem formulation guided treatment. Phase 3 may also include clinical experimentation to verify the formulation for complex, but not routine cases. Baseline data, such as self-report measures, may also be taken at this time. The final two phases of this model were intervention and evaluation of the intervention.

Summary

The Wolpe tradition emphasizes detective-like clinical interviewing, careful observation of the client's personal presentation and an emphasis on history as well as current environment. This reflects the interest in respondent conditioning in Wolpe's work and the centrality of identifying conditioning in guiding the selection of conditioned stimuli for desensitization. In a similar way, Turkat's volume also emphasizes history. This may reflect Turkat's interest in extending Wolpe's work beyond anxiety and mood disorders, where respondent conditioning may be seen clearly from time to time, to problems such as personality disorders, where learning other than respondent conditioning, during the lifespan may be important.

Over time certain changes of emphasis are apparent. As we move from Wolpe to Turkat to Bruch the progressive influence of cognitive models of case formulation is apparent. Whereas, Turkat treads lightly on the assessment of private behavior, Bruch includes unconscious processes, such hidden schemata. Thus, over time the relationship to learning theory has gradually weakened. A second trend related to the empirical rigor of the formulation process. Wolpe's approach included clear tests of case formulation, such as exposing the client to different kinds of CS to identify which were antecedents for anxiety, ratings of anxiety to various stimuli using the Subjective Units of Discomfort (SUDS) scale, as well as research using psychophysiological measures of anxiety. By the time we reach Bruch, testing formulations is not a requirement of the model, but is only used for difficult cases. A final difference is the role of the clinical hypothesis. In Wolpe's and Turkat's work, the clinician may identify a clinical hypothesis within the first few sentences of the first interview. In Bruch's approach the processes is neatly divided into phases. Hypothesis generation is part of phase 3. Thus, the formulation becomes the conclusion of the assessment processes, rather than the driving force behind it.

Chapter 10

SKINNER AND PSYCHOTHERAPY

EARLY BEHAVIORAL ACCOUNTS OF THERAPY

Psychoanalytic and psychodynamic therapies were mainstream psychological treatments until the 1950s. The rise of Rogerian therapy, behavior therapy, ABA, the beginning of modern psychopharmacology and early questioning of the efficacy of psychotherapy (Eysenck, 1952) challenged this orthodoxy. However, challenges to psychotherapeutic orthodoxy date back to the 1920s. Watson and Reyner's (1920) demonstration of the respondent conditioning and respondent extinction of animal phobias in a young child challenged psychodynamic explanations of the acquisition and treatment of neurotic behavior. Mowrer's (1939) two factor theory of the development of anxiety disorders, in which classical conditioning accounted for the acquisition of fears and operant avoidance accounted for their maintenance, was developed in the 1940s and 1950s. This, like Watson and Reyner (1920), also challenged psychotherapy's explanation of the development of neuroses.

Others, not yet directly questioning the efficacy of psychotherapy, attempted to translate psychodynamic concepts into learning processes. For example, Dollard and Miller's (1950) *Personality and Psychotherapy* provided a systematic translation of psychodynamic concepts into learning concepts and sought to explain the process of therapy in learning terms. For example, free association was viewed as the reverse of repression. The job of therapists was to motivate the client to talk about historical and current anxiety-producing material resulting in respondent extinction. Shoben's (1949) account of psychotherapy has many surprisingly modern aspects. Psychotherapy was re-conceptualized as a three-step learning process. In the first step of therapy the therapist reveals the conditioned stimuli that elicit anxiety through their permissive, anxiety-reducing non-punitive behavior. This permits counter-conditioning in which the cues formerly associated with anxiety are now paired with the positive aspects of the therapeutic relationship. Finally, the client and therapist set new healthy goals so that the client may acquire new and effective ways of behaving. Keller and Schoenfeld (1950) noted that psychotherapy was not really a school of psychology at all and was largely uninfluenced by data from experimental psychology. They suggested that

Thorndike's law of effect was "clearly comparable" to Freud's pleasure principle (p. lix.)

SKINNER AND CASE FORMULATION

Skinner and Applied Behavior Analysis

Skinner was not a practicing clinician. Hence, his contribution to case formulation is indirect. Some aspects of Skinner's role in ABA are relatively well known. There are extensive chapters on applied issues in *Science and Human Behavior* (Skinner, 1953), including chapters on therapy, education, government and design of societies. He was extensively involved in the setting up of *Journal of Applied Behavior Analysis* in 1968. Vivid vignettes of early applied projects, such as Project Pigeon, which used pigeons to guide missiles in World War II, and his earlier design of a crib for his daughter with some operant features, are also often cited. These applications are often misrepresented. Perhaps the most amusing recent example was Slater's (2004) description of Skinner confining his daughter in the crib for two years where he administered – worse than punishment – "mean punishments" – which resulted in her subsequent psychosis and suicide in a bowling alley in Billings, Montana. Slater's history-based case formulation of explaining Skinner's daughter's suicide by reference to vivid clinical detail without a good rationale is weak because it depended on unreliable history rather than objective reliable data. The unreliable nature of its history was illustrated convincingly by Skinner's daughter's letter to *The Guardian* – written from this side of the grave – denying the story and reporting her good physical and mental health (Morris, Smith & Altus, 2005.)

Morris et al. (2005) reviewed Skinner's contribution to ABA in greater detail than is generally known and is instructive. Even in the 1930s Skinner noted the possibility of extensions of basic behavioral work to applied questions. Although not published until 1957, Skinner began work on *Verbal Behavior* in the 1930s and published studies of poetry as examples of verbal behavior around that time. Also in the 1930s, he published with Heron, a paper on the effects of caffeine and Benzedrine on operant performance in animals. This became the prototype of later work in behavioral pharmacology (Skinner & Heron, 1937). He also published a model for the token economy in which a rat was taught to drop a marble down a tube to obtain food. Skinner also conducted behavior analytic studies of emotions, such as anxiety. Estes and Skinner (1941) noted that in everyday language we say that anxiety is an emotional state and that the anticipation of the feared stimulus causes us to be anxious. However, they also noted that things that happen in the future cannot cause present behavior. Hence, they argued that some current stimuli associated with the disturbing stimuli – conditioned pre-aversive stimuli – must be the relevant stimuli. Additionally, they noted that such stimuli, in addition to eliciting anxious behavior, also demonstrated that such stimuli had effects on current operant behavior. They showed that stimuli that had been associated with anxiety-provoking stimuli in the past, subsequently suppressed current operant behavior. This model of anxiety was used to identify drugs for anxiety disorders that attenuated the suppressive effects of conditioned pre-aversive stimuli. Skinner's later work investigated cultural design, applications of ABA to animal training and welfare (Bailey & Gillaspy, 2005), including "clicker training" for dogs, as an application of secondary reinforcement, psychiatric patients, teaching machines that now appear like versions of online teaching and the application of self-management to writing (Skinner, 1981).

Morris et al. (2005) make some interesting observations on Skinner's contribution to ABA. First, he never published any typical ABA studies. One may note strategic parallels with *Science and Human Behavior* (1953). The only intervention method he recommended for mental health in this volume was the rather generic self-management. He did not recommend specific technologies to teach self-recording or self-reinforcement or specific intervention techniques, such as shaping, for token economies, etc. Morris et al. suggested that he may have done this in order to focus on basic behavioral principles, to avoid endorsing specific technologies and to allow behavioral interventions to evolve over time as applied behavior analysts collected the data. Rather than being the founder of ABA, Morris et al. concluded that his contribution was to lay the groundwork of the basic science and to point out and foster its applications, but not to directly found the field of ABA.

There was very little clinical research to directly inform Skinner's writings in the 1950s. Nevertheless, *Science and Human Behavior* included a chapter on psychotherapy, which contained the elements of behavioral case formulation and its implications for treatment. Parts of *Beyond Freedom and Dignity* (1971) discussed psychotherapy as a controlling agent in the design of societies and the material in *Verbal Behavior* (1957) is the basis for behavioral verbal therapies, such as those in relational frame theory.

In his chapter on psychotherapy in *Science and Human Behavior*, Skinner presented an analysis of traditional psychotherapy in three parts. Obviously behaviorism had to account for the development of psychopathology. He also seemed to assume that psychotherapy involved some form of client behavior change, at least in the therapist's office, and therefore there was a phenomenon to be explained by reference to learning. He did not discuss behavior change outside the therapist's office, perhaps because such behavior change had not yet been reported. The three parts to his analysis were: (1) an analysis of the nature of psychopathology, (2) an analysis of Freudian psychotherapy from a behavioral perspective, and

(3) the implications for treatment, which mostly emphasized a behavioral conception of self-regulation as a treatment for mental heath problems.

The Nature of Psychopathology

Skinner's analysis began with the important role that society exerts in controlling its member's behavior, especially behavior that is reinforced by primary reinforcers, but that is injurious to other members of society or that may contribute to an unstable society. Societal control of its members can take place through the law, education, religion and psychotherapy. Indeed, Skinner considered psychotherapy to be one of society's mechanisms of behavioral control. Often the mechanism for control is the termination of aversive stimuli. For example, stealing food is reinforced by access to the food, but the social environment punishes food stealing with a variety of primary and secondary punishers, such as time out in prison, removal of secondary reinforcers, such as cash and punishing verbal behaviors from other people. Society also teachers its members rules – private verbal antecedents and establishing operations – that might also control our behavior.

Skinner noted that such controlling strategies may both reduce stealing and also have harmful effects. Societal control may produce by-products such as escape, revolt and passive resistance. Various forms of escape include avoidance, withdrawal, desertion and evasion. These appear to be similar to some forms of psychopathology, such as the withdrawal involved in some forms of depression, avoidance of school in a school phobic or no longer working because of legal disability status. Revolt against control can take the form of complaints and accusations concerning others' wrongdoing. Skinner cited the example of school vandalism, which elsewhere is taken as a symptom of psychopathology, such as Oppositional Defiance or Conduct Disorders (American Psychiatric Association, 2000). Another by-product is passive resistance. Skinner speculated that after escape and revolt have been extinguished, then the person simply exhibits very little behavior. The sullen child and the bland adult with nothing to motivate them may be examples of this. In response to passive resistance, society may have even more aversive methods of control – the sullen child is placed in a locked educational facility and the bland adult is fired and divorced. This intensification of punishment results in even further emotional reactions in the form of anxiety correlated with the new aversive and correlated stimuli. Hence, the formerly bland divorcee hates their spouse, children, former boss and ineffective lawyer and drinks to reduce these aversive private events, but cannot behave sufficiently to find employment of have a meaningful social life.

These forms of societal control of individual behavior also have emotional by-products. The aversive stimuli – the painful slap – and the associated stimuli – the critical glance or parental warning – also elicit fearful behavior. The physiological effects of punishment are referred to as "anxiety" and are accompanied by private behaviors we call worry, shame, guilt or a sense of sin. Certain kinds of operant avoidance behavior are strengthened. Various forms of anger and depression may also relate to the emotional side-effects of punishment, such as the client with depression can do nothing because of the punitive environment. Here, Skinner emphasized punitive societal control, but other forms of punitive environment also come to mind. For example, chronic medical conditions that make moving painful or effortful and poverty that makes everything difficult, effortful and personally expensive. These other forms of punishment may also lead to these emotional side effects.

A history of punishment and its by-products has important effects on operant behavior. The person with a history of punishment learns to avoid these stimuli and over time a person may not speak or behave at all. A variety of stimuli, which in the past preceded punishment, all come to elicit anxiety. In these circumstances avoidance of stimuli associated with punishment may be observed. Avoidance can take a variety of forms, including drug addiction and alcohol use to reduce anxiety in situations formerly associated with punishment, or excessively restrained behavior as shown by the shy, inhibited child or client with an anxiety disorder or even a hysterically paralyzed person. When escape is not possible, the person may engage in high rates of behavior that produce stimuli which evoke reactions incompatible with anxiety, as in thrill-seeking, obsessions and other behaviors that are incompatible with, or at least reduce, anxiety. After severe punishment poor stimulus control may develop, as shown in the child who ignores all parent nagging and instructions. Skinner even speculated that certain forms of psychotic behavior, such as hallucinations and delusions, may function to escape aversive stimulation. A person's verbal behavior may also become distorted when the person is grandiose or brave and this verbal behavior is negatively reinforced by avoidance of talking of one's inadequacies and cowardice. A person may even learn to engage in self-punishment to avoid more intense punishment, as in the bulimic patient who cuts her foot to terminate a highly aversive depressed mood or who vomits to reduce anxiety and guilt after binge eating.

So this is Skinner's initial account of the development of psychopathology. Psychopathology is the result of societal control of its members through aversive contingencies, and perhaps through other naturally occurring aversive contingencies. The negative side effects of punishment include both a variety of forms of avoidance of the punishing stimuli and associated stimuli. Over time the person may behave very little at all or may emit strange behavior that is negatively reinforced in various ways. Skinner's account was generic. It did not address specific forms of psychopathology. Rather, it indicated the directions for future research, but did not provide all the details, which had not yet been worked out in 1953.

Skinner's Account of Emotion and Anxiety

Skinner (1953) gave a general account of emotions which noted that emotions are explanatory fictions – the behavior to be explained, not the explanation of behavior. Thus, we should not say that "she avoided going down town because she was anxious", but rather "she avoided going down town *and* was anxious". Emotions include public behavior, physiological responses and private behavior. For example, a person, whom we describe as angry, threatens and is violent, their heart races and they sweat, they report thinking angry thoughts and feeling angry. When they report feeling angry, part of what the person is doing is describing the behavior of their glands and organs – they describe their racing heart, dilated peripheral blood vessels, their sweaty palms, their gut turning over and stomach churning.

The physiological correlates of emotions are not as highly differentiated: we sweat when anxious and excited. Skinner observes that what differentiated one emotion from another are, in part, the reinforcers for behavior. The angry person's behavior is reinforced by damage and injury to another person. The anxious person's behavior is reinforced by avoidance of aversive stimuli and other stimuli that precede the actual aversive stimuli. The excited, happy child's behavior is reinforced by interaction with people, objects and movement. Emotions are also differentiated by the range of responses affected by that reinforcer. Thus, an angry person is violent to others, smashes objects and threatens because all of these behaviors are reinforced by injury and pain in another person. Different emotions are also distinguished, one from another, by the breadth of impact on the person's behavioral repertoire. Thus, some emotions such as joy or sorrow are characterized by a broad impact on most aspects of a person's behavior. A joyful person approaches many objects and people, smile and is enthusiastic about many different things. Other emotions are characterized by a more limited impact on the person's behavioral repertoire. The amused person smiles modestly and knowingly in response to a few things that only certain people say, but thereafter go on about their life behaving as usual. When analyzing emotional behavior, none of these different aspects of behavior should be isolated from one another. Skinner referred to this as "the total emotion". Skinner (1953, p.166) wrote that:

In describing the fact that criticism of his work "makes an employee mad", for example, we may report: (1) that he turned red, that the palms of his hands sweat, and if the evidence is available, that stops digesting his lunch; (2) that his face takes on a characteristic "expression" of anger; and (3) that he tends to slam doors, to kick the cat, to speak curtly to his fellow workers, to get into a fight, and to watch a street fight or boxing match with special interest. The operant behavior under (3) appears to hang together via a common consequence – someone or something is damaged. The total emotion … is the total effect of the criticism of his work upon his behavior.

Anxiety

Skinner noted that aversive stimuli are those whose removal acts as a negative reinforcer. For example, turning away from a very bright light or the sight of a graveyard is reinforced by removal or reduction in the intensity of these stimuli. Some stimuli are naturally aversive, such as the bright light, and others, such as the graveyard, have acquired their aversive properties during the life of the organism.

Anxiety is one example of an emotion, but one which Skinner gave special attention. Recall that as early as 1941, Estes and Skinner demonstrated that those stimuli, which in the past preceded an aversive stimulus, came to elicit anxiety and inhibit concurrent operant behavior. This analysis invites direct comparison with the effects of clinical anxiety disorders on people's day-to-day lives. Someone asks a person, diagnosed with a social phobia, on the phone if they want to go to a family event. The client freezes, can no longer speak loudly or clearly, terminates that phone call abruptly with in inadequate excuse, only to sit down, "worry" and do nothing appropriate for some time. The client with an obsessive compulsive disorder sees the contaminated mail on the doormat, freezes, walks away and begins engaging in rituals, but also no longer goes about their day-to-day business that they otherwise would have done. For some people, the conditioned pre-aversive stimuli can be both stimuli in the environment – the presence of a critical other person – or internal stimuli – the beginnings of one's heart accelerating or other physiological events.

Pre-aversive stimuli can have profound effects on a person's behavioral repertoire. These include escaping the aversive stimulus by escaping it or otherwise terminating it, and avoiding it by terminating, as well as a general inhibition of ongoing appropriate operant behavior. The most potent pre-aversive stimuli can inhibit behavior so effectively that they can even inhibit effective avoidance behavior. The breadth of pre-aversive stimuli vary greatly from one person to another. One person may be said to have a generalized anxiety disorder or to have a general anticipatory anxiety that "something bad will happen". Another persons' pre-aversive stimuli may be specific to certain places, people or other specific stimuli.

Later, Skinner noted that society designs environments to evoke certain emotional behavior in a variety of ways. The comedian presents stimuli for humor. Your relative kicks you leg to inhibit giggling at a funeral. So-cieties also evoke anxiety in a variety of ways that are useful to societies. Societies promote shame, guilt and a sense of sin to prevent use of pros-titutes, theft and lying. Perhaps societies that inhibit these behaviors and promote their corollaries – fidelity, respect for property and honesty, at least to some extent – are more likely to survive. The physical environ-ment also contains aversive stimuli. These too may generate anxiety. The person who is cold and starving and the person who cannot open the jammed car door, are also anxious.

Skinner was no technocrat. He did not advocate any specific form of treatment for anxiety. Rather, he noted that anxiety must never be elevated to the hidden cause of the problem, but rather that it is the thing to be treated. Thus, treatment should be directed at the circumstances in which anxious behavior is observed.

An Account of Psychotherapy

Skinner noted that traditional clinical psychology focuses on diagnosis as a manner of collecting and organizing facts, but leaves a gap between making the diagnosis and treatment. For Skinner a key element had been omitted, namely the element of identifying the independent variables that control behavior: therapy means the control of problematic client behavior by the therapist and other environmental variables.

How then can we explain traditional psychotherapy, which sometimes does produce behavioral change during the therapy session and some-times even outside the therapy session? Given that the client and therapist have little learning history together, the therapist may exert little control over the client behavior. The possibility of client symptom relief is the main learning mechanism whereby therapists may exert control over cli-ent behavior. Psychodynamic therapists say little to their clients other an occasional grunt or minimal verbal behavior, a nod here and there and per-haps a low frequency interpretation. This non-punishing audience may be contrasted with the client's everyday audience with its history of various forms of punishment in the form of criticism, effort and perhaps primary punishment. A client whose anxieties and behavioral problems result from a history of punishment will begin to emit much behavior that has not been observed for a long time. They may talk about anxiety-provok-ing, unusual topics, long-held secrets or talk in a disorganized way. Like-wise, their previously punished non-verbal behavior may also emerge, as when the inhibited client becomes agitated, assertive or inappropriately sexual.

The most important source of therapist control of client behavior is the possibility of relief of aversive symptoms. To the extent that the thera-pist's behavior results in reduction in aversive stimuli in the client's life, the client's turning to the therapist will be reinforced. If the therapist is directive and gives specific advice, then the efficacy of this advice may begin to exert control over the client's behavior.

The increase in previously punished behavior in therapy leads to another possible therapeutic mechanism: respondent extinction. As the client repeatedly talks about emotionally laden topics, these words – conditioned verbal stimuli – come to elicit negative emotional behaviors such as fear or guilt over time. Hence, avoidance associated with these problems may become less frequent. Another mechanism also exists – inadvertent or explicit therapist reinforcement of client reports of progress. Suffice it to note here that therapists – even therapists such as Carl Rodgers – may be unaware of their use of social reinforcement of client reports of progress (Truax, 1966.)

So for Skinner, psychotherapy was another form of societal control of behavior. Psychotherapy operates principally through the power of symptom relief and respondent extinction of verbal stimuli.

Implications for Treatment

Skinner finally outlined a number of other implications of this model for therapy. The key construction of psychopathology is that the client's behavior results from a history of punishment and its side-effects and that this behavior is disadvantageous to the client or dangerous to society. In non-behavioral approaches to therapy private behavior – their pent up emotions, anxiety and anger – are elevated to the cause of the person's problem. In behavioral accounts of therapy these are private behaviors to be changed, along with public behaviors. They are not the causes of the problem behavior which must be changed in order to produce symptom relief and a better life. Rather, the therapist's job is to identify the environmental events that control both the public and private behaviors of concern and to provide new learning so that the client's behavior no longer has these disadvantageous or dangerous characteristics.

Constructing New Behavioral Repertoires

The most important implication is the construction of new behavioral repertoires by strengthening existing repertoires or constructing new behavioral repertoires. Thus, a therapist may enquire as to when a depressed client was happy in the past and what they did in order to be happy (see LeJuez et al., 2002) or what they have done over the past month that made them happy. Alternatively, if they identify interacting with difficult people makes them feel unhappy, but they are unable to interact effectively with such people, they may decide that the client may need to learn a more effective way to interact with difficult people in a manner that makes them feel happy and more effective. Another strategy that does not involve enhancing behavioral repertoires is teaching the client to avoid anxiety-evoking situations, at least at first. For example, a client might be taught to avoid people and places associated with drug abuse, excessive eating or drinking, or approaching children.

Another area of intervention may be to correct the environmental contingences that support ineffective behavior. Given the person's punitive current environment and a lifelong history of learning avoidance with its accumulating negative side-effects, a lifelong history of ineffective behavior must be unlearned and the current environment that has supported it must be modified. The parents, spouse, coworker or peer who, inadvertently, or even knowingly, maintain the inappropriate behavior through differential reinforcement of the client's unhealthy behavior must be taught to use extinction and differential reinforcement of healthy behavior. If there are other punishing contingencies they too must be corrected. Painful health problems must be rendered painless, punitive jobs replaced with rewarding ones, punitive living situations changed to be more rewarding. (I recall a graduate student who reported a technically excellent functional assessment and its implied treatment plan. He finally commented that before he began implementing the treatment plan he was going to get the family a front door. Presumably his formulation could also include the aversive stimuli that would be removed when the family had one.)

Self-Control

These strategies alone may be insufficient, since the therapist can never completely anticipate all the possible future difficult situations that the client might encounter. Therefore, the therapist and client must work together to construct a repertoire of appropriate self-control in the client so that the client learns to arrange the environment to support their own self-control behavior and the behaviors these self-controlling behaviors in turn control.

Recall that Skinner's analysis of self-control involves two sets of responses: the controlling response and the controlled response. The controlling response changes the future probability of the controlled behavior. For example, one may modify the probability of binge eating (the controlled response) by taking several small snacks to work (the controlling response.) The independent variables controlling posting reminders – such as having healthy food easily available and social consequences for preparing the health snacks – are the focus of intervention. In his account of constructivist tactics, Skinner placed greatest emphasis on teaching the client to arrange their physical and social worlds so that controlling responses that control the healthy behaviors are more likely.

Discovering the Formulation

Skinner advised that the therapist should not deliver the formulation – the analysis of the independent variables controlling their problematic behavior. He gave two reasons. First, the client might reject the excellent advice out of hand. Second, and more subtly, Skinner noted that if the client discovers their own case formulation considerable behavior change has already occurred in making the discovery of the relationship between their own behavior and the environment. By learning to observe and describe one's own behavior in new ways and learning to describe the relationship of their problematic behavior to the environmental variables that control it, by engaging in experiments in which some novel behavior is tried out and the effects on one's own behavior is discriminated and reported, the client's behavior has already changed. Hence, working with a client to make a functional assessment of their presenting problems involves inducing considerable behavior change, which can be the basis of further behavior change toward a healthier happier life.

IMPLICATIONS

Skinner's description of psychopathology is full of implications for understanding psychopathology, psychotherapy, case formulation and intervention. Behavior analysis had a long history of taking concepts from psychotherapy and identifying the learning that might occur during various forms of therapy. Respondent extinction of emotional responding to conditioned stimuli by talking or otherwise exposing clients to conditioned stimuli may be a common element in many forms of psychotherapy. Differential reinforcement of behavior change through client change (Truax, 1966) and simple instruction may also be important common processes. As new forms of psychotherapy are developed and shown to be effective, behavior analysis can examine them and identify the learning that may be taking place. For example, Jacobson et al. (1996) conducted a component analysis of cognitive behavior therapy (CBT) for depression. They decomposed CBT into its behavioral component of behavioral activation and its cognitive component. Although therapist reported being biased in favor of CT, the behavioral activation component of CBT was superior to the cognitive component, both for measures of depression and negative thinking.

Skinner's conceptualization of psychopathology as failure of self-control in the presence of pre-aversive stimuli associated with a history of punishment also has some quite useful implications for case formulation and therapy. It suggests that one of the purposes of taking a history is to identify that history of punishment, to identify the client's self-regulation skills before the onset of the disorder and to identify the failure of their self-regulation skills. This information, if accurate, may form the foundation for case formulation and intervention. It also suggests that intervention should involve teaching self-regulation.

Skinner's explicit avoidance of technocratic answers to intervention methods is noteworthy. Contemporary behavior analysts criticize technically-oriented behavior therapists who learn techniques that match diagnosis, but who fail to understand the conceptual basis of their work. This suggests that behavior analysts should be open to a wide array of intervention methods some of which at first sight might appear non-behavioral, but that might be justifiable on the basis of a behavioral case formulation. (See for example, Hopko et al. (2007) for a case report of behavioral treatment of depression using various treatments, including cognitive methods.)

Skinner suggested that respondent extinction was an important learning process in psychotherapy. If is true, then an important task that a therapist can undertake is to identify the relevant conditioned stimuli and ensure that respondent extinction occurs through exposure. Thus, an effective therapist must accurately identify a range of events and topics that the client avoids talking and thinking about and ensure that exposure to these stimuli take place through talking, writing, or direct exposure to these conditioned stimuli. This must be done until respondent extinction takes place; that is no negative emotional responding occurs in the presence of the conditioned stimuli. (See Chapter 4 for a fuller discussion of this.)

If psychopathology is due to a failure of self-control in the face of stimuli with an associated history of punishment, then one of the therapist's most important jobs is to rebuild or teach these self-control skills. (See Chapter 6 for a further discussion of this approach.) This should be part of a broader effort to use constructional tactics to enhance the client's repertoire (Goldiamond, 1974). Hence, Skinner's generic case formulation emphasized reinforcement-based interventions to reinstate lost behavioral repertoires. (See Chapter 11 for a further discussion.) These interventions should be based on a formulation that, as far as possible, the client apparently discovers for themselves. Thus, is it the therapist's job to teach the client how to discriminate and report the relationship between their own behavior and the environment and to identify the implications of this relationship for behavior change.

Chapter 11

BEHAVIORAL CASE FORMULATION

This chapter will illustrate behavioral approaches to clinical case formulation. In the first section we will consider Skinner's own generic case formulation. This illustrates Skinner's speculations on how behavioral principles could be applied to case formulation and treatment. The next section reviews Kanfer and Phillip's 1970 model of case formulation. The third section reviews Nezu and Nezu's (1989, 1993, Nezu et al., 2004) behavioral approach to case formulation and illustrates it with an example of depression. I then describe Koerner and Linehan's (1997) dialectical behavior therapy (DBT) approaches to case formulation. The next, and perhaps most developed methodology for behavioral case formulation, comes from Haynes and O'Brien's functional analytic clinical case model (FACM). This section will present three illustrations of how the FACM model can be applied to depression, self-injury and psychosis. The fourth section will illustrate Follette, Naugle and Linnerooth (2000) conceptually consistent, behavior analytic approach to case formulation. A case formulation of an eating disorder will illustrate this approach (Farmer & Latner, 2007). The final section will then go on to note some of the differences in the three approaches: it will contrast behavioral with non-behavioral behavior analytic and with Wolpe-type approaches to clinical case formulation.

SKINNER'S GENERIC CASE FORMULATION

Skinner did not publish any case formulations of actual people with clinical problems. As we noted in Chapter 10, Skinner's main contribution to ABA was to lay its foundations, but he was not greatly involved in applied work. Nevertheless, he was quite interested in its potential application to psychopathology.

Let us look at the following passage from *Beyond Freedom and Dignity* (1971), which illustrates how Skinner formulated clinical cases in general terms.

> Consider a young man whose world has suddenly changed. He has graduated from college and is going to work, let us say, or has been inducted into the armed services. Most of the behavior he has acquired up to this point proves useless in his new environment. The behavior he actually exhibits can

be described and the description translated as follows: he lacks assurance or feels insecure or is unsure of himself (his behavior is weak and inappropriate); he is dissatisfied or discouraged (he is seldom reinforced, and as a result his behavior undergoes extinction); he is frustrated (extinction is accompanied by emotional response); he feels uneasy or anxious (his behavior frequently has unavoidable aversive consequences which have emotional effects); there is nothing he want to do or enjoys well, he has no feeling of craftmanship, no sense of leading a purposeful life, no sense of accomplishment (he is rarely reinforced for doing anything); he feels guilty or ashamed (he has previously been punished for idleness or failure, which now evokes emotional responses); he is disappointed in himself and disgusted with himself (he is no longer reinforced by the admiration of other, and the extinction which follows has emotional effects); he becomes hypochondriacal (he concludes that he is ill) or neurotic (he engages in a variety of ineffective modes of escape); and he experiences an identity crisis (he does not recognized the person he once called "I"). (pp.146–147)

A number of observations might be made on this formulation. First, it illustrates how the vernacular, mentalistic language that pervades our description of mental health and behavior disorders can readily be translated into observable behavior. There are corresponding observable behaviors and learning processes for each of the man's problems. For example, "lacks assurance" is reflected in low rates of public, reinforced behavior. Second, it illustrates how such observable behavior may be linked to learning processes. Hence, a "lack of assurance" reflects extinction of previously reinforced behavior and "feeling uneasy or anxious" reflects the emotional side effects of extinction. Third, the possible learning processes that underlie the man's observable behavior have implications for treatment. We might restate Skinner's more prosaic analysis in a behavioral case formulation as follows:

In the previous environment contingencies of reinforcement maintained the man's effective behavior. Following his move to a new job, the contingencies that maintained his previously effective behavior were not present. The new contingencies no longer maintained his effective behavior. He lacked the effective behaviors for the new setting and/or these behaviors did not come into contact with the new contingencies. Hence, his formerly effective behaviors were extinguished. This resulted in low rates of effective behavior and the emotional side effects of extinction. In the new setting there is little reinforcement available to his behavior. The current low rates of effective behavior were previously paired with punishment during his history now evoke emotional responses, such as shame and guilt. Although prior to the change his behavior was reinforced by others, this is no longer the case. Again, there are emotional side effects of this extinction. He has learned a rule "I am ill" that describes the prevailing contingencies as "if I work I will be ignored or punished, if I do nothing, bad things will not happen". His neurotic behavior, which consists of complaining of anxiety and mood symptoms, are ineffective in gaining positive reinforcement.

We could now use this analysis to derive a treatment plan which will be closely based on that analysis. The most telling aspect of this description is that the man's previously effective behavior has undergone extinction.

Thus, one treatment implication is that therapy must reinstate appropriate contingencies to reinforce the man's effective behavior. The therapist and client need to determine if: (1) the effective behavior in the client's repertoire never contacted the contingencies in the new environment; or (2) the client does not have effective behavior for this new setting. If it is the former, then the therapist's job is to be a bridge to contact the existing contingencies by prompting and reinforcing appropriate behavior until the client comes in contact with the existing contingencies. For example, if the client has good administrative skills perhaps a job could be found for him using those skills in a new setting. Alternatively, if the client does not have the skills required for this setting, for example, if he does not know how to take inventory as required in his new job, he may have to seek formal or informal training to do so. His current environment was characterized as one in which his behavior is rarely reinforced. Perhaps, his therapist and the client can discover what behaviors are likely to result in reinforcement from peers and supervisors. Maybe there are social activities with peers he can engage in that he might enjoy. Alternatively, perhaps his supervisor might be open to working with him to give him small manageable tasks and could be taught to give recognition for competently done work. The therapist and client should identify his neurotic forms of behavior and recognize their ineffectiveness in escaping aversive stimuli. They should also identify the aversive stimuli escaped. Perhaps he can be taught other, more effective ways to behave in these situations. Perhaps the aversive stimuli can be removed or attenuated in a more effective way see Table 6.1). If it seems that the client has an inappropriate rule that inaccurately represents the contingencies, perhaps behavioral experiments, cognitive therapy or acceptance-based forms of therapy might be effective in modifying this rule and replacing it with a more accurate or more adaptive rule.

Note that Skinner recommended that these functional relationships should be discovered by the client with assistance from the clinician. He recommended that the clinician should refrain from delivering the formulation and treatment plan to the client. Therefore, in this case the clinician's job is to teach the client how to discover these functional relationships for himself. This can be achieved through standard behavioral methods, such as self-recording. The therapist can teach this to the client through modeling and shaping of client verbal and writing behavior so that the client eventually describes their own functional assessment accurately. For example, they might be taught to write a summary of their day in which they accurately identify the situations that made then feel good and effective and those in which they felt bad and useless, and accurately describe the differences between these situations. (Compare this to Dixon and Johnson's (2007) approach to treating compulsive gambling described in Chapter 6.) During a clinical interview the therapist might ask for ratings of mood during the best and the worst part of the day. This could be the basis for identifying environmental correlates of variability in the client's mood and behavior. For example, suppose the client reported that (1) he felt competent when having lunch with a colleague and (2) miserable after he avoided his supervisor when he saw his supervisor from a distance. This material might be used to identify what was different between these settings. Even this modest amount of information suggests possible intervention strategies, such as scheduling more time with preferred peers, that are associated with better mood and learning some better to way to deal with his supervisor. In short, the therapist would teach the client to identify variations in his own problematic behavior. This self-generated formulation might then be the basis for developing a treatment plan. The hope would be that in future problematic situations, the client would not have to rely on a therapist to conduct a functional assessment and treatment plan. Rather, therapy should strengthen the client's self-regulation skills sufficiently so that he can manage his own life independently.

Skinner's nomothetic formulation of anxiety-depression is remarkable in a number of ways. First, the case formulation was done from first principles with little or no data on human psychopathology to work from, other than perhaps Skinner's observations of people's behavior and reading in psychopathology. At the time there were few empirical reports of behavior therapy in adult mental health and only a handful of reports related to intellectual disabilities and schizophrenia. Second, reflecting its roots in basic learning theory, Skinner's formulation is explicit in the learning processes that underlie the development and maintenance of psychopathology, and its treatment. Third, it takes our mentalistic, vernacular language of emotions and thinking and provides an analysis of those phenomena in terms of the science of behavior. Finally, it foreshadows many developments in ABA and behavior therapy that were to come, including treatment based on reinforcement to reinstate previously extinguished behavior, identifying specific problematic environments for each client, identifying deficiencies in self-management and intervention based on self-management.

SORKC ANALYSIS

Kanfer and Phillips (1970) presented one of the earliest versions of behavioral case formulation. Dissatisfied with earlier behavioral formulations, which referred only to stimulus and response, they expanded this analysis to include five components of an analysis of behavior (see Figure 11.1). They proposed that a complete description of a behavioral unit requires that the specification of the prior stimulation (S), biological state of the organism, (O), response repertoire (R), the contingency (K) and consequences (C.) A complete description must also describe their

S	Prior stimulation
O	Biological state of the organism
R	Response repertoire
K	Contingency
C	Consequence

Antecedent	Behavior	Consequence
S →O →	R→	K → C

Modified from Kanfer and Phillips (1970) *Learning Foundations of Behavior Therapy,* p. 54. Copyright John Wiley and Sons

Figure 11.1. A summary of the SORKC model and its relationship to the antecedent-behavior-consequence model

temporal order. They proposed that the SORKC model could be used to describe both respondent and operant behavior. The S includes that small proportion of all the possible environmental stimuli that do control behavior, including discriminative stimuli and conditioned stimuli. They also noted that stimuli may come both from the environment and may be produced by the organism's own behavior, as in the examples of response chains and self-regulation. They also noted the importance of the social environment as a source of relevant stimulation for behavior. Among organismic variables (O) they included genetics, drugs, the social influence on an organism's physiology that may result in changes in behavior, as well as diseases that may influence learning and behavior. Contingency (K) and consequence (C) both refer to operant aspects of behavior. Chapters 5 and 6 described these. Kanfer and Phillips (1970) went on to illustrate the application of the analysis of behavior based on SORKC analysis to intervention (see their Table 10.1, pp. 511–513).

Application to Bulmia

Ghadheri (2007) reported a narrative case formulation of a woman with bulimia using a conceptual framework strongly influenced by this conceptual framework. He termed this method 'logical functional analysis.' Anna was a 26-year-old woman with a 12 year history of anorexia and subsequent bulimia. She had wanted to start a romantic attachment, but decided she could not until she controlled her bulimia. She had eight episodes of bulimia per week and 10 episodes of vomiting per week. Most occurred in the afternoon. She had restricted patterns of eating, had heightened weight and shape concern, met diagnostic criteria for social phobia and was moderately depressed. Negative affect, such as anger and disappointment were antecedents for binges. She believed that she had a low metabolic rate and that she should restrict eating. Anna responded quite well to manualized cognitive behavior therapy for bulimia. However, exposure therapy failed, perhaps because of failure to be exposed to distressing thoughts. Cognitive therapy was insufficiently effective in achieving this.

Ghaderi used a variety of individualized interventions based on a logical functional analysis. Excessively strong stimulus control included feeling bloated after a meal that was often followed by binging. Poor consequential control included private rules with weak remote consequences, such as "If I follow this treatment, I will slowly lose weight" and weak negative rules, such as negative self-evaluations, that, although distressing, did not motivate her to change her behavior. Inappropriate establishing operations included prolonged periods of not eating, resulting in food being highly reinforcing. Finally, behavioral deficits included lack of generating appropriate rules, avoidance of socially challenging situations and behavioral excesses, such as excessive eating to self-sooth.

Diffusion strategies, identifying goals and values did help. Diffusion was also used to facilitate exposure to fearful social situations. At 18-month follow-up she had gained weight, reduced her preoccupations with weight and appearance, had few episodes of binging and vomiting, did not meet diagnostic criteria and was engaged to her fiancé. Ghaderi distinguished this treatment from standard cognitive behavior therapy (CBT) in the following ways. First, the functional relationships between Anna's private verbal behavior, emotions and their context formed the basis for treatment more than typical CBT. Second, the intervention attempted to modify this private verbal behavior using diffusion and values clarification, rather the cognitive restructuring. Note that this behavioral formulation is similar to Farmer and Latner's below. However, Ghaderi presented this behavioral formulation as a written summary, whereas Farmer and Latner used a diagrammatic presentation.

Commentary on SORKC Analysis

Kanfer and Phillips provided a more sophisticated and detailed analysis of how case formulation could proceed than Skinner's initial analysis. Like Skinner's analysis, it is firmly rooted in the science of learning.

The SORKC acronym is a useful guide for the clinician to analyze presenting problems and their controlling variables. It is also useful to have the SORKC framework to map from problem to intervention in a somewhat abstract way that links practice to theory. SORKC analysis has continued to influence contemporary clinical behavior analysis (Follette et al., 2000).

NEZU AND NEZU'S CLINICAL PATHOGENESIS MAP

Nezu and Nezu (1989, 1993, Nezu et al., 2004) developed a tool to assist in behavioral case formulation called the clinical pathogenesis map (CPM). A CPM should identify all the relevant variables that contributed to the initiation and maintenance of the presenting problems. It should include developmental, historical and recent triggers. It should also include the current system of pathology that elicits and maintains the problematic behavior. Thus, a CPM should include both historical and current variables. A CPM summarizes this information in a diagram that Nezu and Nezu liken to path analysis and causal models of behavior.

Nezu, Nezu, Friedman and Haynes (1999) identified four steps in the CPM approach to case formulation: "(1) problem definition and formulation, (2) generation of alternatives, (3) treatment decision making, and (4) solution implementation and verification" (p. 376). Their approach to problem definition differs from Wolpe's and other methods described in Chapter 10. Rather than identify a clinical hypothesis early on, they used a "funnel approach". This involved a very broad behavioral assessment early on. Only later does the clinician focus down to specific target behaviors. Nezu and Nezu (1989) developed a multi-dimensional framework for assessment including assessment of actual and perceptual data, current and developmental aspects of the problem and person and environmental focal problem areas.

A CPM Formulation of Depression

Nezu et al. (1999) illustrated the application of the CPM to formulate and develop an intervention plan for a client, Paul, with depression. Paul reported that he was depressed more when (1) he was alone, (2) at night in his bedroom and alone, and (3) when he was inactive in the evening. On these occasions he thought about his girlfriends. This triggered a variety of private behavior, including negative self-talk, negative mood, fatigue and some physical sensations of anxiety. When depressed he often found it difficult to get out of bed and he avoided social contact.

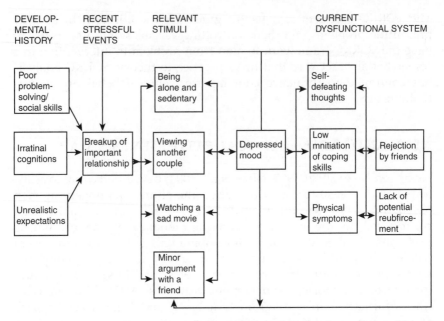

Figure 11.2. A clinical pathogenesis map of Paul's depressed mood. Reproduced from Nezu et al. (1997) Case formulation in behavior therapy. In: T. D. Eells (Ed.). *Handbook of psychotherapy case formulation*. New York: Guilford. p. 383.

Figure 11.2 illustrates Nezu et al.'s CPM for Paul's presenting problems. It summarizes both developmental factors that predisposed toward the development of the problem and recent stressful events. The current environment includes relevant stimuli, such as triggers for depressed mood. It also includes the current dysfunctional system, such as negative cognitions and withdrawal from friends. Nezu et al. (1999) noted that there were a number of causal chains within the current dysfunctional system. One example included: (1) Paul feeling depressed; (2) his friends calling him up; (3) Paul focused on internal states; (4) this irritates his friends who then avoid him; (5) consequently he felt more rejected and isolated. Based on this analysis, Nezu et al. (1999) developed a treatment plan that consisted of five elements. These included (1) reducing the time Paul spend alone; (2) teaching him self-control and self-monitoring to "direct his attention toward positive events and skills" (p. 380); (3) teaching Paul relaxation to counter depression and anxiety; (4) teaching him problem-solving skills to interact more effectively with friends when depressed; and (5) to increase more pleasurable activities.

A CPM Formulation of Anxiety

Nezu et al. (2004) illustrated the use of CPM formulation by describing the case of Henry, a severely anxious, 32-year-old, single man. Henry was a skilled and intelligent accountant. This resulted in rapid career progression and exposure to social situations that he found very frightening. His rapid progression resulted in both a high salary and the requirement to present to groups and meet clients. Nezu et al. used the CPM to organize their information about Henry. Figure 11.3 illustrates this CPM.

Henry's developmental history revealed a history of punishment for social behavior and reinforcement with social withdrawal. This was due to his father having high standards for formal social behavior, his peers ridiculing him for behaving this way and his mother comforting him after his peers ridiculed him. This resulted in him becoming socially anxious, preoccupied about what others thought about him, preoccupied with physical symptoms and with the possibility that others were aware of this.

In the current environment there were several antecedent stimuli. These included being asked to attend a work-related social event, his high school reunion and an invitation to his boss's party. Henry could effectively avoid

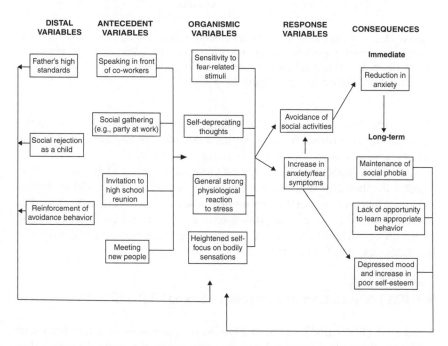

Figure 11.3. A clinical pathogenesis map for social anxiety. Reproduced from Nezu, Nezu & Lombardo (2004), *Cognitive-behavioral Case Formulation and Treatment Design. A Problem Solving Approach.* New York: Springer, Figure 2.1, p. 30.

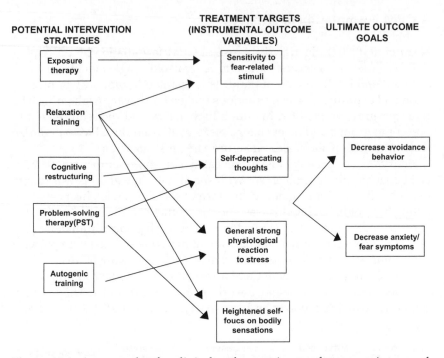

Figure 11.4. An example of a clinical pathogenesis map for aggressive sexual behavior and multiple other problems. Reproduced from Nezu, Nezu & Lombardo (2004), *Cognitive-behavioral Case Formulation and Treatment Design. A Problem Solving Approach*. New York: Springer, Figure 3.1, p. 45.

these situations. For example, he called in sick or got coworkers to make presentations for him. These strategies resulted in reduction in fear but he never learned how to cope with challenging situations.

Nezu et al. (2004) also developed a Goal Attainment Map (GAM). This is used to plan and map where treatment is going. The GAM identifies mutually selected, ultimate treatment goals, treatment targets that lead to those goals and intervention strategies to achieve those treatment targets. It should also identify obstacles to achieving those outcomes. Figure 11.4 illustrates a GAM for Henry.

A CPM Formulation of Aggressive Sexual Behavior

Nezu et al. (1999) also presented a FACM of aggressive sexual behavior in a 27-year-old male sex offender with a diagnosis of personality disorder. He had beaten a woman and attempted to rape a 12-year-old female neighbor. He was referred after a four-month period of hospitalization during which he made suicidal gestures. He had a long history of emotional problems dating back to his teenage years. Other people had regarded him as "borderline retarded". He also had possible neurological damage following a car wreck. Prior to his recent hospitalization his problems worsened significantly. He had failed to respond to trials of lithium and antidepressants.

Nezu et al. conducted an assessment in order to: (1) identify internal and external triggers; (2) identify the behavioral affective and cognitive components of his problems; (3) identify the developmental and environmental variables affecting his current problems; and (4) develop a clinical hypothesis about his problems. They did this using multiple assessment methods. These included: (1) a clinical interview with the client; (2) an intellectual assessment; (3) a psychometric battery assessing life history and social problem solving skills; (4) a role play assessment of assertiveness, heterosexual skills and anger arousing situations; and (5) observational ABC data collected by staff and therapist at his hostel.

These assessments revealed that he scored in the low average range of intellectual functioning. There was little evidence of gross neurological damage, although Nezu et al could not exclude the possibility of some residual brain damage. His history revealed that he felt inadequate, hopeless and lonely. He was fearful, hypersensitive and hostile to women. He had general deficits in social skills. He had a poor understanding of why social situations were difficult, avoided social problems, and had poor ability to inhibit his own behavior. In role play of heterosexual situations he was often inappropriate aggressive, rather than assertive, although he did sometimes demonstrate assertive behaviors.

In their case formulation, Nezu et al. noted that his intellectual limitations may have limited his ability to control his social and sexual behavior. He also reacted out of proportion to everyday triggers and some caregivers may have inadvertently reinforced this in the past. Following his aggressive behavior there were several potential reinforcing consequences. Other people were very frightened of him, interacted with him a great deal and tried to calm him down after a violent episode. When he had problems coping with his sexual impulses he became more focused on work and denied that he had any sexual interests. Sexual aggression was more likely after critical comments at work and after rejection by a woman. Nezu et al presented the CPM for this problem, which is shown in Figure 11.5.

Based on this formulation, the authors developed a treatment plan. The plan's goals were to improve his emotional regulation and problem-solving skills. This plan included (1) avoiding confrontation in therapy by replacing arguments with empathic statements; (2) replacing aggressive responses to triggers, such as insults and rejection, with other more appropriate responses, such as fear or disappointment; (3) teaching better responses to anger than aggression in group and individual therapy; (4) social reinforcement for self-control when distressed; and (5) having a crisis plan for major losses or other triggers, such as taking a day off from his regular routine.

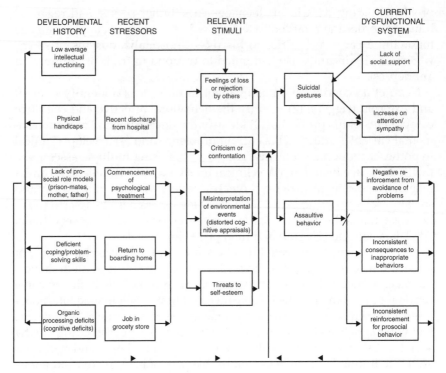

Figure 11.5. An example of a clinical pathogenesis map of DJ. Reproduced from Nezu, Nezu, Friedman & Haynes (1997). In *Handbook of Psychotherapy Case Formulation* (Ed. T.D. Eells). New York: Guilford, Figure 4.4, p. 394.

Commentary on CPMs

A CPM is a useful approach to summarizing a lot of information diagrammatically. A CPM might be helpful in deriving a treatment plan based on both historical and contemporary variables, which many practitioners will find appealing. Some clients might also find such an objective summary of their presenting problems helpful and might be able to participate in treatment planning and/or understand the rationale for their treatment plan better. The use of such a diagrammatic summary could be a useful point of discussion between a therapist and client that circumvents some of the problems of a summary that is only verbal and hence easy to confuse or forget. Discussion of such a summary might be a useful vehicle to prompt clients to participate in their treatment design and to select among the various treatment options that exist. As such, it might be another example of how the pre-intervention activities of assessment and formulation can subtly induce change in client behavior that might facilitate change in later formal therapy. Such a summary may also be good discipline for practitioners to force them to commit their formulation to a permanent medium and this may force practitioners to make relevant distinctions, such as between onset, subsequent development and current factors. Nezu and Nezu also include cognitive factors, such as cognitive deficiencies and distortions, which may be conductive to cognitive therapists using eclectic cognitive-behavioral formulations.

CASE FORMULATION IN DIALECTIVE BEHAVIOR THERAPY

Koerner and Linehan (1997) discussed using DBT concepts to case formulation. They outlined a three-step process which included "(1) gathering information about treatment targets; (2) organizing information into a useful format; and (3) revising the formulation as needed ...". The first target area included five types of behavior "... in descending order of priority ... [are] suicidal crisis behaviors; parasuicidal acts; suicidal ideation and communication; suicide-related expectations and beliefs; and suicide-related affect ..." (pp. 354–355). The second target area included behaviors that interfere with treatment, such as missing appointments, psychiatric inpatient admission and refusal to work in therapy. Therapist behaviors, such as therapists missing appointments and failing to return phone calls are also included here. The third target behavior area included behavior that reduces the client's quality of life. These included mood and anxiety disorder, substance abuse, domestic instability and untreated medical problems.

Koerner and Linehan also used two behavioral concepts in step 1: Chain analysis and task analysis. To facilitate a chain analysis each client keeps their own diary card. This is the basis of the beginning of each DBT therapy sessions. They described that " ... repeated chain analysis identif[ies] the precipitants, vulnerability factors, link, and consequences associated with each primary target ..." (p. 356). They use this chain analysis to develop interventions to teach skillful problem solving, modify contingencies that maintain problems and so on. The chain analysis is used to identify weak links in the chain of events, behavior that leads to dangerous behavior and to intervene at the weak link to teach more functional behavior at that point. A task analysis involves a very detailed step-by-step analysis of how to respond appropriately at the weak link in the chain. This could involve teaching DBT skills, such as mindfulness, self-soothing or self-management skills, use of ideas from the psychological literature or from personal experiences of when one behaved effectively in a similar situation. In Step 2, a written summary of formulation is then developed and shared with the client. The summary may be written or graphic, such as a flow chart. Step 3 involves ongoing revision of the formulation in the light of changes during DBT.

A DBT Case Formulation of Borderline Personality Disorder

Koerner and Linehan (1997) illustrated the use of DBT case formulation with a case formulation of a composite case. "Mary" was a woman with a history of two near-lethal suicide attempts, injuring herself with head banging, ingesting dangerous substances, cutting her arms and legs with razors and taking overdoses of prescribed medications. Child protection services took her and had a long history of disturbed and dangerous behavior. Her diagnoses at various times included alcohol dependence, eating disorder NOS, major depression with psychotic features, dysthymia, and borderline personality disorder. She also experienced panic attacks and was socially avoidant.

By session three, Mary and her therapist identified the following primary stage 1 goals relating to personal safety: (1) to stop cutting herself and making suicide attempts; (2) to reduce psychiatric hospitalizations; (3) to reduce panic attacks; and (4) to replace them with better coping skills. A chain analysis identified the following chain of events as typical of a serious event: (1) at work she had been asked to do a task that was part of her job, but that she could not do; (2) rather than ask for help or have the assignment modified, she set unrealistic goals, covered up her failure, rather than communicating the need for help, left work with a migraine and called in sick; (3) over the weekend she ruminated over work, argued with her partner, who left; (4) when she was alone she began contemplating suicide, got out the razors and then called her therapist; (5) she and her therapist eventually agreed that she could make it through to the next morning and would attend a therapy session at that time.

Koerner and Linehan used this chain analysis to identify several points of intervention. These included: migraine attacks, difficulties at work, arguments with her partner and time alone. Thus, a treatment plan might involve: (1) better management of migraines; (2) some form of assertiveness training to deal with difficult task at work, to ask for assistance and not cover up incompetence; (3) some intervention for rumination about past failures, such as activity scheduling, cognitive therapy, panic management, removing razors and lethal doses of medication from the house, and (4) modifications of beliefs concerning the consequences of suicide as a solution to her problems. The formulation was summarized in a written format (this is shown in Figure 11.6). In step 3 the therapist addressed social avoidance because she feared losing her temper and being violent with others. Additionally, support was given to the therapist who may have inadvertently reduced demands in therapy following Mary's suicidal threats and hostility.

Comment on DBT Case Formulation

The DBT approach to case formulation has several important strengths. Reflecting that it was developed to help people with borderline personality

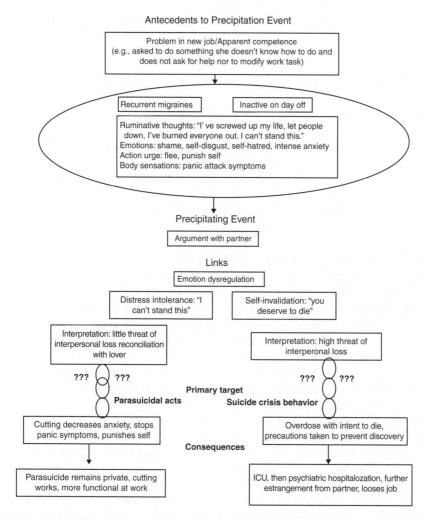

Figure 11.6. An example of a dialectical behavior therapy formulation of parasuicidal behavior. Reproduced from Koerner and Linehan (1997). In *Handbook of Psychotherapy Case Formulation* (Ed. T.D. Eells). New York: Guilford, Figure 13.1, p. 363.

disorder, its explicit guidelines in prioritizing target behavior in terms of safety is very important. It is also practical and may assist both the client and therapists in establishing what is most important early on. Additionally, the use of explicit technology to analyze behavior through diaries, chain analysis and task analysis again directs the therapist and client to be very explicit in their analysis. It is likely to channel them to search for solutions that are directly linked to the environmental variables that control problematic client behavior. Finally, the systematic progression from dangerous behavior, to distressing psychopathology to improved functioning provides the client and therapist a structure to use as therapy progresses. The empirical support for DBT suggests that this approach may be an effective one.

FUNCTIONAL ANALYTIC CLINICAL CASE MODEL

Haynes and O'Brien have written extensively on functional approaches to case formulation (Haynes & O'Brien, 1990, 2000). Their work is one of the most sophisticated accounts of clinical applications of functional analysis. It explicitly addresses its epistemological basis and the limitations to their methods of data collection and inference. It systematically classifies variables and the potential relationships between variables. This approach is also quite developed and useful because there are many illustrations of the application of the FACM to varied problems.

Haynes and O'Brien (1990) defined functional analysis as "the identification of important, controllable, causal and non-causal functional relations applicable to specified behaviors for an individual" (p. 654). They emphasized identifying variables that have a functional relationship to the client's problem, that are causal, can be manipulated and have a large magnitude on the problem. Other variables might be related to the target behavior in various ways. However, they are less important for a clinical formulation because they are correlational, rather than causal, are important, but cannot be manipulated or only have a small impact on the target behavior. Thus, important, but unmodifiable variables, such as life events, biological attributes, medical condition and demographic variables, uncontrollable environmental variables and epidemiological variables, such as economic status, cannot be part of a FACM because they cannot influence the treatment plan. In contrast, variables that can be manipulated, such as the behavior of other people around the client, the activities that the client participates in, the job or education they choose, their self-management skills, etc. are all potentially open to manipulation and may be causal and of large magnitude. Hence, these variables are potentially part of a FACM.

Haynes and O'Brien contrasted nomothetic with idiographic functional analyses. In nomothetic functional analyses a generic model based on the development of psychopathology and learning is proposed for a specific condition. For example, Skinner's generic case formulation is a nomothetic formulation of generic anxiety-depression. Nomothetic functional analyses may provide a framework for assessment and conceptualization of a specific case. However, this approach is limited for clinical work as one of the main purposes of functional assessment is the identification of the relevant variables *for that individual*. One of the tenets of functional analysis is that individual differences within a single diagnostic category are of paramount import. These individual differences between people sharing the same diagnostic label, rather than the diagnostic labels themselves, guide the identification of effective and ineffective treatment strategies. Hence, the role of generic, nomothetic functional analyses is downplayed, other than perhaps as an initial framework to use for each individual client's formulation.

The aims of a FACM are "(a) to organize the assessor's clinical judgments; (b) to encourage a sequential and systematic approach to the multiple judgments involved in clinical case formulation; (c) it helps identify the areas in need of further assessment; (d) it facilitates clinical case presentations and communication between professionals with different backgrounds, and (e) it illustrates variables affecting treatment goals and guides decisions about which variables should be selected as treatment targets" (Virues-Ortega & Haynes, 2005, p. 577). A FACM produces a vector diagram that summarizes all the relevant current variables, their status, direction of influence, strength and modifiability. Unlike other case formulation approaches that also use diagrams to summarize the formulation, the FACM approach only includes variables from the current environment. Historical variables such as unmodifiable historical causal variables are occasionally included, but the FACM diagram clearly indicates these. FACM emphasizes the current, modifiable environment, rather than unmodifiable history.

Hayes and O'Brien (2000, pp. 276–277) identified 11 components to a functional analysis. These are as follows:

1. Identify client behavior problems and intervention goals. Although multiple target behaviors are possible, the focus should be on the major client goal.
2. The behavior problems and goals vary in importance.
3. Client problems may be independent or related to each other. Reciprocal causal relationships between client problems are especially important, because focusing on these problems can lead to large impact on client problems.
4. Client problems have social, legal and medical consequences. One consideration when deciding which problem to focus on is the consequences of the target behavior.
5. Identification of causal variables, such as antecedents, situational events, contingencies, cognitive antecedents and consequences, is important.
6. The modifiability or clinical utility of variables should be identified.
7. The relationship, between the causal variable – whether it is of small or large magnitude, unidirectional or bidirectional, linear or nonlinear – should be identified.
8. Causal variables may affect each other and thus, the relationship between causal variables should be identified and considered.
9. Chains of causal events should be identified. Several points of intervention along a chain of causal events should be noted.
10. Mediating variables are variables through which a causal variable operates. If a causal variable cannot be manipulated, then modification of the medicating variables may be an important strategy to modify client behavior.

11. Moderating variables increase or decrease the strength of a relationship between a causal variable and target behavior. As with mediating variables, modification of moderating variables may be important when the causal variable cannot be manipulated.

Haynes and O'Brien (2000) noted a number of additional characteristics of functional analysis. These include the following:

1. A functional analysis might include multiple functional relationships.
2. A functional analysis is never complete. It is always provisional.
3. The presence of one functional relationship between one independent variable and a dependent variable does not preclude the possibility another functional relationship between the same independent variable and another dependent variable.
4. A functional relationship is dynamic. It changes over time, including the time when intervention takes place.
5. The validity of a functional relationship may be limited to certain domains. For example, a functional relationship may only be present in a certain setting or in when a certain "mood" is present.
6. Functional relationships include both narrow specific variables, such as crying, and broad variables such as depressed mood. Functional analysis should err on the side of specific variables. It should avoid broad variables.
7. A functional analysis should integrate empirical findings from nomothetic functional analyses into idiographic functional analyses.
8. A functional analysis can extend beyond the individual. It may include extended social systems, such as families, classrooms and relevant social systems that are geographically distant.
9. A functional analysis may include noncontiguous causal variables, such as causal historical variables. If they do, then the specific current mechanism must be specified. For example, if child abuse is a distant causal relationship, then the current relevant variables, such as a specific social skills deficit, must be identified.
10. A functional analysis should be goal-oriented and constructivist. It should focus on strengthening desirable behaviors that are alternatives to the problem behavior.
11. A functional analysis can be conducted on a functional response class of topographically different, but functionally equivalent responses (Haynes & O'Brien, 2000, pp. 277–278).

FACM Methodology

The FACM is a much more formal than other previously described modeling procedures. It classifies variables explicitly. For example, variables may be of low, medium and high modifiability. Variables may covary, be unidirectional, bidirectional, moderating or mediating. They may be causal and unmodifiable, causal or moderating, or the target behavior. The FACM indicates the strength of the relationship between the variables on a three-point scale that estimates the correlations as being .2, .4 or .8 (weak, medium and strong respectively). The FACM also estimates how modifiable variables are. The FACM uses these estimations of the modifiability and strength of relationships between variables to estimate the likely impact of manipulating one variable on the target behavior. (See below for an example.) Figure 11.7

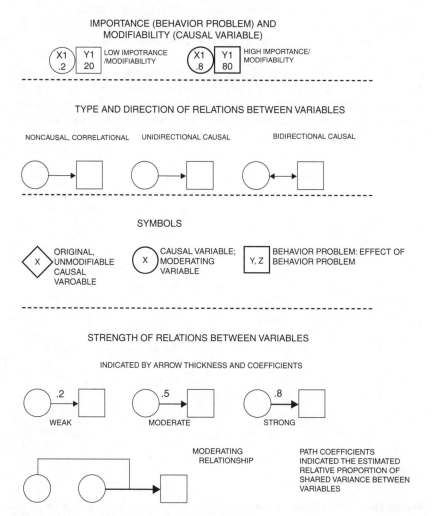

Figure 11.7. The symbols used in a functional analytic clinical case model and the variables they represent. Reproduced from Haynes & O'Brien (2000). *Principles and Practice of Behavioral Assessment.* New York: Kluwer, Figure 13.3, p. 285.

illustrates the symbols used in the vector diagrams. See also Figures 11.8, 11.9 and 11.10 below which illustrate the applications to individual cases.

FACM and A Formulation of Depression

Haynes and O'Brien (2000) presented a FACM of a woman with depression. She had left her home to be with her husband who suddenly died of a heart attack. She subsequently became increasingly isolated, quit her job and developed panic attacks outside the home. Her 8-year-old daughter compensated for her problems by performing household duties and providing reassurance when her mother expressed doubts about herself.

Figure 11.8 identifies two problems: depressed mood and panic episodes. They identified four important, modifiable, causal variables for depressed mood. These were deficient self-help skills, negative self-statements, insufficient social support and reinforcement for depression. The two modifiable causal variables for panic episodes were state anxiety and catastrophic thoughts. The model illustrated that the two problems were correlated with each other, but were non-causal. There were also

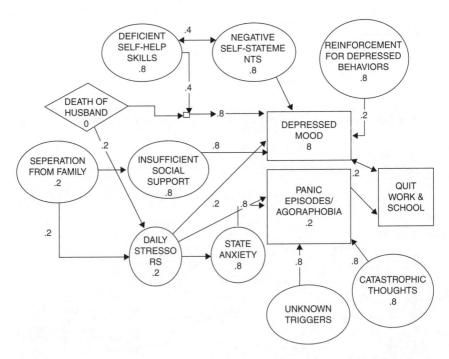

Figure 11.8. A functional analytic clinical case model of depression. Reproduced from Haynes & O'Brien (2000). *Principles and Practice of Behavioral Assessment.* New York: Kluwer, Figure 13.2, p. 284.

significant historical variables, such as the death of her husband and separation from her family. However, these historic variables were unmodifiable. Hence, they cannot be directly addressed in treatment. If current variables related to these historical events were relevant they could be incorporated into the model. For example, if intrusive thoughts were disturbing or if the woman avoided certain places associated with her husband at the time of referral then these problems and the current variables related to them could be incorporated into the FACM for this person. This FACM was also incomplete. There were significant unknown triggers for the panic attacks. Finally, although quitting work and school were effects of behavior problems they also affected these problems. For example, the loss of work and school was supposedly causally related to depressed mood, but not to panic episodes.

This FACM had clear implications for a treatment plan and high treatment utility. Suppose that depressed mood was selected as the primary target behavior. This might be done with the hope that, since it was correlated to panic episodes, successful treatment of depression might also influence panic episodes. One might begin by teaching social skills, since it was furthest back in the chain of causation. Additionally, since the daughter inadvertently maintained her mother's depressed behavior and the mother has no other significant source of social interaction, one might simultaneously target increasing other social support for the mother. At the same time one might also teach the daughter to support her mother's healthy non-depressed behavior. As part of this strategy, one might also attempt to reinstate work that involves pleasurable social contact with others. One might do this because the loss of work, presumably with loss social contact and loss of pleasurable activities, was also causally related to depressed mood.

These strategies might be sufficient to produce a large improvement in the person's life. Given the incomplete nature of the current FACM, perhaps a Wolpe-style interviewer might be able to identify the relevant conditioned stimuli for panic attacks. The information from such an interview could then be the basis of some form of respondent extinction, either by reciprocal inhibition using relaxation or in vivo exposure to the relevant conditioned stimuli.

FACM and a Formulation of Self-injury

Haynes and O'Brien (2000, p. 284) presented a FACM for a boy with self-injurious behavior. The assessment included interviews, questionnaires, self-monitoring and monitoring by the boy's mother and staff, observations in the clinic and in the natural setting. Figure 11.9 illustrates these findings in a FACM.

The variables that were most strongly correlated with self-injury were escape from aversive situations and attention from others. High task

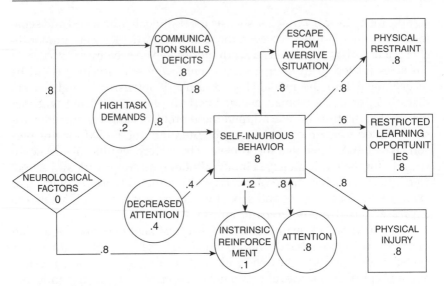

Figure 11.9. A functional analytic clinical case model of self-injurious behavior. Reproduced from Haynes & O'Brien (2000). *Principles and Practice of Behavioral Assessment*. New York: Kluwer.

demands also had a strong impact on self-injurious behavior. However, the impact of communication skills deficits moderated its impact. Self-injurious behavior occupied a pivotal position in the FACM. It strongly resulted in three major problems: physical restraint, restricted learning opportunities and physical injuries. Haynes and O'Brien noted that this FACM is consonant with much of the experimental functional analytic literature on self-injury.

The authors did not spell out the implications for treatment. However, the treatment implications are clear. For example, one could teach communication skills to escape in a safer more appropriate manner. One could remove demands completely and then fade them in gradually. Finally, one might use escape extinction and differential reinforcement of compliance by physically preventing the child to escape from demands and reinforcing compliance with demands with contingent escape.

FACM and Formulation of Psychosis

Virues-Ortega and Haynes (2005) presented a FACM of a 50-year-old man. He was an outpatient who had been diagnosed with schizophrenia and social anxiety. He had a 20-year history of pharmacotherapy, counseling and psychological support. He was currently single and unemployed and took an antidepressant and antipsychotic. His psychiatrist referred him and identified his main problems as being fearful of other people and thinking they may attack him; auditory hallucinations; and negative self-talk. (It is interesting to contrast this formulation of psychotic behavior with Morrison's [1998] cognitive behavioral formulation of a similar problem.)

After initial interviews, assessment included multiple types of assessment, such as interviews with family members and relevant professionals; self-monitoring of symptoms; psychometric assessment of mood, anxiety, obsessive and psychotic symptoms; observation in the natural environment and in analog settings of social behavior with strangers; and a review of his clinical history. This assessment identified five main problems: (1) anxiety as shown by hypervigilance, distress and arousal in the presence of other people, including strangers and his parents; (2) social avoidance; (3) paranoid and delusional beliefs; (4) being socially isolated; and (5) depressed mood (p. 577).

Virues-Ortega and Haynes's formulation included both speculations about the historical development of these symptoms and a FACM diagram of the presenting problem. They speculated that these odd behaviors had been learned because his parents provided poor models of social behavior and modeling of social withdrawal, combined with high rates of punitive interaction in the absence of reinforcing interactions, which were evident during current assessment. They suggested that this led to an impoverished social repertoire as a child, resulting in social rejection and anxiety at that time. Current observations with strangers supported this. His social anxiety may have been exacerbated by caffeine consumption, based on his own self-report. His repeated avoidance of socially anxious situations prevented extinction of anxious responding occurring. The strength of his paranoid beliefs covaried with his anxiety. His poor social skills and social anxiety both resulted in lack of social reinforcement and depressed mood. They concluded that paranoid beliefs and anxious responses were functionally equivalent responses, since they both were triggered by similar stimuli and both were maintained by the avoidance of anxiety. The FACM for this case formulation is shown in Figure 11.10.

Virues-Ortega and Haynes went on to estimate which variables would have the greatest impact on increasing comfort in social situations. Their model suggested that increasing the reinforcing value of interacting with other would have the greatest impact on the target behaviors. Thus, all other things being equal, this would be the preferred method of intervention.

Commentary on FACMs

As these examples illustrate, FACMs have been applied to a wide variety of clinical problems, including mixed depression and anxiety, self-injury

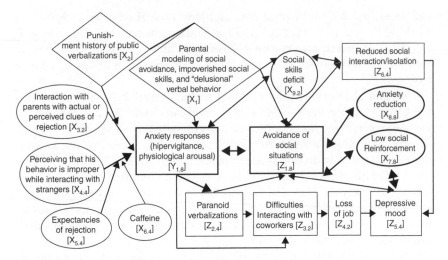

Figure 11.10. A functional analytic clinical case formulation of a case of psychosis and anxiety. From Virues-Ortega & Haynes (2005). Functional analysis in behavior therapy: behavioral foundations and clinical applications. *International Journal of Clinical and Health Psychology*, **5**(3), 575. Asociacion Espanola de Psicologia Conductual.

in a child with learning disabilities, aggressive sexual behavior, psychosis, migraine and marital problems (Floyd, Haynes & Kelly, 1997; Haynes, Leisen & Blaine, 1997; O'Brien & Haynes, 1995). FACMs are also highly practical in that they focus on current variables, preferably causal ones, with large effects on the problem(s) of interest. FACMs are very explicit in identifying the status of each variable in the model as causal, correlational, or a consequence of target behaviors. As with Nezu and Nezu's CPMs, a diagrammatic summary of a formulation has the benefits of forcing the clinician into writing a formulation and being explicit about the status of the variables. It also provides the client and clinician with a tool to use to understand and plan treatment in a constructive, participatory way.

FOLLETTE ET AL.'S METHODOLOGY

Follette et al. (2000) argued that behavioral case formulation should be closely based on behavioral and learning concepts. These include (1) basing the formulation on function, rather than topography; (2) analyzing functional rather than topographical classes of behavior; (3) that history can result in a wide range of topographies resulting from a complex link between historical antecedents and current topography; (4) that behavior

Classical Functional Analysis

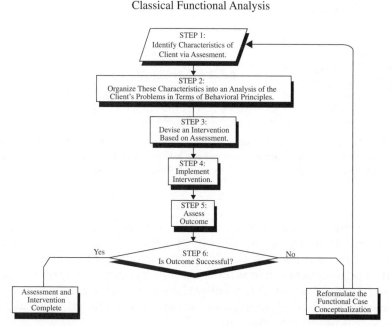

Figure 11.11. A six-step protocol for conducting a behavioral assessment. From Follette, Naugle and Linnerooth (2000). In *Clinical Behavior Analysis* (Ed. M.J. Dougher). Reno, NV: Context Press, Figure 1, p. 103.

is merely a sample of the person's behavioral repertoire, not a sign of an underlying problem; and (e) the entire person must be analyzed as a whole and understood within the context of the person's history. They describe a six-step protocol to conduct a classic functional analysis. Figure 11.11 illustrates this. These six steps include:

1. Identify the client's presenting problems, organize them into a problem list that prioritizes them, and identify the client's assets and liabilities.
2. Organize the information from step 1 using the learning concepts based on respondent and operant conditioning.
3. Identify intervention strategies based on step 2.
4. Implement the intervention.
5. Continuously evaluate the outcome of treatment.
6. Decide if the outcome was successful or not. If successful the process is complete. If the intervention was unsuccessful, then reformulate the case.

Follette et al. recommend using a simple schematic to organize the information using behavioral principles. This is illustrated in Figure 11.12.

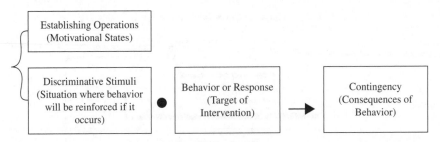

Figure 11.12. A classical functional analysis. From Follette, Naugle and Linnerooth (2000). A schematic of operant behavior. In *Clinical Behavior Analysis* (Ed. M.J. Dougher). Reno, NV: Context Press, Figure 2, p. 106.

This schematic is used to organize the information in Step 1 using the behavioral concepts of establishing operation, discriminative stimuli, response and contingency. Follette go on to note that formulations may include private events, such as thoughts and physiology. They refer back to Kanfer and Grimm's work to identify client problems in behavior analytic terms, such as lack of appropriate contingencies, interfering behaviors, and deficits in self-regulation etc.

A Formulation of A Case of Bulimia

Farmer and Latner (2007) adopted Follette et al.'s methodology to present a formulation and account of treatment of bulimic behavior. Jill was an 18-year-old woman with a four-year history of bulimia. She kept a behavioral diary that identified five recent episodes of binge eating. Farmer and Latner used the information about these five episodes to conduct a functional assessment. They observed that Jill engaged in restricted eating for two or more days prior to important social events. As the event approached she engaged in binge eating on highly preferred food, such as ice cream. She would feel bloated and uncomfortable thereafter. Subsequently engaging in purging terminated these aversive consequences. This left her feeling slightly demoralized, but not as unpleasant as the bloated feelings. Figure 11.13 summarizes this formulation.

Farmer and Latner used this formulation to guide Jill's treatment. For example, the establishing operation of food deprivation made food highly reinforcing. Hence, one component of intervention was removed these periods of reinforcer deprivation. To do this, Jill's gradually ate meals more often. To make binges more difficult, the response effort of binge eating was increased. This was done by limiting the amount of ice cream at home. They also used behavioral activation and social support to increase pleasurable activities. Since some of Jill's binge eating related to

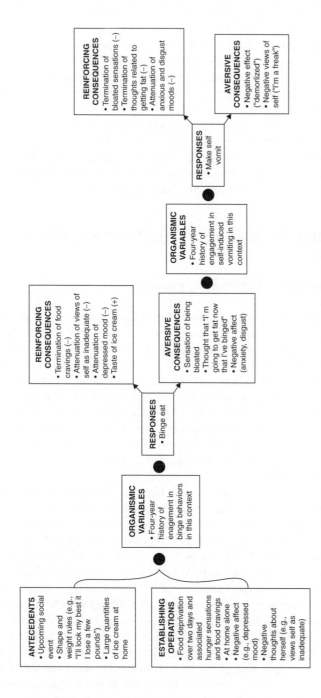

Figure 11.13. A functional analytic model of a case of an eating disorder. From Farmer and Latner (2007) In Sturmey (Ed.) *Functional Analysis in Clinical Treatment.* Academic Press/Elsevier, p. 397.

regulation of emotion, Farmer and Latner taught Jill problem solving and emotional regulation skills. The therapists identified some of Jill's rules related to binge eating. These included rules related to the effectiveness of binging in reducing calorie intake. The therapists provided Jill information to counter such rules. Farmer and Latner also used a variety of exposure-based treatment to address problematic antecedent stimuli. One example included Jill progressively wearing tighter clothes and not checking her appearance.

Follette et al.'s methodology is closest to behavior analysis. It explicitly refers to behavior analytic concepts and is explicit concerning private behavior. Farmer and Latner's case study nicely illustrates its application to bulimia and how private behavior typical of bulimia can be conceptualized and treated within a behavior analytic framework.

RADICAL BEHAVIORAL AND OTHER APPROACHES COMPARED

Commonalities in Behavioral Approaches

The behavioral approaches to case formulation described in previous parts of this chapter share some common elements, and also differ in a number of significant ways. Thus, all approaches tend to be empirical, involve data collection, and are very goal-oriented. They all describe the relationship between the client's problematic and other behavior to environmental events, as well as response–response relationships, such as response chains and self-regulation. They all involve functional relationships that describe the relationship between current independent variables and client behavior. All these approaches to case formulation use the formulation to develop an individual treatment plan that is directly linked to that formulation.

There are also important differences between behavioral approaches to case formulation. The earlier approaches are most behavior analytic. Thus, Skinner's generic case formulation is explicit in its link to theory, by referencing operant extinction, the side effects of operant extinction, and so on. Kanfer and Phillips's SORKC analysis and Follette et al.'s (2000) approach are similarly analytic in their use of behavioral concepts. Thus, these early approaches meet one of the Baer et al's criteria for ABA, namely that ABA should use the concepts and not merely the technology of behavior analysis. Notable is the absence of explicit behavioral concepts or indeed the confusion in terminology in some of the later approaches to behavioral formulation. For example, although Haynes and O'Brien's FACM approach is very systematic in its categorization of variables in its formulation, it is not always explicit if the causal variables should be considered establishing operations, discriminative stimuli, or contingencies, etc. For example, their formulation of depression does include variables such as "reinforcement for depressed behavior", but it is unclear what the function(s) of "insufficient social support" or "catastrophic thoughts" might be. Greater analytic precision might be helpful in that it might result in formulations that identified the controlling variables even more precisely than current formulations do. For example, "insufficient social support" could refer to (1) a lack of opportunity to engage in some competing pleasurable behavior to compete with depression; (2) inadequate reinforcement for non-depressed behavior; or (3) the result of having poor client social skills. If these differences could be determined, different treatment plans would result.

The Radical Behavioral and the Wolpe traditions

The Wolpe tradition focused on respondent conditioning and the putative mechanism of reciprocal inhibition as the basis for treatment of phobias and related problems. It shares with radical behavioral approaches an emphasis on learning as an important aspect of the acquisition of psychopathology and as the basis for treatment. It differs from radical behavioral approaches in a number of ways. For example, this approach is often content to use office-based assessment and client self-reports of change, such as SUDS ratings. It rarely uses observational data on client fearful behavior in the natural environment, either as the basis for its formulations or to evaluate its treatments. As noted at the end of the previous chapter, as this tradition became influenced by cognitive behavior therapy and attempted to account for private verbal behavior, it adopted the cognitive model of private verbal behavior as the cause of public behavior and as the broken computer to be fixed.

The Radical Behavioral and Cognitive Formulations Compared

Radical behavioral and cognitive behavioral approaches share some general features, such as commitment to empiricism, including the use of client data in therapy and scientific evaluation of therapy and the use of some learning concepts. They differ most clearly in the status they give to client verbal behavior and to the mechanisms of change during treatment. A comparison of Morrison's (1998) cognitive behavioral case formulation, Virues-Ortega and Haynes (2005) behavioral formulation of psychosis and Wilder et al., (2001) functional analysis of bizarre speech in an adult with schizophrenia illustrate these differences.

Morrison's (1998) formulation is couched in terms of "heuristic models of the links between cognitive, behavioral, emotional and physiological factors … The cognitive formulation … should be used as an alternative explanation of symptoms, along with others that can be generated by the patient (in collaboration with the therapist) …" (p. 197). Thus, avoidance of fearful or otherwise aversive stimuli is construed as a "safety behavior". These safety behaviors maintain the problem because not experiencing the avoided stimuli fails to provide evidence to disconfirm a maladaptive belief. Morrison uses behavioral experiments, such as exposure to avoided stimuli which may be effective in producing change. However, Morrison construed the mechanism of change as a mechanism to contradict beliefs and reduce client conviction in these beliefs.

Such cognitive approaches to case formulation may result in effective treatments. However, from a radical behavioral perspective they have a number of limitations. For example, many of the mechanisms are described in everyday language. For example, events that precede an intrusive thought are described as "triggers", rather than discriminative stimuli. The term "discriminative stimuli" implied a learning mechanism to explain why that stimulus preceded the intrusive thought, but the meaning of the term "trigger" is unclear. The preference for cognitive explanations of behavior seems weak because of the circular reasoning. Further, there are more parsimonious explanations of observed behavior available. For example, instead of hypothesizing that safety behavior inhibits cognitive change we could write more simply that "varying the route when shopping was negatively reinforced by avoidance of walking past an Irish pub and thoughts about the IRA".

Virues-Ortega and Haynes (2005) formulation is illustrated in Figure 11.10. They collected data from multiple sources and focused their formulation on the environmental events and observable behavior of the client that could be readily modified. Thus, although their formulation did include hypervigilence, perceptions and expectations, it also included important roles for social behavior, lack of social reinforcement and job loss as important parts of the formulation. Such events are sometimes absent or underplayed in cognitive formulations. For example, Morrison's formulation focuses on the clients cognitions, but gives little weight to the social or other consequences of this man's strange behavior, even though there are extensive data demonstrating this (Wilder et al., 2001; Wilder & Wong, 2007).

Chapter 12

BEHAVIORAL ASSESSMENT

CONCEPTUAL ASPECTS OF BEHAVOURAL ASSESSMENT

Structuralist and Functional Approaches to Assessment

Assessment is a characteristic activity of psychologists, and may include assessment of intelligence, aptitude, personality, or adaptive behavior; as well as diagnostic assessment. Structural approaches emphasize or overtly purport to identify hidden traits or diseases within the person. These constructs are often assumed to be relatively enduring across time and situations. Both structural and functional assessments emphasize objectivity, reliability and validity of measurement. However, they differ in the status they give to assessment observations. For structuralists, observations are seen as indicators that are relatively unimportant in themselves. They are important rather as indicators of hidden constructs. For functionalists, it is the observations that are important. They are simply a sample of the person's behavioral repertoire.

Several authors have expressed concern about the role of assessment in clinical activity noting that clinicians may maintain assessment and treatment as separate activities. For example, treatment may be uninfluenced by assessment. Clinicians may tend to use the kinds of therapy they were taught during their professional training, irrespective of the client's assessment and some clinicians explicitly deny that assessment influences their treatment (Nelson-Gray, 2003).

Diagnostic-based approaches supposedly use the diagnosis itself to guide treatment. This is a relatively common practice, as shown in anxiety management groups and parent skills classes for parenting children with ADHD. Many services are organized by assigning staff to groups of clients with common diagnoses. One might argue that evidence-based practice indicates that this is justified since certain diagnoses predict response to some treatments and not others. For example, many reviews of evidence-based practice are organized around diagnostic labels and the goal of recent reviews of evidence-based practice is to produce a list of effective treatments *for each diagnostic category* (Fonagy et al., 2002; Nathan & Gorman, 1995; Roth & Fonagy, 2004). For example, the American Psychological Association's

Task Force on Psychological Interventions identified behavior therapy, cognitive therapy and interpersonal therapy as effective for unipolar depression and dialectical behavior therapy as "probably efficacious" for personality disorders. It did not conclude that dialectic behavior therapy was effective for unipolar depression and did not conclude that behavior therapy, cognitive therapy and interpersonal therapy were effective for personality disorders. So, all other things being equal one might argue that clinicians should use diagnostic-based treatment. One might make other pragmatic arguments in favor of such an approach. Diagnostic-based interventions and services might lead to concentrated expertise and development of specialized clinical skill. Diagnostic-based services might also lead to treatments that are conducted better than in generic services, because of the extensive practice that clinicians would gain by seeing many clients with the same diagnosis.

Functional-based approaches note that even when there is evidence to prefer one kind of therapy over another for a particular diagnosis, the clinician still must make significant decisions beyond the diagnosis. Indeed some books on case formulation make exactly this point when the authors entitle their book as "beyond diagnosis" (Bruch & Bond, 2001.) For example, behavior therapy is an indicated therapy for unipolar depression; what should the target behavior(s) and goals of therapy be? Do these questions make any difference, or should the therapist and client merely work their way through a standardized behavior therapy treatment manual with little individualization? A related question is what to do when clients do not or only partially respond to an evidence-based treatment; should the therapist move down the list of evidence-based treatments? What if there is only one or no treatment on the list? A third problem that limits a clinician's use of diagnostic driven treatment is that many clients do not come with prepackaged problems that fit neatly into one and only one diagnosis. If some one is depressed *and* has a personality disorder *and* does not meet the criteria for diagnosis but clearly has a significant problem, where should the clinician begin?

Several studies have tested the hypothesis that basing treatment on the functions of the target behavior predicts effective treatment *for individual clients*. (See Chapter 13 for a more detailed discussion of this issue.) Paul's (1967) oft quoted question is "What treatment, by whom, is most effective for this individual with that specific problem, under which sets of circumstances, and how does this come about? " (p. 111). The answer from function-based treatments is: "the treatments that the therapist and client can implement that match the function of the client's presenting problem". Thus, the central tenet of functional approaches to assessment is that function, not diagnosis or topography, should direct treatment. Therefore, the primary aim of functional assessment is to detect the individual differences in function that direct clinicians to the maximally effective treatment for each client.

General Characteristics of Behavioral Assessment

Behavioral assessment emerged as a distinct field in the mid-1970s. Since that time, there have been many text books and entire journals, such as *Behavioral Assessment, Journal of Behavioral Assessment*, and special issues of the *Journal of Applied Behavior Analysis* (Nelson & Hayes, 1979) on this topic. Nelson and Haynes (1979) defined behavioral assessment as

> the identification of meaningful response units and their controlling variables (both current environmental and organismic) for the purpose of understanding and altering human behavior (p. 491).

They noted that, although traditional and behavioral assessment do share some common methods, such as interviews, questionnaires and observation, they differ in their assumptions and level of inference. For behaviorists, the data are a sample of behavior in a particular context. Behavior assessment focuses on the behavior of the individual organism to define and quantify the problem of interest; define and design the intervention; monitor progress; and evaluate response to treatment at follow-up. It tends to deemphasize screening and nomothetic comparisons and focuses on comparing the organism's behavior with its own at different points in time.

Cone's Model

Cone (1997) proposed that behavioral assessment should include descriptive, interpretative and verification phases. During the descriptive phase, the clinician gathers information to identify the target behaviors, antecedents and consequences. The clinician may use a wide range of assessment methods at this point. During the hypothesis formulation or interpretative phase, the clinician estimates the relationship between the behavior and environmental events, perhaps using conditional probabilities or other methods. Finally, during the hypothesis testing or verification phase, the clinician makes predictions based on these hypotheses and then tests them. This can be done using simple predictions of behavior based on environmental manipulations as well as using formal, experimental analyses. (See below for a further discussion of clinical applications of experimental analyses of behavior.)

Cone's distinctions between description, interpretation and verification are useful aspects of the clinician's activities when conducting a behavioral assessment. However, dividing behavioral assessment neatly into three phases seems artificial and runs counter to Wolpe and Turkat's hypothesis-driven approach. For example, in hypothesis-driven interviewing, the hypothesis guides the interviewer to ask certain kinds of questions and not others. Thus, it may be useful to consider these three functions of behavioral assessment, but perhaps artificial to divide behavioral assessment into three separate compartments. The clinician can use these three important functions of behavioral assessment to ensure that the assessment includes all three tasks.

Applied Behavior Analysis

Assessment within ABA gives primary emphasis to observational data. Thus, it typically uses fewer assessment modalities than other approaches to behavioral assessment. It emphasizes observational data and to a lesser extent reliable and valid perhaps permanent product, mechanical or telemetric measures of behavior. Other methods are usually viewed as suspect. When self-report data changes it is not clear if behavior actually changes, or if it is the behavior of the person reporting the behavior – whether it is the client themselves or a third party who have changed (Baer et al., 1968). Thus, verbal self-reports or reports from others, including psychometric data, even if reliable, are suspect. When the client says or writes "I am less depressed" or circles a number on a rating scale indicating less depression, it is unclear if the therapist or someone else prompted or reinforced this response, or if the client is accurately tacting some private behavior.

This emphasis on observational and other reliable and objective data sources has enabled ABA to make considerable inroads into areas where behavior can be observed, such as classrooms, residential, treatment and other public settings. However, behavior analysis's unswerving commitment to the use of these kinds of data has meant that the applications of ABA to some areas of mental health, such as outpatients with depression and anxiety, have been limited so far.

METHODS OF BEHAVIORAL ASSESSMENT

Clinicians use a wide variety of methods when conducting a behavioral assessment. This section reviews the use of interviews, psychometric measures of function, observational methods and the analysis and synthesis of data in behavioral assessment.

Interviewing

There are two broad approaches to behavioral interviewing: semi-structured and hypothesis-driven interviewing. In semi-structured interviewing, a number of predetermined topics are covered, but in no fixed order or with no precisely determined questions. Kanfer and Saslow (1969) and Kanfer and Phillips (1970, p. 508) outlined seven topics that should be covered in behavioral interviews. These included:

1. Analysis of the problem situation, including the major client's complaints classified as behavioral excesses, or deficits, with the frequency, duration, stimulus conditions and client strengths notes.

2. Clarify the problem situation to specify the role that other people may play in maintaining the major client complaints and what may occur of change take place.
3. Identify a hierarchy of reinforcers and aversive stimuli that result in relevant approach and avoidance behaviors that may be incorporated into a treatment plan.
4. Take a developmental history of the problem to evoke past habitual behavior, identify environmental correlates of change, and related them to the presenting problem.
5. Analyze the client's repertoire of self-control responses, including other people who maintain the client's self-control repertoire and excesses or deficits in self-control.
6. Analyze the client's social relationships and networks that may influence the presenting problem and may participate in treatment. Prompt the client to consider what social relationships they actually need.
7. Identify the norms of the client's social and physical environment and determine the importance of these factors in formulating treatment goals.

Morganstern (1988) and Sturmey (1996) also outlined broadly similar components to semi-structured behavioral interview (see Table 12.1).

Table 12.1. The common elements of a semi-structured behavioral interview. (From Sturmey, 1996, Table 4.3, *Functional analysis in clinical psychology*. Chichester, UK: Wiley UK; p. 85.

Section	Purpose/topic
Open interview	Introduce participants; explain purpose of interview; explain ground rules; establish initial rapport
Ascertain current problem(s)	Elicit target behaviors, group into potential response classes, establish priority amongst problems; establish antecedents, consequences, frequency and duration; identify current strategies and their effectiveness
History	Identify onset (clear/traumatic vs insidious), development (gradually worsening, variable, periods of remission), reasons for seeking treatment (self-referral, other-referral, recent traumatic problem); previous treatments
Assets & goals for change	Elicit strengths such as personal characteristics, interests, hobbies, achievements and resources; elicit goals for change related to the problem and more general life goals
Close interview	Summarize interview; explain how treatment might go; how often appointments are; the expectations of therapist and client; who will be informed, how; confidentiality

More recently, several structured interviews have been developed for use with people with developmental disabilities, such as O'Neil et al.'s (1997) functional assessment interview; McGill, Teer, Rye and Hughes's (2003) *Setting Events Interview*; March and Horner's (2002) *Functional Assessment Checklist for Teachers and Staff*; and Reed, Thomas, Sprague and Horner's (1997) *Student Guided Functional Assessment Interview*. These structured interviews are a useful source of model questions for behavioral interviewing and have been useful with a wider range of populations with varying minor modifications (Sturmey, 2007). Other examples of clinical behavioral interviews can be found in Dixon and Johnson (2007) on gambling and Dixon and Bihler (2007) on traumatic brain injury.

As part of a study to teach interview skills, Miltenberger and Fuqua (1985) provided more detailed operationalized definitions of interviewer skills that should be used in semi-structured behavioral interviewing. These included:

1. Ask for a general description of the problem using open-ended questions
2. Ask for other problems using open-ended questions
3. Set priorities using open-ended questions
4. Ask for specification of the problems using open-ended questions
5. Ask about the onset using open-ended questions and events around the onset
6. Ask about the frequency, duration, magnitude and latency of the problem behaviors using open-ended questions
7. Ask about the antecedents for the occurrence and non-occurrence of the problem using open-ended questions
8. Ask about the consequences after the problem behavior occurs
9. Ask about correlated verbal behavior, such as client thoughts, self-talk and internal dialog when the problem occurs.

Social validity ratings from experienced behavior therapists supported the validity of these interview skills. Sessions that had few of these interview behaviors in them were rated as incomplete, interpersonally ineffective, used open-ended questions inappropriately and questions were timed poorly. In contrast, sessions with high rates of these interviewer behaviors were rated positively on all these dimensions.

Other aspects of semi-structured behavioral interviewing that are important include establishing rapport early in the interview process. Early opening statements that explain the purpose, format and duration of the interview may be helpful. Some clients find talking about their problems difficult at first. Turkat (1988) used the following statements to try and loosen an unresponsive client:

Let me explain a little bit about what I'm trying to do. What I'm trying to do now is get an idea of what's going on with you. And, if there are any problems you are having, try to see what they are, and perhaps, why they developed, and then see if there is something we can do about it. Okay? And, if so, I'll tell you what I think. I'll tell you if there is something we can do and if there is no problem, I'll tell you that. So, I'm just trying to get an idea of whether or not you need to do something about it. And if you do, what the options might be and how one might do that. I'm not here to say that you're crazy or mentally ill or anything like that, because you're obviously not. (p. 352)

It may also be useful to think of the interview as a series of sections or paragraphs which begin with a transition statement that directs the interviewer's and client's attention to a new topic. An open-ended question is then used to explore the issue, followed by a series of open-ended questions until specific issues need to be clarified. Then there is a summary and a check for agreement and clarification and, if the issue is completed for now, another transition statement is made to move on to another topic (see Figure 12.1).

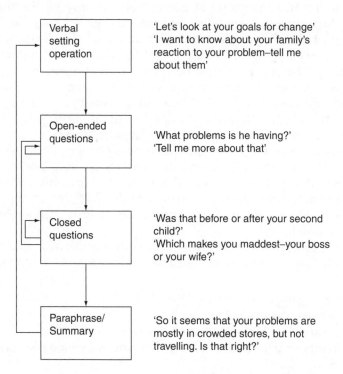

Figure 12.1. A common pattern of the use of interview techniques. Reproduced from Sturmey, 1996, Figure 4.1, *Functional analysis in clinical psychology*. Chichester, UK: Wiley UK, p. 80.

Hypothesis-driven Interviewing

Turkat (1988) stated that:

> Time and again I have observed initial interviews that produce much information but provide little understanding of the patient's psychopathology ... I have found it especially disturbing to watch a beginning student being trained by a technology-oriented behavior therapist. The student having spent four or five session collecting information, runs out of questions for the patient, and then asks the supervisor, 'Now, what should I do?' The reply is to begin implementing ("pet") techniques matched to a patient's complaints. (p. 349)

Hypothesis-driven interviewing is a response to the more technique-driven semi-structured interviewing described in the previous passage. Hypothesis-driven interviewing is at once the most impressive kind of behavioral interviewing, but paradoxically the most elusive to define. Rather that follow a set script of questions, or even following the more fluid outlines and strategies of semi-structured behavioral interviewing, hypothesis-driven interviewing *begins* with a hypothesis. We saw in Chapter 9 how Wolpe sized up a client and her presenting problem almost before she sat down, but certainly by the time she had spelled out her name letter by letter, and gave her age as "thirty four and a half" Wolpe had already decided that "The clinician adopts a preliminary hypothesis, namely, that the patient is a perfectionist. Accordingly, he expects her to be fearful of making mistakes, being criticized, failing. He further expects interpersonal difficulties and perhaps depression. With this beginning hypothesis, the clinician moves on with the inquiry" (Wolpe & Turkat, 1985, p.12). Several papers exist that can act as models for hypothesis-driven interviews, including examples with anxiety disorders (Wolpe, 1980b; Wolpe & Turkat, 1985; Levine, 1987), sexual disorders (Wolpe, 1980b), eating disorders (Brady, 1986; Chioda, 1987), behavior disorders (Sturmey, 1991), traumatic brain damage (Dixon & Bihler, 2007), gambling (Dixon & Johnson, 2007) and borderline personality disorder (Cuper, Merwin & Lynch, 2007).

Turkat's (1988) transcript of an initial interview with a freshman student referred for an injection phobia illustrates this approach to interviewing.

Dr: What is going on with you?
Pr: Trying to go to school I guess
Dr: Are you doing that okay, or having a rough time of it?
Pr: It's pretty rough. I'm only taking 13 hours, everyone else is taking 15 or 16.
Dr: Why only 13?
Pr: Just to see if I can take it or not.
Dr: Notice any difficulties in taking what you have now?
Pr: At times, like when they force me to have lack of sleep. (p. 350)

From this Turkat made the following preliminary formulation: "Charles is angry about insulin injections because they make him appear weak" (p. 350).

So how did Wolpe and Turkat derive these hypotheses so early on in the interview process? First, I expect they already had a conceptual framework that functioned as a menu of limited options available to them. This conceptual framework defined potentially relevant variables and mechanisms for etiology, maintenance and treatment, before the therapist sees the client and provides the therapist with a world view of psychopathology and treatment. Second, treatment plans flowed directly from that conceptual framework. For example, Wolpe focused on conditioning events and subsequence avoidance of anxiety. That two factor model guides much of his questioning of patients with anxiety disorders. Indeed, Wolpe and Turkat (1985) described one example of extensive interviewing before they discovered a potential conditioning event. In the previous chapter we reviewed four examples of behavioral case formulation, all of which can be characterized as providing a conceptual framework that guides and limits the options available to clinicians.

Skinner's generic formulation used the framework of operant extinction and its already known affects on human behavior. This formulation can guide the clinician to search for: (1) losses of sources of reinforcement prior to the onset of the problem, such as transitions or life events characterized by loss of reinforcement; (2) interpretation of emotional problems as the side effects of extinction; (3) a lack of reinforcement for effective behavior in the current environment; and (4) a lack of effective behavior, such as social or other relevant skills, to contact existing contingencies. Because of the treatment implications of such a conceptual framework, the potential elements of an intervention plan may flow directly from the discovery of these elements of a formulation. For example, if the person is in a new environment because of a transition from a previous environment where they had been effective, a treatment plan would probably consist of discovering those behaviors that are needed to be effective in the new environment and learning those. Exactly how these behaviors would be taught would depend on whether these behaviors are already in the client's repertoire.

In a similar way, Kanfer and Phillip's SORCK analysis provides exactly that there are five groups of relevant variables to investigate. As we saw, these five variables map directly onto treatment options. Nezu and Nezu's CPMs and Haynes and O'Brien's FACM also do the same. They limit the range of variables that can enter into a formulation. Hence, if one were using a FACM framework, one would explicitly identify current variables that had a large effect on the client's problems and that were manipulable and preferably causal.

A second aspect of hypothesis-driven interviewing is that predictions can be made from the current hypothesis and questions can be used to test those predictions. For example, in Wolpe's case he predicted that his client will be fearful of making errors, being criticized and failing. Thus, one might ask questions such as what was her reaction to criticism from her spouse, children, coworkers and family members, and expect her to be fearful and avoidant in these situations, but not others, such in crowds, traveling, being trapped, with animals and so on. Likewise, with Turkat's young man angry about injections because they make him seem weak. Thus, one might predict that he would not like it if an authority figure yelled at him but that he would be especially angry if an authority figures ridiculing and humiliating him, especially in front of others. These predictions could be tested by asking him to rate vignettes or personal experiences that vary along these dimensions.

Self-recording

Skinner (1953) noted that self-control was the key to treating psychopathology. Most self-control occurs through private verbal behavior that is difficult to access. However, clinicians often used self-recording as a proxy for accessing private verbal behavior, including the client's private self-management behavior. Thus, some self-monitoring merely asks the client to record the frequency of the target behavior.

This approach can be modified in a number of ways to meet the needs of each individual behavioral assessment. An example comes from Hopko, Armento, Cantu, Chambers, and Lejuez (2005), who investigated the relationship between activity and mood in people with and without clinical depression. They asked their participants to rate their ongoing activity level and its immediate and future reward value. As predicted, people with depression were less active and reported reduced immediate and future reward value of the activities in which they participated. Such information has direct implications for individual treatment of depression using brief behavioral activation treatment for depression (BATD; LeJuez et al., 2002). Most importantly of all, it could be used to teach the client to self-regulate by first discriminating between pleasurable and non-pleasurable activities and then to engage in self-regulation to increase participation in pleasurable activities and increase overall activity level (Skinner, 1953).

Self-recording is often reactive and this can be helpful in beginning intervention. Self-recording has been used alone or in combination with other methods of self-management, such as setting goals, self-reinforcement and self-punishment to change a wide range of clinically relevant behaviors including academic performance in children (Kirby, Fowler & Baer, 1991; Lloyd, Bateman, Landrum & Hallahan, 1989; Rosenbaum

& Drabman, 1979), promoting generalization of social skills in youth with severe emotional disturbances (Ninness, Fuesrst, Rutherford & Glen, 1991), increasing interactions between mothers with intellectual disabilities and their children (Feldman et al., 1986) and improving staff performance. Thus, self-recording can be used both in behavioral assessment prior to formal intervention, to produce data for discussion with a client to help teach self-management skills and as a form of intervention.

Self-recording can be inaccurate and compliance can be a problem. Some clients may be reluctant to report certain kinds of behavior or may be too busy or too unfocused to record data. It may be possible to gradually shape up reliable self-recording over time or to use new technologies, such as email or hand-held electronic devices to record data more conveniently. For example, Stein and Corte (2003) and Wegner et al. (2002) both used ecological momentary assessment to conduct a functional assessment of eating disorder related behavior. In ecological momentary assessment, a pager or other device prompts the client to record ongoing behavior and its context at the time it occurs. These methods of self-recording are new, attractive and could be applied to many problems. However, there are few published studies on their use and hence their status is not yet known.

Psychometric Measures of Function

Researchers have now developed a number of measures of the function of target behaviors, especially in the area of intellectual disabilities (Sturmey, 1994; Sturmey & Bernstein, 2004), including the motivational assessment scale (MAS; Durand & Crimmons, 1988), the stereotypy analysis scale (Pyles, Riordan & Bailey, 1997), the functional analysis checklist (van Houten, Rolider & Ikowitz et al., 1989) and the detailed behavior report (Groden & Lantz, 2001) For example, Matson and Vollmer (1995) developed the Questions About Behavioral Function (QABF) to assess the functions of a wide range of maladaptive behavior in people with intellectual disabilities. The QABF has good inter-rater and test–retest reliability (Applegate, Matson & Cherry, 1999; Dawson, Matson & Cherry, 1998; Paclaskyj, Matson, Rush, Smalls & Vollmer, 2001).

An interesting recent development has been that these scales have been modified for use with other populations. For example, Kearney and Silverman (1990) developed a school refusal scale to assess the function of school refusal. This was directly modeled on the MAS. Dixon and Johnson (2007) also modified the MAS to identify the contingencies maintaining gambling. Finally, Williams, Rose and Chisolm (2006) modified the QABF to assess the functions of nail biting. They also found some evidence of validity in that the modified QABF item that rated nail biting when bored correlated at the .0001 level with observed frequency of nail biting when subjects were left alone, Thus, these measures, developed primarily for use with people with intellectual disabilities, are a useful source of items for the development of scales for other populations.

Several researchers have also developed questionnaires to identify the functions of various psychiatric conditions that are related to behavioral issues. For example, Daffern and Howells have developed a behavior-diagnostic questionnaire measure to assess the functions of aggressive behavior in psychiatric inpatients (Daffern & Howells, 2002; Daffern, Howells & Ogloff, 2007). The assessment and classification of function (ACF) is a rating scale that assesses nine possible functions of aggression. These functions are (1) demand avoidance; (2) to force compliance; (3) to express anger; (4) to reduce tension; (5) to obtain tangibles; (6) to reduce social distance (attention seeking); (7) to enhance status or social approval; (8) compliance with instruction; and (9) to observe suffering.

Daffern et al. (2007) assessed the reliability of the ACF. Six forensic clinical psychologists and two doctoral clinical psychology students participated. They had copies of the ACF, written instructions and a one-hour lecture on how to score the ACF. They then rated 300-word descriptions of incidents of aggressive behavior by scoring the presence or absence of each of the nine functions on the ACF. The intra-class correlation for single raters was .64 and for all raters was .94. Daffern et al. (2007) went on to suggest that this behavioral diagnostic approach might be used to identify effective and ineffective interventions for aggressive behavior. Table 12.2 illustrates this approach to basing treatment on the results of the ACF. Daffern went on to develop the Functional Review of Aggressive Behaviors (FRAB), which is an abbreviated assessment of aggression that captures, the topography, function and consequences of aggressive behavior.

Klonsky (2006) identified nine different questionnaire measures of the function of self-harm. However, he noted that none was comprehensive and few had any reported psychometric properties.

Psychometric scales to assess the functions of behavior and psychiatric symptoms are often quick and easy to administer and may be a useful component of a more comprehensive array of assessment methods. However, several studies have found poor reliability (Paclawskyj et al., 2000; Sigafoos, Kerr, & Roberts, 1995; Sturmey, 1994, 2001). Klonsky (2006) noted that the accuracy of self-reports may be questionable on a number of grounds. For example, people may be unable to report some functions of their behavior. Others may be reluctant to do so out of embarrassment or for other reasons. Hence, these questionnaires should be used with caution as one component of a functional assessment.

Table 12.2. Intervention strategies indicated by the function of aggressive behavior in psychiatric inpatients. From Daffern et al., 2007, *A functional analysis of psychiatric in patient aggression*. Doctoral Dissertation, University of South Australia, p. 143.

Purpose	Intervention
Demand for activity	Increase assertion; enhance anger management skills and develop more adaptive communication. Reinforce adaptive expression of dissatisfaction with treatment. Minimise reinforcement of aggression by allowing avoidance of demand. Ensure patients understand why demands are required. Identify less provocative means of demanding activity.
Denial of a request	Increase assertion; enhance anger management skills and develop more adaptive communication. Reinforce adaptive expression of dissatisfaction with treatment. Minimise reinforcement of aggression by acquiescing to requests. Explain why requests cannot be granted. Identify less provocative means of denying requests.
Following provocation	Provide anger management programs that reduce or help patients manage emotional arousal, challenge beliefs supporting the use of aggression, and increase assertion. Develop adaptive communication skills. Challenge dysfunctional or distorted beliefs, particularly where these beliefs consist of appraisals of events as malevolent and deliberate.
Following frustration	Teach and encourage the use of adaptive methods for reducing arousal. Encourage alternative means of discharging tension or preventing tension.
To observe suffering	Assist patients identify more adaptive and pro social means through which they can gain pleasure. Punish aggression, so that the reinforcement potential of observing suffering comes at significant and certain cost.
To enhance status	Encourage alternative means of enhancing status, and punish aggression. Where ward culture supports the use of aggression then these values need to be challenged.

(continued)

Table 12.2. (*Continued*).

Purpose	Intervention
For instrumental purposes	Punish aggressive behaviour; ensure aggression is not reinforced. Challenge individual and community views about the legitimacy of aggression, and teach more adaptive means of securing needs. Avoid reinforcement of aggression by allowing patients to receive tangible rewards.
To reduce social distance	Teach and reinforce adaptive, assertive methods to socialise through social skills training. Differentially reinforce prosocial attempts to elicit attention. Avoid reinforcement of aggression by providing attention following aggression. Provide individual time for patients vulnerable to aggression if socially isolated.
Following instruction	Develop assertion skills so that patients can resist instructions to harm others.

Observational Methods

General Features

During direct observations, observers enter the settings and maintain minimal interactions with the observees, usually by sitting or standing quietly and unobtrusively. To reduce observee reactivity, time is given for observees to habituate to being observed. Sometimes observers give an innocuous explanation to explain their presence that does not explain which behaviors are being observed. For example, when Wilder et al. (2001) conducted a functional assessment of psychotic speech, they told the client that they were evaluating his work behavior.

Observers make observations using predetermined behavior categories which have been developed during pilot observations. They use coding systems, such as time-sampling or frequency counts, to estimate behavior parameters, such as rate or duration. They also observe the relationship between behavior and the environment to determine variables that are systematically related to the behaviors of interest. They then use the information on the behavior-environment relationship to design an individual treatment.

The Parameters of Behavior

Clinicians may develop draft definitions of target behaviors from other assessment sources, such as interviews, or from published research. During pilot observations, the observers develop, evaluate and refine operationalized behavioral definitions of target behaviors, using inter-observer agreement (IOA). IOA is used to evaluate the adequacy of the definitions and to pinpoint problematic aspects of a definition. For example, when defining "social interaction" in older adults an initial definition might inadvertently omit interaction with peers and fail to define precisely what constitutes one episode of engagement. After pilot data with poor IOA, observers might refine their definition of "social interaction" to clarify whether or not the other person must respond to a social bid, whether an episode is counted as one or two episodes of social interaction if there is an interruption from another person or telephone or the person looks away, etc. Typically, behavior categories are continually refined until observers reach some predetermined level of IOA. Table 12.3 gives several illustrations of behavior definitions related to psychopathology.

Behavior is a physically present phenomenon that is real, exists in time and space and can be measured. Thus, we can measure certain parameters of behavior including frequency, duration and intensity. From these measures we can also derive rate, by dividing frequency by time. We can also derive the proportion of time spent in a behavior by dividing the time spent in behavior by total time. The intensity of behavior is somewhat

Table 12.3. Some illustrations of behavioral definitions
of psychopathology

Diagnostic category	Behavior	Definition
Depression	Smiling	a slight opening of the lips, an upward turn of the corners of the mouth, and an increase in the protrusion of the skin covering the cheek bones
	Crying	inarticulate sounds accompanied by tears from the patient's eyes (Reisinger, 1972, p. 125–130)
Tic disorder	Vocal tic	rapidly bringing the elbows together, foot stomping, and arm flapping above the head (Woods et al., 2001, p. 354.)
Schizophrenia	Bizarre vocalization	Sentences that … (a) … referred to stimuli n present of not being discussed, or (b) … referred to one of five specific topics(i.e. karate [etc.]) (Wilder et al., 2001, p. 67)
Pediatric feeding disorder	Inappropriate behavior	head turns, batting or blocking the spoon or cup (Piazza et al., 2003, p. 311)

more difficult to capture, but has something to do with the energy associated with the behavior. For example, some studies have used voice volume as a measure of behavior intensity (Fleece et al., 1981).

In order to measure frequency, the observer must define individual episodes of behavior with clear onsets and offsets. This may not be too difficult for certain brief behaviors, such as screaming or banging a toy. For other behaviors, such as number of episodes of interaction or talking, it may take some work to develop clear rules specifying the onset and offsets of behavior. Observers may record frequency by simple hash marks on a piece of paper divided into time blocks, known as frequency-within-interval recording, using golf counters, or other kinds of event recorders. Observers may record duration by using stopwatches or similar devices.

Miltenberger, Rapp and Long (1999) described a very simple, low-technology approach to measuring duration and frequency of behavior using videotaped behavior. They used the time base on the video camera to measure the onset and offset of each behavior on a data sheet that consisted of a grid of 600 cells, which corresponded to 10 minutes divided into one second blocks. This method enabled them to record the duration, frequency, rate and proportion of time spent in each behavior and to convert them to time-sampling data, (see below) if so desired.

Time Sampling

It is preferable to record the frequency and duration of behavior directly. However, if one is recording several or many behaviors or the behavior is complex or fast moving, this may not be possible or desirable in live recording. For this reason several methods of observation collectively known as time sampling are commonly used. In time sampling, time is divided into intervals and the intervals are scored using some predetermined rule. Observers then calculate the proportion of intervals scored. Figure 12.2 illustrates and defines the commonly used methods. Thus, when using time sampling, observers must decide ahead of time which time sampling method will be appropriate to their purpose, how often to make observations, and when to schedule breaks in the observation schedule.

There is an extensive literature evaluating time sampling methods which may be briefly summarized as follows. Momentary time sampling estimates duration. It does so quite accurately if there are a large number of observations and the duration of the behavior is moderate. Estimating low duration behaviors may be less accurate. Hence, estimating low duration behaviors requires a larger number of observations. Although MTS does have error variance attached to it, it is not biased in estimating duration. Partial interval time sampling overestimates duration, and grossly so, if the intervals are long and the behavior observed is brief. However, this may not matter if one is collecting data for an intervention to *reduce* a target behavior, since such a method will be nonconservative. Whole-interval sampling consistently underestimates duration, but is rarely used. None of these time-sampling methods estimate frequency or rate accurately in any simple fashion. Thus, if observers are not going to measure behavior directly, then they should use MTS to estimate duration and should measure frequency directly.

MTS	X	X	✓	X	✓	✓	X	X	✓	✓	50%
PIR	X	✓	✓	✓	✓	✓	✓	✓	✓	✓	90%
O & R	X	R	✓	R	✓	R	✓	R	✓	R	80%
WIR	X	X	X	X	X	✓	X	X	X	X	10%

Figure 12.2. Four different time-sampling methods and their relationship to frequency and duration of the target behavior. Reproduced from Sturmey, 1996, *Functional analysis in clinical psychology.* Chichester, UK: Wiley UK, p. 107.

ABC Recording

Bijou, Peterson and Ault (1968) described a method of collecting natural-istic observations that has become one of the most commonly used meth-ods of behavior analysis: the antecedent–behavior–consequence (ABC) record. The ABC record can be used to observe behavior in the natural environment and organize observation using behavioral concepts. Bijou noted that if the teacher was describing the behavior of Timmy, the teacher might write "Timmy is playing by himself in a sandbox in a play yard in which other children are playing. A teacher stands nearby. Timmy tires of the sandbox and walks over to climb on the monkey bars. Timmy shouts at the teacher, saying, 'Mrs. Simpson, watch me.' Timmy climbs to the top of the apparatus and shouts again to the teacher, 'Look how high I am. I'm higher that anybody' ..." (p. 178). Bijou et al. noted that this narrative can be converted into a more organized and analytic description using antecedent, behavior and consequences. This is shown in Figure 12.3. They went on to note that such observations must be reliable, as shown by good IOA. ABC records can be very useful because they can be used to derive frequency graphs, and more importantly, describe the relationship between behavior and its antecedents and consequences.

ABC records have been widely used and there are many procedural variations available. For example, Groden and Lantz (2001) reported the development of the *Detailed Behavior Record (DBR)*. The DBR included data on:

- The target behavior, its frequency, intensity and severity, and behaviors that may occur before the target behavior that may be earlier members of the response chain.
- General antecedent stimuli, such as day, date, time, activity and loca-tion of the occurrence of the target behavior.
- Specific antecedents, such as the client's actions and thoughts, and physical events that preceded the target behavior.
- Setting events, such as events distant in time, that may be relevant.
- Programmatic and naturally occurring consequences of the target be-havior.
- The probably function of the target behavior.

Groden and Lantz reported data on the reliability of the DBR from 38 staff who had been trained to use it over a one-year period with children with autism. Staff included professional and non-professional staff working in day programs, in home programs and residential settings. They trained the staff in class training in behavior theory, using written exercises and observing videotapes of varying degrees of complexity. They scored the accuracy of the use of DBRs using a points system in which staff could earn up to 100 points for accurate completing of the DBR. The scoring system was highly reliable. After training, staff uniformly made 80–100 points, suggesting that training resulted in a high degree of accuracy, regardless of their professional training. Coding of all components was accurate, although some components were more difficult than others to score accurately.

Time	Antecedent Event	Response	Consequent Social Event
9:14		1. T. throws bucket and shovel into corner of sandbox.	
		2. . . . stands up.	
		3. . . . walks over to monkeybars and stops.	
		4. . . . turns toward teacher.	
		5. . . . says, "Mrs. Simpson, watch me."	
			6. Mrs. S. turns toward Timmy.
	6. Mrs. S. turns toward Timmy.	7. T. climbs to top of apparatus.	
		8. . . . looks toward teacher.	
		9. . . . says, "Look how high I am. I'm higher than anybody."	
9:16			10. Mrs. S. says, "That's good, Tim. You're getting quite good at that."
	10. Mrs. S. says, That's good, Tim. You're getting quite good at that."	11. T. climbs down	
		12. . . . runs over to tree.	
		13. . . . says, "Watch me climb the tree, Mrs. Simpson."	
			14. Mrs. S. turns and walks toward classroom.
	14. Mrs. S. turns and walks toward classroom.	15. T. stands, looking toward Mrs. S.	
9:18	16. Girl nearby trips and falls, bumping knee.		
	17. Girl cries.		
		18. T . proceeds to sandbox	
		19. . . . picks up bucket and shovel.	
		20. . . . resumes play with sand.	

Figure 12.3. An example of an ABC chart. Reproduced from S. W. Bijou, R. F. Peterson & M. A. Ault (1968). A method to integrate descriptive and experimental field studies at the level of data and empirical concepts. *Journal of Applied Behavior Analysis*, **1**, p. 179–180.

Many people use ABC records and their variants of ABC. There are a number of commonly encountered problems that practitioners should address. First, the people taking ABC data require training. Groden and Lantz's study is a good model here. Training took place on actually practicing observation skills with an objective criterion for observer accuracy. Practitioners should continue such observer training until observers reach some predetermined level of mastery. Bijou et al.'s early study also used IOA data to ensure that observers were reliable. This too should be part of observer training. Similarly, Groden and Lentz trained their staff and measured the completeness and accuracy of staff recordings. Hence, practitioners should use effective training procedures, such as modeling rehearsal and feedback to mastery to ensure the staff have the skills to record accurately. As well as having the skill to use ABC records, staff must also record consistently. For example, if no records are available for a particular time period, it may be unclear if no target behaviors occurred or if staff failed to record or lost the data. It is always a good idea to ask observers to record that no incidents occurred to ensure whether the problem is lack of recording. In order to maintain staff behavior in keeping ABC records, staff performance should be monitored, frequently at first, and less frequently later on. Feedback can them be given to the staff and their supervisors on their data collection performance. A final area that clinicians must address is that the ABC data must be analyzed, interpreted and used to design an intervention. It is not unusual for a staff member who has diligently collected ABC data to be unable to describe the relationship between the target behavior and the environment. Others may not be able to develop a treatment strategy based on that information. A clinician should be able to provide further training in this or to be able to do this for the staff themselves. This issue is discussed more generally below.

Scatterplots

Touchette, MacDonald and Langer (1985) developed a graphical aide to assist in developing hypotheses about the possible function of a target behavior. A scatterplot is a grid of day plotted along the x-axis and time of day plotted on the y-axis. (See Figure 12.4 for an example.) Touchette et al. reported a scatterplot for assaults in a 14-year-old teenager with autism with a long history of assaulting others. When Touchette et al. plotted the data as a scatterplot, several patterns were important. First, the target behavior was very likely to occur Monday through Thursday between 1 and 4pm when she attended group classes. It was also very unlikely to occur during the mornings when she was engaged in one-to-one teaching and on Fridays, when she was engaged in field trips. On the basis of this functional assessment Touchette et al. eliminated the group activities and replaced them with leisure activities that she typically engaged in at the weekends.

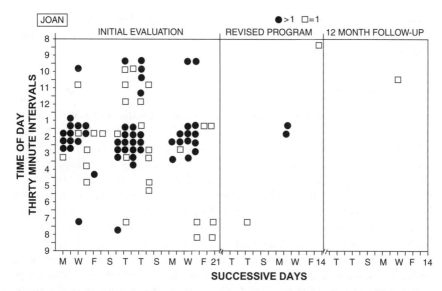

Figure 12.4. An example of a scatterplot. Reproduced from Touchette et al., (1985). A scatter plot for identifying stimulus control of problem behavior. *Journal of Applied Behavior Analysis*, 18, p. 343–351.

This resulted in the near elimination of aggression. Touchette et al. reported similar analyses and interventions for two other participants.

Scatterplots are often used in service for people with intellectual disabilities but lend themselves readily to other applications. For example, one might use scatterplots to analyze the occurrence of binge eating, panic attacks or angry outbursts in adults in mental health settings.

Sequential Analysis of Data

Sequential analysis of data was relatively difficult until the advent of laptop computers. Since that time, sequential analysis of data has been used in many contexts, such as violent and unhappy marital interactions (Cordova, Jacobson, Gottman, Rushe & Cox, 1993) and functional assessment of challenging behavior in people with intellectual disabilities (Thompson, Felce & Symons, 2000; Yoder, Short-Meyerson & Tapp, 2004).

In sequential analysis, observers collect data typically using laptop computers coding the frequency of brief behaviors, the onset and offset of longer behaviors, and potentially related environmental events. The temporal relationships between environmental events and behavior can be calculated from these data. For example, one might calculate the overall probability of a behavior of interest. Then, one might observe the probability of that behavior, given the occurrence of some environmental event of interest. This is termed the conditional probability of that behavior.

This analysis can be made more elaborate by graphing the conditional probability of the behavior of interest for some period of time before and after the environmental event of interest.

Inter-observer Agreement

In order to ensure that observations are indeed public and not based on the idiosyncrasies of individual observers, observers routinely collect IOA (Bijou et al., 1968). To do this, two observers simultaneously and independently collect observations. These data are then compared for agreement. Agreement should be defined conservatively. For example, if at the end of 10 min of observations, both observers agree that there were three occurrences of the target behavior, it might be tempting to conclude that there was good IOA, especially if one calculated IOA as 100%. However, Table 12.4 demonstrates that an agreement must be defined as conservatively as possible, using interval-by-interval agreement instead of session totals. In sample 1, shown in the figure, both observers agree that the behavior occurred three times. If the observers calculate IOA based on the column totals, then IOA will be 100%, even though they never agreed that the behavior occurred at the same time. If agreement is based on an interval-by interval basis, the observers agreed on only 40% of the intervals and never during the six intervals that the behavior was recorded. In sample 2 in Table 12.4, IOA is 100% when calculated on an interval by interval basis. This is because the observers agreed at

Table 12.4. The effects of liberal and conservative definitions of agreement on inter-observer agreement data

Observation	Sample 1		Sample 2	
	Observer A	Observer B	Observer A	Observer B
1	+	−	+	+
2	+	−	−	−
3	+	−	−	−
4	−	−	+	+
5	−	−	−	−
6	−	−	−	−
7	−	−	+	+
8	−	+	−	−
9	−	+	−	−
10	−	+	−	−
Total	3	3	3	3

every observation that the behavior did or did not occur. This interval-by-interval definition of IOA is preferred.

IOA is very useful at the beginning of any study in order to help observers define and refine their behavior categories. It is often necessary to take extensive pilot data to obtain adequate IOA and to obtain reliable behavior categories. Minimally, observers should have an average IOA of 80%, but generally an IOA of at least 90% is preferable.

IOA observations should be distributed throughout a study. One cannot assume that good IOA early on will be maintained later. Additionally, and especially during intervention, behavior changes in ways that do not occur early in a study, Hence regular IOA data distributed throughout the study are essential.

Other Artifacts

Being observed may make observees behave differently. Such observee reactivity can be reduced by taking sufficient pilot data so that observees habituate to the presence of the observer. Sometimes minor deception may be used as to the exact purpose of the observations, which may also reduce observee reactivity.

Observers may drift in accuracy over time. For example, they may inadvertently learn to cue each other as to what they are recording. This can be minimized by introducing new observers as the study continues. Rotating observers across subjects may be helpful. It may also be useful to have only a certain proportion of observations being IOA observations. Observers may also be reactive to the presence of the IOA observer. Again, attempts to keep the observers blind to which sessions are IOA observations, or scoring videotape independently, may minimize these problems.

Permanent Product, Mechanical and Telemetric Measures

Behavior often produced some trace, such as trash, damage or records. Such permanent products of behavior can often be highly reliable measures of behavior. Common examples include the products of academic (Kelly, 1976) work behavior, record keeping of various kinds, such as telephone records, receipts and bills. An example of true dedication to the use of reliable, permanent product measures comes from Dalhquist and Gil (1986). They asked children to place used dental floss in a bag next to the sink. They then examined it to ensure that it was "flattened shredded and discolored" (p. 257).

Another approach is to use mechanical or electro-mechanical devices to produce permanent product. For example, actometers have been used to measure activity levels in children with ADHD. Van Wormer (2004) used pedometers to measure obese clients' activity levels. Azrin, Rubin, O'Brien,

Ayllon and Roll (1968) taught children with disabilities to maintain correct posture using mercury switches to measure posture. Ingeniously, Dallery and Glenn (2005) used webcam recordings of teenagers exhaling into CO detectors to measure smoking behavior – something clients are unlikely to report accurately. Roll (2005) used a hand-held CO detector to measure smoking behavior as part of a contingency management approach to reduce smoking in 22 adolescents. Some of these methods have the additional advantage of measuring behavior outside of the office.

Functional Assessment and Functional Analysis

Researchers usually distinguish descriptive or functional assessment methods that do not systematically manipulate independent variables and functional analyses that do (Baer et al., 1968). Functional assessments necessarily produce correlational data. They do not clearly identify the independent variable that controls the observed behavior. For example, if one reliably observes a high rate of a target behavior at home, but not at work, and the client complains that being alone at home is difficult, it is tempting conclude that the lack of reinforcement at home for appropriate behavior sets the occasion for the target behavior. However, there may be other reasons, such as the tasks being carried out at home, that occasion the problem instead. A functional assessment cannot disentangle these possibilities.

In a functional analysis the independent variable is systematically manipulated and its effects on the target behavior is observed. For example, Fyffe, Kahng, Fittro and Russell (2004) conducted an experimental functional analysis of inappropriate sexual behavior (ISB) in Matt, a nine-year-old boy with traumatic brain damage and a seizure disorder. He had been placed in residential treatment because of ISB toward his siblings. ISB included touching or attempting to touch others in the groin, buttocks or breasts. Fyffe et al. used functional analyses based on work by Iwata et al. (1982/1994). They counted the number of instances of ISB and divided this by time to calculate the rate of ISB. Using laptop computers, IOA was 89–99%.

During the functional analysis attention condition, the experimenter gave Matt a brief reprimand contingent on ISB. In the demand condition Matt had a break contingent on ISB. In the play condition he had access to preferred toys and received attention on a FT-30 s schedule. The top panel of Figure 12.5 shows that during the analog baseline assessment, Matt only showed ISB during the four attention condition sessions. There was no ISB during the other conditions. Therefore, intervention consisted of functional communication training and attention extinction. This consisted of giving Matt a card attached to his wheelchair that he could hand over to request attention. If Matt handed the card over, the therapist interacted with him for 30 s of attention. They blocked and ignored any attempt at ISB. Over time, the availability of the card was reduced by progressively removing it for 5 s and eventually for 5 minutes. The lower panel of Figure 12.5 shows that ISB was high in the two baseline conditions. Functional communication training and attention extinction resulted in near elimination of ISB, including during gradual fading of the card to request attention. At the end of treatment ISB was nearly

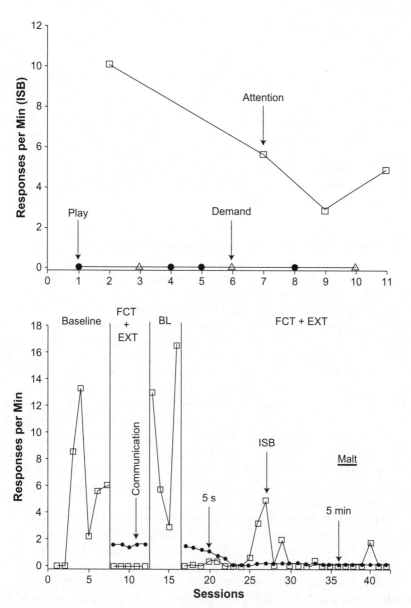

Figure 12.5. A functional analysis of inappropriate sexual behavior. C. E. Fyffe, S. W. Kahng, E. Fittro & D. Russell (2004). Functional analysis and treatment of inappriate sexual behavior. *Journal of Applied Behavior Analysis, 37,* p. 401–404.

eliminated with an overall 94% reduction in ISB and Matt requested attention at an acceptably low frequency.

Meta-analyses of outcome research with people with intellectual disabilities have consistently shown that using a functional assessment or analysis is associated with larger effect sizes and that experimental functional analyses are associated with the larger effect sizes (e.g. Didden, Duker & Korzilius, 1997; Didden, Korzilius, van Oorsouw & Sturmey, 2006). Several studies in mental health and school refusal also indicate that treatments based on the results of functional assessments produce larger effects that those that are not (see Chapter 13, for a further discussion of this point). However, Desrochers, Hile and Williams-Moseley (1997) found that practitioners in intellectual disabilities services consistently reported using descriptive methods, such as interviews and questionnaires. Rarely did they report using experimental functional analyses. Thus, even in the field where functional approaches to problems have the strongest history, experimental analyses are not commonly used. However, it is noteworthy that basing treatments on functional assessments was widespread.

Analyzing and Synthesizing Assessment Data

A common problem in behavioral assessment is how to analyze and synthesize assessment data and use it to design an individually-based intervention. Recall that Turkat bemoaned the problem of the technique-oriented clinician who collects large amounts of data only to implement their pet therapies. Using the information from a behavioral assessment can be problematic. First, data come from multiple sources that may be difficult to reconcile and that may conflict with one another. Second, there may a large amount of data that can be tedious to analyze and interpret. Third, there may be conflicting demands placed on the clinician regarding prioritizing target behaviors and selecting the target behavior that may produce the greatest change in the client in the quickest most efficient manner. Finally, there are probably existing coping strategies and implicit treatment procedures that may be powerfully reinforced in the short term, even if they are not completely effective in the long term.

Wolpe and Turkat's solution is to begin with the hypothesis. This may seem difficult or not even positively a bad thing to some. Turkat and Wolpe would probably argue that even if the initial hypothesis is incorrect, it may still be the best way to guide behavioral assessment than mechanically checking off a list of assessment procedures that have no hypothesis to guide them. Further, the skillful clinician will generate, entertain and evaluate multiple hypotheses as they assess. Thus, the hypothesis driven approach is not necessarily blinkered by only one, potentially incorrect hypothesis. The alternate approach is to reach some conclusion after gathering assessment data and testing the model (Cone, 1997; Haynes & O'Brien, 1990). Even if a clinician makes a hypothesis that is only partially correct, incomplete or is only a partial analysis of the problem, it is still possible to proceed with intervention, evaluate the hypothesis and the treatment and revise it as necessary.

A final key component to analyzing and synthesizing the data from behavioral assessment is to translate it into a treatment plan that is based on that hypothesis. Clinical formulations can fail at many points, but this is one key place where a formulation may falter. A formulation must generate a treatment plan that is better and more effective than that which would otherwise have been done if the functional assessment had not taken place (Nelson-Gray, 2003). This issue is discussed further in the last section of this chapter.

ILLUSTRATIONS OF BEHAVIORAL ASSESSMENT

After discussing the methods and process of conducting a behavioral assessment in somewhat abstract terms it would be useful to illustrate the variety of approaches to behavioral assessment and illustrate how clinicians use behavioral assessment to develop individual treatment plans. The following illustrations describe the application of behavioral assessment to pediatric feeding disorders, depression, nail biting, self-harm, aggression in psychiatric patients, bulimia and hypochondriasis.

Pediatric Feeding Disorder

Piazza and Addison (2007) described a case of functional analysis and treatment of a food refusal in a three-year-old girl, Peyton, who did not eat enough, frequently refused bites of food and showed behavior problems during mealtimes. Medical evaluations failed to identify any medical reason for food refusal and also indicated that she was able to swallow food. Piazza and Addison conducted an experimental functional analysis of food refusal using analog baseline conditions modified from those of Iwata et al. (1982/1994). They conducted this analysis in a clinic when her parents fed her as they usually did. Peyton showed the highest rates of food refusal in the escape condition, indicating that perhaps removal of the spoon was the reinforcer maintaining her food refusal.

Based on this functional analysis and previous research validating the use of escape extinction, Piazza and Addison treated the food refusal with escape extinction; that is, non-removal of the spoon until Peyton swallowed a bite of food. This treatment resulted in Peyton eating bites of food and large reductions in disruptive behaviors during mealtimes. Piazza and Addison then trained her parents and teachers to implement the procedure and provided monthly outpatient follow-up appointments. At follow-up Peyton continued to eat food, showed little disruptive behavior at mealtimes and the length of mealtimes was substantially reduced. Her parents reported that this treatment plan was highly effective and acceptable.

Depression

Hopko et al. (2007) described treatment of a woman with a long history of depression, which had been at its worse for the preceding six years. Kim was a professor who was married with two children. She reported cognitive, physiological and behavioral manifestations of depression, such as excessive worry, tachycardia and binge drinking, gambling, episodes of angry behavior and social withdrawal. Behavioral assessment included a structured diagnostic interview, a psychometric self-report measure of quality of life and one week of self-recording of mood and activities. This revealed that she was very active professionally, and with her family, but gained little pleasure from these activities. It also indicated episodes of binge drinking and gambling. Hopko et al. conducted an assessment of her core values, which she identified as her role as an academician, mother and her Christian values. An interview with Kim identified environmental factors that correlated with her depressed behaviors. Specifically, her high level of professional activity resulted both in avoidance of failure at work but also resulted in her being isolated from her family. Following periods of negative affect Kim drank and gambled, which removed her negative affect. Episodes of anger with her husband resulted in removal of demands to engage in child care, which she felt were unreasonable, given her active professional career.

Based on this functional assessment, Hopko et al. developed a treatment plan with the goal of increasing her contact with positive reinforcement through goals that were consonant with her core values. They used BATD (Lejuez et al., 2002) to increase activity progressively from easy to more challenging tasks related to increased time in family activities, spiritual and health-related activities. Kim kept a log of these activities. Hopko et al. also used ACT-related interventions, such as accepting unpleasant thoughts. Kim's engagement in family-related activities resulted in the removal of the antecedent for anger episodes and related drinking and gambling, which also reduced during BATD. After 15 weeks of BATD, Kim's scores on psychometric measures of depression reduced to sub-clinical levels, she enjoyed life much more and her anger, gambling and drinking were substantially reduced.

Nail Biting

Williams et al. (2006) reported a functional analysis of nail biting. Forty undergraduates, who reported biting their nails regularly, volunteered to take part for research participation credits. They first completed a modified QABF. They then participated in four analog conditions based on Woods and Milternberger's (1998) study of nail biting in children. In the alone condition, the observers videotaped the participant when they were alone in a room. In non-contingent interaction, the experimenter and participant engaged in conversation about everyday topics. In the academic demand condition, the participants completed math problems with an experimenter in the room who did not interact with them. In the social disapproval condition, the participant watched a videotape and answered questions about it at the end. If they bit their nails the experimenter told them to stop. They defined a nail bite as "a finger entering the mouth" (p. 3). They recorded that the frequency of nail bites during IOA was 83%.

On average the participants bit their nails 6.5, 3.2, 0.3 and 0.2 times in the alone, social interaction, demand and disapproval conditions respectively. Most participants bit their nails most frequently in the alone condition, but some bit their nails frequently in the demand condition. A few participants also reported "a sense of relief" from nail biting on the modified QABF. Thus, Williams et al. observed individual differences in the functions of nail biting that may have implications for treatment. Suppression of nail biting was greatest when other people were present. This suggested that the presence of other people, especially during the social interaction and social disapproval conditions, was a discriminative stimulus for not biting nails.

Self- harm

Deliberate self-harm is a very distressing problem, both for people who self-harm, their family members and staff. There is an extensive literature on the functions of self-harm. Linehan's DBT addresses this issue, and Chapter 11 described Koerner and Linehan's (1997) behavioral case formulation of a composite case of self-harm.

Klonsky (2006) conducted a comprehensive review of studies using functional approaches to self-harm. He identified 18 empirical studies conducted with a variety of populations, such as people with depression, anxiety, eating disorders, several personality disorders, prisoners, adolescents, schizophrenia and post traumatic stress disorder. This literature review identified seven possible functions. The most commonly reported functions all involved termination of negative private events, such as negative mood, aversive arousal, tension, suicidal intentions, depersonalization, derealization and other dissociative symptoms. Studies reported positive internal consequences less commonly, such as excitement, exhilaration and positive mood. Fewer studies reported that self-harm resulted in social consequences, such as getting other people to realize the severity of the person's suffering and to take action. A minority of studies found evidence that some people reported self-harming in order to self-punish for bad thoughts.

This review found good evidence of the functional nature of self-harm in a wide range of populations and contexts. Although termination of aversive private events was reported most commonly, the role of social consequences was unclear. It is possible that client reports of social consequences may be inaccurate because they are unaware of these consequences or because they minimized the inter-personal nature of such behavior. The literature was also limited in that the treatment implications of these individual differences in the functions of self-harm had not been extensively explored. For example, Klonsky reported no treatment studies that matched interventions to functions. For example, if a client self-harmed after an adverse interpersonal interaction that resulted in negative mood and self-harm terminates this negative mood, then one might teach the person how to deal with the interpersonal interaction more effectively and/or manage negative mood in other ways. Alternatively, if someone self-harms after periods of boredom in order to gain excitement, one might develop a treatment plan to insert stimulating activities during periods of boredom and/or teach some more effective way to gain stimulation when bored.

Aggression in Psychiatric Patients

As noted earlier, Daffern and colleagues published a number of papers on functional assessment of aggression in psychiatric inpatients. They noted that aggression in psychiatric inpatients is often attributed to their psychiatric illness and many people often assume that this is not determined by environmental variables. These structural assumptions often lead to management exclusively by psychotropic medication and restrictive reactive strategies, such as restraint and seclusion. Daffern et al. (2007) reported data using the ACF to assess the function of aggressive behavior in 232 psychiatric inpatients. Of these inpatients, 105 were aggressive at least once. There were a total of 502 incidents of aggression. Unit staff completed an ACF on 476 (95%) of these incidents. A function was reported in 97% of incidents. Daffern et al. analyzed the data by comparing incidents of aggression to staff compared to incidents of aggression to other patients.

There were large differences in the function of aggression to staff compared with the function of aggression to other patients. The function of aggression to staff was most likely to be related to expression of anger (73% of incidents), reduction in tension (64% of incidents), to force compliance (47% of incidents), demand avoidance (44% of incidents), to enhance status (25% of incidents) and to obtain tangibles (16%). In contrast, aggressive incidents involving other patients were most likely related to express anger (87% of incidents), to enhance status (54% of incidents) to reduce tension (36% of incidents) and to obtain tangibles (16% of incidents). Chi-squared tests indicated that the functions of aggressive incidents involving staff were more likely to be due to demand avoidance, to force compliance and to reduce tension rather than incidents involving other patients. Also, the function of aggressive incidents involving other patients were more likely to be to express anger, enhance status and for compliance with instruction rather than incidents involving staff. Daffern et al. concluded that, since many of the incidents were related to interpersonal interactions between staff and patients, the most common examples were as requests from staff to engage in activities and patient requests being denied. Patient arousal also preceded many incidents of aggression. They suggested that management of patient arousal through relaxation and teaching inter-personal skills to both patients and staff were promising interventions.

Bulimia

Miltenberger and colleagues have addressed the functional nature of bulimic symptoms (Lee & Miltenberger, 1997). Stickney, Miltenberger and Wolff (1999) used self-report measures in 16 female undergraduates to identify the antecedents and consequences of binge eating. Common antecedents included negative mood states such as depression anger, and so on. The most commonly reported consequence was removal of these negative mood states, and decrease in hunger and craving. Deaver, Miltenberger, Smyth, Meidinger and Crosby (2003) asked young women who did and who did not engage in binge eating to record their affect every two minutes before, during and after meals. These results confirmed the earlier study's retrospective findings that eating results in removal of negative affect in people with binge eating. Engel et al. (2006) extended these findings by showing that antecedent anger was also related to binge eating. Ghaderi (2007) developed a typological approach to functional assessment of bulimia, which is similar to the work of Kanfer and Phillips (1970) and Daffern and Howells (2002). Ghaderi (2007) noted that bulimic symptoms could be a function of:

- poor stimulus control, poor contingency control, such as absence of discriminative stimuli for appropriate eating and presence of discriminative stimuli for binging

- inappropriate consequential control, such as weak and ineffective private verbal consequences for appropriate eating and other behavior and inappropriate rule governed behavior that is insensitive to its consequences, such as "I have to be thin to be attractive"
- inappropriate establishing operations, such as long periods of food deprivation
- inadequate behavioral repertoires due to skills deficits, such as poor exercise habits.

Ghaderi (2006, 2007) subsequently used this typology to design individually tailored interventions, For example, poor stimulus control related to verbal stimuli could be corrected by teaching appropriate private rules through educational and cognitive interventions. Inappropriate stimulus control related to non-verbal stimuli could be corrected by exposure treatment, for example exposure to bloated feelings and eating fatty foods. Poor consequential control could be corrected by contingency management, goal setting and self-control training. Finally, inadequate response repertoires could be corrected by educational, and skills training interventions (see Ghaderi, 2007, Figure 1).

These studies strongly support the functional nature of bulimic symptoms in commonly regulating negative affect. (Other functions are not precluded.) These studies suggest two promising strategies to manage bulimic symptoms: self-management of mood and prevention of hunger and associated cravings. Thus, teaching self-regulation skills to manage negative mood to compete with bulimic symptoms may be an effective strategy to treat bulimia. Further, these studies also point to significant individual differences in the nature of the negative mood that interventions should address. Thus, some intervention plans should address depression, whereas others should address anger or loneliness. Similarly, the reinforcing power of relief from hunger and cravings can be reduced by more frequent access to food and prevention of prolonged periods of not eating. These empirical findings on groups of clients are consonant with Farmer and Latner's (2007) case formulation described in the preceding chapter. They are also supported by Ghaderi's (2006) RCT which demonstrated the superiority of function-based treatment over manualized treatment for bulimia. (See Chapter 13 for detailed discussion of this study.)

Hypochondriasis

Abramowitz and Moore (2006) reported a functional analysis of hypochondriasis. Twenty-seven adult outpatients who met DSM-IV-TR diagnostic criteria for hypochondriasis, but who did not meet DSM-IV-TR criteria for OCD, major depression, psychotic or manic disorders participated. None had received adequate cognitive behavior therapy or educational materials related to cognitive behavioral formulation of hypochondriasis. An interviewer elicited three triggers for illness-related behavior, such as dry mouth, eating food past its sell-by date or feeling dizzy. The interviewer then elicited three coping behaviors, such as asking for reassurance, checking moles on the body or swallowing until feeling normal. Finally, interviewers identified a response prevention strategy, such as engaging in a distracting activity, such as reading non-health related materials or feeding one's baby.

The experimenters assigned participants randomly to two conditions. Participants in the safety behavior condition engaged in three conditions in a laboratory setting: before exposure to a trigger, after exposure to a trigger and after engaging in a safety behavior. Participants in the response prevention group took part in the same conditions, but did not engage in the safety behavior. Participants reported their anxiety behavior and urge to engage in a safety behavior during these three conditions and every five minutes thereafter for an hour. They reported these measures on a seven-point Likert scale.

Self-reports of anxiety were a function of these three conditions, time after engaging in response prevention and whether or not the participant engaged in the response prevention strategy. In the safety behavior group, anxiety was low before exposure (mean = 1.7) and rose significantly after exposure (mean = 5.3). Immediately after engaging in the safety behavior, the mean anxiety ratings fell to 2.6 and then gradually fell to 1.6 at 60 minutes post exposure. In the response prevention group mean anxiety ratings before, immediately after and 5 minutes after exposure were 1.9, 4.7 and 6.1. Participants in this group then reported that anxiety ratings fell gradually to 2.8 at 60 minutes post exposure. Thus, engaging in the safety behavior appeared to terminate anxiety. Failure to engage in the safety behavior resulted in very high ratings of anxiety, which decreased over a one-hour period. These data parallel similar data for exposure and response prevention for OCD (Rachman, de Silva and Röper, 1976) suggesting similarities in the functional nature of these two disorders.

Comment

The preceding sections all illustrate the variety of approaches to conducting and using a behavioral assessment. Piazza and Addison's approach to pediatric feeding disorders is very close to work done in intellectual disabilities since the mid-1980s, as it involved functional analysis, tight experimental control and a close relationship of the assessment and treatment to basic behavioral concepts, such as extinction of operant behavior. Hopko et al.'s behavioral assessment was most obviously different from Piazza and Addison's. They did not involve direct observation in the natural environment, but rather relied on more traditional clinical assessment methods, such as interviews and self-report data. Nevertheless, these assessments were both based on behavioral concepts. Hopko et al.'s approach involved idiographic assessment and treatment, but built around their semi-standardized treatment package for depression, BATD. This approach does however, incorporates individual functional assessment since it described the possible contingencies maintaining Kim's problematic behavior. It also incorporated individually meaningful goals and behavioral approaches to private verbal behavior through the use of ACT.

These preceding sections also illustrate the flexibility and variety of applications of a functional approach to psychopathology. The same assessment technology and conceptual framework readily transfer from one problem to another. Thus, questionnaires first developed for use with people with developmental disabilities can be used as models for questionnaires to assess gambling, school refusal and nail biting. Iwata's functional analysis methodology, developed to assess self-injury has been extended to assess pediatric food refusal and psychotic speech. Conceptual similarities are apparent as one compares Klonsky's work on self-harm and Miltenberger's on bulimia. In both cases problematic behavior is often negatively reinforced by termination of negative affect. In both cases, these results indicate that teaching more effective ways to manage negative affect may be appropriate methods of intervention.

SUMMARY

Clinicians can use a wide variety of methods to assess the functions of psychopathology. Although ABA gives pride of place to observational data and experimental analysis, there are a wide range of other methods that clinicians may find very useful in developing behavioral case formulations and individually designed, function-based treatment plans. Researchers and practitioners have applied these approaches to a very wide range of clinical problems and contexts beyond developmental disabilities, children and severe psychiatric disorders. Models for clinicians to use are now available for almost all common clinical problems (Sturmey, 2007).

Chapter 13

OUTSTANDING ISSUES AND FUTURE DIRECTIONS

This chapter reviews outstanding issues in behavioral case formulation. These include professional performance in case formulation, such as writing and using a case formulation to guide treatment design and to work with clients and third parties, the reliability and validity of case formulations and the behavioral model of therapy. All of these issues have implications for professional training which will also be discussed. The final section of this chapter will identify future directions in behavioral case formulation.

PROFESSIONAL PERFORMANCE

Developing a case formulation is a badge of professionalism – to understand and construe a client's presenting problem in a way that lay people or other professionals cannot; to caste new light on a client's problem that others previously have not; to show that you have a special skill, something to offer that others do not – effective case formulation is one way to show your professional worth. Yet, despite the centrality of case formulation to the clinical psychologist and a variety of other mental health professionals, there has been surprisingly little research into some of the fundamental questions that case formulation begs. Is there much evidence to back up the claim that clinicians can indeed formulate cases and that this makes a meaningful difference to treatment? Are case formulations reliable and valid? Even if they are reliable and valid, do clinicians use them to implement treatments that are more effective than the treatment that would have happened, if the case formulation had not been used? Put bluntly, if the client was going to go into a cognitive behavior anxiety management group with six standard lessons, learn about anxiety, how to relax, how to make better attributions for maladaptive cognitions and how to self-expose progressively and probably do fairly well, what does a case formulation have to offer that makes treatment better than this?

Quality of Case Formulations

Concern over the quality of case formulation comes from the results of Eells et al. (1998) evaluation of case formulations in routine clinical practice. They evaluated a random sample of 56 intake reports from a larger sample of approximately 300 reports written by 14 practitioners – nine psychiatry residents, four social workers, and a psychiatric nurse. Six identified themselves as psychodynamic, three as cognitive-behavioral, three as eclectic mixes of more than one school of psychotherapy and two did not identify an orientation. The clients were adults aged 20–66 years. Most had high-school education. Half were unemployed.

Scoring the intake was quite reliable with kappas varying from 0.74 to 0.88 for content categories and 0.67 to 0.82 for quality measures. The overall completeness and quality of the formulations was disappointing. For example only two-thirds included a problem list, two-thirds included identifying information and only 41% included past psychiatric history. Approximately one-third included reference to a life event related to the presenting problem, and only 4% referred to a recent life event. Only 42% noted a psychological mechanism. Hence, these formulations focused on description, rather than inference and on symptoms and history. Quality ratings were also disappointing. For example, only 45% included any psychological mechanism and 29% only contained rudimentary mechanisms but did not link symptoms, problems, stressors, and life events into a synthesized formulation. Only 5% of the formulations had a strong mechanism. This study lends support to the notion that these formulations were incomplete and of poor quality. The results should be qualified in that they were based on written records – it is possible that clinicians actually made more sophisticated formulations privately or verbally. A second limitation is that the sample of clinicians and clinical contexts was small and not representative of any population of interest.

Guidelines for Writing Case Formulations

Eells (1997) noted that case formulations should be brief, abstract out only the relevant features of the case, and guide treatment. In additions to these three guidelines a written behavioral case formulation should be behavioral and analytic (Baer et al., 1968). That is they should refer to behavior and use the conceptual framework and concepts of behavior analysis discussed in Chapters 3–7 of this book. Eells et al's (1998) rating scale might be useful in teaching professionals to write better case formulations. However, their ratings scales are described in general terms and are not operationalized. Thus, they might be a useful part of a broader feedback mechanism, but cannot provide very clear guidelines to clinicians.

Kuyken, Fothergill, Musa and Chadwick (2005) also developed criteria for cognitive behavioral formulations of depression, which are discussed in greater detail later in this chapter.

Behavioral Case Formulation Guidelines

Sturmey (1996) proposed guidelines for writing functional analyses of individual cases (see Table 13.1). These included a 250 word limit, only brief mention of demographic variables, an operationalized target behavior, which could be a behavior, cognition of physiological problem, a consequence, description of the onset and maintenance, a brief history, description of secondary gains, description of the function of the behavior and an implied treatment.

New Guidelines

In the light of the material earlier in this book we can now provide more detailed guidelines for behavioral case formulations. Behavioral case formulations should meet the following criteria:

1. They should specify
   (a) target behavior(s)
   (b) may include overt and covert behavior
   (c) whether the target behaviors are respondent, operant, or rule-governed behavior
   (d) the organization of the responses as a single response, a responses class with multiple, topographically distinct members, or a response hierarchy
2. Specify any functionally equivalent potential replacement behaviors
3. Describe the target behavior's controlling variables, including
   (a) reinforcer deprivation and satiation and other distal antecedent stimuli
   (b) conditioned stimuli for respondent behavior
   (c) discriminative stimuli for the presence and absence of the target behavior
   (d) other relevant antecedent stimuli
4. Describe the contingencies
   (a) maintaining the target behavior
   (b) maintaining or failing to maintain the functionally equivalent behaviors
5. Describe the learning processes in behavior analytic terms, such as extinction, differential reinforcement, stimulus control that may account for the target behavior
6. Translate the functional assessment into a treatment plan that reflects the functions identified in the formulation.

Table 13.1 Sturmey's (1996) guidelines for writing a functional analysis of individual clinical cases. From P. Sturmey (1996) *Functional Analysis in Clinical Psychology*. Chichester: Wiley, Table 8.1, p. 180.

1. A word limit of 250 words.

2. A *brief*, demographic and psychiatric description of problem, e.g., 'A four-year-old child was referred for fecal incontinence. The family consisted of mother (divorced) and two other children.'

3. At *least* one operationalized target 'behavior' which might be an overt behavior (e.g., 'crying'), cognitive (e.g., 'recurrent thoughts of worthlessness'), or physiological (e.g., 'feelings of tension').

4. At least one operationalized antecedent which must include examples, e.g., 'feelings of worthlessness' most often happened when alone (early morning/late at night) and after failures to assert herself (giving in to her husband), *or* state 'antecedents unknown'.

5. At least one operationalized consequence which must include examples, e.g., The pain behavior appeared to be maintained by both positive reuiforcers, primarily social in nature (e.g., frequent visits to GP, attention from family) and negative reinforcers (excessive use of anxiolytics such as minor tranquilizers, alcohol and analgesics, avoidance of driving in certain cases and certain social activities described as stressful', *or* state 'consequences unknown'.

6. A stated distinction between onset and maintenance which may or may not require separate functional analyses, e.g., 'No clear onset could be identified, although the problem got considerably worse after he changed his job.'

7. A brief history to include (a) the onset (traumatic/insidious) e.g., 'this problem began about 15 years ago, but with no clear point of onset'; and (b) factors which have been associated with an increase or decrease in the severity of the problem during its development, e.g., 'this person's control of his temper has always been poor, but has got considerably worse, following the loss of his job and moving house.'

8. Describe the secondary gains that may often be relevant and important for design of treatment, e.g., The adoption of the role of a person with an incurable and mysterious illness gained the person considerable status in her family and neighborhood.'

9. Describe the functions of the behaviors in terms of the purposes that they serve for the subject, e.g., The agoraphobic symptoms appeared to keep her husband at home more often than otherwise might have happened.'

10. State a treatment, either planned or implemented, which is explicitly linked to (3), (4), or (5) e.g., 'Rational emotive therapy was selected to modify the dysfunctional cognitions which maintain the depression', or 'A Patterson-style behavior management program was implemented in order to change the patterns of instructions given to the child *and* to increase parental use of praise.'

Using Case Formulations

Using Typologies of Functions

One approach to translating a behavioral case formulation into a treatment plan is to develop a typology of functions and list indicated and contraindicated treatments for each function. This approach is sometimes known as behavioral diagnostics. Chapter 12 included several examples of this approach. There are a number of advantages of limiting the number of possible functions available to the clinician. The clinician then uses the selected function to identify indicated and contraindicated treatments. Kanfer and Phillips developed behavioral diagnostics as a generic approach to case formulation. Several others have extended this to developmental disabilities and aggression in psychiatric inpatients.

SORC Analysis and Treatment Design

Kanfer and Phillips (1970) illustrated the application of the analysis of behavior based on SORKC analysis to intervention (see their Table 10.1, page 511–513). Here are some of their examples.

- *Response*: If the response is absent use shaping, modeling and imitation to instate the response
- *Response*: If the response is excessive, consider extinction.
- *Stimulus*: If stimulus control is ineffective, then use stimulus discrimination training. Begin with clear and effective discriminative stimuli
- *Consequence*: If the consequence is too potent use aversive conditioning to change the S-Ds to S-deltas
- *Contingency*: If the current contingency required to support new behavior is too demanding, for example, a person learning a new social skill is initially rebuffed, then place the new response on 100% reinforcement. Gradually thin the schedule until the response is resistant to extinction.
- *Organism*: The state of the organism interferes with appropriate behavior or learning, change the state of the organism. For example, through drugs, modification of painful stimuli, etc.

Thus, SORKC analysis is used to closely map interventions from the analysis of behavior to the intervention plan. Table 13.2 illustrates some of these mappings. The reader can also refer back to Chapter 11 for several other examples of this approach.

Table 13.2. Examples of Kanfer and Grimm's (1977) typological approach to translating type of clinical function to treatment plan. From P. Sturmey (1996) *Functional Analysis in Clinical Psychology*. Chichester: Wiley, Table 3.1, p. 66.

Type	Sub-type	Description	Treatment
Behavior deficit	Information	Person does not know details of correct performance or social standards for behavior (e.g., sexual problem)	Provide information
Behavior excesses	Excessive self-monitoring	Client attends too frequently, too long or too intensely to own behavior (e.g., somatic- or evaluation-based fears)	Thought stopping; provide incompatible response; satiation
Problems in environmental stimulus control	Restrictive environment	Lack of opportunity for desired behavior; no reinforcement or punishment provided (e.g., college student living at home with dating problems)	Modifying current environment or seeking new environment
Inappropriate self-generated stimulus control	Discrimination internal stimuli	Internal states are incorrectly labelled (e.g., sexual arousal as anxiety)	Train client in better discrimination of more correct labelling of own behavior
Inappropriate contingency arrangements	Non-contingent reinforcement	Temporal arrangement of behavior and reinforcement is incorrect (e.g., low motivation, blandness, low affect)	Rearrange contigencies; use of short-term goals; self-management

Iwata's Functional Analyses

Iwata's work on functional analysis of self-injury in people with intellectual disabilities has provided extensive evidence of the important of selecting interventions based on functions. Identifying the function of self-injury can accurately predict treatments that will be effective, ineffective and in some cases treatments that will increase self-injury. Iwata et al, (1994) reported data on the analysis of functional analysis of 152 children and adults with intellectual disabilities who self-injured. Using single-subject experimental analyses of behavior, they identified functions in 95% of the cases. They compared a variety of treatments, some of which were indicated and some of which were contraindicated. They collapsed the outcomes for all subjects and reported treatment outcome by function and treatment. Figure 13.1 summarizes these results. This figure shows important treatment by function interactions. For example, for self-injury maintained by social-positive reinforcement, non-contingent reinforcement, attention extinction, differential reinforcement and time out were almost always effective. However, verbal reprimands and response interruption were almost always ineffective. Attention extinction was almost always ineffective to behavior that was maintained by social-negative reinforcement, automatic reinforcement and that was multiply controlled or undifferentiated. Figure 13.1 contains many such examples.

These results have been replicated for many different behavior problems in people with intellectual disabilities, autism, and typically developing children and adolescents with behavior problems. Furthermore, demonstrations that these analyses predict effective and ineffective treatments have been extended to other populations and problems, such as pediatric feeding disorders (Piazza & Addison, 2007), psychotic speech (Wilder and Wong, 2007), ADHD (Neef & Northup, 2007), school refusal (Chorpita, Albano, Heimberg & Barlow, 1996; Kearney & Silverman, 1990) and has influenced the assessment and treatment of many forms of psychopathology (Sturmey, 2007). Hence, this conceptual framework may be the basis for a general approach to behavioral case formulations with modifications as needed to different populations and contexts.

Other Typologies of Function in Developmental Disabilities

Other researchers and practitioners have used functional assessments and analyses to structure treatment design. For example, O'Neill et al. (1997) summarized the results of functional assessments and provided guidelines for clinicians to use to build a support plan. The aim of the support was to build competing behavior support paths to make the target behavior less likely and the alternate behavior more likely. This competing behavior model prompts the clinician to identify setting event, predictor, teaching

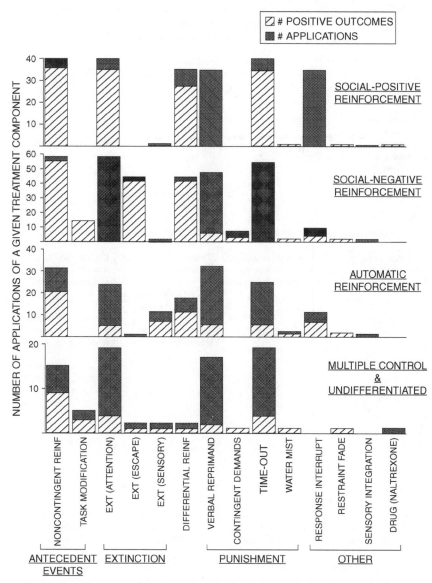

Figure 13.1. The relationship between functions and indicated and contraindicated treatments. Reproduced from Iwata et al. (1994), *Journal of Applied Behavior Analysis*, p. 232, Figure 6.

and consequence strategies. Figure 13.2 illustrates this. Pyles and Bailey (1989) also provided an example of this behavioral diagnostic approach. Daffen and Howells's work on aggression in psychiatric inpatients discussed in Chapter 12 also used a behavioral diagnostic approach.

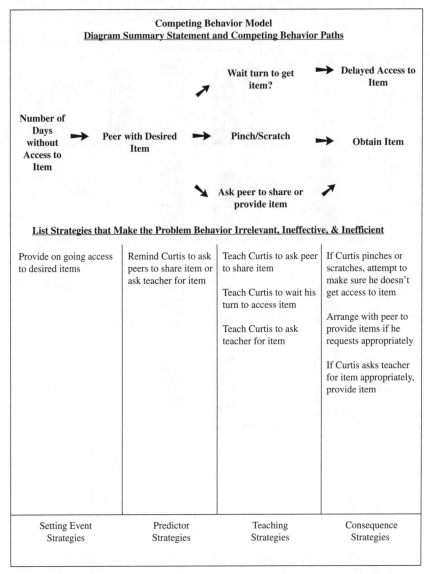

Figure 13.2. O'Neill et al.'s Competing Behavior Model, which indicates how to translate a functional assessment into a treatment plan. Reproduced from O'Neill et al. (1997) *Functional Assessment and Program Development for Problem Behavior. A Practical Handbook.* New York: Brooks/Cole, p. 83, Figure 3.13

Reformulating Cases

A case formulation should not be set in stone. Haynes and O'Brien noted that formulations have limited validity. Hence, a currently valid formulation may be invalid in the future. New information may change the formulation. Unpredicted events may change the person's behavior and its relationship to the environment. Intervention may bring the client into contact with new environments that may give rise to new behavior or new functions. Treatment failure and relapse may also be informative in reformulating a problem. Relapse may be due to either a failure to maintain implementation of effective treatment or to a true change in function (Lerman, Iwata, Smith, Zarcone & Vollmer, 1994). Likewise, for complex behaviors, where there are multiple functions, treating one function successfully may mean that other formerly secondary functions later become more significant (Sturmey, 1996).

Using Case Formulations with Clients

Many advise sharing the formulation with clients and working collaboratively with them on the formulation. Recall that Skinner exhorted therapists *not* to deliver the formulation to the clients, but rather to shape clients' self-regulation so that they could describe their own functional assessment. More recently clinical lore has suggested that sharing the formulation may be a desirable practice. For example, Kinderman and Lobban (2000) provided a client with an initial generic formulation of psychotic behavior: vulnerability + stress = distress or disorder. They then used this stimulus to guide assessment and develop a more elaborate and individually-based case formulation. They reported that this enabled them to work collaboratively with their client and facilitated his participation in the process of case formulation. This is similar to Dixon and Johnson's (2007) collaborative use of ABC and other data to develop a behavioral case formulation with their client. Chadwick, Williams and Mackenzie (2003) cited research suggesting that sharing the formulation with a client might result in positive gains for the client, such as an improved therapeutic alliance and reduction of distress. Thus, several authors have recommended using case formulations with clients in various ways.

There is very little research on evaluating ways of using case formulations with clients. Case formulations could be used in a variety of ways. They could be used educationally to teach the client their formulation to provide a rationale for treatment. This could be done with collaboratively or authoritatively with less client participation. If case formulations are used with client active participation in data collection, writing and interpretation in therapy, this may be a useful way to begin to induce change in client behavior early on and perhaps make formal intervention easier, since some behavioral change has already occurred (Skinner, 1953.)

Possibly the only empirical evaluation of sharing the case formulation with clients comes from Chadwick et al. (2003) who conducted two studies evaluating sharing case formulations Their study tested the hypotheses that sharing a case formulation strengthened the therapeutic alliance and reduced client distress. They worked with 16 people with drug-resistant schizophrenia and schizo-affective disorder. The therapists were two highly experienced cognitive behavior therapists with six and 15 years of experience. In baseline, the therapists conducted routine assessments without any intervention or sharing of the formulation. Chadwick et al. then devoted two sessions to case formulation. These sessions consisted of "exploring and refining an individualized [C]ase [f]ormulation" (2003, p. 673). This included developing a developmental diagram and accompanying letter. The diagram included information on analysis and maintenance of current problems, including links between thoughts, feelings, behavior and physical signs, triggers, onset and critical incidents, core beliefs and key formative experiences. The letter had four components. These were:

1. describing the case formulation in non-technical language using the client's language where possible
2. identifying target behaviors
3. pointing out that beliefs such as delusions were reactions to experiences, but not necessarily facts
4. identifying risks to the therapeutic alliance based on the formulation.

A second clinician familiar with the case checked the case formulation for consistency. The client took the case formulation home. The authors encouraged them to make changes to the formulation, which half did. The authors then interviewed the clients using semi-structured interviews to ascertain the client's reaction to the formulation. The dependent variables were psychometric measures of the therapeutic alliance, anxiety and depression. Thirteen clients completed data collection on all four accessions.

The results were disappointing. Client ratings of the therapeutic alliance improved over time, but there was no specific impact of sharing the formulation on the therapeutic alliance. Only *therapist* ratings of the therapeutic alliance improved significantly after sharing the formulation. Client reports of anxiety and depression remained on the borderline of mild and mild-moderate respectively, but were uninfluenced by sharing the formulation.

Client interviews revealed both positive and negative reactions to formulations. Nine of 11 clients reported that it was helpful in understanding their problems. Six reported positive reactions, such as feeing reassured, seeing a way out of their problems and feeling that their therapist understood them. Six also reported negative reactions, including a realization that their problems were longstanding, that their problems dated back to childhood, that there were too many factors in the formulation and not being able to see any way out of their problems. Therapists reported several positive reactions to formulations. These included validation at the client endorsing their formulation, feeling hopeful about the therapy, increased sense of alliance and collaboration with the client, increased confidence, feeling that they adhered to the cognitive behavioral model and better understanding of their client.

Chadwick et al.'s second study was a multiple baseline design across four adult clients with distressing auditory hallucinations and paranoid delusions. The dependent variables were client ratings of the strength of their beliefs, anxiety and depression. The experiment consisted of three phases: a baseline when the therapists conducted assessment; an intervention phase involving sharing the case formulation; and a cognitive intervention phase when beliefs were challenged. Again the results were disappointing. Sharing the formulation had no impact on strengths of delusional beliefs, even though these ratings did later respond to therapy that challenged the strength of their beliefs. Thus, the authors concluded that sharing formulations alone were ineffective in changing the strengths of delusional beliefs. Overall, sharing the formulation had no statistically significant impact on anxiety and depression. Sharing the formulation had no impact on anxiety and depression for two clients. However, one person's anxiety *worsened* during sharing the formulation and one or perhaps three of the clients reported increases in depression. Despite this negative evidence, Chadwick et al. concluded both that "the two experiments found no evidence that C[ase] F[ormulation] has a direct impact on any of the main targets of C[ognitive] B[ehaviour] T[herapy] for psychosis" and that "the present research assuredly is not evidence that CF has little or no value" (p. 679).

Comment

There is little evidence to support the common clinical lore that sharing the case formulation with a client is an effective or desirable strategy. This conclusion is primarily justified on the absence of evidence on this point. Indeed, the rather mixed response to sharing the case formulation from Chadwick et al.'s study suggests that sharing the case formulation may also have some negative effects on some clients.

Careful review of Chadwick et al.'s method suggests many procedural variations in sharing a case formulation. These variations may be very important, but research has not yet evaluated the relative efficacy of these procedural differences in sharing case formulations with clients. Sharing formulations could be done in a number of ways. First, the formulation can be written by the client, by the client with varying degrees of support and input from the therapist or by the therapist alone. Second, the formulation formats may vary considerably. They may be written, spoken or diagrammatic. Thus, they may vary in their complexity. Written formulations may vary in their readability, length and presentation format. There is a robust literature indicating that professionals generally write in language that is too complex for the general public (Hartley, 1994; Sturmey, 1990). Simplifying this language has numerous benefits for the reader, such as increased comprehension and recall (Hartley, 1994; Lorenc, Sturmey & Brittain, 1992; McGaw & Sturmey, 1989). As noted elsewhere (Sturmey, 1996), some diagrammatic case formulations are very complex, may be difficult for both the therapist and client to understand and use and can sometimes be readily simplified. Future research should evaluate the impact of these procedural variations in sharing case formulations on client ability to report their own formulation and its implications for treatment, its acceptability, and its effectiveness in changing client behavior.

There is no research yet on these specific points. However, based on research in other areas one might make the following recommendations. First, clinicians should be explicit in the purpose of sharing a formulation. This will guide their evaluations of whether sharing the formulation has achieved these goals. Second, clinicians should involve the client in development of the formulation in some way in order to promote discrimination of their target behaviors and the relationship of these problems to modifiable, causal, large independent variables unless there are indications that this is not desirable. Involving clients in writing the formulation has an important advantage in that the client's behavior is observable and there is a permanent product that is easy to work with. Third, written and diagrammatic formulations are likely to be superior to spoken formulations. Permanent product formulations obviate therapist and client memory problems. They give the client a permanent antecedent stimulus they can take away to perhaps prompt further self-regulation. A permanent product formulation can also be a guide to the rationale for treatment. Fourth, formulations that are shared with the client should be kept simple. Clinicians should check their written English for readability and human interest. They should check the layout to assure that it maximizes the goals of the written formulation. Fifth, clinicians should also check that diagrammatic formulations are sufficiently simple for clients to understand and use. Sixth, clinicians should check with clients that (1) they understand the formulation and its implications for treatment; and (2) that it is acceptable to them. Finally, the manner in which clinicians use a case formulation over time may change. Perhaps early formulations should be very simple and later formulations more detailed as the client and therapist build a better formulation (Kindermand & Lobban, 2000). A therapist might be able to use a very simple early formulation as a tool to work with the client to shape up more careful self-observation that might lead to the client developing more detailed formulations of their own problems. Readers should regard these recommendations with caution as they have not yet been empirically evaluated, although they do reflect research in other areas such as doctor–patient communication and text design.

RELIABILITY OF CASE FORMULATION

Reliability of observation is a necessary condition for scientific approaches to knowledge. It is a test that the information considered is public rather than idiosyncratic and subjective. It is also a necessary condition for validity. If we conduct case formulation in order to improve treatment beyond that which we would have done, then reliability of the case formulation and reliability of translating it into a treatment plan are necessary conditions for adequate case formulation. However, the issue of reliability is a somewhat complex one. Merely showing that clinicians agree on the target behavior is insufficient if they cannot also agree on other aspects of the formulation. Likewise agreeing on the formulation is insufficient, if clinicians cannot also reliably agree on the treatments implied and contraindicated by that formulation. What is the evidence on the reliability of case formulation?

Wilson and Evans (1983) mailed clinical vignettes describing anxiety, conduct and withdrawal problems to 118 members of the American Association of Behavior Therapy. They asked them to describe the child's major difficulty and to specify and rank order treatment targets. These apparent behaviorists frequently used intrapsychic processes, such as 'internalizing hostility', and diagnostic labels instead of operationalized target behaviors and frequently inferred situations information not present in the vignettes. Only 20% of responses identified any target behavior and inter-observer agreement on target behaviors was an unimpressive 39% (range 18–73%) and was equally poor for both simple and complex cases.

In contrast two studies by Persons found rather better agreement on target behaviors. Persons, Mooney and Padesky (1995) asked 46 clinicians to listen to audiotapes of initial interviews of two patients and to identify two and five problems in each case. The proportions of clinicians who correctly identified the first client's three problems were 98%, 83% and 13%. For the second client, the analogous figures were 100%, 96%, 67%, 93% and 72%. Agreement by individual clinicians on patient schemas and core beliefs was poor (0.46). Only when it was averaged across five clinicians did it begin to approach acceptability (0.76), although of course in practice five clinicians do not conduct formulations on individual clients. Persons and Bertagnolli (1999) found similar results with a second sample of clinicians making formulations of audiotapes of clients with depression. In this study inter-observer agreement on target behaviors was only 67%. Reliability on schemas was only 0.37 for single judges and 0.72 when pooled across five clinicians.

Kuyken et al. (2005) compared the formulations of a group of 115 clinicians attending three workshops on case formulations with an expert's standard cognitive behavioral formulation. Approximately half had completed professional mental health training and 21% were accredited cognitive behavior therapists. Thirty per cent were clinical psychologists, 17% were psychiatric nurses and 12% were counselors. One-quarter had doctorates and one-quarter had Masters degrees. Of those with professional training the average person had seven years post-qualification experience. Thus, the participants were quite varied and included well trained and relatively untrained professional staff. The clinicians read case description material, and observed videotapes of therapist–client interaction. In these videotapes, the therapist identified core beliefs, assumptions and compensatory strategies, and linked adverse developmental experiences to core beliefs. Kuyken et al. rated the formulations using a questionnaire measure of the quality of the formulations. This rating scale had quite good reliability based on 10 independently coded formulations. Kappas were 0.85 for overall quality and ranged from 0.70 to 0.97 for individual elements of the formulations.

The clinicians' overall performance was quite varied. Clinicians identified some elements of the formulation most of the time and other elements, including essential elements, rarely. For example, although 72% identified core beliefs of incompetency and worthlessness, only 37% identified the core belief of unlovability. (All three were essential aspects of the expert's formulation.) In terms of identifying essential elements of the history, participants identified essential elements between 71% and 15% of the time. Kuyken et al. rated 22%, 34%, 35% and 10% as very poor, poor, good enough, and good. Formulations were most competent on content, but weakest on parsimony, coherence and integration of information. There was a very modest relationship between competency years of experience (Spearman rho = 0.22.) However, the quality of formulation was quite strongly related to professional accreditation with 25%, 46% and 63% of clinicians who were prequalified, qualified and qualified and accredited in cognitive behavior therapy making good enough or better formulations. (One might still wonder as to the validity of professional accreditation, if a third of accredited therapists did not make an adequate clinical formulation.)

These studies are disturbing. They provide a very modest test of clinician's ability to formulate cases. Clinicians appear to have acceptable, though rather variable agreement on identifying target behaviors. However, such tests are at most modestly challenging. For example, none of the studies asked the clinicians to combine different topographies with the same function into one response class or to identify more than one function for the same topography. Similarly, none of the studies required clinicians to translate the formulation into a plan reliably, which is a key function of the formulation. To date there have been no reliability studies of the several behavioral methods of case formulation described in Chapters 10 and 11, such as Wolpe's work, FACMs and CPMs. This state of affairs has led some to describe case formulation as another case of the Emperor's clothes (Kuyyen, 2005).

ABA, such as that published in the *Journal of Applied Behavior Analysis*, is deeply concerned with the reliability of functional relationships (Skinner, 1953; Sidman, 1960). This approach is different from traditionally psychological approaches that emphasize agreement between two observers or tests on one occasion across many subjects. ABA demonstrates the reliability of its functional analysis through single subject experimental design and by turning the behavior on and off through systematic manipulation of independent variables across time within one subject. Thus, it proceeds systematically, but slowly, one independent variable at a time. However, since the relationship between the independent and dependent variables as shown repeatedly, this strategy results is a very high degree of confidence that such relationships are indeed highly reliable.

DOES CASE FORMULATION IMPROVE TREATMENT OUTCOME?

Adult Mental Health

The evidence supporting the use of individualized functional-based intervention in mental health is more limited than in the area where it has been most frequently applied, such as intellectual disabilities, child behavior disorders, etc. Indeed, the need and desirability of providing individualized treatments has been challenged in adult mental health. For example, Wilson (1996a) pointed out that manualized cognitive behavior therapy is highly effective for many disorders. He also pointed out a number of other important advantages. Namely, that manualized treatments are focused and easy to disseminate. They are also consonant with the idea of actuarial approaches to predicting treatment response. Many studies of actuarial prediction of treatment response have often shown that actuarial prediction is superior to clinician opinion. He argued that the effectiveness of manualized treatment depends primarily on effective training in the use of the manual, rather than clinical experience. Schulte (1992) has also proposed that diagnosis may be the superior basis to predict treatment response than individualization. Wilson also noted that there are several arguments in support of individualization of treatment. These include:

- that cognitive behavior therapy requires individual formulation;
- that manuals preclude this individualization
- they limit the creativity of the clinician in implementing therapy

- manuals are limited and are only applicable to research population, but have limited application to clinical populations
- manualized treatments promote a particular school of psychology's approach to therapy.

Wilson (1996b), however, noted that, although manualized cognitive behavior therapy treatment of bulimia nervosa was a first choice treatment, that only approximately 50% of patients refrain from binge eating and purging after treatment. This raised the issue of what to do with patients who fail manualized therapy. In this context Wilson (1996b) suggested alternate empirically supported therapies, such as anti-depressants or inter-personal psychotherapy, although there was no evidence that these therapies were effective with this particular problem in patients who had failed manualized therapy. He did not recommend psychotherapy, since there was no evidence of its effectiveness. Finally, alternatives included more intense cognitive behavior therapy, such as inpatient supervised exposure therapy or individual case formulation.

Bulimia

Ghadheri (2006) reported a randomized controlled trial for treatment of bulimia nervosa. Ghaderi screened 146 people recruited from advertisements, psychiatric clinics and student health centers. Ghaderi excluded people who did not meet the binge and purge criteria for bulimia, people taking psychotropic medications, those taking psychotropic medication or who were already participating in psychological treatment and those with other psychiatric disorders, such as anorexia or psychoses. Those with comorbid anxiety or depression were retained. Fifty patients with bulimia nervosa participated in the trial of whom 48 completed. The mean age patient's age was 27 years. Their eating disorder began at 18 years on average. The average duration of the problem was nine years. Half had received previous treatment for this problem.

Ghaderi (2006) randomly assigned participants to two conditions and told all participants that both treatments were effective. Ghaderi administered both treatments over 19 weekly, 50-minute sessions. The first group received Fairburn's manualized cognitive behavior therapy for bulimia. The second group received a more individualized version of Fairburn's manual. Ghaderi described the functional analysis in the following way:

> The treatment condition showed to be very similar to the manual-based C[ognitive] B[ehavior] T[herapy] in some cases, but different in other case by a more intense focus on rule governed behavior, acceptance strategies, interpersonal relations, and the issue that maintained the eating disorder (e.g., trauma, abusive relationships and social isolation) ... standardized

CBT was used as a base, and strategies were added and removed from that protocol dependent on what the functional analysis showed for that individual participant ... (2006, p. 278.)

Ghaderi (2007) described this process in more detail. The study also addressed treatment adherence. Two observers, trained in the delivery cognitive behavior therapy, coded 10 randomly selected sessions summaries and audiotapes. The manualized treatment did not include acceptance and other strategies that were used in the functional analysis treatment condition.

Both treatments produced large reductions in symptoms compared with baseline on both self-report psychometric measures and reports of binging and vomiting. For example, both groups reported statistically significant improvements on the Eating Disorders Examination (Cooper & Fairburn, 1987) both post treatment and at six-month follow-up. Impressively, participants in both groups showed little regression at follow-up.

There were some differences between standardized and individualized treatments. All favored the individualized interventions. For example, 92% of participants in the individually tailored treatment met criteria as responding to treatment, whereas only 69% of those in the standardized treatment did. Additionally, 80% of non-responders were in the standardized rather than individualized treatment group. Additionally, at post treatment, participants in the individualized treatment group showed more consecutive weeks with no binging. However, this difference was not significant at follow-up.

This study supported the efficacy of individualization of treatment. Participants who received individualized treatment were more likely to no longer meet diagnostic criteria and to refrain from binging post treatment. On other measures of functioning they did as well as those receiving standardized treatment. Indeed, this study was a relatively tough, but very meaningful, test of the effects of treatment individualization, in that the comparison treatment was an "industry standard", empirically supported treatment that was already quite effective. Hence, it left only modest room for individualization to improve beyond the effects of standard, empirically validated treatment. Ghaderi suggested that individualization was effective because it was more likely to address interpersonal difficulties, regulation of affect and increased acceptance of thoughts and emotion that the manualized cognitive behavior therapy. Ghaderi noted a number of limitations to the study. These included using only one therapist, the possibility of allegiance effects, since the therapist probably favored individualization, insufficient experimental power to detect difference that might have remained at follow-up.

One additional possible limitation is that the description of individualization is necessarily brief. Individualization took place. However, it is difficult to ascertain if Ghaderi based the individualization on the baseline functions of symptoms, such as those described in studies by Miltenberger and others discussed in Chapter 12.

Marital Therapy

Jacobson, Follette, Follette, Holtzworth-Munroe, Wood and Follette (1989) also provided support for treatment individualization of marital therapy. They randomly assigned 30 distressed married couples to one of two forms of social learning-based treatment of marital distress. One was standardized and the other permitted greater flexibility and individualization. Both were equally effective at post treatment in terms of marital satisfaction, spouse reports of the relationship and observations of interactions. However, at 6-month follow-up couples in the standardized treatment were more likely to regress than those who received individualized treatment.

Phobias

Two other studies have found *no* evidence of the effectiveness of individualization of treatments in mental health. The Bochum Anxiety-Therapy Project (Schulte, et al., 1992) evaluated the effects of individualization of treatment of phobias. One hundred and twenty patients with phobias, including mostly complex phobias such as agoraphobia participated. The participants' average age was 39 years and most (64%) were women. The phobias had lasted on average about 17 years. The authors excluded people with depression. The majority had also already experienced pharmacological and psychological treatments. Hence, the sample had clinically significant problems.

The authors randomly assigned participants to one of three conditions. One group received standardized exposure treatment that was not based on any individualized assessment. A second group received individualized therapy based on a behavior-diagnostic interview. This treatment could be revised as therapy progressed. A yoked control group received the same therapies as the individualized treatment group. That is, they received an individualized treatment plan based on someone else's functional assessment. Thus, this treatment plan, though individualized, should mostly be irrelevant to the functions of their own problems.

All treatment groups improved compared to baseline. At post treatment, those receiving standardized exposure treatment made the most rapid progress. At six-month follow-up all groups were equivalent. Thus, there was no support for treatment individualization. Indeed, when Schulte et al. compared all subjects receiving exposure therapy with those who did not from all three groups, they found that exposure therapy was more effective than all other interventions. Thus, this study found no evidence to support treatment individualization.

Depression

Several studies have demonstrated the importance of matching function and intervention in depression. McNight, Nelson, Haynes and Jarrett (1984) evaluated matching treatment to function in nine women with depression. Pre-intervention assessments showed that three women had irrational cognitions, three had social skills deficits and three had both. McNight et al. gave all nine women two treatments: social skills training and cognitive therapy. They compared the effectiveness of these two treatments in a within-subject multi-element experimental design. Matched treatments were most effective. That is, for the three participants with irrational cognitions, cognitive therapy was superior to social skills training. However, for the three who had social skills deficits, the opposite was true. For participants with both irrational cognitions and social skills deficits, both treatments were equally effective.

In a similar study, Nelson-Gray et al. (1989) assessed nine women with depression as having either irrational cognitions, social skills deficits or too few pleasant events. These women then received either treatments that matched the reasons for their depression, a treatment that did not match their depression or a cognitive behavioral treatment package. For example, a woman with social skills deficits in the matched treatment group would receive social skills training, whereas a woman with social skills deficits in the mismatched group might receive cognitive therapy. Subjects in the matched group and the group that received the treatment package all responded better to treatment than the group that received the mismatched treatment.

Intellectual and Other Developmental Disabilities

Functional approaches to the assessment and treatment of a wide range of behavioral and psychiatric disorders in people with intellectual and other developmental disabilities are well established. Indeed, hundreds of such studies have been published. Recent meta-analyses have consistently demonstrated that interventions based on functional assessments and especially functional analyses result in larger changes than interventions not based on pretreatment functional assessments and analyses (Didden et al., 1997, 2006).

Summary

The evidence that has accumulated since Wilson's challenge on the effectiveness has been mixed. Two studies of bulimia and marital therapy have provided evidence that individualization may be *more* effective than manualized therapy. Two studies of anxiety (Schulte et al., 1992) and OCD (Emmelkamp, Bouman and Blaaw [1994], cited in Ghaderi [2006]) reported no effects of individualization of treatments. Several factors may account for these disparate outcomes. When individualized treatments are compared to evidence-based manualized treatments, a comparison is made between an established, effective treatment with moderate to fairly large effective sizes. In such comparison, there is less room for individualization to improve over a standardized treatment protocol than comparisons with no treatment baseline or contraindicated treatments. When treatments indicated by a functional assessment are compared with those contra-indicated by the functional assessment, as in the two studies of depression, the comparison is most likely to favor function-based treatments as contrain-dicated treatments are likely to be at least ineffective, if not potentially harmful. Another important point in the comparisons of individualized with manualized, evidence-based treatments is that a failure to detect a difference between the two procedures permits no conclusions about the effectiveness of individualization. This is so on two grounds. First, the failure to detect differences may be due to the lack of experimental power or choice of insensitive dependent variables. Tarrier and Calem (2002) reported power calculations showing that very large samples would be needed to detect differences between effective manualized and individualized treatments. Hence, although no difference may have been detected, they may still exist. Given that two of four studies with low power that have made this comparison found effects of individualization one might be modestly optimistic that such effects are indeed there. Second, a failure to produce an effect of individualization may reflect the poor quality of the function-based assessment and treatments. For example, Schulte et al.'s individual-based treatments were conducted by relatively inexperienced graduate-level therapist. They had treated only a median of nine patients (range 0 – over 200) prior to the study. A related question, raised by Wilson (1996a, 1996b), is how to operationalize the process of individualization. Thus, Wilson characterized this as "allowing therapists free reign in individual case formulation" (p. 197). Although this is perhaps an inaccurate description of individualized case formulation, it does throw the gauntlet down to proponents of individualization to operationalize these procedures. Studies such as those by McKnight et al. (1994) and Nelson-Gray et al. (1989) have demonstrated how this can be done.

CASE FORMULATION AND DIAGNOSIS

Psychiatric diagnosis is now entrenched in everyday language. It is a pervasive explanation of behavioral phenomena, not just in clinical settings, but also in education and other organizations. Its use is enshrined in billing and communications among professionals and between professionals and non-professionals. Behavior analysts too freely communicate with these words to organize book chapters within books (Dougher, 2000; Sturmey, 2007), review articles (Nelson-Gray & Farmer, 1999) and to label behavioral treatment manuals (Hopko et al., 2003; Linehan, 1993) and treatment trials (Linehan, 1993). Doubtless, this is partly done expeditiously to communicate with non-behaviorists in the common vernacular language without necessarily abandoning any conceptual integrity.

There has been debate about the role of diagnosis in behavior analysis. Several have noted that many elements of psychiatric diagnosis are incompatible with behavioral concepts. For example, diagnostic criteria for personality disorders require that the behavior is relatively uninfluenced by situations and endures across time. It is often assumed that they reflect biological processes that are highly genetic (Nelson-Gray & Farmer, 1999). For example, behavior analysts have often presented functional analysis as an alternative to psychiatric diagnosis (Follette et al., 2000; Bissett and Hayes, 1999).

Nelson-Gray and Farmer (1999a) presented a SORC analysis of personality disorders that gave rise to debate between behavior analysts, which provoked responses (Bissett and Hayes, 1999; Staats, 1999) and a reply (Nelson-Gray & Farmer 1999b). Bissett and Hayes noted that, whereas as psychiatric diagnosis is topographically or structurally based, functional analysis focuses on function rather than topography. Thus, one topography, such as excessive drinking, can serve multiple functions, such as compliance and avoidance of emotional problems. Likewise many topographies can serve one function. Thus, avoiding aversive emotions can control multiple behaviors, such as overdrinking, binging, or sexual promiscuity. This suggests the inutility of psychiatric diagnosis for treatment design and the incoherence of attempting to combine the oil and water of structural and functional approaches.

A BEHAVIORAL MODEL OF THERAPY

Kanfer and Phillips (1970) extended Skinner's analysis of psychotherapy in a number of ways. They noted that most classic behavior therapy modifies behavior directly, for example by identifying and modifying contingencies maintaining the behavior of interest. Therapy is usually not like that. The therapist and client hope that, through the exchange of words and through other behavior in therapy, future problematic behavior outside of therapy will be less likely and that desirable, effective behavior will increase. Thus, therapy is an *indirect* approach to modifying client behavior primarily through therapist and client verbal behavior. Verbal behavior is an integral part of many classic behavioral procedures. A therapist gives verbal and written instructions to engage in some therapeutic procedure and verbally praises or punishes progress or the lack thereof. Verbal behavior may also be a target behavior, as in the treatment of psychotic speech, depressed speech or language deficits. Therapy is one example of social behavior where the behavior of one person influences another person's behavior. One difference perhaps is that in therapy the client often seeks out the therapist as a source of relief from aversive stimulation.

Kanfer and Phillips noted that client verbal reports are an important component of verbal therapy. "I had a panic attack last Wednesday", says the client. What can we make of such verbal behavior? Research has evaluated some of the variables controlling such client verbal reports. The event itself may be one controlling variable. Unfortunately, it is not the only one. We learn to describe our private behavior through our social environment. A child has not eaten for a long time and eagerly looks at food. Someone says "You must be hungry", the child says "yes", is given food and the aversive state of food deprivation is removed. On other occasions the child walks into the kitchen and an adult notices that his eyes are droopy, and knows that he only slept for five hours the previous night, and the adult says "you look tired", the child says "I *am* tired", and the adult takes the child to have a nap and the aversive sleep deprivation is removed. Later the child says "I am hungry" and received snacks, or "I am tired" and gets a nap. On other occasions the adults may carelessly make and error by asking the child if the child wants a snack when the child is sleep deprived. The child then provides the incompetent adult with a consequence to shape more accurate discriminations of the child's behavior. In this ways the social environment teaches us to label (tact) private events such as "hunger" and "tired". Later, we can ask the question "how do you feel?" Thus, following some stimulus, the person learns to emit two responses, a private one (privately tacting the internal stimuli) and an observable verbal response. If the language learning environment is an effective one, we can progressively learn to discriminate and label many private events (Skinner, 1953, 1957).

A problem arises when the learning environment fails to teach people to discriminate and report their private experiences, or when the learning environment reinforces inaccurate self-reports. Thus, a person's verbal behavior may be reinforced with analgesics, both when they feel pain accurately and inaccurately. Inaccurate public verbal behavior may be maintained by reinforcement with reinforcing analgesics. Clinical interviews may like this too. For example, Braginsky and Braginsky (1967, cited in Kanfer and Phillips, 1970) reported that people with schizophrenia described more healthy behavior when they were told the purpose of the interview was to determine if they were to be assigned to a locked unit and reported more unhealthy behavior when they were told that the purpose of the interview was to determine discharge to the community. Such observations strongly suggest environmental control of client reports of symptoms.

Client verbal behavior may be strongly influenced by therapist approval and disapproval (Truax, 1966). Other variables too control client verbal behavior. Given the absence of verification of facts it is easy to see how the therapist could inadvertently reinforce inaccurate reports of client progress, including gross inaccuracies, such as lying about homework completion, and more subtle inaccuracies, such as inaccurately reporting the amount of homework assignments completed. Given the likelihood that therapists may be susceptible to client reports of progress and gratitude, and that other important variables, such as disability status, insurance and legal claims, may also control client verbal reports, we can assume that client verbal behavior may often be inaccurate.

The learning environment may not teach people to discriminate, control and report their own motor behavior very accurately. Consider the difficulty that many of us would have in reporting accurately even everyday actions, such as driving where there are few obvious contingencies for inaccurate verbal behavior. Thus, clients may come to therapy with a limited repertoire of verbal behavior to report their own actions accurately. Note that this issue is not merely a problem in terms of determining what is truly happening in a client's life. More seriously yet is the problem that if the therapist is to gain control of client behavior outside of therapy, they must be able to accurately determine what the client's behavior is outside of therapy.

Implications for Therapy

Psychoanalytic, psychodynamic and psychotherapy see the purpose of verbal therapy being to uncover the hidden forces and defective personality that cause their psychopathology. The relationship between the therapist and client is paramount and behavior change occurs because of the therapists' insights and interpretation. Behavioral approaches to therapy emphasize the environment as the causes of all behavior, including problematic behavior. In behavioral approaches to therapy the therapeutic relationship is a necessary, but insufficient condition for change. The therapist must establish themselves as a powerful reinforcer for client behavior and must establish stimulus control over the client behavior. Skinner (1953) noted that the most important reinforcer that a therapist has to change client behavior is relief from aversive stimulation. Clients come to therapy because of aversive stimuli. The development of psychopathology and waiting for an appointment constitute a period of aversive stimulation. Clients have often been exposed to this aversive stimulation for extensive periods of time prior to therapy. Hence, any relief from this aversive stimulation that the therapist can offer is likely to be a consequence that is highly reinforcing to any client behavior that may result in the shaping of client compliance with therapy and positive behavior change. However, the therapeutic relationship alone is insufficient to promote client self-regulation and change client behavior. In behavioral approaches to therapy the main goal is to teach the client to analyze the relationship between their own behavior and the environment and to provide opportunities for more effective client action.

Kanfer and Phillips (1970) outlined three assumptions for behavioral approaches to psychotherapy. First, the modification of client behavior consists of the therapist applying external controls, such as verbal conditioning, not by promoting internal change but by processes such as insight or growth. Kanfer and Phillip's second assumption is that learning in therapy consists of two stages. In the first stage the client must learn to discriminate the relationship between the environment and its relationship to their own behavior. The job of the therapist is to teach accurate and realistic discriminations. For example, a person with depression might learn to report the changes in their mood with different people and activities and to describe this relationship accurately. A parent of a child with behavior problems might learn to describe correctly the relationship between the child's adaptive and problem behaviors and environmental events, such as being left alone or being asked to do a familiar or unfamiliar task. A person with an eating disorder might learn to describe accurately the relationship between being with other people or being alone and their binge eating. In the second stage, operant conditioning is used to teach new behaviors, such as self-control and social or verbal behaviors that address behavioral deficits. If this is not possible within a therapy session, then a plan can be developed with the client to do so in the natural environment. The third assumption is that client verbal and other behaviors during the interview are the dependent variables of interest, as well as client behavior outside the interview. For example, during therapy some traditional behavior therapy interventions, such as systematic desensitization, can be used to modify client behavior in the interview.

Teaching Clients Self-regulation

Recall that behavioral accounts of self-regulation distinguish a controlling and controlled response. Analysis and intervention focus on the variables that control the controlling response. Skinner (1953) posited that mental health problems arise from ineffective self-regulation that leads to inappropriate or ineffective forms of avoidance of aversive stimulation. Thus, a person may fail to avoid criticism, feel anxious and avoid other people and drink to reduce anxiety. If this person learns to arrange their environment to behave so that criticism does not occur, or learns to reduce anxiety by listening to music, rather than drinking, then this person has learned an effective form of self-regulation.

This could be done in two stages. First, the person might learn to discriminate the relationship between the environment and their behavior through self-recording. For example, they might keep ABC records or behavioral diaries of their behavior. The therapist would then use these materials to get the client to state verbally or in writing their own functional assessment. The second stage would be to teach the client to emit a controlling response. This might be to write a plan and carry it with them, self-instruct, or present a task that is easier to complete with another otherwise threatening person. A second approach would be to remove stimuli that occasion the problem. Examples might include only talking to moderately critical people or about moderately difficult topics at first and initially to avoid the most challenging situations that could be dealt with later. The therapist's job in this stage is to provide supplementary prompts and consequences to increase the frequency and appropriate stimulus control of the controlling response. For example, the therapist might shape the client's verbal behavior in therapy to accurately describe their own functional assessment. A plan might be written with the client, but the client should have to state the elements of the plan before they are written. The therapist might then prompt the controlling response by giving the client a summary of the plan to carry with them and to check off each day which elements of the plan they have and have not done. When the client returns for future appointments, the therapist's job is to: (1) reinforce accurate emission of controlling responses; (2) teach rule governed behavior that supports the plan, such as statement rules that are congruent with the plan; and (3) prompt the client to refine the plan. Chapter 6 contains examples of self-regulation in a variety of mental health problems.

Say-Do Correspondence Training

One approach to ensure the accuracy of client verbal reports and produce actual client change has been say-do correspondence training. Here, the client is asked to state what they will do and their behavior is then observed. If their behavior corresponds to their stated intention, accurate correspondence, their behavior is reinforced. If their observable behavior does not correspond to their verbal behavior then their verbal behavior is not reinforced. Refinements in the procedure include progressively fading reinforcement. This is done by gradually increasing the time between accurate doing and the delivery reinforcement, progressively fading from continuous to intermittent schedules of reinforcement (Baer, Blount, Detrich & Stokes, 1987) and fading out the promise (Luciano-Soriano, Molina-Cobos & Gomez-Becera, 2000). Say-do correspondence training has been used to improve children's healthy eating (Luciano-Soriano et al., 2000), increase appropriate play (Baer, Detrich & Weninger, 1988), increase social behavior in withdrawn children (Osnes, Guevremont & Stokes, 1986), increase self-help skills in adolescent living in group homes (Paniagua, 1985). It has also been used to increase on-task behavior in children with ADHD (Paniagua, Morrison & Black, 1990), autism and learning disabilities and improve a number of behavioral deficits in children and adults with learning disabilities, such as lack of exercise (Wilson, Rusch & Lee, 1992), lack of appropriate social behavior (Osnes, Guevremont & Stokes, 1987; Ralph & Birnbrauer, 1986) and lack of academic on task behavior (Whitman, Scibak, Butler, Richter & Johnson, 1982). So far, the use of correspondence training has been limited to typical and atypical children and adults with intellectual disabilities. No examples of application to adult mental health and interviewing specifically were found. However, it might provide a model for future exploration of therapist control of client behavior through therapy.

The implications for therapy are clear. Client verbal reports of progress or engagement in therapy require verification. To some extent agreement between client report and the report of others may be used, but that data may only be reliable but not valid. For various reasons one or both parties might be inaccurate or similarly biased. One possible solution might be to confirm client reports with other data sources, such as permanent products of client behavior, for example tickets indicating travel, actual items purchased or copies of documents, such as job applications.

FUTURE DIRECTIONS

Training Case Formulation Skills

Several authors have noted the absence of effective training in case formulation skills (Sim, Gwee and Bateman, 2004). For example, Fleming and Patterson (1993) surveyed the teaching of case formulation to psychiatry residents in Canada. Most programs did teach case formulation skills, although less than half provided guidelines for case formulations, even though residents were unanimous in their view that standardization and guidance was needed. Although a biopsychosocial format was preferred, there was little agreement on what the content of formulation should be. Surveys of clinicians' performance in case formulation also suggest the need for further training in this area, both before and after professional training (Eells et al., 1998; Kuyken et al., 2004).

Several studies have begun to address teaching case formulation skills. Unfortunately, the studies are poorly designed, lack control groups and have used self-report measures of acceptability, rather than clinician skill (Guerrero, Hishinuma, Serrano & Ahmed, 2003; Kuyken et al., 2005; Ross, Leichner, Matas & Anderson, 1990) and have not yet addressed the key function of case formulation, namely, developing an appropriate treatment plan. However, several of these studies offer models for future work in the area. Miltenberger and Fuqua (1985) and Milternberger and Veltum (1988) taught clinical trainees interview skills necessary to conduct a functional assessment of a clinical problem using modeling, rehearsal and feedback. Clinicians practiced on several scripts so they could learn the clinical skills with several different clinical problems. Miltenberger and Veltum also demonstrated that for some trainees written and verbal instructions were sufficient. Kuyken et al.'s (2004) study also included two positive features that future studies should incorporate. The use of a standard of performance defined by clear criteria allowed them to compare the performance of workshop participants against a standard. Research in the area could be improved by the use of multiple exemplars for clinical training and the use of generalization probes. For example, training clinicians on formulation skills should enable them to produce adequate formulations not only on materials used during training, but also on novel clients and problems that they have not been trained on. Research in this area should also strive toward ensuring that the material that is used to train is valid. For example, written and some role play material may be incomplete or inadequate. Video models' interviews with live clients or well-trained actors or clinicians may be more effective.

Clinical Judgment in Case Formulation

Several authors have noted that individualization of cases involves many complex decisions. These include identifying target behaviors, selecting assessment methods, integrating the information, selecting a function, translating it into a workable treatment plan, implementing and evaluating that plan. Clinicians are notoriously weak at such complex decision making, which has been used as an argument to support manualized treatment (Wilson, 1996a, 1996b.)

Waddington and Morely (2000) conducted a unique study of clinical judgment during case formulation. They investigated one possible bias, namely the possibility that clinicians give the first hypothesis undue weight. They identified two sources of such bias, namely the clinician's theoretical orientation and information in a referral letter. Sixty-four qualified and trainee clinicians read a mock referral letter and clinical materials describing a client with attachment issues and post traumatic stress disorder. Unsurprisingly, clinicians who identified themselves with attachment theory were more likely to use ideas related to attachment theory. However, the study found no evidence of selective bias, either from therapist orientation or from the content of the mock letter. Waddington and Morely noted that this was a preliminary and imperfect study with negative results and hence no strong conclusions could be drawn. Future research could begin to study clinical judgments during case formulation. This is an under-researched and important area. Understanding clinical decisions during case formulation might enable clinicians to improve their individualization of treatment in order to give rise to treatments that are superior to manualized treatments.

SUMMARY

Behavioral case formulation has been applied to a very wide range of mental health and behavioral issues (Sturmey, 2007). Future research should expand this research to address issues of professional performance and training, evaluating how to share formulations most effectively with clients, improving client outcome beyond manualized treatment and clinical judgment during case formulation.

REFERENCES

Abramowitz, J.S. & Moore, E.L. (2007). An experimental analysis of hypochondriasis. *Behavior Research and Therapy*, **45**, 413–424.

Adams, H.E. (1985). Chronic headache. In *Behavioral Case Formulation* (Ed. I.D. Turkat). New York: Plenum, pp. 87–110.

Allen, K.D.E. & Evans, J.H. (2001). Exposure–based treatment to control excessive blood glucose monitoring. *Journal of Applied Behavior Analysis*, **34**, 497–500.

Anataki, C., Young, N. & Finlay, M. (2002). Shapeng clients' answers: Departures from neutrality in care-staff interviews with people with a learning disability. *Disability and Society*, **17**, 435–455.

American Psychiatric Association (1996). Committee on the practice of psychotherapy. 11/30/96. RESOURCE DOCUMENT ON MEDICAL PSYCHOTHERAPY. William, H. Sledge, MD Chair, Committee on the practice of psychotherapy, 1992–96. Downloaded on June, 24, 2007.

American Psychiatric Association (2000). *The diagnostic and statistical manual of the American Psychiatric Association*. (Fourth Edition, text revision). Washington: Author.

Applegate, H., Matson, J.L. & Cherry, K.E. (1999). An evaluation of functional variables affecting severe problem behaviors in adults with mental retardation by using the Questions about Behavioral Function Scale (QABF). *Research in Developmental Disabilities*, **20**, 229–237.

Atkinson, R.P., Jenson, W.R., Rovner, L., Cameron, S., Van Wagenen, L. & Petersen, B.P. (1984). Brief report, validation of the autism reinforcer checklist for children. *Journal of Autism and Developmental Disorders*, **14**, 429–433.

Auguston, E.M. & Dougher, M.J. (1997). The transfer of avoidance evoking functions through stimulus equivalence classes. *Journal of Behavior Therapy and Experimental Psychiatry*, **28**, 181–191.

Ayllon, T. (1963). Intensive treatment of psychotic behavior by stimulus satiation and food reinforcement. *Behavior, Research and Therapy*, **1**, 53–61.

Ayllon, T. & Azrin, N.H. (1965). The measurement and reinforcement of behavior of psychotics. *Journal of the Experimental Analysis of Behavior*, **8**, 357–383.

Ayllon, T. & Haughton, E. (1964). Modification of symptomatic verbal behavior of mental patients. *Behavior, Research and Therapy*, **2**, 87–97.

Ayllon, T.M. & Michael, J. (1959). The psychiatric nurse as a behavioral engineer. *Journal of the Experimental Analysis of Behavior*, **2**, 323–334.

Ayllon, T. & Haughton, E. (1962). Control of the behavior of schizophrenic patients by food. *Journal of the Experimental Analysis of Behavior*, **5**, 343–52.

Ayllon, T., Haughton, E. & Hughes, H.B. (1965). Interpretation of symptoms, Fact or fiction? *Behavior, Research and Therapy*, **3**, 1–7.

Azrin, N.R., Rubin, H. O'Brien, F. Ayllon, T. & Roll, D. (1968). Behavioral engineering, Postural control by a portable operant apparatus. *Journal of Applied Behavior Analysis*, **1**, 99–108.

Bach, P.H. & Hayes, S.C. (2002). The use of acceptance and committment therapy to prevent the rehospitalization of psychotic patients. *Journal of Consulting and Clinical Psychology* **70**, 1129–1139.

Baer, D.M. & Guess, D. (1971). Receptive training of adjectival inflections in mental retardates. *Journal of Applied Behavior Analysis*, **4**, 129–139.

Baer, D.M., Wolf, M.M. & Risley, T.R. (1968). Some current dimensions for applied behavior analysis. *Journal of Applied Behavior Analysis*, **1**, 91–97.

Baer, R.A., Blount, R.L., Detrich, R. & Stokes, T.F. (1987). Using intermittent reinforcement to program maintenance of verbal/nonverbal correspondence. *Journal of Applied Behavior Analysis*, **20**, 179–184.

Baer, R.A., Detrich, R. & Weninger, J.M. (1988). On the functional role of the verbalization in correspondence training procedures. *Journal of Applied Behavior Analysis*, **21**, 345–335.

Bailey, R.E. & Gillaspy, J.A. (2005). Operant psychology goes to the four: Manan and Keller Breland in the popular press, 1947–1966. *The Behavior Analyst*, **28**, 143.

Barretto, A., Wacker, D.P., Harding, J.L. & Berg, W.K. (2006). Using telemedicine to conduct behavioral assessments. *Journal of Applied Behavior Analysis*, **39**, 333–340.

Baron, A., DeWaard, R.J. & Galizio, M. (1981). Factor-analytically derived subscales for the reinforcement survey schedule reinforcer preferences as a function of drug use and sex. *Behavior Modification*, **5**, 203–222.

Baron–Cohen, S. (1997). *Mind Blindness. An Essay on Autism and Theory of Mind.* Cambridge, MA: The MIT Press.

Baum, W.M. (1974). On two types of deviation from the matching law, Bias and undermatching. *Journal of the Experimental Analalysis of Behavior*, **22**, 231–242.

Bentall, R.P., Lowe, C.F. & Beasty, A. (1985). The role of verbal behavior in human learning, II. Developmental differences. *Journal of the Experimental Analysis of Behavior*, **43**, 165–181.

Bernstein, D.J. & Micheal, R.L. (1990). The utility of verbal behavioral assessment of value. *Journal of the Experimental Analysis of Behavior*, **54**, 173–184.

Bernstein, H., Brown, B. & Sturmey, P. (May, 2007). *The effects of fixed ratio values on concurrent mand and play responses.* Paper presented to the

Annual convention of the Association for Applied Behavior Analysis internaional, San Diego, California.

Bicard, D.F. & Neef, N.A. (2002). Effects of strategic versus tactical instructions on adaptation to changing contingencies in children with ADHD. *Journal of Applied Behavior Analysis*, **35**, 375–389.

Biglan, A. (1995). *Changing Cultural Practices: A Contextualist Framework for Intervention Research*. Reno, NV: Context Press.

Bihm, E.M., Poindexter, A.R., Kienlen, T.L. & Smith, B.L. (1992). Staff perceptions of reinforcer responsiveness and aberrant behaviors in people with mental retardation. *Journal of Autism and Developmental Disorders*, **22**, 83–93.

Bijou, S.W., Peterson, R.F. & Ault, M.H. (1968). A method to integrate descriptive and experimental field studies at the level of data and empirical concepts. *Journal of Applied Behavior Analysis*, **1**, 175–191.

Binder, L.M., Dixon, M.R. & Ghezzi, P.M. (2000). A procedure to teach self-control to children with Attention Deficit Hyperactivity Disorder. *Journal of Applied Behavior Analysis*, **33**, 233–237.

Bissett, R.T. & Hayes, S.C. (1999). The likely success of functional analysis tied to the DSM. *Behavior, Research and Therapy*, **37**, 379–383.

Blampied, N.M. & France, K.G. (1993). A behavioral model of infant sleep disturbance. *Journal of Applied Behavior Analysis*, **26**, 477–492.

Bowman, L.G., Fisher, N.W., Thompson, R.H. & Piazza, C.C. (1997). On the relation of mands and the function of destructive behavior. *Journal of Applied Behavior Analysis*, **30**, 251–265.

Bourgeois, M.S. (1990). Enhancing conversation skills in patients with Alzheimer's disease using a prosthetic memory aid. *Journal of Applied Behavior Analysis*, **23**, 29–42.

Bouton, M. (2002). Context, ambiguity, and unlearning, sources of relapse after behavioral extinction. *Biological Psychiatry*, **52**, 976–986.

Brady, J.P. (1986). Invited case transcript: Behavioral analysis of a case of psychogenic nausea and vomiting. *Journal of Behavior Therapy and Experimental Psychiatry*, **17**, 271–274.

Brantley, P.J.C. & Callon, E.B. (1985). Histrionic personality. In *Behavioral Case Formulation* (Ed. I.D. Turkat). New York: Plenum, pp. 199–252.

Bruch, M. (1998). The development of case formulation approaches. In *Beyond Diagnosis. Case Formulation Approaches in CBT* (Eds M.B. Bruch & F.W. Bond). Chichester: Wiley, pp. 1–18.

Bruch, M.B. & Bond, F.W. (Eds) (1998). *Beyond Diagnosis, Case Formulation Approach in CBT*. Chichester: Wiley.

Buchanan, J.A. & Fisher, J.E. (2002). Functional assessment and noncontingent reinforcement in the treatment of disruptive vocalization in elderly dementia patients. *Journal of Applied Behavior Analysis*, **35**, 99–103.

Budzinski, T.H. & Stoyva, S. (1973). An electromyographic feedback technique for teaching voluntary relaxation of masseter muscle. *Journal of Dental Research*, **52**, 116.

Cammilleri, A.P. & Hanley, G.P. (2005). Use of a lag differential reinforcement contingency to increase varied selections of classroom activities. *Journal of Applied Behavior Analysis*, **38**, 111–115.

Carr, E.G., Taylor, J.C. & Robinson, S. (1991). Social control of self–injurious behavior of organic etiology. *Behavior Therapy*, **11**, 402–409.

Carroll, K.M., Rounsaville, B.J., Nich, C., Gordon, L. & Gawin, F. (1996). Integrating psychotherapy and pharmacotherapy for cocaine dependence, results from a randomized clinical trial. *NIDA Research Monograph*, **150**, 19–35.

Carroll, K.M., Nich, C., Ball, S.A., McCance, E. & Rounsaville, B.J. (1998). Treatment of cocaine and alcohol dependence with psychotherapy and disulfiram. *Addiction*, **93**, 713–727.

Cautela, J.R. (1972). Reinforcement survey schedule: Evaluation and current applications. *Psychological Reports*, **30**, 683–690.

Cautela, J.R. (1990). *Behavior Analysis Forms for Clinical Intervention*. Volume 2. Cambridge, MA: Cambridge Center for Behavior Analysis.

Cautela, J.R. & Brion-Meisels, L. (1979). A children's reinforcement survey schedule. *Psychological Reports*, **44**, 327–338.

Cautela, J.R., Cautela, J. & Esonis, S. (1981). *Forms for Behavior Analysis with Children*. Champaign, Il: Research Press.

Cautela, J.R. & Kastenbaum, R.A. (1967). Reinforcement Survey Schedule for use in therapy, training, and research. *Psychological Reports*, **20**, 115–1130.

Cautela, J.R. & Lynch, E. (1983). Reinforcement survey schedules: Scoring, administration, and completed research. *Psychological Reports*, **53**, 447–465.

Chadwick, P., Williams, C. & Mackenzie, J. (2003). Impact of case formulation in cognitive behavior therapy for psychosis. *Behavior, Research and Therapy*, **41**, 671–680.

Chiesa, M. (1994). *Radical Behaviorism: The Philosophy and the Science*. Boston, MA: Authors Cooperative.

Chioda, J. (1987). Invited case transcript. Bulimia. An individual behavioral analysis. *Journal of Behavior Therapy and Experimental Psychiatry*, **18**, 41–49.

Chomsky, N. (1959). A review of B.F. Skinner's *Verbal Behavior. Language*, **35**, 26–58.

Chorpita, B.F., Albano, A.M., Heimberg, R.G. & Barlow, D.H. (1996). A systematic replication of the prescriptive treatment of school refusal behavior in a single subject. *Journal of Behavior Therapy and Experimental Psychiatry*, **27**, 281–290.

Comer, S.D., Collins, E.D. & Fischman, M.W. (1997). Intravenous buprenorphine self–administration by detoxified heroin abusers. *Journal of Pharmacology and Experimental Therapy*, **301**, 266–276.

Cone, J.D. (1997). Issues in functional analysis in behavioral assessment. *Behavior Research and Therapy*, **35**, 259–275.

Conners, F.A. (1992). Reading instruction for students with moderate mental retardation: Review and analysis of research. *American Journal on Mental Retardation*, **96**, 577–597.

Cooper, Z. & Fairburn, C. (1987). The eating disorder examination: A semi–structured interview for the assessment of the specific psychopathology of eating disorders. *International Journal of Eating Disorders*, **6**, 1–8.

Cordova, J.V., Jacobson, N.S., Gottman, J.M., Rushe, R. & Cox, G. (1993). Negative reciprocity and communication in couples with a violent husband. *Journal of Abnormal Psychology*, **102**, 559–564.

Corrigan, P.W. (2001). Getting ahead of the data. A threat to some behavior therapies. *The Behavior Therapist*, **24**, 189–193.

Cowley, B.J.G., Green, G. & Braunling–McMorrow, D. (1992). Using stimulus equivalence procedures to teach name–face matching to adults with brain injuries. *Journal of Applied Behavior Analysis*, **25**, 461–475.

Caudill, B.D. & Lipscomb, T.R. (1980). Modelling influences on alcoholics' rate of alcohol consumption. *Journal of Applied Behavior Analysis*, **13**, 355–365.

Cuper, P., Merwin, R. & Lynch, T. (2007). Personality disorders. In *Functional Analysis in Clinical Treatment* (Ed. P. Sturmey). New York: Academic, pp. 403–428.

Daffern, M. & Howells, K. (2002). Psychiatric inpatient aggression: A review of structural and functional assessment approaches. *Aggression and Violent Behavior*, **7**, 477–497.

Daffern, M., Howells, K. & Ogloff, J. (2007). What's the point? Towards a methodology for assessing the function of psychiatric inpatient aggression. *Behavior Research and Therapy*, **45**, 101–111.

Dahlquist, L.M. & Gil, K.M. (1986). Using parents to maintain improved dental flossing skills in children. *Journal of Applied Behavior Analysis*, **19**, 255–260.

Dallery, J. & Glenn, I.M. (2005). Effects of an internet–based voucher reinforcement program for smoking abstinence: A feasibility study. *Journal of Applied Behavior Analysis*, **38**, 349–357.

Dawson, J.E., Matson, J.L. & Cherry, K.E. (1998). An analysis of maladaptive behaviors in persons with autism, PDD–NOS, and mental retardation. *Research in Developmental Disabilities*, **19**, 439–448.

De Houwer, J., Baeyens, F. & Eelen, P. (1994). Verbal evaluative conditioning with undetected US presentations. *Behavior, Research and Therapy*, **32**, 629–633.

De Peuter, S., Van Diest, I., Lemaigre, V., Li, W., Verleden, G., Demedts, M. & Van den Bergh, O. (2005). Can subjective asthma symptoms be learned? *Psychosomatic Medicine*, **67**, 454–461.

Deaver, C.M., Miltenberger, R.G., Smyth, J., Meidinger, A. & Crosby, R. (2003). An evaluation of affect and binge eating. *Behavior Modification*, **27**, 578–599.

Deb, S. & Iyer, A. (2005). Clinical interviews. In *Mood Disorders in People with Mental Retardation* (Ed. P. Sturmey). Kingston, NY: NADD Publications, pp. 159–174.

DeLeon, I.G., Fisher, W.W., Catter, V.R., Maglieri, K., Herman, K. & Marhefka, J. (2001). Examination of relative reinforcement effects of stimuli identified through pretreatment and daily brief preference assessments. *Journal of Applied Behavior Analysis*, **34**, 463–473.

DeLeon, I.G., Iwata, B.A., Goh, H. & Worsdell, A.S. (1997). Emergence of reinforcer preference as a function of schedule requirements and stimulus similarity. *Journal of Applied Behavior Analysis*, **30**, 439–449.

Derby, K.M., Wacker, D.P., Peck, S., Sasso, G., DeRaad, A., Berg, W. et al. (1994). Functional analysis of separate topographies of aberrant behavior. *Journal of Applied Behavior Analysis*, **27**, 267–278.

Desrochers, M.N., Hile, M.G. & Williams–Moseley, T.L. (1997). Survey of functional assessment procedures used with individuals who display mental retardation and severe problem behaviors. *American Journal on Mental Retardation*, **101**, 535–546.

Dewhurst, D.L. & Cautela, J.R. (1980). A proposed reinforcement survey schedule for special needs children. *Journal of Behavior Therapy and Experimental Psychiatry*, **11**, 109–112.

Devriese, S., Winters, W., Stegen, K., Van Diest, I., Veulemans, H., Nemery, B., Eelen, P., Van de Woestijne, K. & Van den Bergh, O. (2000). Generalization of acquired somatic symptoms in response to odors, a pavlovian perspective on multiple chemical sensitivity. *Psychosomomatic Medicine*, **62**, 751–759.

Diamond, J. (1999). *Guns, Germs and Steel, The Fates of Human Societies*. New York: Norton.

Diamond, J. (2004). *Collapse, How Societies Choose to Fail or Succeed*. New York: Penguin.

Didden, R., Duker, P.C. & Korzilius, H. (1997). Meta–analytic study on treatment effectiveness for problem behaviors with individuals who have mental retardation. *American Journal on Mental Retardation*, **101**, 387–399.

Didden, R., Korzilius, H., van Oorsouw, W. & Sturmey, P. (2006). Behavioral treatment of challenging behaviors in individuals with mild mental retardation, Meta–analysis of single–subject research. *American Journal on Mental Retardation*, **111**, 290–298.

Didden, R. (2007). Functional analysis methodology in developmental disabilities. In *Functional Analysis in Clinical Treatment* (Ed. P. Sturmey). New York: Academic Press, pp. 65–86.

Dixon, M. & Bihler, H.L. (2007). Brain injury. In *Functional Analysis in Clinical Treatment* (Ed. P. Sturmey). New York: Academic Press, pp. 261–282.

Dixon, M.R. & Johnson, T.E. (2007). Impulse control disorders. In *Functional Analysis in Clinical Treatment* (Ed. P. Sturmey). New York: Academic, 429–454.

Dixon, M.R. & Falcomata, T.S. (2004). Preference for progressive delays and concurrent physical therapy exercize in an adult with acquired brain injury. *Journal of Applied Behavior Analysis*, **37**, 101–105.

Dixon, M.R., Hayes, L.J., Binder, L.M., Manthey, S., Sigman, C. & Zdanowski, D.M. (1998). Using a self-control training procedure to increase appropriate behavior. *Journal of Applied Behavior Analysis*, **31**, 203–210.

Dixon, M.R. & Holcoumb, S. (2000). Teaching self-control to small groups of dually diagnosed adults. *Journal of Applied Behavior Analysis*, **33**, 611–614.

Dixon, R.M., Horner, M.J. & Guercio, J. (2003). Self-control and the perference for delayed reinforcement: An example in brain injury. *Jornal of Applied Behavior Analysis*, **36**, 371–374.

Dollard, J. & Miller, N.E. (1950). *Personality and psychotherapy: An analysis in terms of learning, thinking and culture*. New York: McGraw Hill.

Dougher, M.J. & Hayes, S.C. (2000). *Clinical Behavior Anlaysis*. Reno, NV: Context Press.

Dougher, M.J. & Hayes, S.C. (2000). Clinical behavior analysis. In *Clinical Behavior Analysis* (Ed. M.J. Dougher). Reno, NV: Context Press, pp. 11–25.

Dowrick, P.W. & Dove, C. (1980). The use of self-modelling to improve the swimming performance of spine befida children. *Journal of Applied Behavior Analysis*, **13**, 51–56.

Drebing, C.E., Van Ormer, E.A., Krebs, C., Rosenheck, R., Rounsaville, B., Herz, L. & Penk, W. (2005). The impact of enhanced incentives on vocational rehabilitation outcomes for dually diagnosed veterans. *Journal of Applied Behavior Analysis*, **38**, 359–379.

Drummond, D.S. & Glautier, S. (1994). A controlled trial of cue exposure treatment in alcohol dependence. *Journal of Consulting and Clinical Psychology*, **62**, 809–817.

Dryden, W. (1998). Understanding persons in the context of their problems. A rational emotive behavior therapy perspective. In. M. Bruch & F.W. Bond (Eds.) *Beyond diagnosis. Case formulation approaches in CBT*, (pp. 43–64). Chichester, UK: Wiley UK.

Ducharme, K.M. & Feldman, M.A. (1992). Comparison of staff training strategies to promote generalized teaching skills. *Journal of Applied Behavior Analysis*, **25**, 165–179.

Durand, V.M. & Crimmons, D.B. (1988). Identifying the variables maintaining self–injurious behavior. *Journal of Autism and Developmental Disorders*, **18**, 99–117.

Dymond, S., O'Hara, D., Whelen, R. & O' Donvan, A. (2006). Citation analysis of Skinner's *Verbal Behavior*. 1984–2004. *The Behavior Analyst*, **29**, 75–88.

Eells, T.D. (Ed.) (1997). *Handbook of Psychotherapy Case Formulation*. New York: Guilford.

Eells, T.D. (Ed.) (2007). *Handbook of Psychotherapy Case Formulation, (second edition)*. New York: Guilford.

Eells, T.D., Kandjelic, E.M. & Lucas, C.P. (1998). What's in a case formulation? Development and use of a content coding manual. *Journal of Psychotherapy Practice and Research*, **7**, 144–153.

Eifert, G.H. & Heffner, M. (2003). The effects of acceptance versus control contexts on avoidance of panic–related symptoms. *Journal of Behavior Therapy and Experimental Psychiatry*, **34**, 293–312.

Ellis, N.R., Bamett, C.D. & Pryer, M.W. (1960). Operant behavior in mental defectives: Exploratory studies. *Journal of the Experimental Analysis of Behavior*, **3**, 63–69.

Engel, S.G., Boseck, J.J., Crosby, R.D., Wonderlich, S.A., Mitchell, J.E., Smyth, J., Miltenberger, R. & Steiger, H. (2006). The relationship of momentary anger and impulsivity to bulimic behavior. *Behavior, Research and Therapy*, **45**, 437–447.

Epstein, R. (1997). Skinner as self-manager. *Journal of Applied Behavior Analysis*, **30**, 545–568.

Estes, W.K. & Skinner, B.F. (1941). Some quantitative properties of anxiety. *Journal of Experimental Psychology*, **29**, 390–400.

Eysenck, H.J. (1952). The effects of psychotherapy: An evaluation. *Journal of Consulting Psychology*, **16**, 319–324.

Eysneck, H.J. (1960). *Handbook of abnormal psychology*. London, United Kingdom: Pitman.

Eysenck, H.J. & Rachman, S. (1965). *The Causes and Cures of Neuroses*. San Diego, CA, Robert R. Knapp.

Farmer, R.F. & Latner, J.D. (2007). Eating disorders. In *Functional Analysis in Clinical Treatment* (Ed. P. Sturmey). New York, Academic Press, pp. 379–402.

Farmer, R.F. & Nelson-Gray, R.O. (1999). Functional analysis and response covariation in the assessment of personality disorders, a reply to Staats and to Bissett and Hayes. *Behavior, Research and Therapy*, **37**, 385–394.

Feldman, M.A., Towns, F., Betel, J., Case, L., Rincover, A. & Rubino, C.A. (1986). Parent education project II. Increasing stimulating interactions of developmentally handicapped mothers. *Journal of Applied Behavior Analysis*, **19**, 23–37.

Fields, L. & Verhave, T. (1987). The structure of equivalence classes. *Journal of the Experimental Analalysis of Behavior*, **48**, 317–332.

Fisher, J.E., Drossel, C., Yury, C. & Cherup, S. (2007). A contextual model of restraint–free care for persons with dementia. In *Functional Analysis in Clinical Treatment* (Ed. P. Sturmey). New York: Academic Press, pp. 211–238.

Fisher, W.W., Kuhn, D.E. & Thompson, R.H. (1988). Establishing disoiminative control of responding using functional and alternative reinforces during functional communication training. *Journal of Applied Behavior Analysis*, **31**, 545–560.

Fisher, W.W., Lindauer, S.E., Alterson, C.J. & Thompson, R.H. (1998). Assessment and treatment of destinctive behavior maintained by stereotypic object manipulation. *Journal of Applied Behavior Analysis*, **31**, 513–527.

Fisher, W.W., Piazza, C.C., Bowman, L.G., Hanley, G.P. & Adelinis, J.D. (1997). Direct and collateral effects of restraints and restraint fading. *Journal of Applied Behavior Analysis*, **30**, 105–119.

Fitterling, J.M., Martin, J.E., Gramling, S., Cole, P. & Milan, M.A. (1988). Behavioral management of exercise training in vascular headache patients, An investigation of exercise adherence and headache activity. *Journal of Applied Behavior Analysis*, **21**, 9–19.

Fleece, L.G., Gross,A., O'Brien, T., Kistner, J., Rothblum, E. & Drabman, R. (1981). Elevation of voice volume in young developmentally delayed children via an operant shaping procedure. *Journal of Applied Behavior Analysis*, **14**, 351–355.

Fleming, J.A. & Patterson, P.G. (1993). The teaching of case formulation in Canada. *Canadian Journal of Psychiatry*, **38**, 345–350.

Flor, H., Knost, B. & Birbaumer, N. (2002). The role of operant conditioning in chronic pain, an experimental investigation. *Pain*, **95**, 111–118.

Floyd, F.J., Haynes, S.N. & Kelly, S. (1997). Marital assessment, A dynamic functional–analytic approach. In *Clinical Handbook of Marriage and Couples Intervention* (Eds W.K.M. Halford & H.J. Markman). New York: Wiley, pp. 349–378.

Foa, E.B., Liebowitz, M.L., Kozak, M.J., Davies, S., Campeas, R., Franklin, M.E. et al. (2005). Randomized, placebo controlled trial of response and ritual prevention, Damipramine, and their combination in the treatment of obsessive–compulsive disorders. *American Journal of Psychiatry*, **162**, 151–161.

Follette, W.V., Naugle, A.E. & Linnerooth, P.J. (2000). Functional alternatives to traditional assessment and diagnosis. In M.J. Dongher, (Ed.) *Clinical behavior analysis*, (pp. 99–126).

Fonagy, P., Target, M., Cotrell, Phillips, J. & Kurtz, Z. (2002). *What Works for Whom? A Critical Review of Treatments for Children and Adolescents*. New York: Guilford.

Fosbury, J.A., Bosley, C.M., Ryle, A. Sönsksen, P.H. & Jadd, S.L. (1997). A trial of cognitive analytic therapy in poorly controlled Type I patients. *Diabetis Care*, **20**, 959–964.

Foster, M.A., Owens, R.G. & Newton, A.V. (1985). Functional analysis of the gag reflex. *British Dental Journal*, **158**, 369–370.

Foster, S.L. & Ritchey, W.L. (1979). Issues in the assessment of social competence in children. *Journal of Applied Behavior Analysis*, **12**, 625–638.

Fox, E. (2006). RFT tutorial. Downloaded June 24, 2007. http://www.contextualpsychology.org/rft_tutorial.

Fox, R.A. & De Shaw, J.M. (1993). Milestone Reinforcer Survey. *Education and Training in Mental Retardation*, **28**, 257–261.

Frederiksen, L.W., Jenkins, J.O., Foy, D.W. & Eisler, R.M. (1976). Social skills training to modify abusive verbal outbursts in adults. *Journal of Applied Behavior Analysis*, **9**, 117–125.

Friman, P.C. (2007). The fear factor, A functional perspective on anxiety. In *Functional Analysis in Clinical Treatment* (Ed. P. Sturmey). New York: Academic Press, pp. 335–357.

Friman, P.C., Hayes, S.C. & Wilson, K.G (1998a). Why behavior analysts should study emotion, The example of anxiety. *Journal of Applied Behavior Analysis*, **31**, 137–156.

Friman, P.C., Wilson, K.G. & Hayes, S.C. (1998). Behavior analysis of private events is possible, progressive, and nondualistic, A response to Lamal. *Journal of Applied Behavior Analysis*, **31**, 707–708.

Fulcher, R.C. & Cellucci, T. (1997). Case formulation and behavioral treatment of chronic cough. *Journal of Behavior Therapy and Experimental Psychiatry*, **28**, 291–296.

Fyffe, C.E., Kahng, S., Fittro, E. & Russell, D. (2004). Functional analysis and treatment of inappropriate sexual behavior. *Journal of Applied Behavior Analysis*, **37**, 401–404.

Galeazzi, A., Fanceschina, E., Cautela, J., Holmes, G.R. & Sakano, Y. (1998). A comparison of Italian, Japanese, and American students' responses to the adolescent reinforcement survey schedule. *Journal of Clinical Psychology*, **54**, 267–278.

Ghaderi, A. (2006). Does individualization matter? A randomized trial of standardized (focused) versus individualized (broad) cognitive behavior therapy for bulimia nervosa. *Behavior, Research and Therapy*, **44**, 273–288.

Ghaderi, A. (2007). Logical functional analysis in the assessment and treatment of eating disorders. *Clinical Psychologist*, **11**, 1–12.

Glenn, S.S. (1988). Contingencies and meta–contingencies, Toward a synthesis of behavior analysis and cultural materialism. *The Behavior Analyst*, **11**, 161–179.

Goldiamond, I. (1959). In statement of laboratory stuttering in normally fluent individuals through operant conditioning procedures. *Journal of the Experimental Analysis of Behavior*, **2**, 269.

Goldiamond, I. (1974). Toward a constructional approach to social problems, ethical and constitutional issues raised by applied behavior analysis. *Behaviorism*, **2**, 1–84.

Goldstein, M.H., King, A.P. & West, M.J. (2003). Social interaction shapes babbling: Testing parallels between birdsong and speech. *Proceedings of The National Academy of Science USA*, **100**, 8030–8035.

Grandi, S., Fabbri, S., Panattoni, N., Gonnella, E. & Marks, I. (2006). Self–exposure treatment of recurrent nightmares, waiting–list–controlled trial and 4–year follow–up. *Psychotherapy Psychosomatics*, **75**, 384–388.

Green, C.W., Reid, D.H., White, L.K., Halford, R.C., Brittain, D.P. & Gardner, S.M. (1988). Identifying reinforcers for persons with profound handicaps, Staff opinion versus systematic assessment of preferences. *Journal of Applied Behavior Analysis*, **21**, 31–43.

Green, C.W., Reid, D.H. Canipe, V.S. & Gardner, S.M. (1991). A comprehensive evaluation of reinforcer identification processes for persons with profound multiple handicaps. *Journal of Applied Behavior Analysis*, **24**, 537–552.

Greene, P.G. & Seime, R.J. (1987). Stimulus control of anticipatory nausea in cancer chemotherapy. *Journal of Behavior Therapy and Experimental Psychiatry*, **18**, 61–64.

Greenspoon, J. (1955). The reinforcing effect of two spoken sounds on the frequency of two responses. *American Journal of Psychology*, **68**, 409–416.

Gresswell, D.M. & Hollin, C.R. (1992). Toward a new methodology of makiing sence of case material. *Clinical Behavior and Mental Health*, **2**, 329–341.

Griffen, A.K., Wolery, M. & Schuster, J.W. (1992). Triadic instruction of chained food preparation responses: Acquisition and observational learning. *Journal of Applied Behavior Analysis*, **25**, 193–204.

Groden, G. & Lantz, S. (2001). The reliability of the Detailed Behavior Report (DBR) in documenting functional assessment observations. *Behavioral Interventions*, **16**, 15–25.

Grodnitzky, G.R. & Tafrate, R.C. (2000). Imaginal exposure for anger reduction in adult outpatients, a pilot study. *Journal of Behavior Therapy and Experimental Psychiatry*, **31**, 259–279..

Guerrero, A.P.S., Hishinuma, E., Serrano A.C. & Ahmed I. (2003). Use of the "Mechanistic Case Diagramming" technique to teach the bio–psycho–social–cultural formulation to psychiatric clerks. *Academic Psychiatry*, **27**, 88–92.

Guess, D.S., Sailor, W., Rutherford, G. & Baer, D.M. (1968). An experimental analysis of linguistic development: The productive use of the plural morpheme. *Journal of Applied Behavior Analysis*, **1**, 297–306.

Hadwin, J., Baron–Cohen, S. Howlin, P. & Hill, K. (1997). Does teaching theory of mind have an effect on the ability to develop conversation in children with autism? *Journal of Autism and Developmental Disorders*, **27**, 519–537.

Hagopian, L.P. & Thompson, R.H. (1999). Reinforcement of compliance with respiratory treatment in a child with cystic fibrosis. *Journal of Applied Behavior Analysis*, **32**, 233–236.

Halle, P.A., De Boynson–Bardies, B. & Vihman, M.M. (1991). Beginnings of prosodic organization, intonation and duration patterns of disyllables produced by Japanese and French infants. *Language and Speech*, **34**, 299–318.

Harding, J.W., Wacker, D.P., Berg, W.K., Rick, G. & Lee, J.F. (2004). Promoting response variability and stimulus generalization in martial arts training. *Journal of Applied Behavior Analysis*, **37**, 185–196.

Haring, T.G. & Kennedy, C.H. (1988). Unit of analysis in task analytic research. *Journal of Applied Behavior Analysis*, **21**, 207–215.

Hartley, J. (1994). *Designing Instructional Text* (3rd edn). London: Kogan Page.

Hastie, M & Nelson, A. (2005). Teaching the Art of Case Conceptualization Using the "Case Conceptualization Grid": *A Practical Tool for Clinical Supervision*. Downloaded http://www.austinchildguidance.org/news, December 22, 2007.

Hayes, S.C., Barnes–Holmes, D. & Roche, B. (2001a). *Relational Frame Theory. A Post-Skinnerean Account of Human Language and Cognition*. New York: Kluwer.

Hayes, S.C., Blackledge, J.T. & Barnes–Holmes, D. (2001b). Language and cognition, Constructing an alternative approach within the behavioral tradition. In *Relational Frame Theory. A Post-Skinnerean Account of Human Language and Cognition* (Eds S.C. Hayes, D. Barnes–Holmes & B. Roche). New York: Kluwer, pp. 3–20.

Hayes, S.C., Fox, E., Gifford, E.V. & Wilson, K.G. (2001c). Derived relational responding as learned behavior. In *Relational Frame Theory. A Post-Skinnerean Account of Human Language and Cognition* (Eds S.C. Hayes, D. Barnes–Holmes & B. Roche). New York: Kluwer, pp. 21–50.

Haynes, S.N., Leisen, M.B. & Blaine, D.D. (1997). Functional analytic case models and clinical descision–making. *Psychological Assessment*, **9**, 334–348.

Hayes, S.C., Masudo, A., Bissett, R., Luomo, J. & Guerrero, L.F. (2004). DBT, FAP, and ACT: How empirically oriented are the new behavior therapy technologies? *Behavior Therapy*, **35**, 35–54.

Haynes, S.N. & O'Brien, W.H. (1990). The functional analysis in behavior therapy. *Clinical Psychology Review*, **10**, 649–668.

Haynes, S.N. & O'Brien, W.H. (2000). *Principles and Practice of Behavioral Assessment*. New York: Kluwer.

Heard, K.W. & Watson, T.S (1999). Reducing wandering by persons with dementia using differential reinforcement. *Journal of Applied Behavior Analysis*, **32**, 381–384.

Heimberg, R.G., Salzman, D.G., Holt, C.S. & Blendel, K.A. (1993). Cognitive behavioral treatment for social phobia: Effectiveness at five year follow up. *Cognitive Therapy and Research*, **17**, 325–339.

Henry, W.P. (1997). Interpersonal case formulation: Describing and explaining interpersonal patterns using the structural analysis of social behavior. In T.D. Eells (Ed.) *Handbook of psychotherapy care formulation*, (pp. 223–259). New York: Guilford.

Hergenhahn, B.R. (2001). *An Introduction of the History of Psychology*. New York: Wadsworth.

Hermans, D., Dirikx, T., Vansteenwegen, D., Baeyens, F., Van den Bergh, O. & Eelen, P. (2005). Reinstatement of fear responses in human aversive conditioning. *Behavior, Research and Therapy*, **43**, 533–551.

Herrnstein, R.J. (1961). Relative and absolute strength of response as a function of frequency of reinforcement. *Journal of the Experimental Analysis of Behavior*, **4**, 267–272.

Higgins, S.T., Delaney, D.D., Budney, A.J., Bickel, W.K., Hughes, J.R., Foerg, F. & Fenwick, J. (1991). A behavioral approach to achieving initial cocaine abstinence. *American Journal of Psychiatry*, **148**, 1218–1224.

Higgins, S.T., Budney, A.J., Bickel, W.K., Hughes, J.R., Foerg, F. & Badger, G. (1993). Achieving cocaine abstinence with a behavioral approach. *American Journal of Psychiatry*, **150**, 763–769.

Higgins, S.T., Budney, A.J., Bickel, W.K. & Badger, G. (1994). Participation of significant others in outpatient behavioral treatment predicts greater cocaine abstinence. *American Journal of Alcohol and Drug Dependence*, **20**, 47–56.

Higgins, S.T., Heil, H.H., & Sigmon, S.C. (1997). The influence of alternative reinforcers on cocaine use and abuse: A brief review. *Pharmacology Biochemistry and Behavior*, **57**, 419–427.

Higgins, S.T., Heil, H.H., & Sigmon, S.C. (2007). A behavioral approach to the treatment of substance use disorders. In *Functional Analysis in Clinical Treatment* (Ed. P. Sturmey). New York: Academic, pp. 261–282.

Higgins, S.T., Wong, C.J., Badger, G.J., Haug Ogden, D.E. & Dantona, R.L. (2000). Contingent reinforcement increases cocaine abstinence during outpatient treatment and one year of follow–up. *Journal of Consulting and Clinical Psychology*, **68**, 64–72.

Hollandsworth, J.G. Jr., Glazeski, R.C. & Dressel, M.E. (1978). Use of social-skills training in the treatment of extreme anxiety and deficient verbal skills in the job-interview setting. *Journal of Applied Behavior Analysis*, **11**, 259–269.

Holmes, G.R., Heckel, R.V., Chestnut, E., Harris, N. & Cautela, J. (1987). Factor analysis of the Adolescent Reinforcement Survey Schedule (ARSS) with college freshmen. *Journal of Clinical Psychology*, **43**, 386–390.

Homes, G.R., Heckel, R. V.,Chestnut, E., Harris, N. & Cautela, J. (1987). Factor analysis of the Adolescent Reinforcement Survey Schedule (ARSS) with college freshmen. *Journal of Clinical Psychology*, **43**, 386–390.

Hopkinson, J. & Neuringer, A. (2003). Modifying behavioral variability in moderately depressed students. *Behavior Modification*, **27**, 251–264.

Hopko, D.R., Bell, J.L. Armento, M.E., Hant, M.K. & Lejuez, C.W. (2005). Behavior therapy for depressed cancer patients in primary care. *Psychotherapy: Theory, Research, Practice and Training*, **42**, 236–243.

Hopko, D.R., Lejuez, C.W., LePage, J.P., Hopko, S.D. & McNeil, D.W. (2003). A brief behavioral activation treatment for depression. A randomized pilot trial within an inpatient psychiatric hospital. *Behavior Modification*, **27**, 458–469.

Hopko, D.R., Armento, M.E., Cantu, M.S., Chambers, L.L. & Lejuez, C.W. (2005). The use of daily diaries to assess the relations among mood state, overt behavior, and reward value of activities. *Behavior, Research and Therapy*, **41**, 1137–1148.

Hopko, D.R., Hopko, S.D. & LeJuez, C.W. (2007). Mood disorders. In *Functional analysis in clinical treatment* (Ed. P. Sturmey). New York: Academic Press, pp. 307–334.

Horcones, L. (2006). Communidad Los Horcones Walden Dos. Founed in 1973. Retrieved 15 Janury 2007, from http://www.loshorcones.org.mx/.

Horowitz, M.J. (1997). *Formulation as a Basis for Planning Psychothereapy Treatment*. Washington, DC: American Psychiatric Association Press.

Houlihan, D., Schwartz, C., Miltenberger, R. & Heuton, D. (1991). The rapid treatment of a young man's balloon (noise) phobia using in vivo flooding. *Journal of Behavior Therapy and Experimental Psychiatry*, **24**, 233–240.

Howlin, P., Baron–Cohen, S. & Hadwin, J (1998). *Teaching Children With Autism to Mind-Read: A Practical Guide for Teachers and Parents*. Chichester: Wiley.

Ingham, R.J. & Andrews, G. (1973). Behavior therapy and stuttering, a review. *Journal of Speech and Hearing Disorders*, **38**, 405–441.

Ingram, B.L. (2002). Clinical case formulation: Matching the integrative treatment plan to the client. Chichester, UK: Wiley UK.

Iwata, B.A., Dorsey, M.F., Slifer, K.J., Bauman, K.E. & Richman, G.S. (1982/1994). Toward a functional analysis of self–injury. *Journal of Applied Behavior Analysis, 27, 197–209.*

Iwata, B.A., Pace, G.M. Cowdery, G.E. & Miltenberger, R.G. (1994). What makes extinction work, An analysis of procedural form and function. *Journal of Applied Behavior Analysis, 27, 131–144.*

Jacobs, S., Daly, N.D., King, D.W. & Chermamie, G. (1984). The accuracy of teacher predictions of student reward preferences. *Psychology in the Schools, 21, 520–524.*

Jacobson, N.S., Dobson, K.S., Truax, P.A., Addis, M.E., Koerner, K., Gollan, J.K. et al. (1996). A component analysis of cognitive-behavioral treatment for depression. *Journal of Consulting and Clinical Psychology*, **64**, 295–304.

Jacobson, N.S., Follette, V.M., Follette, W.C., Holtzworth–Munroe, A., Katt, J.L. & Schmaling, K.B. (1989). A component analysis of behavioral marital therapy, 1-year follow–up. *Behavior Research and Therapy*, **23**, 549–555.

Jolliffe, C.D. & Nicholas, M.K. (2004). Verbally reinforcing pain reports, an experimental test of the operant model of chronic pain. *Pain*, **107**, 167–175.

Jackson, H.F., Glass, C. & Hope, S. (1987). A functional analysis of recidivist asson. *British Journal of Clinical Psychology*, **26**, 175–185.

Jones, K.M. & Friman, P.C. (1999). A case study of behavioral assessment and treatment of insect phobia. *Journal of Applied Behavior Analysis*, **32**, 95–98.

Jones, R.N., Mandler–Provin, D., Latkowski, M.E. & McMahon, W.M. (1988). Development of a reinforcement survey for inpatient psychiatric children. *Child & Family Behavior Therapy*, **9**, 73–77.

Kale, R.J., Kaye, J.H., Whelan, P.A. & Hopkins, B.L. (1968). The effects of reinforcement on the modification, maintenance, and generalization of social responses of mental patients. *Journal of Applied Behavior Analysis*, **1**, 307–314.

Kanfer, F.H. & Phillips, J.S. (1970). *Learning Foundations of Behavior Therapy*. New York, Wiley.

Kanfer, F.H. & Saslow, G. (1969). Behavioral diagnosis. In *Behavior Therapy, Appraisal and Status* (Ed. C.M. Franks). New York: McGraw–Hill, pp. 417–444.

Kanter, J.W., Landes, S.J., Busch, A.M., Rusch, L.C., Brown, K.R., Baruch, D.E. & Holman, G. (2006). The effect of contingent reinforcement on target variables in outpatient psychotherapy for depression: A successful and unsuccessful case using functional analytic psychotherapy. *Journal of Applied Behavior Analysis*, **39**, 463–467.

Kazdin, A.E. (1982). The token economy: A decade later. *Journal of Applied Behavior Analysis*, **15**, 431–445.

Kearney, C.A. & Albano, A.M. (2004). The functional profiles of school refusal behavior. Diagnostic aspects. *Behavior Modification*, **28**, 147–161.

Kearney, C.A. & Silverman, W.K. (1990). A preliminary analysis of a functional model of assessment and treatment for school refusal behavior. *Behavior Modification*, **14**, 340–366.

Keehn, J.D., Bloomfield, F.F. & Hug, M.A. (1969). Use of the reinforcement survey schedule with alcoholics. *Quarterly Journal of Studies on Alcoholism*, **31**, 602–615.

Keijers, G.P., Van Minner, A., Hoogduin, C.A., Klaasen, B.N., Hendriks, M.J. & Tanis–Jacobs. J. (2005). Behavioral treatment of trichotillomania: Two-year follow-up results. *Behavior, Research and Therapy*, **44**, 359–370.

Keller, F.S. & Schoenfeld, W.N. (1950). *Principles of Psychology*. Acton, MA: Copley.

Kelly, M.B. (1976). A review of academic permanent - product data collection and reliability procedures in applied behavior analysis research. *Journal of Applied Behavior Analysis*, **9**, 211.

Kennedy, C.H. (2007). Stereotypic movement disorder. In *Functional Analysis in Clinical Treatment* (Ed. P. Sturmey). New York: Academic Press, pp. 193–210.

Kinderman, P. & Lobban, F. (2000). Evolving formulations: Sharing complex formulations with clients. *Behavioural and Cognitive Psychotherapy*, **28**, 307–310

Kirby, K.C., Fowler, S.A. & Baer, D.M. (1991). Reactivity in self–recording: Obtrusiveness of recording procedure and peer comments. *Journal of Applied Behavior Analysis*, **24**, 487–498.

Klein Knecht, R.A., McCormick, C.E., Thorndike, R.M. (1973). Stability of stated reinforces as measured by the Reinforces Survey Schedule. *Behavior Therapy*, **4**, 407–413.

Klonsky, E.D. (2006). The functions of self-harm. *Clinical Psychology Review*, **27**, 226–239.

Koerner, K. & Linehan, M.B. (1997). Case formulation in dialective behavior therapy for borderline personality disorders. In *Handbook of Psychotherapy Case Formulation* (Ed. T.D. Eells). New York: Guilford, pp. 340–367.

Kohlenberg, R.J. & Tsai, M. (1991). *Functional Analytic Psychotherapy: Creating Intense and Curative Therapeutic Relationships*. New York: Plenum.

Krantz, P.J., MacDuff, M.T. & McClannahan, L.E. (1993). Programming participation in family activities for children with autism: Parents' use of photographic activity schedules. *Journal of Applied Behavior Analysis*, **26**, 89–97.

Kuyken, W., Fothergill, C.D., Musa, M. & Chadwick, P. (2005). The reliability and quality of cognitive case formulation, Behavior Research Therapy, **43**, 1187–1201.

Lalli, J.S., Casey, S. & Kates, K. (1995). Reducing escape behavior and increasing task completion with functional communication training, extinction and response chaining. *Journal of Applied Behaviour Analysis*, **28**, 261–268.

Lalli, J.S., Mace, F.C., Wohn, T. & Livezy, K. (1995). Identification and modification of a response-class hierarchy. *Journal of Applied Behavior Analysis*, **28**, 551–559.

Lam, K., Marra, C. & Salzinger, K. (2005). Social reinforcement of somatic versus psychological description of depressive events. *Behavior, Research and Therapy*, **43**, 1203–1218.

Lamal, P.A. (1997). *Behavioral Analysis of Societies and Cultural Practices*. New York: Hemisphere.

Lamal, P.A. (1998). Advancing backwards. *Journal of Applied Behavior Analysis*, **31**, 705–706.

Lane, D.A. (1997). Context focused analysis: An experimentally derived model for working with complex problems with children, adolescents and systems. In M. Bruch & F.W. Bond (Eds.) *Beyond diagnosis*. Case formulation approaches in CBT, (pp. 103–140). Chichester, UK: Wiley UK.

Lang, P.J. (1979). A bio–informational theory of emotional imagery. *Psychophysiology*, **16**, 495–512.

Lang, P.J. & Melamed, B.G. (1969). Avoidance conditioning therapy of an infant with chronic ruminative vomiting. *Journal of Abnormal Psychology*, **74**, 1–8.

Larson, K. & Ayllon (1990). The effects of contingent music and differential reinforcement on infantile colic. *Behavior, Research and Therapy*, **28**, 119–125.

Lavie, T. & Sturmey, P. (2002). Training staff to conduct a paired–stimulus preference assessment. *Journal of Applied Behavior Analysis*, **35**, 209–211.

LeBlanc, L.A.C., Coates, A.M., Daneshvar, S., Charlop–Christy, M.H., Morris, C. & Lancaster, B.M. (2003). Using video modeling and reinforcement to teach perspective–taking skills to children with autism. *Journal of Applied Behavior Analysis*, **36**, 253–257.

Lee, L. & Miltenberger, R.G. (1997). School refusal behavior, Classification, assessment, and treatment issues. *Education and Treatment of Children*, **19**, 474–486.

Lee, M.I. & Miltenberger, R.G. (1997). Functional assessment and binge eating. *Behavior Modification*, **21**, 159–17.

Lee, R., Sturmey, P. & Fields, L. (2007). Schedule–induced and operant mechanisms that influence response variability, A review and implications for future investigations. *The Psychological Record*.

Lee, R. & Sturmey, P. (2006). The effects of lag schedules and preferred materials on variable responding in students with autism. *Journal of Autism and Developmental Disorders*, **36**, 421–428.

Lee, R. & Sturmey, P. (in preparation). The effects of script–fading and a lag–1 schedule on varied social responding in children with Autism.

Lejuez, C.W., Hopko, D.R. & Hopko, S.D. (2001). A brief behavioral activation treatment for depression. *Behavior Modification*, **25**, 255–286.

Lejuez, C.W., Hopko, D.R. & Hopko, S.D. (2002). *The Brief Behavioral Activation Treatment for Depression (BATD): A Comprehensive Patient Guide*. Boston, MA: Pearson Custom Publishing.

Lerman, D.C., Iwata, B.A. Smith, R.G. Zarcone, J.R. & Vollmer, T.R. (1994). Transfer of behavioral function as a contributing factor in treatment relapse. *Journal of Applied Behavior Analysis*, **27**, 357–370.

Leslie, J.C. & O'Reilly, M.F. (1999). *Behavior Analysis. Foundations and Applications to Psychology*. Amsterdam, Netherlands: Harwood.

Letham, J., Slade, P. D., Troup, J.D. & Bentley, G. (1983). Outline of a Fear-Avoidance Model of exaggerated pain perception. – I. *Behaviour, Research and Therapy*, **21**, 401–408.

Levenson, H. & Strupp, H.H. (1997). Cyclical maladptive behavior patterns: Case formulation in time-limited dynamic psychotherapy. In: T. D. Eells (Ed.) *Handbook of psychotherapy case formulation*. New York: Guilford.

Levine, B.A. (1987). Invited case transcript. The importance of checking the assumptions of the professional referral source. *Journal of Behavior Therapy and Experimental Psychiatry*, **18**, 241–244.

Liberman, R.P.T., Teigen, J., Patterson, R. & Baker, V. (1973). Reducing delusional speech in chronic paranoid schizophrenics. *Journal of Applied Behavior Analysis*, **6**, 57–64.

Linehan, M.M. (1993). *Cognitive Behavioral Treatment of Borderline Personality Disorder*. New York: Guilford.

Lloyd, J.W., Bateman, D.F. Landrum, T.J. & Hallahan, D.P. (1989). Self-recording of attention versus productivity. *Journal of Applied Behavior Analysis*, **22**, 315–323.

Loeber, S., Croissant, B., Heinz, A., Mann, K. & Flor, H. (2006). Cue exposure in the treatment of alcohol dependence, Effects on drinking outcome, craving and self–efficacy. *British Journal of Clinical Psychology*, **45**, 515–529.

Loftus, E.F. (1993). Desperately seeking memories of the first few years of childhood, the reality of early memories. *Journal of Experimental Psychology General*, **122**, 155–165.

Loftus, E.F. (1994). The repressed memory controversy. *American Psychologist*, **49**, 443–445.

Lorenc, L., Sturmey, P. & Brittain, H. (1992). Evaluation of a meta-cognitive strategy to improve the information gained from a stroke information pack. *Stress Medicine*, **8**, 111–112.

Loro, A. D. Jr. Fisher, E. B. Jr. & Levenkron, J. C. (1979). Comparison of established and innovative weight-reduction treatment procedures. *Journal of Applied Behavior Analysis*, **12**, 141–155.

Luborsky, L. (1997). The core conflictual relationship theme: A basic case formulation method. In T. D. Eells (Ed.) *Handbook of Psychotherapy case formulation*, (pp. 52–83). New York: Guilford.

Luciano-Soriano, M.C., Molina-Cobos, F.J. & Gomez-Becerra, I. (2000). Say-do-report training to change chronic behaviors in mentally retarded subjects. *Research in Developmental Disabilities*, **21**, 355–366.

MacCorquodale, K. (1970). On Chomsky's review of Skinner's *Verbal Behavior. Journal of the Experimental Analysis of Behavior*, **13**, 83–99.

MacDuff, G.S., Krantz, P.J. & McClannahan, L.E. (1993). Teaching Children with autism to use photographic activity schedules: Maintanence and generalization of complex response chains. *Journal of Applied Behavior Analysis*, **26**, 89–97.

Maisto, S.A. (1985). Alcohol abuse. In *Behavioral Case Formulation* (Ed. I.D. Turkat). New York: Plenum, pp. 37–86.

Malatesta, V.J. (1985). Formulation of geriatric organic syndrome. In *Behavioral Case Formulation* (Ed. I.D. Turkat). New York: Plenum, pp. 259–308.

Malatesta, V.J. (1990). Behavioral case formulation: An experimental assessment study of transient tic disorder. *Journal of Psychopathology and Behavioral Assessment*, **12**, 219–232.

Mann, R.A. & Baer, D.M. (1970). The effects of receptive language training on articulation, 3 291–298.

Mann, R.A. B., D.M. (1971). The effects of receptive language training on articulation. *Journal of Applied Behavior Analysis*, **4**, 291–298.

March, R.E. & Horner, R. H. (2000). Feasibility and contributions of functional behavior assessment in schools. *Journal of Emotional & Behavior Disorders.* **10**, 158–170.

Marks, I. (1981). *Cure and care of neurosis.* New York: Wiley.

Mathews, J.R.H., Hodson, G.D., Crist, W.B. & LaRoche, G.R. (1992). Teaching young children to use contact lenses. *Journal of Applied Behavior Analysis*, **25**, 229–235.

Matson, J.L., Bielecki, J., Mayville, E.A., Smalls, Y., Bamburg, J.W. & Baglio, C.S. (1999). The development of a reinforcer choice assessment scale for persons with severe and profound mental retardation. *Research in Developmental Disabilities*, **20**, 379–384.

Matson, J.L. & Vollmer, T.R. (1995). *Questions About Behavioral Function.* Batorn Rouge, LA: Scientific Publishers.

Mawson, D., Marks, I.M., Ramm, L. & Stern, R.S. (1981). Guided mourning for morbid grief: A controlled study. *The British Journal of Psychiatry,* **138,** 185–193.

McClannahan, L.E. & Krantz, P.J. (2006). *Teaching Conversation to Children With Autism: Scripts And Script Fading.* Bethesda, MD: Woodbine.

McClannahan, L.E. & Krantz, P.J. (1993) On systems analysis in autism intervention programs. *Journal of Applied Behavior Analysis,* **26,** 589–596.

McComas, R., Lee, J.J. & Jawor, J. (2002). The effects of differential and lag reinforcement schedules on varied verbal responding by individuals with autism. *Journal of Applied Behavior Analysis,* **35,** 391–402.

McGaw, S. & Sturmey, P. (1989). The effects of text readability and summary exercises on parent knowledge of behavior therapy: The Portage parent readings. *Educational Psychology,* **9,** 127–132.

McGee, G.G.K., Krantz, P.J. Mason, D. & McClannahan, L.E. (1983). A modified incidental-teaching procedure for autistic youth, Acquisition and generalization of receptive object labels. *Journal of Applied Behavior Analysis,* **16,** 329–338.

McGill, P. (1999). Establishing operations: Implications for the assessment, treatment, and prevention of problem behavior. *Journal of Applied Behavior Analysis,* **32,** 393–418.

McGill, P. Teer, K., Rye, L. & Hughes, D. (2003) Staff reports of setting events associated with challenging behavior. *Behavior Modification,* **27,** 265–282.

McNight, D.L., Nelson, R.O., Haynes, S.C. & Jarrett, R.B. (1984). The importance of treating individually assessment response classes in the amelioration of depression. *Behavior Therapy,* **15,** 315–335.

McPherson, A., Bonem, M., Green, G. & Osborne, J. (1984). A citation analysis on the influence on research of Skinner's *Verbal Behavior. The Behavior Analyst,* **19,** 19–27.

McWilliams, N. (1999). *Psychotherapy Case Formulation.* New York: Guilford.

Messer, S.B. & Wolitzky, D.L. (1997). The traditional psychoanalytic approach to case formulation. In I.D. Eells (Ed.) *Handbook of psychotherapy case formulation,* (pp. 26–57). New York: Guilford.

Meyer, V. & Turkat, I.D. (1979). Behavioral analysis of clinical cases. *Journal of Behavior Therapy and Experimental Psychiatry,* **1,** 259–270.

Miltenberger, R.G. (2003). Behavior modification: Principles and procedures. (3rd. ed). Belmont, Ca: Wadsworth.

Miltenberger R.G. & Veltum, L.G. (1998). Evaluation of an instructions and modeling procedure for training behavioral assessment interviewing. *Journal of Behavior Therapy and Experimental Psychiatry,* **19,** 31–41.

Miltenberger, R.G., Rapp, E.S. & Long, E. S. (1999). A low–tech method for conducting real–time recording. *Journal of Applied Behavior Analysis,* **32,** 119–120.

Miltenberger, R.G. & Fuqua, R.W. (1985). Evaluation of a training manual for the acquisition of behavioral assessment interviewing skills. *Journal of Applied Behavior Analysis*, **18**, 323–328.

Mitchell, W.S. & Stoffelmeyer, B.E. (1973). Application of the Premack principle to the behavioral control of extremely inactive schizophrenics. *Journal of Applied Behavior Analysis*, **6**, 419–423.

Morganstern, I.P. (1988). Behavioral interviewing, the initial stages of assessment. In Behavioral Assessment, A Practical Handbook, 3rd edn (Eds M.B. Hersen & A.S. Bellack). Oxford: Pergamon.

Morris, E. K., Smith, N.G. & Altus, D.E. (2005). B.F. Skinner's contributions to applied behavior analysis. *The Behavior Analyst*, **28**, 99–132.

Morrison, A.P. (1998). Cognitive behavior therapy for psychotic symptoms of schizophrenia. In *Treating Complex Cases. The Cognitive Behavioural Approach (Eds* N.W. Tarrier, A. Wells & G. Haddock). Chichester: Wiley, pp. 195–216.

Mowrer, O. H. (1939). A stimulus-response analysis of anxiety and its role as a reinforcing agent. *Psychological Review*, **46**, 553–565.

Nathan, P. & Gorman, J.M. (2002). *A Guide To Treatments that Work*. Oxford: Oxford University Press.

Neef, N.A., Marckel, J., Ferreri, S.J., Bicard, D.F., Endo, S., Aman, M.G., Miller, K.M., Jung, S., Nist, L. & Armstrong, N. (2005). Behavioral assessment of impulsivity: A comparison of children with and without attention deficit hyperactivity disorder. *Journal of Applied Behavior Analysis*, **38**, 23–37.

Neef, N. A. & Northup, J. (2007). Attention deficit hyperactivity disorder. In *Functional Analysis in Clincal Psychology* (Ed. P. Sturmey). New York: Academic Press, pp. 87–110.

Neef, N.A., Parrish, J.M., Hannigan, K.F., Page, T.J. & Iwata, B.A. (1989). Teaching Self-catheterization skills to children with neurogenic bladder complications. *Journal of Applied Behavior Analysis*, **22**, 237–243.

Nelson, R.O. & Hayes, S.C. (1979). The nature of behavioral assessment: A commentary. *Journal of Applied Behavior Analysis*, **12**, 491–500.

Nelson–Gray, R.O. (2003). Treatment utility of psychological assessment. *Psychological Assessment*, **15**, 521–531.

Nelson–Gray, R.O. & Farmer, R.F. (1999). Invited essay. Behavioural assessment of personality disorders. *Behavior, Research and Therapy*, **37**, 347–368.

Nelson–Gray, R.O., Herbert, J.D., Herbert, D.L. Sigmon, S.T. & Brannon, S.E. (1989). Effectiveness of matched, mismatched, and package treatments of depression. *Journal of Behavior Therapy and Experimental Psychiatry*, **20**, 281–294.

Neuringer, A. (2002). Operant variability, evidence, functions, and theory. *Psychonomic Bulletin and Review*, **9**, 672–705.

Neuringer, A. (2004). Reinforced variability in animals and people, Implications for adaptive action. *American Psychologist*, **59**, 891–906.

Newman, A. & Bloom, R. (1981). Self-control of smoking — I. Effects of experience with imposed, increasing, decreasing and random delays. *Behavior, Research and Therapy*, **19**, 187–192.

Nezu, A.M. & Nezu, C.M. (1989). *Clinical Decision Making in Behavior Therapy: A Problem Solving Approach.* Champaign, IL: Research Press.

Nezu, A.M. & Nezu, C.M. (1993). Identifying and selecting target problems for clinical interventions, A problem solving model. *Psychological Assessment*, **5**, 254–263.

Nezu, A.M., Nezu, C.M., Friedman, S.H. & Haynes, S.N. (1997). Case formulation in behavior thereapy, Problem solving and functional analytic strategies. In *Handbook of Psychotherapy Case Formulation* (Ed. T.D. Eells). New York: Guilford, pp. 368–401.

Nezu, A.M., Nezu, C.M. & Lombardo, E. (2004). *Cognitive–behavioral Case Formulation and Treatment Design. A Problem Solving Approach.* New York: Springer.

Ninness, H.A.C., Fuerst, J., Rutherford, R.D. & Glenn, S.S. (1991). Effects of self-management training and reinforcement on the transfer of improved conduct in the absence of supervision. *Journal of Applied Behavior Analysis*, **24**, 449–508.

Northup, J. (2000). Further evaluation of the accuracy of reinforcer surveys: A systematic replication. *Journal of Applied Behavior Analysis*, **33**, 335–338.

Northup, J., George, T., Jones, K., Broussard, C. & Vollmer, T.R. (1996). A comparison of reinforcer assessment methods: The utility of verbal and pictorial choice procedures. *Journal of Applied Behavior Analysis*, **29**, 201–212.

Novacco, R.W. (1997). Preface. In *Cognitive Behavior Theapy for People with Learning Disabilities* (Eds B. Stenfert Kroese, D. Dagnan & R.M. Loumidis). New York: Brunner-Routledge, pp. x–xii.

O'Brien, W.H. & Haynes, S.N. (1995). A functional analytic approach to the conceptualization, assessment and treatment of a child with frequent migraine headaches. *In Session*, **1**, 65–80.

O'Callaghan, P.M., Allen, K.D., Powell, S. & Slama, F. (2006). The efficacy of noncontingent escape for decreasing children's disruptive behavior during restorative dental treatment. *Journal of Applied Behavior Analysis*, **39**, 161–171.

O'Neill, R.E., Horner, R.H., Albin, R.W., Sprague, J.R., Storey, K. & Newton, J.S. (1997). *Functional Assessment and Program Development for Problem Behavior. A Practical Handbook.* New York: Brooks/Cole.

Oliver, C., Hall, S. & Murphy, G. (2005). The early development of self–injurious behavior: evaluating the role of social reinforcement. *Journal of Intellectual Disabilities Research*, **49**, 591–599.

Orlando, R. & Bijou, S.W. (1960). Single and multiple schedules of reinforcement in developmentally retarded children. *Journal of the Experimental Analysis of Behavior*, **3**, 339–348.

Osnes, P.G., Guevremont, D.C. & Stokes, T.F. (1987). Increasing a child's proso-cial behaviors: Positive and negative consequences in correspondence training. *Journal of Behavior Therapy and Experimental Psychiatry*, 8, 71–76.

Owens, R.G. & Ashcroft, J.B. (1982). Functional analysis in applied psy-chology. *British Journal of Clinical Psychology*, 21, 181–189.

Paclawskyj, T.R., Matson, J.L., Rush, K.S., Smalls, Y. & Vollmer, T.R. (2001). Assessment of the convergent validity of the Questions About Behavioral Function scale with analogue functional analysis and the Motivation Assessment Scale. *Journal of Intellectual Disabilities Research*, 45, 484–494.

Paclawskyj, T. R., Matson, J. L., Rush, K. S., Smalls, Y. & Vollmer, T.R. (2000). Questions about behavioral function (QABF), a behavioral checklist for functional assessment of aberrant behavior. *Research in Developmental Disabilities*, 21, 223–229.

Palmer, D.C. (2006). On Chomsky's appraisal of Skinner's *Verbal behavior*. A half century of misunderstanding. *The Behavior Analyst*, 29, 253–268.

Paniagua, F.A. (1986). Management of hyperactive children through cor-respondence training procedures. *Behavioral and Residential Treatment*, 2, 1–23.

Paniagua, F.A., Morrison, P.B. & Black, S.A. (1990). Management of a hy-peractive–conduct disordered child through correspondence training, a preliminary study. *Journal of Behavior Therapy and Experimental Psychia-try*, 21, 63–68.

Partington, J.W. & Sundberg, M.L. (1998). *The Assessment of Basic Language and Learning Skills, An Assessment, Curriculum Guide, and Tracking System for Children with Autism or Other Developmental Disabilities*. Danville, CA: Behavior Analysts.

Partington, J.W., Sundberg, M.L., Newhouse, L. & Spengler, S.M. (1994). Overcoming an autistic child's failure to acquire a tact repertoire. *Jour-nal of Applied Behavior Analysis*, 27, 733–734.

Patterson, P.L. & Teigen, J.R. (1973). Conditioning and post–hospital gen-eralization of nondelusional responses in a chronic psychotic patient. *Journal of Applied Behavior Analysis*, 6, 65–70.

Paul, G.L. (1967). Strategy of outcome research in psychotherapy. *Journal of Consulting Psychology*, 31, 109–118.

Paunovic, N. (1999). Exposure counterconditioning (EC) as a treatment for severe PTSD and depression with an illustrative case. *Journal of Behavior Therapy and Experimental Psychiatry*, 3, 105–117.

Pelios, L.M., Morren, J., Tesch, D. & Axelrod, S. (1999). The impact of func-tional analysis methodology on treatment choice for self–injurious and aggressive behavior. *Journal of Applied Behavior Analysis*, 32, 185–195.

Persons, J.B. (1997). *Cognitive Therapy in Practice: A Case Formulation Approach*. New York: W.W. Norton.

Persons, J.B. & Bertagnolli, A. (1999). Inter-rater reliability of cognitive-behavioral case formulations of depression. *Cognitive Therapy and Research*, 23, 271–283.

Persons, J.B., Mooney, K.A. & Padesky, C.A. (1995). Inter-rater reliability of cognitive-behavioral. Case formulations. *Cognitive Therapy and Research*, **19**, 21–34.

Persons, J.B. & Thompkins, M.A. (2007). Cognitive-behavioral case formulation. In T.D. Eells (Ed.) *Handbook of psychotherapy case formulation.* (Second edition), (pp. 290–316).

Phillips, D., Fischer, S.C. & Singh, R. (1977). A children's reinforcement survey schedule. *Journal of Behavior Therapy and Experimental Psychiatry*, **8**, 131–134.

Piazza, C.C. & Addison, L.R. (2007). Function-based assessment and treatment for pediatric feeding disorders. In *Functional Analysis in Clinical Treatment* (Ed. P. Sturmey). New York: Academic Press, pp. 129–150.

Piazza, C.C., Patel, M.R., Gulotta, C.S. Sevin, B.M. & Layer, S.A. (2003). On the relative contributions of positive reinforcement and escape extinction in the treatment of food refusal. *Journal of Applied Behavior Analysis*, **36**, 309–324.

Pierce, W.D. & Epling, W.F. (1995). The applied importance of research on the matching law. *Journal of Applied Behavior Analysis*, **28**, 237–241.

Prochaska, J.O. & Norcross, J.C. (2002). *Systems of psychotherapy. A transtheoretical analysis.* Belmont, Ca: Wadsworth.

Pyles, D.A. & Bailey, J.S. (1989). Behavioral diagnostics. *Monograph of the American Association on Mental Retardation*, **12**, 85–107.

Pyles, D.A., Riordan, M.M. & Bailey, J.S. (1997). The Stereotypy Analysis Scale: An instrument for examining environmental variables associated with differential rates of stereotypic behavior. *Research in Developmental Disabilities*, **18**, 11–38.

Rachman, S., De Silva, P. & Röper, G. (1976). The sponteneous decay of impulsive urges. *Behavior, Research and Therapy*, **14**, 445–4.

Ralph, A. & Birnbrauer, J.S. (1986). The potential of correspondence training for facilitating generalisation of social skills. *Applied Research in Mental Retardation*, **7**, 415–429.

Redin, J.A., Miltenberger, R.G., Crosby, R.D., Wolff, G.E. & Stickney, M.I. (2002). Functional assessment of binge eating in a clinical sample of obese eaters. *Eating and Weight Disorders*, **7**, 106–115.

Reed, H., Thomas, E., Sprague, J.R. & Horner, R.H. (1997). Student guided functional assessment interview: An analysis of student and teacher agreement. *Journal of Behavioral Education*, **7**, 33–49.

Reid, D.H., Everson, J.M. & Green, C.W. (1999). A systematic evaluation of preferences identified through person–centered planning for people with profound multiple disabilities. *Journal of Applied Behavior Analysis*, **32**, 467–477.

Reisinger, J.J. (1972). The treatment of anxiety–depression via positive reinforcement and response cost. *Journal of Applied Behavior Analysis*, **5**, 125–130.

Richman. D.M. & Lindauer, S.E. (2005). Longitudinal assessment of stereotypic, proto-injurious, and self-injurious behavior exhibited by young children with developmental delays. *American Journal on Mental Retardation*, **110**, 469–450.

Risley, T.R. & Hart, B. (1968). Developing correspondence between the non–verbal and verbal behavior of preschool children. *Journal of Applied Behavior Analysis*, **1**, 267–281.

Roll, J.M. (2005). Assessing the feasibility of using contingency management to modify cigarette smoking by adolescents. *Journal of Applied Behavior Analysis*, **38**, 463–467.

Roscoe, E.M., Fisher, W.W., Glover, A.C. & Volkert, V.M. (2006). Evaluating the relative effects of feedback and contingent money for staff training of stimulus preference assessments. *Journal of Applied Behavior Analysis*, **39**, 63–77.

Rosenbaum, M.S. & Drabman, R.S. (1979). Self–control training in the classroom, A review and critique. *Journal of Applied Behavior Analysis*, **12**, 467–485.

Ross, C.A., Leichner, P., Matas, M. & Anderson, D. (1990). A method of teaching and evaluating psychiatric case formulation. *Academic Psychiatry*, **14**, 99–105.

Roth, A.F. & Fonagy, P. (Eds) (2004). *What Works for Whom? A Critical Review of Psychotherapy Research*, 2nd edn. New York: Guilford.

Ryle, A. (1982). Psychotherapy: *A cognitive integration of theory and practice*. London, UK: Academic.

Ryle, A. (1997). Case formulation in cognitive analytic case formulation. In T.D. Eells (Ed.) *Handbook of psychotherapy case formulation*, (pp. 289–313). New York: Guilford.

Salzinger, K. (1996). Reinforcement history: A concept underutilized in behavior analysis. *Journal of Behavior Therapy and Experimental Psychiatry*, **27**, 199–207.

Saussure, F. de (1916, 1977). *Course in general psycholinguistics*. Glasgow, United Kingdom: Fontana/Collins.

Schaeffer, H.H. (1970). Self-injurious behavior: Shaping head-banging in monkeys. *Journal of Applied Behavior Analysis*, **3**, 111–116.

Schindler, F.E. (1980). Treatment of systematic desensitization of a recurring nightmare of a real life trauma. *Journal of Behavior Therapy and Experimental Psychiatry*, **11**, 53–54.

Schulte, D. (1992). Tailor–made and standardized therapy, complementary tasks in behavior therapy. A contrarian view. *Journal of Behavior Therapy and Experimental Psychiatry*, **27**, 119–126.

Schulte, D.K., R., Pepping, G. Schulte-Bahrenberg, T. (1992). Tailor-made versus standardized therapy of phobic patients. *Advances in Behavior Research and Therapy*, **14**, 67–92.

Sherman, J.A. (1965). Use of reinforcement and imitation to reinstate verbal behavior in mute psychotics. *Journal of Abnormal Psychology*, **70**, 155–164.

Shoben, E.J. (1949). Psychotherapy as a problem in learning theory. *Psychological Bulletin*, **46**, 366–392.

Sidman, M. (1960). *Tactics of Scientific Research*. New York: Basic Books.

Sidman, M. (1994). *Equivalence Relations and Behavior. A Research Story*. Boston, MA: Authors Cooperative.

Siegel, G.M.L., Lenske, J. & Broen, P. (1969). Suppression of normal speech disfluencies through response cost. *Journal of Applied Behavior Analysis*, **2**, 265–276.

Sigafoos, J., O'Reilly, M., Schlosser, R. & Lancioni, G.E. (2007). Communication intervention. In *Autism Spectrum Disorders, Applied Behavior Analysis, Evidence and Practice* (Eds. P. Sturmey & A. Fitzer). Austin, TX: Pro–ed.

Sigafoos, J., Kerr, M. & Roberts, D. (1995). Interrater reliability of the Motivation Assessment Scale, failure to replicate with aggressive behavior. *Research in Developmental Disabilities*, **15**, 333–342.

Silverman, K., Watanake, K., Marshall, A.M. & Baer, D.M. (1984). Reducing self-injury and corresponding self-restraint through the strategic use of protective clothing. *Journal of Applied Behavior Analysis*, **17**, 545–552.

Sim, K., Gwee, K.P. & Bateman, A. (2004). Case formulation in psychotherapy, Revitalizing its usefulness as a clinical tool. *Academic Psychiatry*, **29**, 289–292.

Simpson, H.B., Huppert, J. D., Petkova, E., Foa, E.B. & Liebowitz, M.R. (2006). Response versus remission in obsessive–compulsive disorder. *Journal of Clinical Psychiatry*, **67**, 269–276.

Sireling, L., Cohen, D. & Marks, I (1988). Guided mourning for morbid grief, A controlled replication. *Behavior Therapy*, **19**, 121–132.

Skinner, B.F. (1948). *Walden Two*. New York: MacMillan.

Skinner, B.F. (1950). Are psychological theories of learning necessary? *Psychological Review*, **57**, 193–216.

Skinner, B.F. (1953). *Science and Human Behavior*. New York: McMillan.

Skinner, B.F. (1957). *Verbal Behavior*. New York: Prentice–Hall.

Skinner, B.F. (1969). *Contingencies of Reinforcement*. Englewood Cliff, NJ: Prentice–Hall.

Skinner, B.F. (1971). *Beyond Freedom and Dignity*. New York: Alfred Knopf.

Skinner, B.F. (1974). *About behaviorism*. New York: Random.

Skinner, B.F. (1981). A thinking aid. *Journal of Applied Behavior Analysis*, **20**, 379–380.

Skinner, B.F. (1990). Can psychology be a science of mind? *American Psychologist*, **45**, 1206–1210.

Skinner, B.F. & Heron, W.T. (1937). The effects of caffeine and benzedvine upon conditioning and extinction. *The Psychological Record*, **1**, 340–346.

Skinner, B.F. & Vaughn, M.E. (1983). *Enjoy old age: A program of self-management*. New York: Norton.

Slade, P. (1982). Toward a functional analysis of anorexia nervosa. *British Journal of Clinical Psychology*, **21**, 167–179.

Slade, P.D., Troup, J.D., Letham, J. & Bertley, G. (1983). The Fear-Avoidance Model of exaggerated pain perception — II. *Behavior, Research and Therapy*, **21**, 409–416.

Slater, L. (2004). *Opening Skinner's boy: Great psychological experiments of the twentieth century*. New York: Norton.

Smeets, P.M.L., Lancioni, G.E., Ball, T.S. & Oliva, D.S. (1985). Shaping self-initiated toileting in infants. *Journal of Applied Behavior Analysis*, **18**, 303–308.

Smith, R.G., Iwata, B.A., Vollmer, T.R. & Pace, G.M. (1992). On the relationship between self-injurious behavior and self-restraint. *Journal of Applied Behavior Analysis*, **25**, 433–445.

Sperry, L., Gudeman, J.E., Blackwell, B. & Faulkner, L.R. (2004). *Psychiatric Case Formulation*. Washington, DC: American Psychiatric Association Press.

Staats, A.W. (1999). Valuable, but not maximal, it's time behavior therapy attend to its behaviorism. *Behavior, Research and Therapy*, **37**, 369–378.

Stein, K.F. & Gorte, C.M. (2003). Ecologic momentary assessment of eating-disordered behaviors. *International Journal of Eating Disorders*, **34**, 349–360.

Stemmer, N. (1990). Skinner's verbal behavior, Chomsky's review, and mentalism. *Journal of the Experimental Analalysis of Behavior*, **54**, 307–315.

Stenfert Kroese, B. (1997). Cognitive-behavior therapy for people with learning disabilities: Conceptual and contextual issues. In: B. Stenfert Kroese, Dagnan, D. & Loumidis, K. (Eds.) *Cognitive Behavior Therapy for People with Learning Disabilities*, (p. 1–15). New York: Brunner-Routledge.

Stenfert Kroese, B., Dagnan, D. & Loumidis, R.M. (1997). Cognitive-behavior therapy of people with learning disabilities. Conceptual and contextual issues. In *Cognitive Behavior Therapy for People with Learning Disabilities* (Eds B. Stenfert Kroese, D. Dagnan & R.M. Loumidis). Amsterdam: Brunner-Routlege, pp. 1–15.

Stickney, M.I., Miltenberger, R.G. & Wolff, G. (1999). A descriptive analysis of factors contributing to binge eating. *Journal of Behavior Therapy and Experimental Psychiatry*, **30**, 177–189.

Stokes, T.F. & Baer, D.M. (1977). An implicit technology of generalization. *Journal of Applied Behavior Analysis*, **10**, 349–367.

Sturmey, P. (1990). Goal planning manuals: Their readability, human interest and content. *Mental Handicap Research*, **3**, 70–80.

Sturmey, P. (1991). Assessment of challenging behaviour: An annotated semi–structured behavioural interview. *Mental Handicap*, **19**, 56–60.

Sturmey, P. (1994). Assessing the functions of aberrant behaviors: A review of psychometric instruments. *Journal of Autism and Developmental Disorders*, **24**, 293–304.

Sturmey, P. (1996). *Functional Analysis and Clinical Psychology*. Chichester: Wiley.

Sturmey, P. (2001). The reliability of the Functional Analysis Checklist. *Journal of Applied Research in Intellectual Disabilities*, **14**, 141–146.

Sturmey, P. (2004). Cognitive therapy with people with intellectual disabilities: A selective review and critique. *Clinical Psychology and Psychotherapy*, **11**, 223–232.

Sturmey, P. (2005). Against psychotherapy with people with mental retardation. *Mental Retardation*, **43**, 55–57.

Sturmey, P. (2006a). Against psychotherapy with people who have mental retardation: In response to the responses. *Mental Retardation*, **44**, 71–74.

Sturmey, P. (2006b). On some recent claims for the efficacy of cognitive therapy for people with intellectual disabilities. *Journal of Applied Research in Intellectual Disabilities*, **19**, 109–118.

Sturmey, P. (2006c). In response to Lindsay and Emerson. *Journal of Applied Research in Intellectual Disabilities*, **19**, 125–129.

Sturmey, P. (Ed.) (2007). *Functional Analysis in Clinical Treatment*. New York, Academic Press.

Sturmey, P. & Bernstein, H. (2004). Functional analysis of maladaptive behaviors: Current status and future directions. In J.L. Matson, R.B. Laud & M.L. Matson (Eds.) *Behavior modification for persons with developmental disabilities*. Volume 1. (pp. 101–129). Kingston. NY: NADD Press.

Sturmey, P., Matson, J.L. & Lott, J.D. (2003). The internal consistency and factor structure of the Choice Assessment Scale. *Research in Developmental Disabilities*, **24**, 317–322.

Sturmey, P. & McGlynn, A.P. (2003). Restraint reduction. In *Responding to Challenging Behavior in Persons with Intellectual Disabilities: Ethical Approaches to Physical Intervention* (Ed. D. Allen). Kidderminster: BILD Publications, pp. 203–218.

Sturmey, P. & Fitzer, A., Ed. (2007). *Autism Spectrum Disorders: Applied Behavior Analysis, Evidence and Practice*. Austin, TX: Proed.

Sugai, G. & White, W.J. (1986). Effect of using object self-stimulation as a reinforces on the prevocational work rates of an autistic child. *Journal of Autism and Developmental Disabilities*, **16**, 459–471.

Tarrier, N. & Calem, R. (2002). New developments in cognitive-behavioural case formulation. Epidemiological, systemic and social context: An integrative approach. *Behavioural and Cognitive Psychotherapy*, **30**, 311–328.

Tarrier, N.W., Wells, A. & Haddock, G. (Ed.) (1998). *Treating Complex Cases. The Cognitive Behavioural Approach*. Chichester: Wiley.

Tarrier, N. & Wykes, Y. (2004). Is there evidence that cognitive behavior therapy is an effective treatment for schizophrenia? A cautions or cautionary tale? *Behavior, Research and Therapy*, **42**, 1377–1401.

Taylor, I. & O'Reilly, M.F. (1997). Toward a functional analysis of private verbal self-regulation. *Journal of Applied Behavior Analysis*, **30**, 43–58.

Taylor, J.L. (2005). In support of psychotherapy for people who have mental retardation. *Mental Retardation*, **43**, 450–453.

Taylor, J.L. & Lindsay, W.R. (2007). Developments in the treatment and management of offenders with intellectual disabilities. *Issues in Forensic Psychology*, 23–31.

Thompson, R.H., Fisher, W.W. Piazza, C.C. & Kuhn, D.E. (1998). The evaluation and treatment of aggression maintained by attention and automatic reinforcement. *Journal of Applied Behavior Analysis*, **31**.

Thompson, T., Felce, D. & Symons, F. (Eds) (2000). *Computer–assisted Behavioral Observation in Developmental Disabilities*. Baltimore, MD: Brooks.

Thompson, T.J., Braam, S.J. & Fugua, R.W. (1982). Training and generalization of Country skills: A multiple probe evaluation with handicapped persons. *Journal of Applied Behavior Analysis*, **15**, 177–182.

Thorndike, R.M. & KleinKnecht, R.A. (1974). Reliability of homogneous scales of reinforcers: A cluster analysis of the reinforcement survey schedule. *Behavior Therapy*, **5**, 58–63.

Touchette, P.E., MacDonald, R.F. & Langer, S.N. (1985). A scatter plot for identifying stimulus control of problem behavior. *Journal of Applied Behavior Analysis*, **18**, 343–351.

Townend, M. (2002). Individual exposure therapy for delusional disorder in the elderly: A case study of a 71 year old man. *Behavioral and Cognitive Psychotherapy*, **30**, 103–109.

Truax, C.B. (1966). Reinforcement and non–reinforcement in Rogerian psychotherapy. *Journal of Abnormal Psychology*, **71**, 1–9.

Turkat, I.D. (Ed.) (1985a). *Behavioral Case Formulation*. New York: Plenum.

Turkat, I.D. (1985b). Formulation of parnoid personality disorder. In *Behavioral Case Formulation* (Ed. I.D. Turkat). New York: Plenum, pp. 155–198.

Turkat, I.D. (1988). Issues in the relationship between assessment and treatment. *Journal of Psychopathology and Behavioral Assessment*, **10**, 185–197.

Turkat, I.D. & Wolpe, J. (1985). Behavioral formulation of clinical cases. In *Behavioral Case Formulation* (Ed. I.D. Turkat). New York: Plenum, pp. 5–36.

Ullman, L.P. & Krasner, L. (1965). *Psychological Approaches to Abnormal Behavior*. New York: Prentice–Hall.

Ulrich, R.E. & Azrin, N.H. (1962). Reflexive fighting in response to aversive stimulation. *Journal of the Experimental Analysis of Behavior*, **5**, 511–520.

Van den Bergh, O., Kempynck, P. J., van de Woestijne, K. P., Baeyens, F. & Eelen, P. (1995). Respiratory learning and somatic complaints, a conditioning approach using CO_2-enriched air inhalation. *Behavior, Research and Therapy*, **33**, 517–527.

Van den Bergh, O., Stegen, K., Van Diest, I., Raes, C., Stulens, P., Eelen, P., Veulemans, H., Van de Woestijne, K.P. & Nemery, B. (1999). Acquisition and extinction of somatic symptoms in response to odours, a Pavlovian paradigm relevant to multiple chemical sensitivity. *Occupational and Environmental Medicine*, **56**, 295–301.

Van Houten, R., Rolider, A. & Ikowitz, J. (1989). The Functional Analysis Checklist. Unpublished manuscript. Reprinted in Sturmey, P. (2001). The reliability of the functional analysis checklist. *Journal of Applied Research in Intellectual Disabilities*, **14**, 141–146.

Van Houten, R. & Nau, P.A. (1980). A comparison of the effects of fixed and variable ratio schedules of reinforcement on the behavior of deaf children. *Journal of Applied Behavior Analysis*, **13**, 13–21.

VanWormer, J.J. (2004). Pedometers and brief e-counseling, Increasing physical activity for overweight adults. *Journal of Applied Behavior Analysis*, **37**, 421–425.

Virues–Ortega, J. (2006). The case against B.F. Skinner 45 years later: An encounter with N. Chomsky. *The Behavior Analyst*, **29**, 243–252.

Virues–Ortega, J. & Haynes, S.N. (2005). Functional analysis in behavior therapy, Behavioral foundations and clinical application. *International Journal of Clinical and Health Psychology*, **5**, 567–587.

Vogel, W. & Peterson, L.E. (1991). A variant of guided exposure to mourning for use with treatment resistant patients. *Journal of Behavior Therapy and Experimental Psychiatry*, **22**, 217–219.

Vollmer, T.R. (2002). Punishment happens: Some comments on Lerman and Vorndran's review. *Journal of Applied Behavior Analysis*, **35**, 469–473.

Vollmer, T.R., Borrer., J.C., Lalli, J.S. & Daniel, S.D. (1999). Evaluating self-control and impulsivity in children with severe behavior disorders. *Journal of Applied Behavior Analysis*, **32**, 451–466.

Waddington, L. & Morely, S. (2000). Availability bias in clinical formulation: The first idea that comes to mind. *British Journal of Clinical Psychology*, **73**, 117–127.

Waller, G. (2000). *Psychological Case Formulation in Clinical Practice.* Chichester: Wiley.

Walters, R.H., Marshall, W.E. & Shooter, J.R. (1960). Anxiety, isolation and susceptibility to social influence. *Journal of Personality*, **28**, 518–529.

Walters, R.H. & Ray, E. (1960). Anxiety, social isolation, and reinforcer effectiveness. *Journal of Personality*, **28**, 358–367.

Watanabe, S.S., Sakamoto, J. & Wakita, M. (1995). Pigeons' discrimination of paintings by Monet and Picasso. *Journal of the Experimental Analysis of Behavior*, **63**, 165–174.

Watson, J.B. & Rayner, R. (1920). Conditional emotional reactions. *Journal of Experimental Psychology*, **3**, 1–14.

Weerasekera, P. (1996). *Multiperspective Case Formulation. A Step Towards Treatment Integration.* Malabar, FL: Kreiger.

Wegner, K.E., Smyth, J.M., Crosby, R.D., Wittrock, D., Wonderlich, S.A. & Mitchell, J.E. (2002). An evaluation of the relationship between mood and binge eating in the natural environment using ecological momentary assessment. *International Journal of Eating Disorders*, **32**, 352–361.

Wells, A. (1998). Cognitive therapy of social phobia. In N. Tamier, A. Wells & G. Haddock (Eds.) Treating complex cases. The cognitive behavioral therapy approach, (pp. 1–26). Chichester: Wiley.

Whitehead, W.E., Lurie, E. & Blackwell, B. (1976). Classical conditioning of decreases in human systolic blood pressure. *Journal of Applied Behavior Analysis*, **9**, 153–157.

Whitman, T.L., Scibak, J.W., Butler, K.M., Richter, R. & Johnson, M.R. (1982). Improving classroom behavior in mentally retarded children through correspondence training. *Journal of Applied Behavior Analysis*, **15**, 545–564.

Wilder, D.A., Masudo, A., O'Connor, C. & Baham, M. (2001). Brief functional analysis and treatment of bizarre vocalizations in an adult with schizophrenia. *Journal of Applied Behavior Analysis*, **34**, 65–68.

Wilder, D.A. & Wong, S.E. (2007). Schizophrenia and other psychotic disorders. In *Functional Analysis in Clinical Treatment* (Ed. P. Sturmey). New York: Academic Press, pp. 307–334.

Williams, T.I., Rose, R. & Chisolm, S. (2006). What is the function of nail biting, An analog assessment study. *Behavior Research and Therapy*, **45**, 989–995.

Wilson, E.O. (1975). *Sociobiology. The New Sysnthesis*. Harvard, MA: Harvard Press.

Wilson, G.T. (1996a). Treatment of bulimia nervosa, when CBT fails. *Behavior Research and Therapy*, **34**, 197–212.

Wilson, G.T. (1996b). Manual-based treatments, the clinical application of research findings. *Behavior, Research and Therapy*, **34**, 295–314.

Wilson, K.G. & Blackledge, J.T. (1999). Recent developments in the behavioral analysis of language, Making sense of clinical phenomena. In *Clinical Behavior Analysis* (Ed. M.J. Dougher). Reno, NV: Context Press, pp. 27–46.

Wilson, F.E. & Evans, I.M. (1983). The reliability of target behavior selection in behavioral assessment. *Behavioral Assessment*, **5**, 15–32.

Wilson, K.G., Hayes, S.C., Gregg, J. & Zettle, R.D. (2001). Psychopathology and psychotherapy. In *Relational Frame Theory. A post Skinneran account of human language and cognition* (Eds S.C. Hayes, D. Barnes–Holmes & B. Roche) New York: Kluwer, pp. 211–238.

Wilson, P.G., Rusch, F.R. & Lee, S. (1992). Strategies to increase exercise-report correspondence by boys with moderate mental retardation, Collateral changes in intention-exercise correspondence. *Journal of Applied Behavior Analysis*, **25**, 681–690.

Winters, N.C., Hanson, G. & Stoyanova, V. (2007). The case formulation in child and adolescent psychiatry. *Child and Adolescent Psychiatric Clinics of North America*, **16**, 111–132.

Wolf, M.M. (1978). Social validity: The case for subjective measurement or How applied behavior analysis is finding its heart. *Journal of Applied Behavior Analysis*, **11**, 203–214.

Wolpe, J. (1958). *Psychotherapy by Reciprocal Inhibition*. Stanford, CT: Stanford University Press.

Wolpe, J. (1980a). This week's citation classic. Wolpe's *Psychotherapy by Reciprocal Inhibition. Current Contents*, **25**(23), 253.

Wolpe, J. (1980b). Behavioral analysis and therapeutic strategy. In *Handbook of Behavioural Intervention* (Eds A.F. Goldstein & E.B. Foa). New York: Wiley, pp. 7–37.

Wolpe, J. (1986). Individualization, the categorical imperative of behavior therapy practice. *Journal of Behavior Therapy and Experimental Psychiatry*, **17**, 145–153.

Wolpe, J. (1989). The derailment of behavior therapy, a tale of conceptual misdirection. *Journal of Behavior Therapy and Experimental Psychiatry*, **20**, 3–15.

Wolpe, J. & Turkat, I. (1985). Behavioral formulation of clinical cases. In *Behavioral Case Formulation* (Ed. I.D. Turkat). New York: Plenum, pp. 5–36.

Wong, S.E. & Wodsey, J.E. (1989). Reestablishing conversational skills in overtly psychotic, chronic schizophrenic patients. *Behavior Modification*, **13**, 415–431.

Woods, D.W. & Himle, M.B. (2004). Creating tic suppression: Comparing the effects of verbal instruction to differential reinforcement. *Journal of Applied Behavior Analysis*, **37**, 417–420.

Woods, D.W. & Miltenberger, R.G. (1995). Habit reversal: A review of applications and variations. *Journal of Behavior Therapy and Experimental Psychiatry*, **26**, 123–131.

Woods, D.W., & Miltenberger, R. (1996). Are people with nervous habits nervous? A preliminary examination of habit function in a nonreferred population. *Journal of Applied Behavior Analysis*, **29**, 259–261.

Woods, D.W., Miltenberger, R.G. & Lumley, V.A. (1996). Sequential application of major habit-reversal components to treat motor tics in children. *Journal of Applied Behavior Analysis*, **29**, 483–493.

Woods, D.W., Twohig, M.P., Flessner, C.A. & Roloff, T.J. (2003). Treatment of vocal tics in children with Tourette syndrome, Investigating the efficacy of habit reversal. *Journal of Applied Behavior Analysis*, **36**, 109–112.

Woods, D.W., Watson, T.S., Wolfe, E., Twohig, M.P. & Friman, P.C. (2001). Analyzing the influence of tic-related talk on vocal and motor tics in children with Tourette's syndrome. *Journal of Applied Behavior Analysis*, **34**, 353–356.

www.contextualpsychology.org (2006). Contextual psychology.org. On line research and learning community. Available from http://www. contextualpsychology.org/, Downloaded June 23, 2007.

Yoder, P.J., Short–Meyerson, K. & Tapp, J. (2004). Measurement of behavior with a special emphasis on sequential analysis of behavior. In *International Handbook of Research Methods in Intellectual Disability* (Eds E. Emerson, T. Parmenter & C. Hatton). New York: Wiley, pp. 179–202.

Young, J.M., Krantz, P.J., McClannahan, L.E. & Poulson, C.L. (1994). Generalized imitation and response class formation in children with antism. *Journal of Applied Behavior Analysis, 27*, 685–697.

Zettle, R.D. (2003). Acceptance and commitment therapy (ACT) vs. systematic desensitization in the treatment of mathematics anxiety. *The Psychological Record, 53*, 197–215.

Zlutnick, S., Mayville, W.J. & Moffat, S. (1975). Modification of seizure disorders: The interuption of behavioral chains. *Journal of Applied Behavior Analysis, 8*, 1–12.

INDEX

ABC charts 64, 116, 242–244
Acceptance and Commitment
    Therapy 132–133, 252
Acquired brain damage
    See brain damage
ACT See Acceptance and
    Commitment Therapy
Activity schedules 105–106
ADHD
    See Attention Deficit
        Hyperactivity Disorder
Adjustment disorder 39
Aggression 47, 101
    Clinical Pathogenesis Map
        and 204–207
    Functional assessment of 236,
        254–255
    See also anger
Alcohol abuse 47–48
    Behavioral formulation
        of 177–180
Alzheimer disease 11, 64, 82
Anger 47
    Case formulation and 171
    Cognitive analytic case
        formulation of 166–167
    Interview and 232–233
Anorexia
    See eating disorders
Anxiety
    Hypochondriasis and 256–257
    Skinner and 184–185, 188–190
Anxiety disorder 63
    Clinical Pathogenesis Map
        and 203–204
    Wolpe's case formulation
        of 173

Attention Deficit Hyperactivity
    Disorder 7, 10, 60, 61, 62, 67,
    71–72, 113, 115, 118–119
    Actometer and 247
    Psychiatric case formulation
        of 155–154
Applied behavior analysis 32–33
Asthma 39, 40
Autism 11, 57, 60, 68, 92–93,
    105–106
    Verbal behavior and 137–138
Autoclitics 125
Aversive stimuli 41

Baron-Cohen
    See Theory of mind
Behavioral activation 67, 88, 251–252
Behavioral assessment
    ABA and 228
    Bulimia 255–256
    Cone's model of 227–228
    Depression and 252
    Hypochondriasis 256–257
    Interviewing and 228–234
        Hypothesis-driven 232–234
        Semi-structured 228–231
        Self-recording 234–235
    Nail biting 253
    Observation 239–248
    Pediatric feeding disorder
        251–252
Behavioral definitions 240
Behavioral skills training 62
Behaviorism
    See Radical behaviorism
Bereavement 84
    See also Morbid grieving

Bladder control
See Incontinence
Blocking 39
Blood pressure 41–42
Bowel control
See incontinence
Brain damage 11, 57, 113, 114–115,
121–122
Psychiatric case formulation
of 154–155
Functional analysis of sexual
behavior and 248–249
Bulimia 110
Behavioral assessment
and 255–256
Behavioral formulation
and 199–200, 220–222
Validity of case formulation
276–278
See also eating disorders

Case formulation
ADHD and 155–156
Anger and 166–167
Anxiety 280
Behavioral 195–198
Bulimia 199–200, 220–222,
276–278
Client and 193, 197, 269–271
Compulsive gambling 197–198
Cognitive 156–162
Cognitive-analytic 165–167
Common features 146–150
Clinical judgment 287–288
Definitions of 145–146
Depression and 166, 195–198,
214–215, 279
Eating disorder and 163–165
Functional analytic clinical case
model (FACM) 210–218
Depression and 214–215
General characteristics 210–213
Methodology 213
Psychosis and 216–217
Self-injury and 215–216

History of xi-xii 143–145
History, role of 172–173
Integrationist 162–165
Marital therapy 278
Obesity and 151–153
Phobia and 171, 278–279
Professional performance
259–273, 288
Psychoanalytic 150–153
Psychosis and 158–162, 171–172,
216–217
Reliability 273–275
Self-injury and 215–216
Translating to treatment 264–271
Validity 275–279
Writing 260–263
Causes of behavior 23
See also functional analysis and
functional relations
Chaining
See Response chain
Chemotherapy 42
Chiesa 21–22, 29, 33–35
Child effect 31
Cholic 86
Chomsky 5, 10–11, 127–128
Chronic cough 48–49
Classical conditioning
See respondent conditioning
Clinical behavior analysis 131
Clinical judgment 287–288
Clinical Pathogenesis map 201–207
Anxiety and 203–204
Depression and 201–204
Sexual aggression and 204
Cognitive analytic case formulation
See Case Formulation
Cognitive behavior therapy xi-xii
Cognitive case formulation
Radical behavioral case
formulation and 223–224
See Case formulation
Combinatorial entainment 129–130
Competing response
See habit reversal

Compliance 89–90
Compulsive gambling
　See gambling
Constructional approaches 18
Correspondence training 285–286
Cue-dependent extinction 48
Cue exposure
　See cue-dependent exposure,
　　alcohol and substance abuse
Cultural design 26–29
　Los horsones and 26
Cultural evolution 26–29

Darwin
　See evolution
Dental floss 247
Depression 3–5, 16–20, 57, 67–68,
　　84, 88, 98
　Behavioral formulation of
　　175–176, 252
　Cognitive analytic case
　　formulation of 165–166
　Clinical Pathogenesis Map and
　　201–204
　Functional Analytic Clinical
　　case Formulation of 214–215
Deprivation
　See reinforcer deprivation
Dementia
　See Alzheimer disease
Detailed Behavior Record 242–243
Desensitization 48–49
　See also Wolpe
Diagnosis
　Case formulation and 4–5, 7,
　　16–17, 281
　Circular arguments and 9, 53
Dialectic behavior therapy 112–
　　113, 134–135
　Case Formulation and 207–210
Diamond 26–29
Differential Reinforcement of
　　Other Behavior 56
Discrimination
　Classical conditioning and 38

DRA
　See Schedules of Reinforcement
DRO
　See Schedules of Reinforcement
DRI
　See Schedules of Reinforcement
DRL
　See Schedules of Reinforcement
DRO
　See Schedules of Reinforcement
Duration 239–241

Eating disorders 57
　Ecological momentary
　　assessment and 235
　Integrationist case formulation
　　of 163–165
Echoic 125, 138
Ecological momentary
　　assessment 235
Emergent relationships 121
Escape behavior 81–82, 84–85,
　　215–216, 251
Establishing operations 79–81
　See also Reinforcer satiation
　See also Reinforcer deprivation
Emotional behavior 30
Equivalence 121
　See also Stimulus equivalence
Exercize 89–90, 114–115
Exposure therapy 42–52
　See Respondent extinction,
　　Phobia, Obsessive
　　Compulsive Disorder,
　　Nightmare, and Morbid
　　grieving
Extinction
　Operant extinction 83–87
　　Depression and 84
　　Escape extinction 85
　　Pediatric Feeding
　　　Disorders 86
　　Resistance to extinction 84
　　Respondent behavior and 39,
　　　42–50

Evidence-based practice 17, 66–67, 183
    ACT and 133–134
    Functional analysis and 250
Evolution 13, 15–16
    Skinner and 25–29

FAP
    See Functional analytic psychotherapy
FCT
    See Functional Communication Training
Fear 49–52
    See also phobia
Fixed Interval schedule
    See Schedule of reinforcement
Fixed Ratio schedule
    See Schedule of reinforcement
Flooding 41, 43
Frequency 239–241
Functional analysis 82
    Extinction and 84–85
    Mathematics and 29–32
    Sexual behavior and 248–249
Functional analytic psychotherapy 135–136
Functional assessment 248–250
Functional communication training 71–72, 108–109, 252
Functional relations 23–24
    See also causes of behavior
Functionalism 13–16
    Assessment and 225–226
    See also Structuralism
Freud xi

Gag 42
Gambling 115–116
Generalization 32–33, 73–77
    Classical conditioning and 38
    Modeling and 100
    Operant behavior and 69–70
    Response generalization 74
    Stimulus generalization 69–70

Generalization gradient 30
Group designs 31

Habit reversal 24–25
    See also tics, Tourette disorder
Headaches 89–90
Herrnstein's equation 56, 64–65, 67–69
History of case formulation
    See Case formulation
History
    Role of in case formulation See case formulation
Hording 81–82
Human operant behavior 57–58
Hypochondriasis 256–257
Hypoglycemia 72–73
Hypothesis-driven interviews
    See Interview
Hypothetic-deductive method 31

Identity 121
Incontinence 40
Individual differences 12, 15
Insect phobia 50–52
Intellectual disabilities (mental retardation) 11, 57, 60, 71–72, 74–76, 84–85, 104, 113, 114
    Evidence-based practice and 250
    Verbal behavior and 137–138
Intent 53
Inter-observer agreement 239, 246–247
Interviews 18
    Hypothesis driven 170–171, 232–234, 250
    Semi-structured 228–231
Introspection 6, 9
Iwata 30, 266–269

James, William 13–14, 15

Lag schedules
    See Schedules of reinforcement

Language interventions 11
Law of Least Effort 91
Listener 124–125
Los horcones 26

Mand 124–125, 138
Marital therapy 278
Match to sample training 120–121,
123
Matching law
See Herrnstein's equation
Mental retardation
See intellectual disabilities
Modeling 100–101
Mood 18, 30
Morbid grieving 39, 46
Motivation 13, 14, 61
Multiple chemical sensitivities 40
Murder 87–89

Nail biting 253
Neobehaviorism 34
Nightmares 39, 43, 45–46

Obesity 113
Psychoanalytic case formulation
of 151–153
OCD
See Obsessive compulsive
disorder
Obsessive Compulsive disorder 39,
43–44
Office-bound therapists 13, 58
Older adults 57, 113
See also Alzheimer disease
Operant behavior
Acquisition 53–54
Case formulation and 58–59
Human operant behavior 57–58,
70
Maintanence 54–56
Stimulus control 69–77
Establishing stimulus
control of operant
behavior 71–72

See also Schedules of
reinfrocement
Overshadowing 39

Pain 57
Panic 171
Pavlovian conditioning
See Respondent conditioning
Pediatric feeding disorders 86,
251–252
Permanent product 247–248
Personality disorder 110,
Behavioral formulation
of 174–177
Cognitive analytic case
formulation of 166–167
Dialectic behavior therapy
and 135
Dialectic behavior therapy case
formulation and 208–210
Phobias 37, 43, 50–52
Case formulation and 171
Interview and 232–233
Validity of case formulation
278–279
Physical disabilities 100
Physical therapy 114–115
Post traumatic stress disorder 39,
44–45, 153
Preference assessment
See Reinforcer assessment
Private events
See Radical behaviorism, Private
behavior and
Problem list 17–18, 176, 219
Professional performance and case
formulation 259–263
Prompting and fading 77
Psychoanalytic case formulation
See Case formulation
Psychotic behavior
See schizophrenia
Psychotherapy
Behavioral explanations of 183–184
Eysenck and effectiveness of 183

PTSD
  See Post traumatic stress
    disorder
Punishment 93–98
  Ethics and 94
  Secondary punisher 40

QABF
  See Questions About Behavioral
    Function
Questions About Behavioral
  Function 235–236
  Nail biting and 253

Radical behaviorism xii 21–35
  Definition of 22
  Private behavior and xii 13–14,
    33, 126
  Thinking – see Behaviorism,
    Private behavior and
  Misrepresentations of 21, 33–35,
    73
  Theory and 21
  See Behaviorism
Randomized controlled trials
  See evidence-based practice
Reciprocal inhibition 52, 144
  See Wolpe
Respiratory behavior 40
  See Asthma
Reinforcer
  Deprivation 30, 79–81, 112
  Satiation 79–82, 112
  Secondary 40
  Self-control and 112
  Token 82–83, 169–170
  See also Establishing operations
Reinforcer Assessment 59–63
  See also Stimulus preference
    assessments
Reinforcer Surveys 59–62
  See also Stimulus preferences
    assessments
Reinforcement
  Spencer and 16
  Thorndike and 16

Relational frame theory 128–103
Reliability of case formulation
    273–275
Resistance to extinction
  See Extinction
Respondent behavior 37–54
  Acquisition of 37–38, 41–42
  Anger 47
  Blocking 39
  Blood pressure 41–42
  Case formulation and 169–173
  Chemotherapy 42
  Extinction 39, 41, 43–49
    See also Flooding and Sensate
      Focus
  Overshadowing 39
  Psychopathology 39–40
  Respiratory behavior 40
  Spontaneous remission 39
  Stimulus control 38–39
  See also Wolpe
Respondent conditioning
  See respondent behavior
Response chain 102–111
Response cost 97
Response generalization
  See Generalization
Response stereotypy
  See Variability
Restraint 112
Retrospection 7–8
  See also introspection
Rule governed behavior 70,
    118–119
Rumination 96

Sally-Ann task 11
Say-do correspondence
    training 285–286
Scatterplots 244–245
Schedules of reinforcement 54–58,
    64
  Case formulation and 58–59, 64
  Compound schedules 56–58
  Concurrent schedules
    See Hernstein equation

Differential reinforcement of alternate behavior (DRA) 86
Differential reinforcement of high rates of behavior (DRH) 56
Differential reinforcement of incompatible behavior (DRI) 63, 86
Differential reinforcement of other behavior (DRO) 55–56, 63–64, 84–87
Differential reinforcement of lower rates of behavior (DRL) 56
Fixed Interval schedule 55
Fixed time schedule 81–82, 248
Fixed Ratio schedule 55, 64, 70
Lag schedules 92–93
Non-contingent reinforcement See Fixed time schedules
Progressive ratio schedules 66
Simple schedules 55–56
Variable Interval schedule 55
Variable Ratio schedule 55
See also Extinction
Schizophrenia 11, 57, 77, 86–87
    Case formulation and 171–172
    Cognitive behavioral case formulation of 158–162
    Functional Analytic Clinical case Formulation of 216–217
    Shaping and 87
    Sharing case formulation 269–271
    Token economy and 83–84
School refusal 57
Science and behavior 22–23
Secondary Punisher See Punisher
Secondary reinforcer See Reinforcer
Seizure disorders 107–108
Selection See evolution
    Operant and 28–29
Self-catheterization 105

Self-control 111–116
Self-harm 236, 253–254
Self-recording 234–235
Self-regulation 34, 284–285
    See also Skinner and self-regulation
Self-report
    Reinforcer assessment and 61
Self-injury 57, 84–85, 87–88, 108–109
    Functional Analytic Clinical case Formulation of 214–215
Sequential analysis of data 245–246
Semi-structured interviews See Interview
Sensate focus 41
Sexual behavior 39
    Clinical pathogenesis map and 205–206
    Functional analysis of 248–250
Shaping 87–90
Sharing case formulation 269–271
Skinner
    ABA and 184
    Anxiety 184–185
    Case formulation and xi-xii 195–198, 233
    Chomsky and see Chomsky
    Cultural evolution and 26–29
    Psychotherapy and 190–194
    Psychopathology and xii 186–190
        Self-regulation and 18–20, 192–193
    Self-control and 111–113, 192–193
    Self manages 114
    Three sources of behavior 25–28
    See Radical behaviorism
    See Theory
    See *Verbal Behavior* (Skinner 1958)
Sleep disorders 87
Smoking 90, 113
    Carbon monoxide monitoring and 248

Social validity 82
Social skills 63, 103
   Case formulation and 175
SORK analysis 199–201, 222, 233
   Bulimia and 199–200
   Translating to treatment 264–265
Spencer 16
Speaker 124–125
Spina bifida 100, 104
Spontaneous remission 39
Staff training 60, 74–76
Stereotyped behavior 57, 110
Stimulus control
   See Generalization
   See Operant behavior
   See Respondent behavior
Stimulus equivalence xii–xiii
      119–123
Stimulus generalization
   See Generalization
Stimulus preferences
      assessments 62
   See also Reinforcer surveys
Structuralism 4, 5–13
   Assessment and 225–226
   Psychology and 6–7
   See also Functionalism
Stuttering 97
Subjective units of discomfort
      (SUDS) 51, 181, 223
Substance abuse 47–48, 65–67
SUDS
   See Subjective units of
      discomfort
   See Wolpe
Suicide 110
Systematic desensitization
      170, 173

Tact 124–125, 138
Task analysis 102
Therapy and behaviorism 281–283
Theory 21–22

Theory of mind 11–12
   Behavioral approaches to 12
Tics 24
   See also habit reversal
Time sampling 241
Token economy 82–83
Tourette disorder 24–25
   See also Habit reversal
Transfer of function 122–123, 132
   See also Stimulus equivalence
Transitivity 121
Traumatic brain injury
   See brain damage
Trichotillomania 113
Turkat xi, xiii

University College of London
      model of case formulation
      180–181

Variability 90–93
Variable Interval schedule
   See Schedule of Reinforcement
Variable Ratio Schedule
   See Schedule of reinforcement
Verbal behavior (Skinner 1958)
      123–124, 127–128
Verbal behavior 123–138, 184
   Case formulation and xii
   Developmental disabilities
      and 137–138
   Shaping 57
   See also Rule governed behavior
Video modeling 100

Wandering 64
Watson 24
Wolpe xiii 52, 147
   Case formulation and 169–174
   Radical behavioral approaches
      and 223
Words as conditioned stimuli 41
Wundt 6